AF248697

The Humboldt Forum in the Berlin Palace

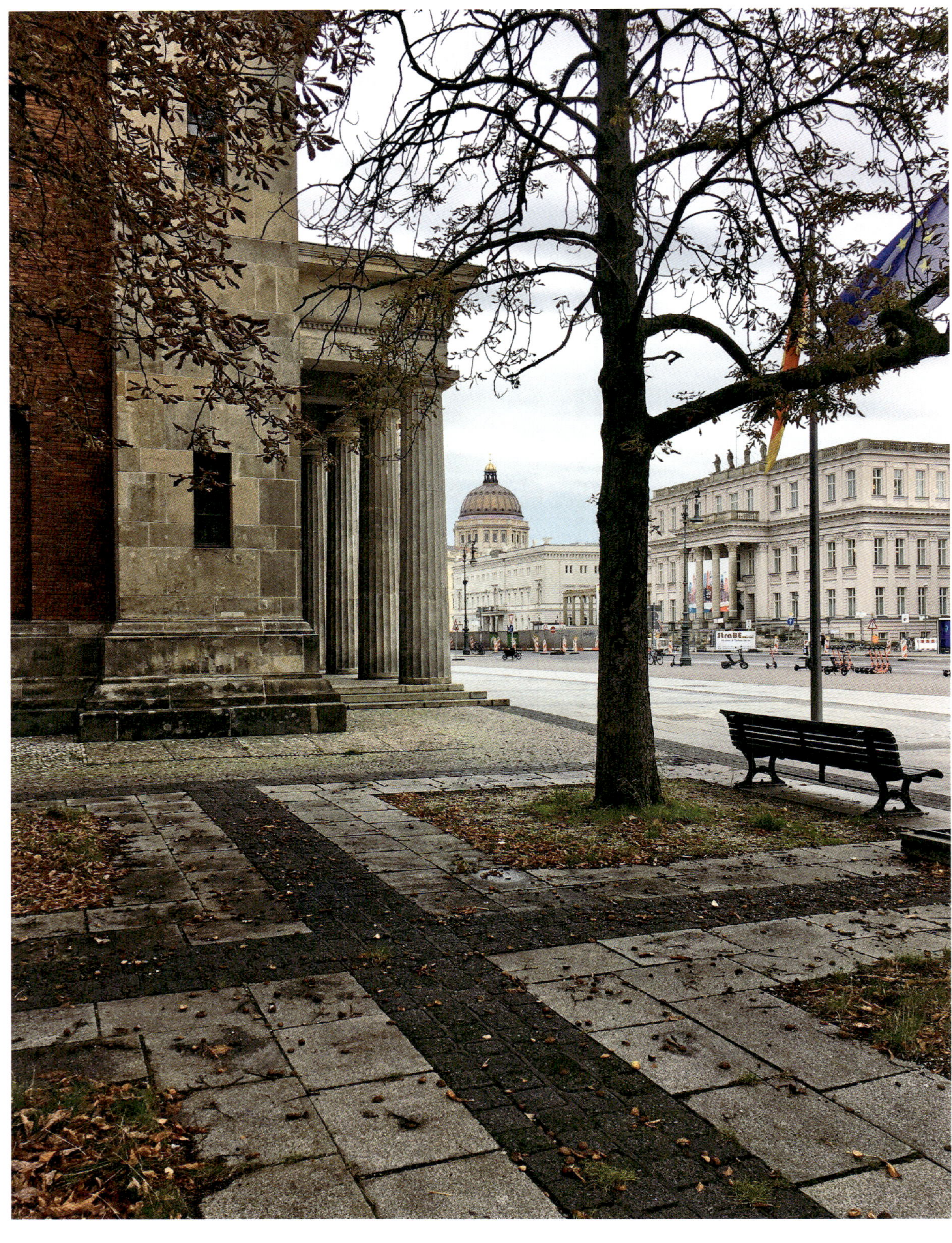

The Humboldt Forum
in the Berlin Palace

Edited by
Stiftung Humboldt Forum
im Berliner Schloss

PRESTEL

MUNICH · LONDON · NEW YORK

Contents

Foreword
Monika Grütters

Cross-party majorities can hardly be taken for granted in the context of parliamentary affairs. Yet precisely such of broad consensus emerged in July of 2002, when the German Bundestag voted for the reconstruction of the Berlin Palace and its use as a cultural centre under the name 'Humboldt Forum': there was unequivocal approval for a visionary plan for a museum of world cultures at the heart of the German capital. Now, nearly twenty years later, the goal is in sight: at long last, the Humboldt Forum is opening its gates to the public. Here, at the centre of Berlin, all interested individuals are invited to come into contact with the wider world, entirely in the spirit of the Humboldt brothers, whose name stands for rapprochement between human communities and for the ideal of a dialogue between the various world cultures on the basis of equality.

Viewed from the outside, the Humboldt Forum is a source of fascination by virtue of its spectacular conjunction of Baroque and contemporary architecture. Within, the building will offer a stage to the cultures of the world, provide a setting to exemplify current scientific and scholarly discourses, and showcase interdependencies between Berlin and the world at large, while at the same time inviting visitors to explore the history of the site. As a place of public debate which not only portrays society, but contributes to its ongoing development, the Humboldt Forum embodies the self-conception of Germany as a cultural nation in the twenty-first century. Here, at the heart of the German capital, we do not position ourselves at the forefront of attention, but instead define ourselves through exchange with others. Furthermore, the Humboldt Forum demonstrates the responsible confrontation with the deep historical abysses and ruptures of our democracy. Rather than remaining purely self-referential, Germany strives to be a partner to the larger world – a driving force for mutual understanding between different peoples. Not least of all, the Humboldt Forum is designed to serve as a model and benchmark for the treatment of cultural properties from colonial contexts in museums.

In conjunction with the neighbouring Museum Island, with its cultural treasures from Europe and the Middle East, the non-European collections owned by the Stiftung Preussischer Kulturbesitz (Prussian Cultural Heritage Foundation) reveal that there is a 'we' not just within, but also beyond national borders. In this spirit, the Humboldt Forum invites visitors to become citizens of the world. My thanks to all of the fellow campaigners, who put their body and soul into making this visionary idea a reality. We owe an enormous debt of gratitude to our generous donors: of over 600 million euros in building costs, 80 million euros is being generated by private donations for the historical facade. This goal has meanwhile nearly been attained. An additional 20 million euros in donations is required for architectural options such as the cupola.

With a tremendous sense of expectation, we look forward to this place of encounter, whose abundance of exhibitions and events will serve as a spur to confront one's own identity, to stimulate curiosity about the Other, to reflect on one's own standpoint, as well as to embrace shifts of perspective. It is my hope that the Humboldt Forum will welcome numerous visitors who will find themselves receptive to the core insight that ultimately, despite all of our differences and despite all of the conflict, more connects us – the peoples of the world – than divides us.

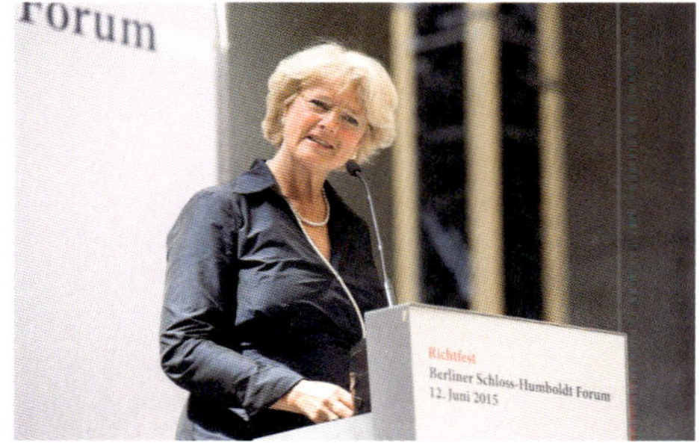

Prof. Monika Grütters, Member of the German Bundestag, State Minister for Culture and Media

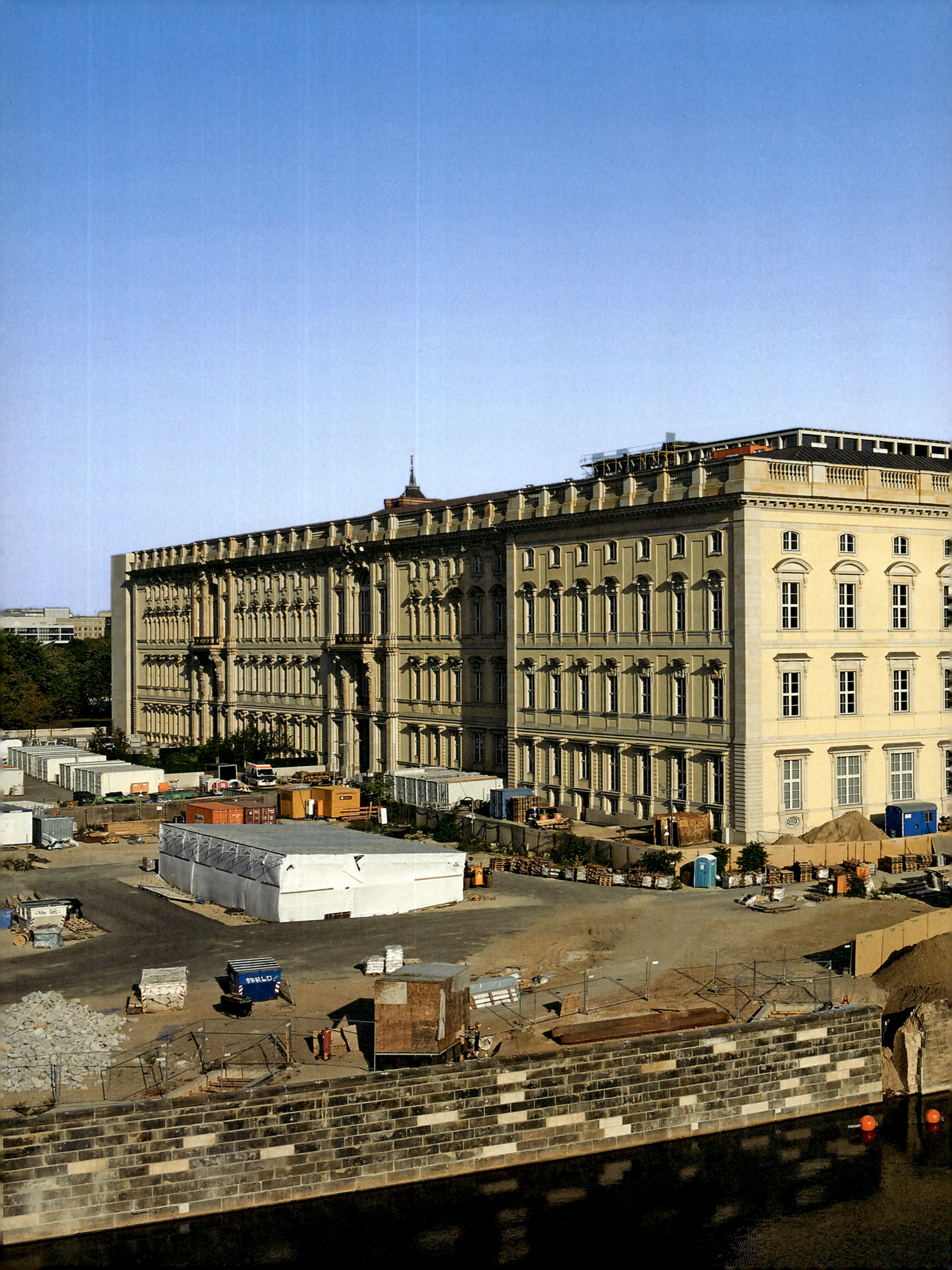

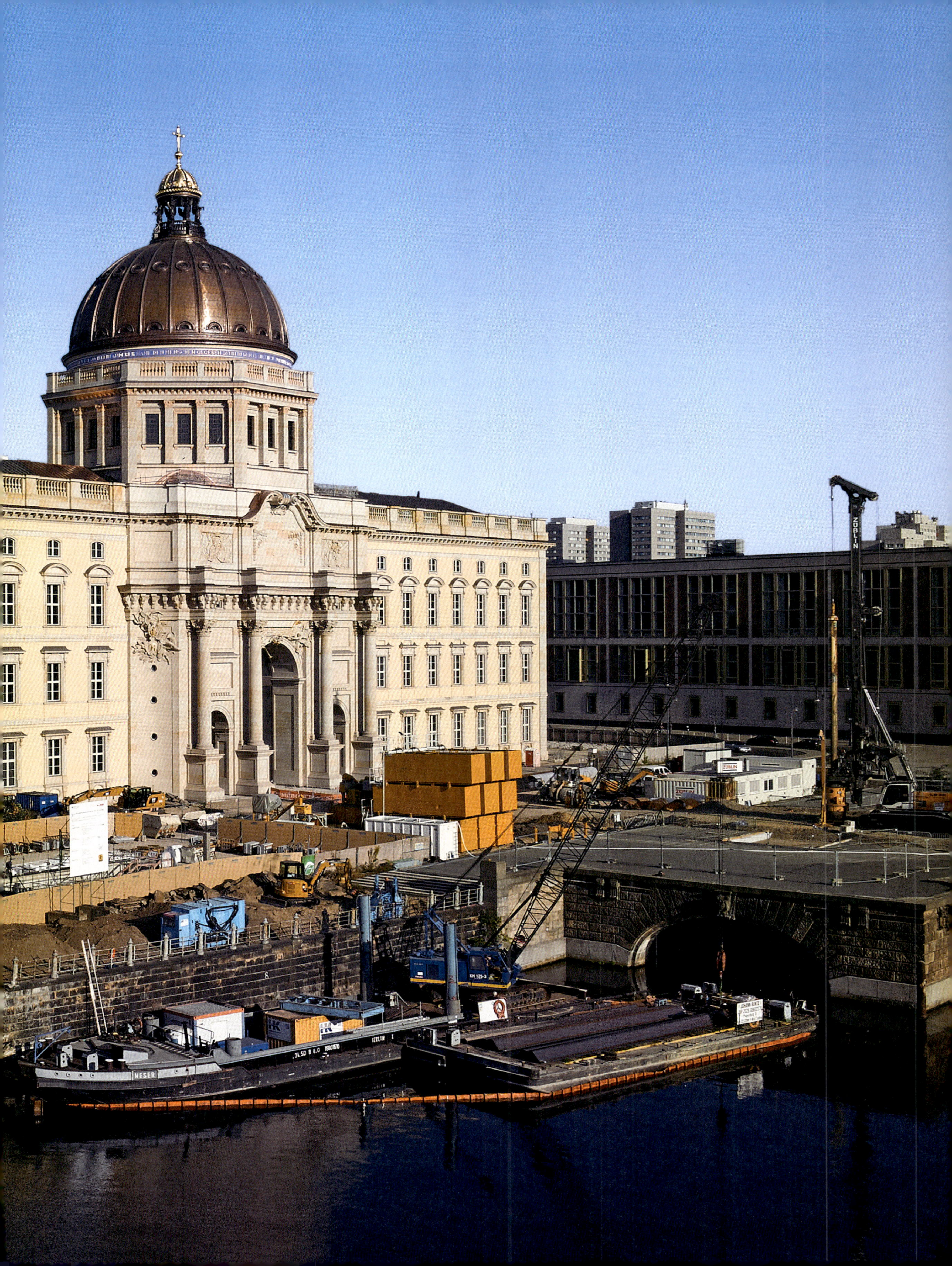

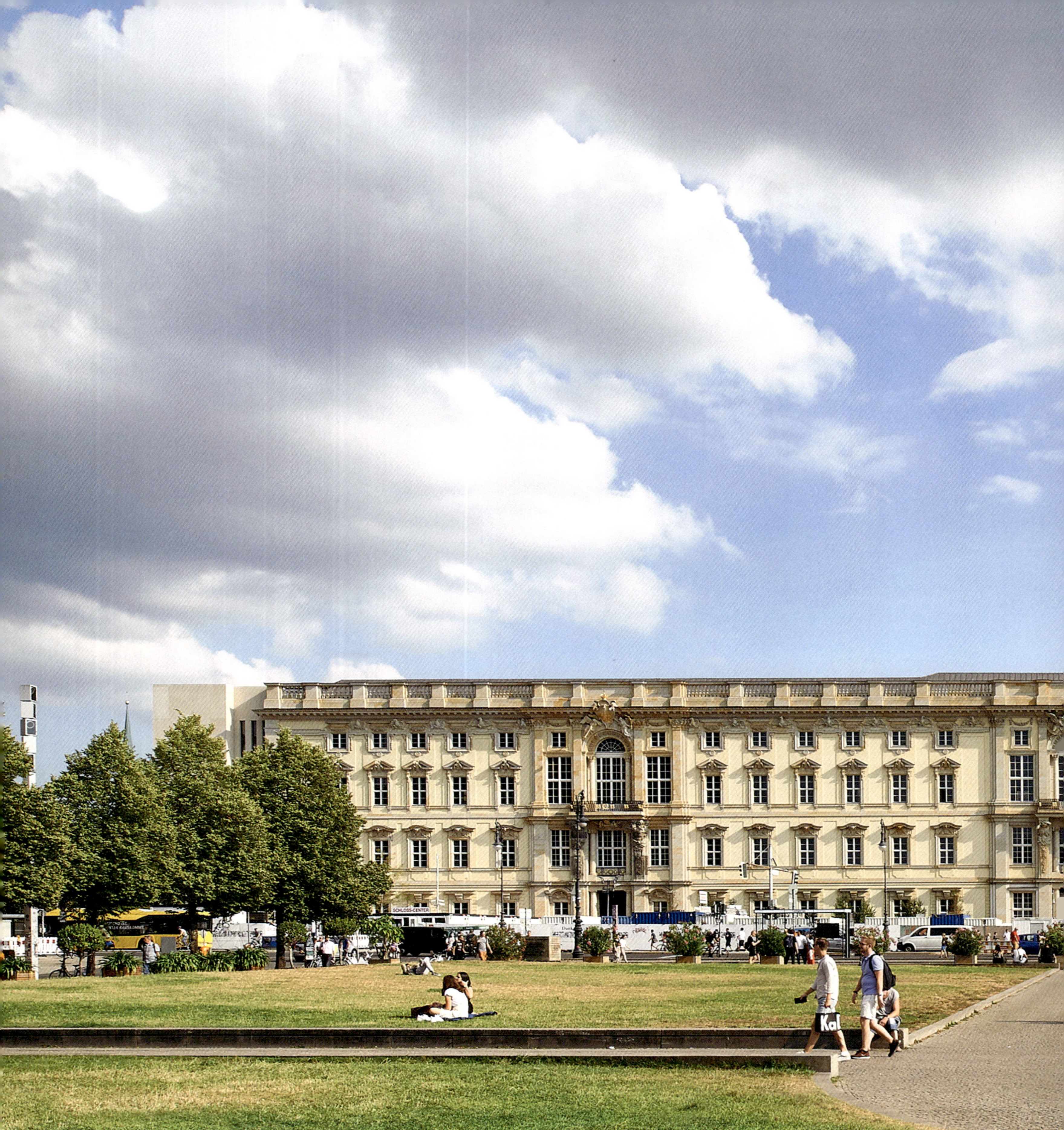

Fig. pp. 8–9:
Looking from the Brandenburg Gate towards Spreegraben and Königsbrücke, the reconstructed Berlin Palace on Spree Island has restored the point de vue to the boulevard Unter den Linden.

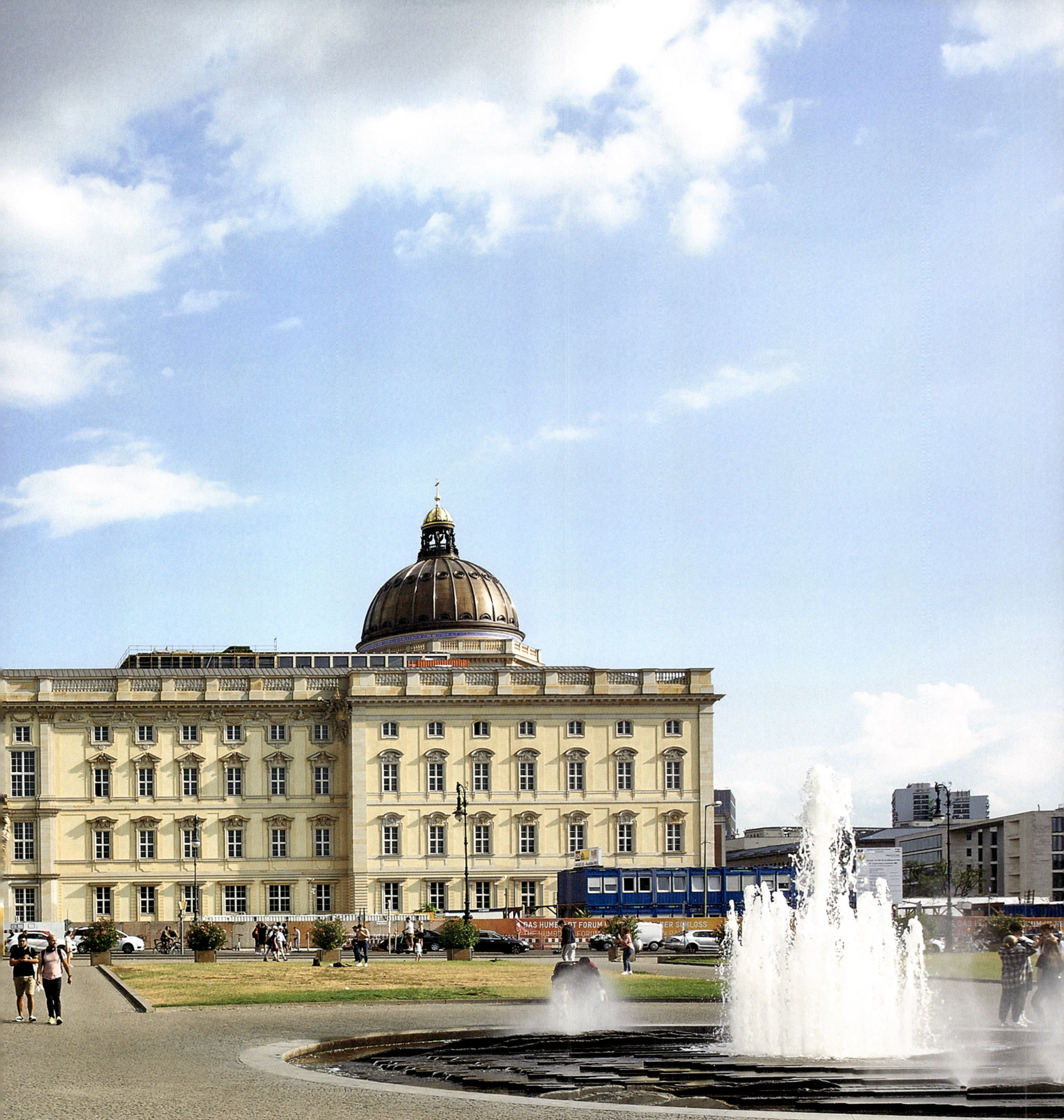

The facade of the Palace facing the Lustgarten (Pleasure Garden) towards the north is characterized by two large portals, the one on the left providing access to the Schlüter Courtyard (Portal 5), the one at the centre to the Passage (Portal 4). To the right, the projecting section, the 'Eosander shoulder', with its large corner cartouche, articulates the long section of the facade.

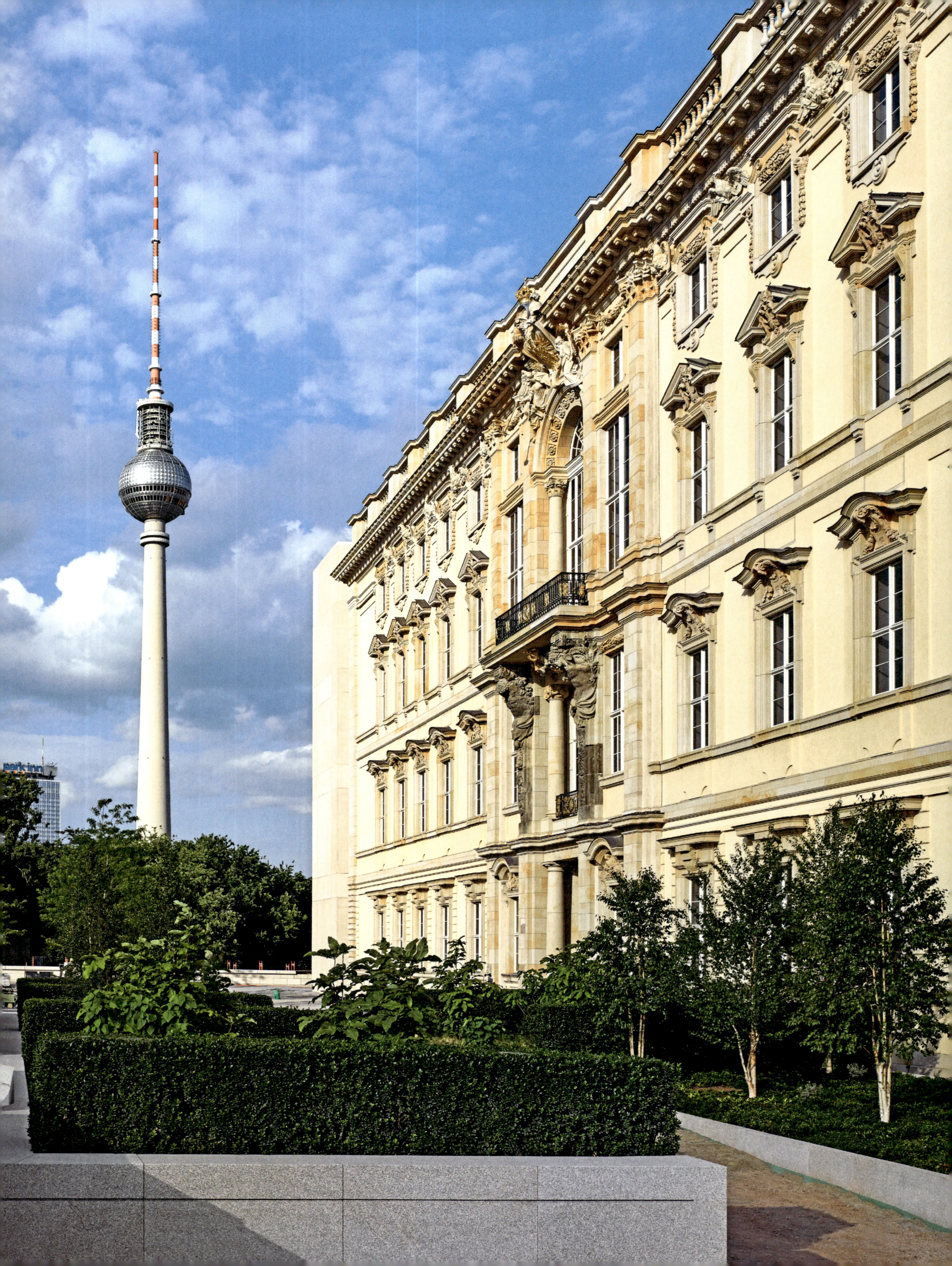

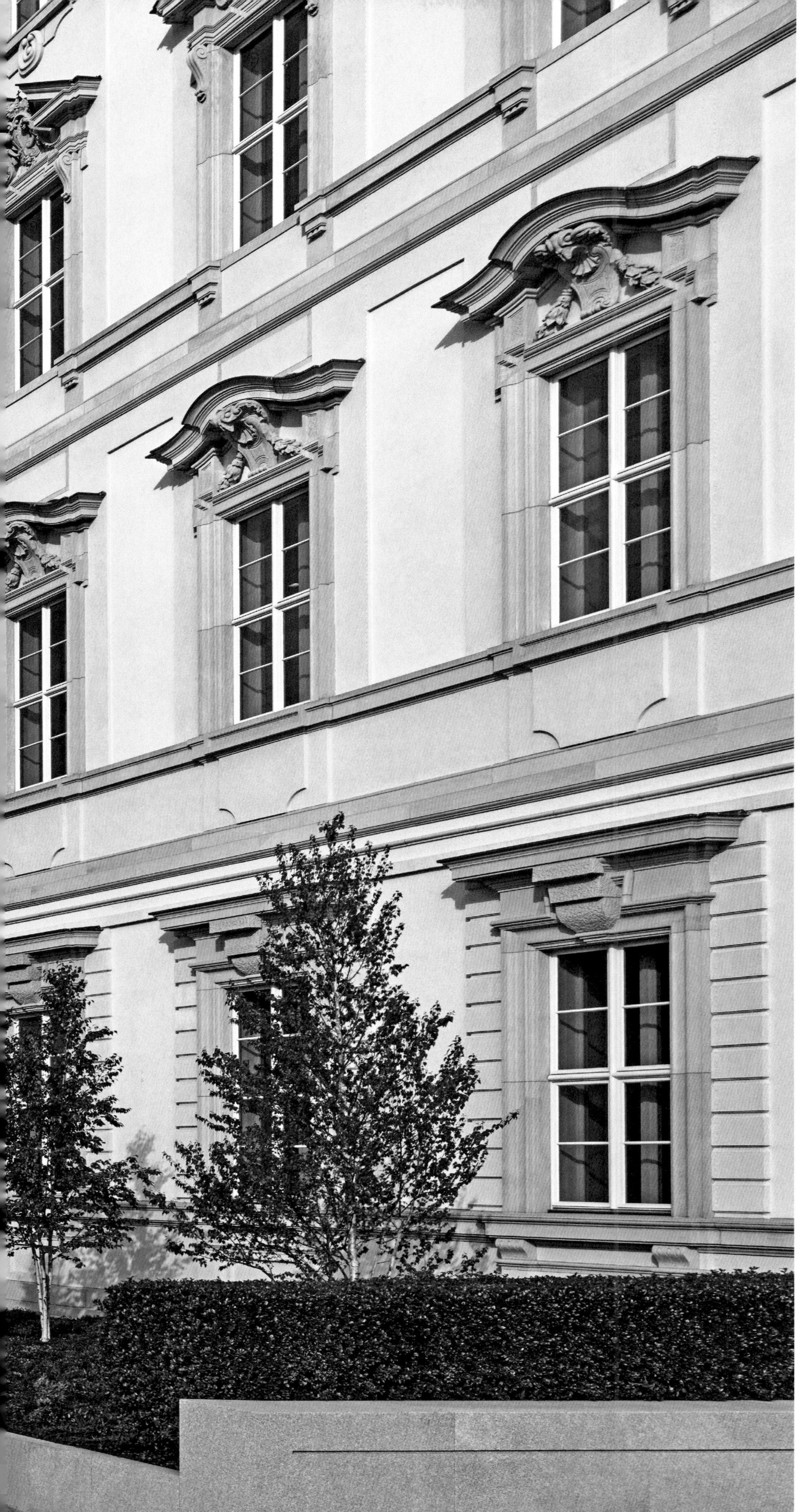

Making an appearance beyond the eastern section of the Lustgarten front – past the raised beds of the Palace terraces, based on historical models by Peter Joseph Lenné – is the 20th century, in the form of the Television Tower.

Integrated into Portal 5 are numerous surviving sculptures from the old Palace, in particular the atlantes supporting the balcony. Appropriately for the garden side, the atlas on the left displays the attributes of Spring, and the one on the right those of Summer. Autumn and Winter follow on Portal 4.

Fig. pp. 16–17:
As though keeping watch over the post-communist world, the Television Tower thrusts itself into this view from the southwest, which includes Portals 1 and 2, both decorated with massive columns.

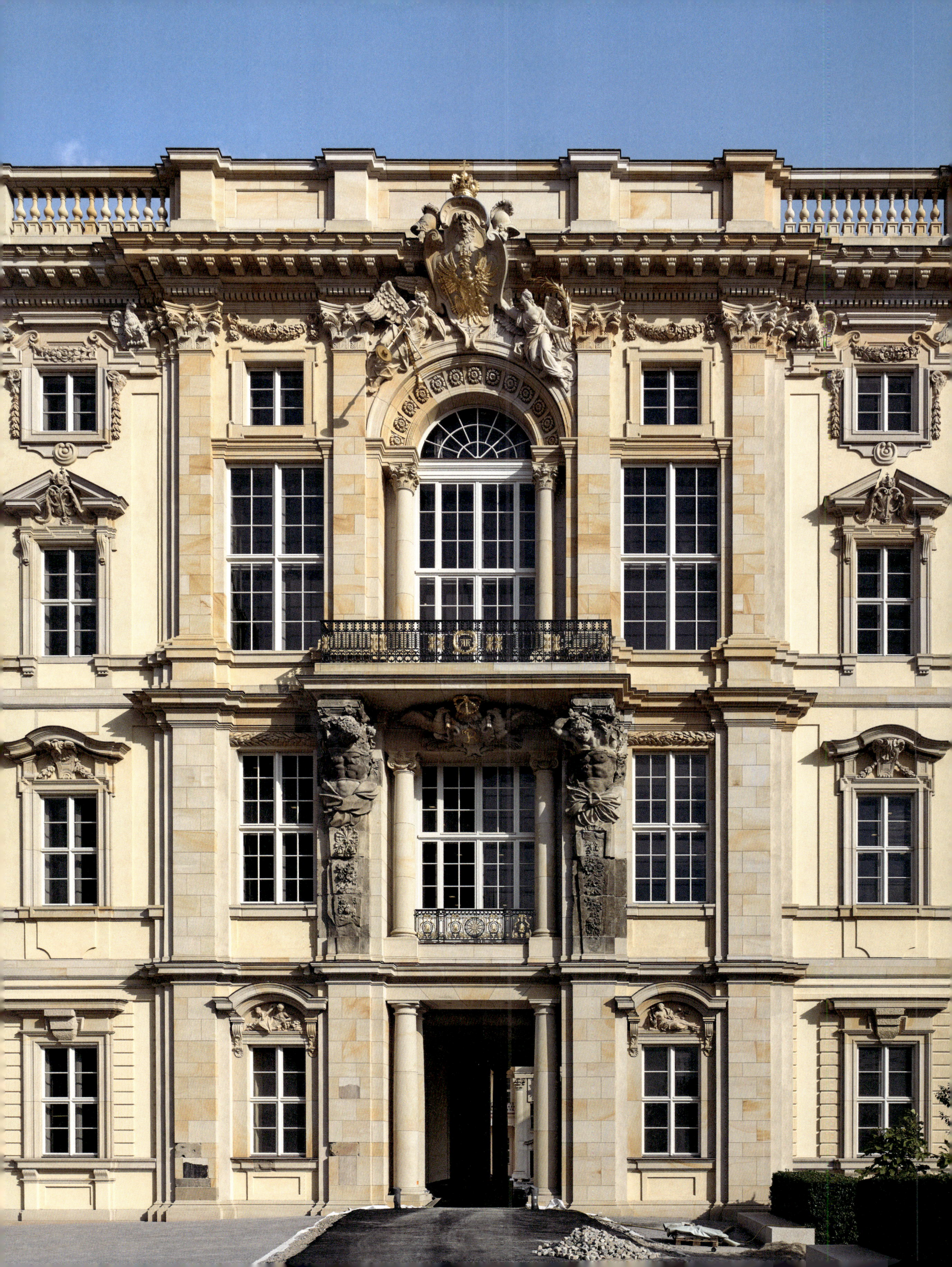

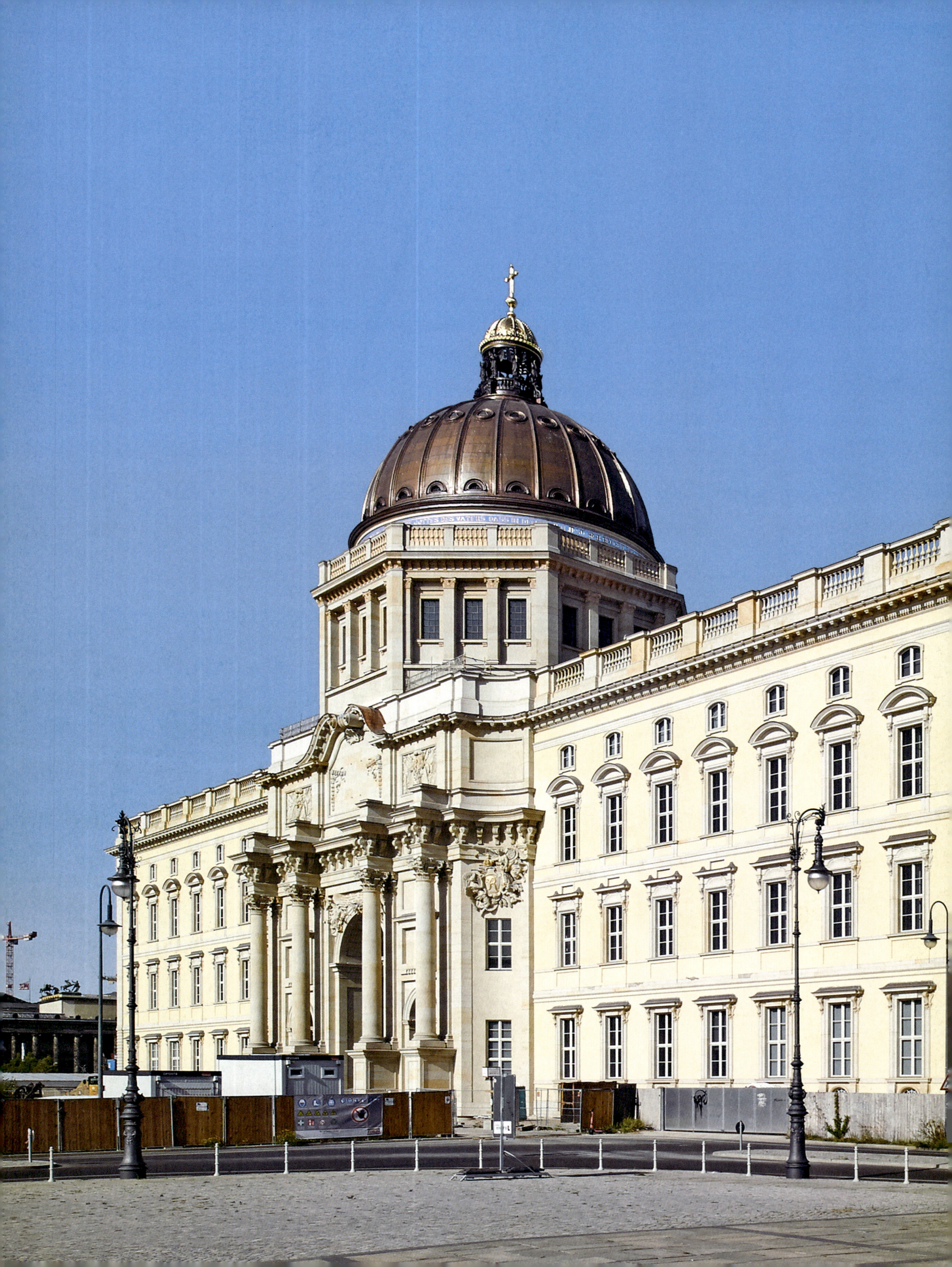

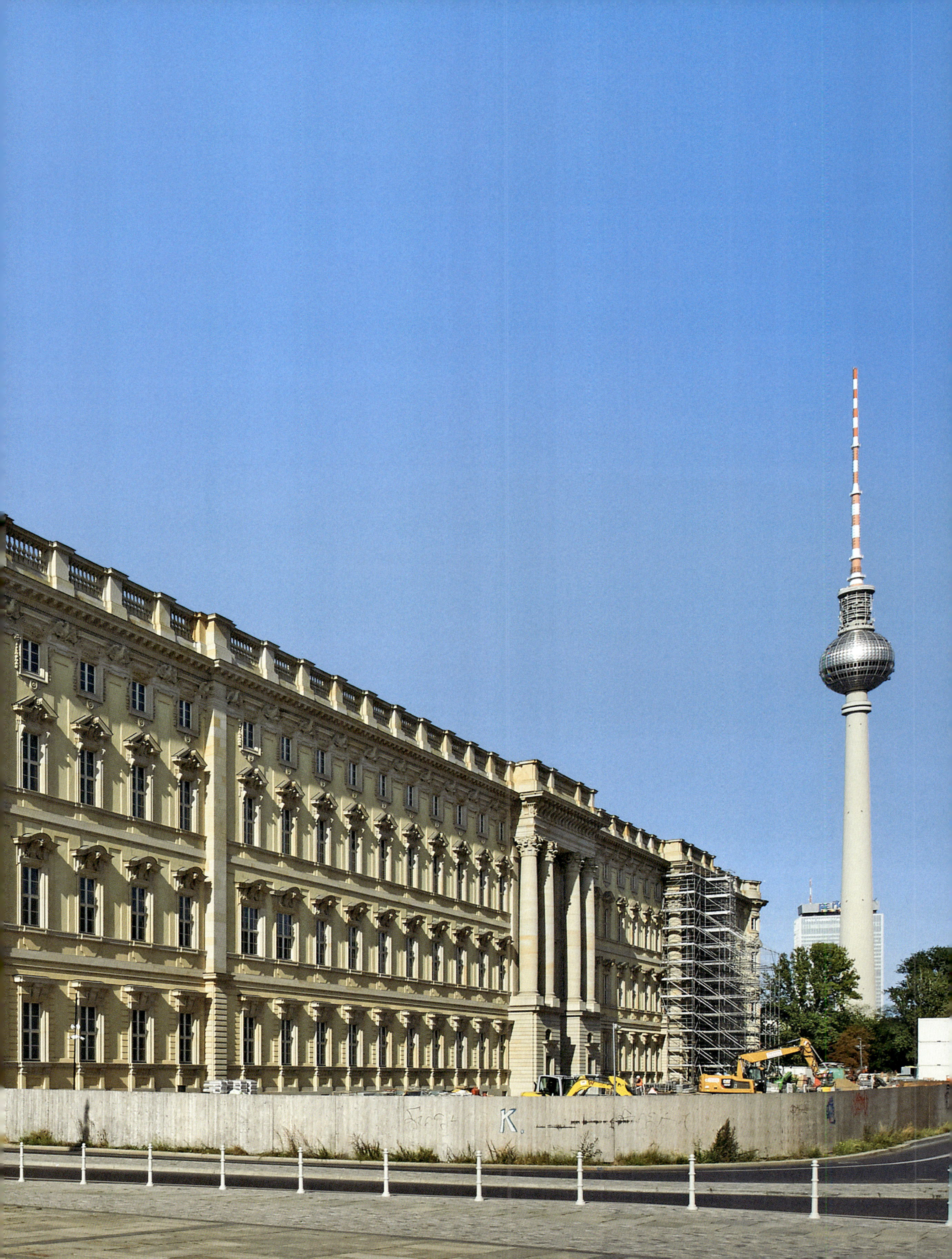

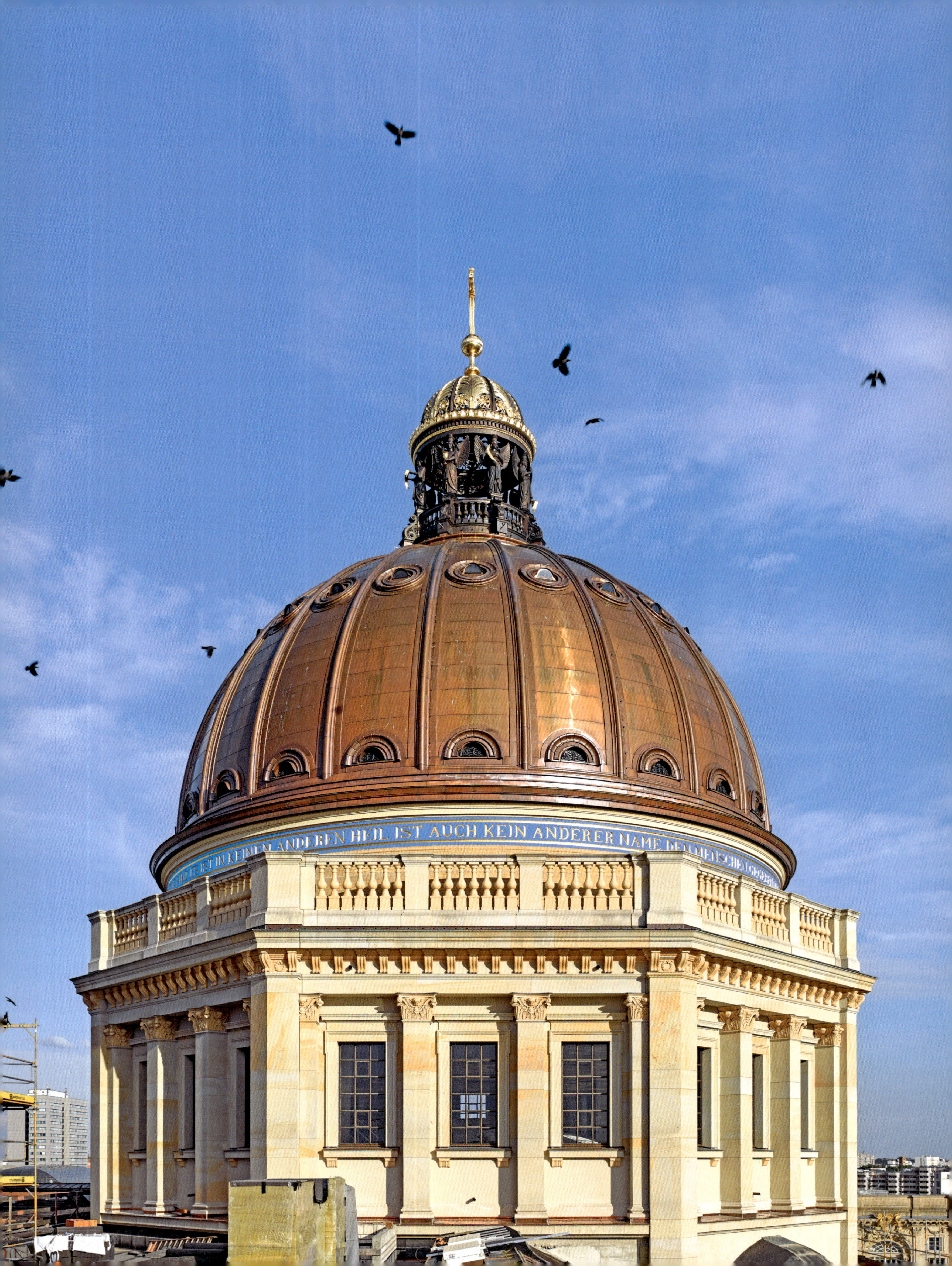

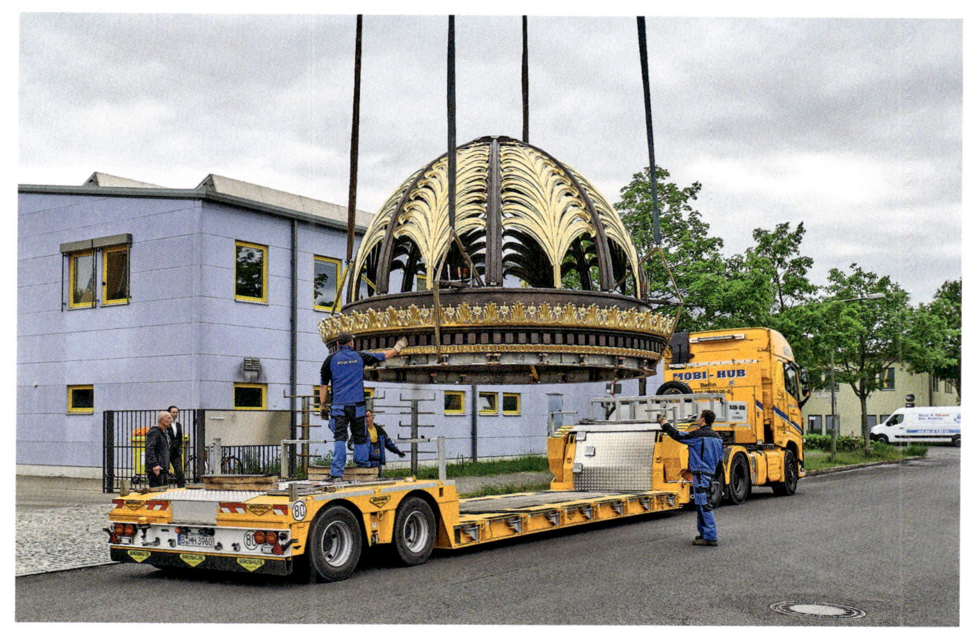

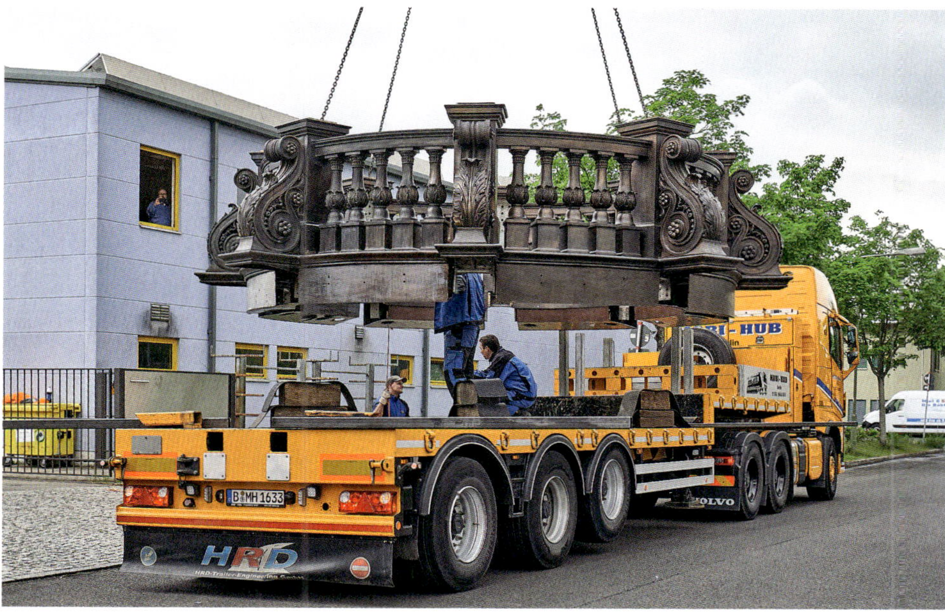

The classical cupola above the triumphal arch of Portal 3 was set into place by Friedrich August Stüler only in the mid-19th century, embellishing the Baroque Palace constructed in the early 18th century by Andreas Schlüter and Johann Friedrich Eosander.

The cupola on the reconstructed Berlin Palace acquired its crowning terminus, namely the lantern and golden cross, in late May of 2020. Work on this part of the building alone – consisting of steel, bronze and a half kilo of gold leaf – lasted two years.

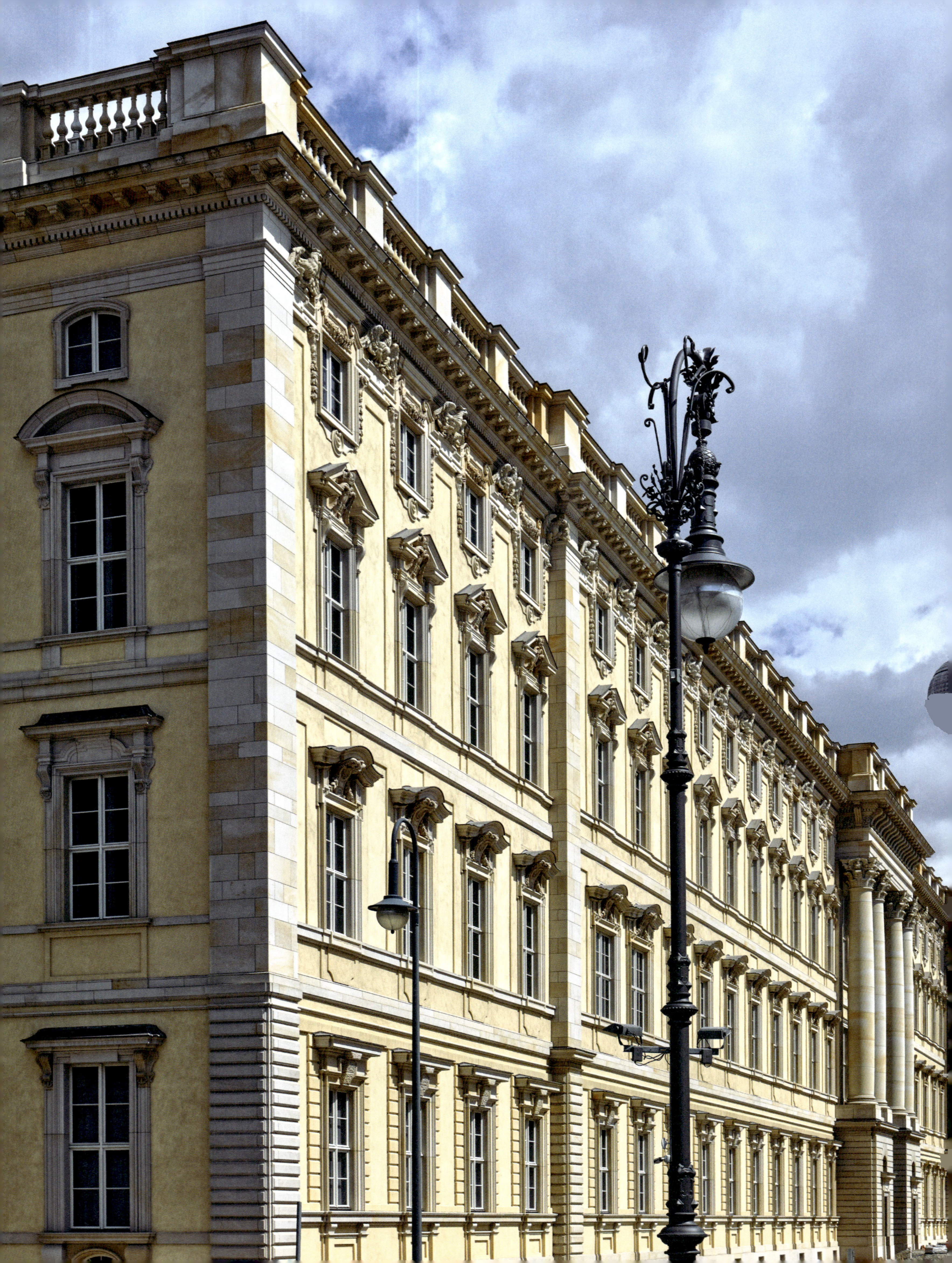

The facade facing the former
Schlossplatz (Palace Square) to
the south was erected under the
generous rule of the first Prussian
King, Friedrich I. Under his more
parsimonious son, the Soldier King
Friedrich Wilhelm I, the facade
ornamentation assumed a far bleaker
aspect, a contrast highlighted by a
comparison between the southern
facade on the right and the western
facade on the left.

Fig. pp. 22–23:
The aesthetic contrast between
Baroque reconstruction and
contemporary facade at the northeast
corner of the building illustrates the
challenge faced by the architect.
Located here in the historical building
was the apothecary wing.

Fig. pp. 24–25:
Harboured behind the contemporary
grid facade along the Spree River, with
its closed windows, are elongated
exhibition halls; the 1st upper storey,
shown here, houses the Berlin
Exhibition.

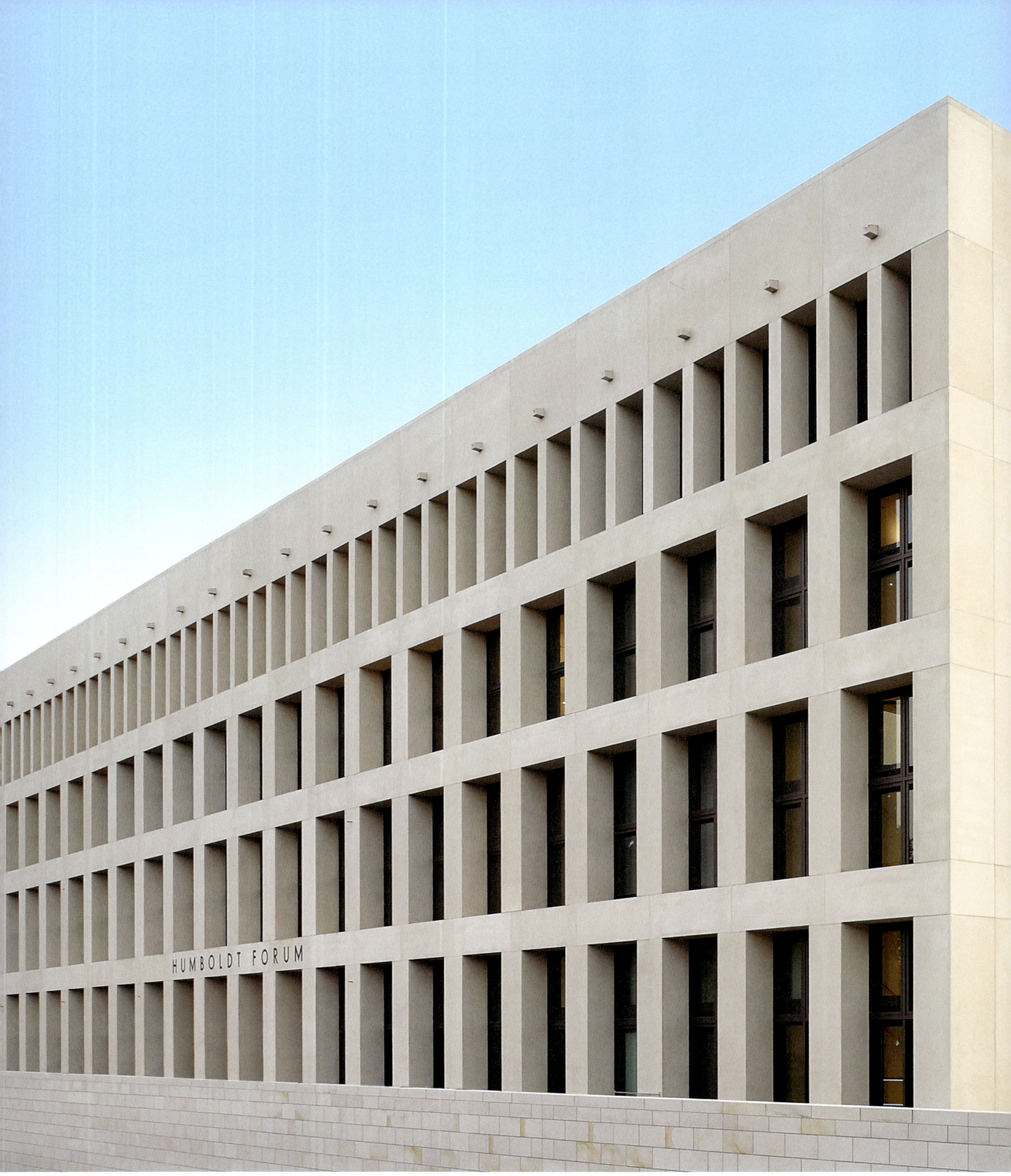
HUMBOLDT FORUM

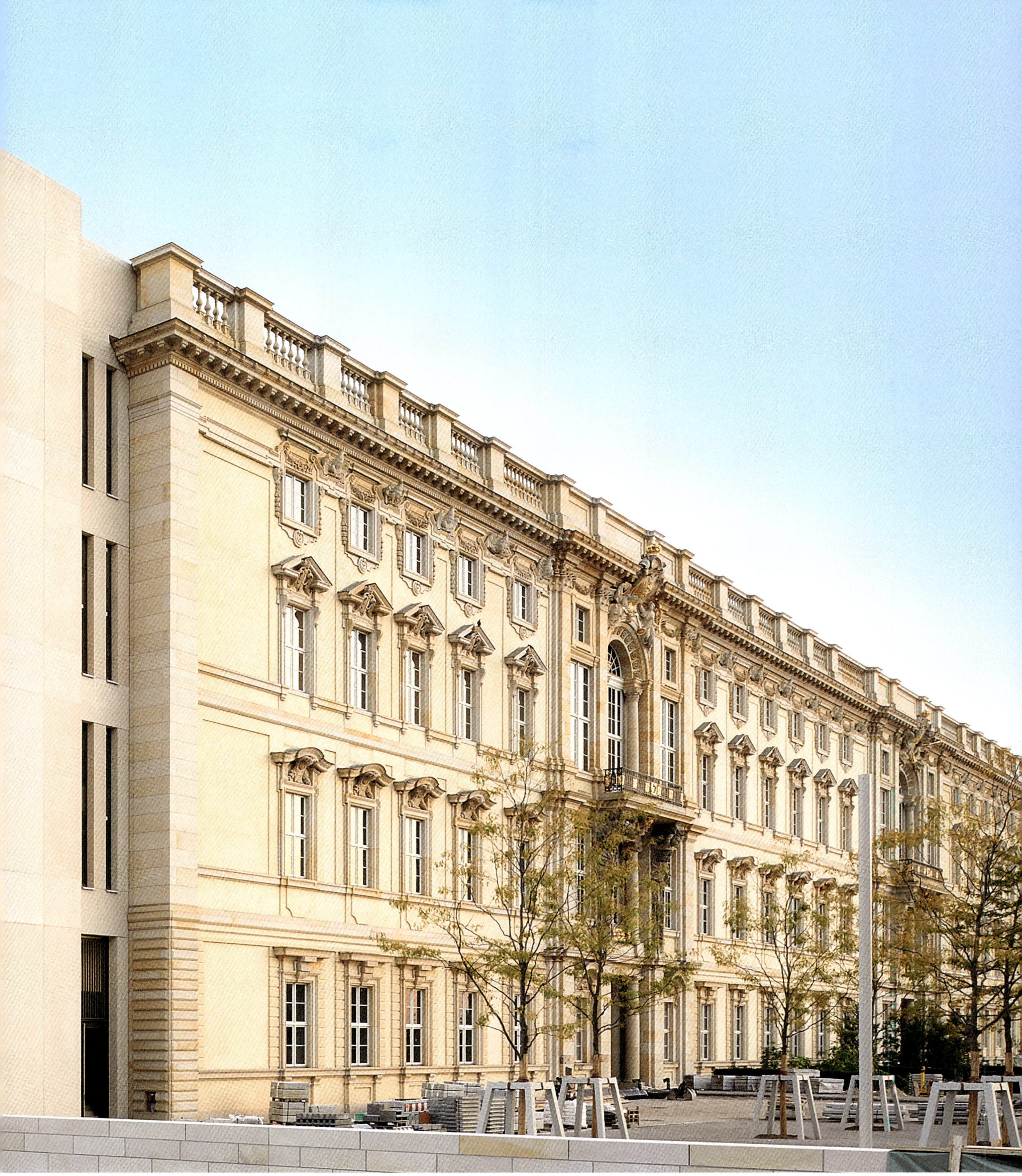

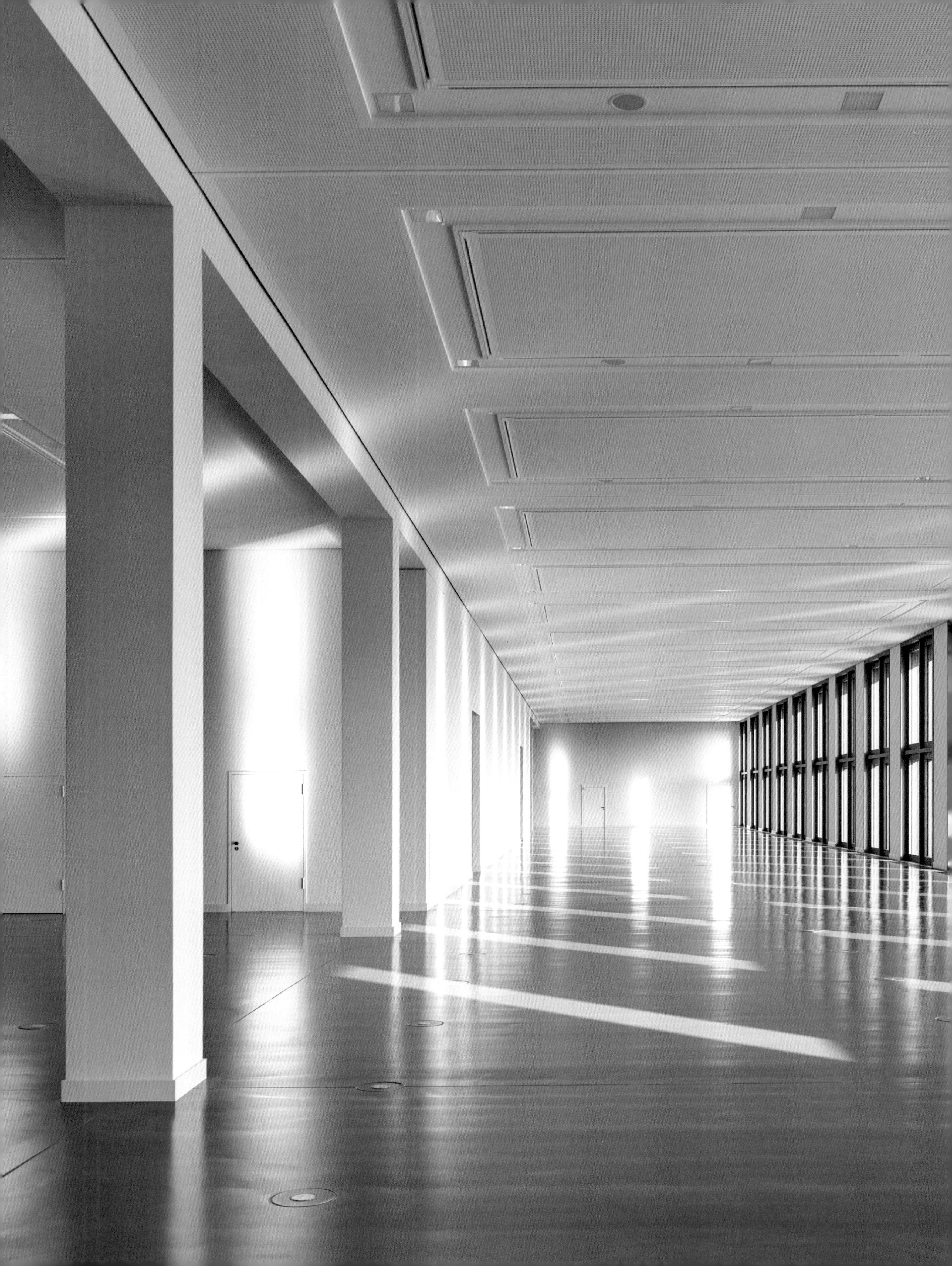

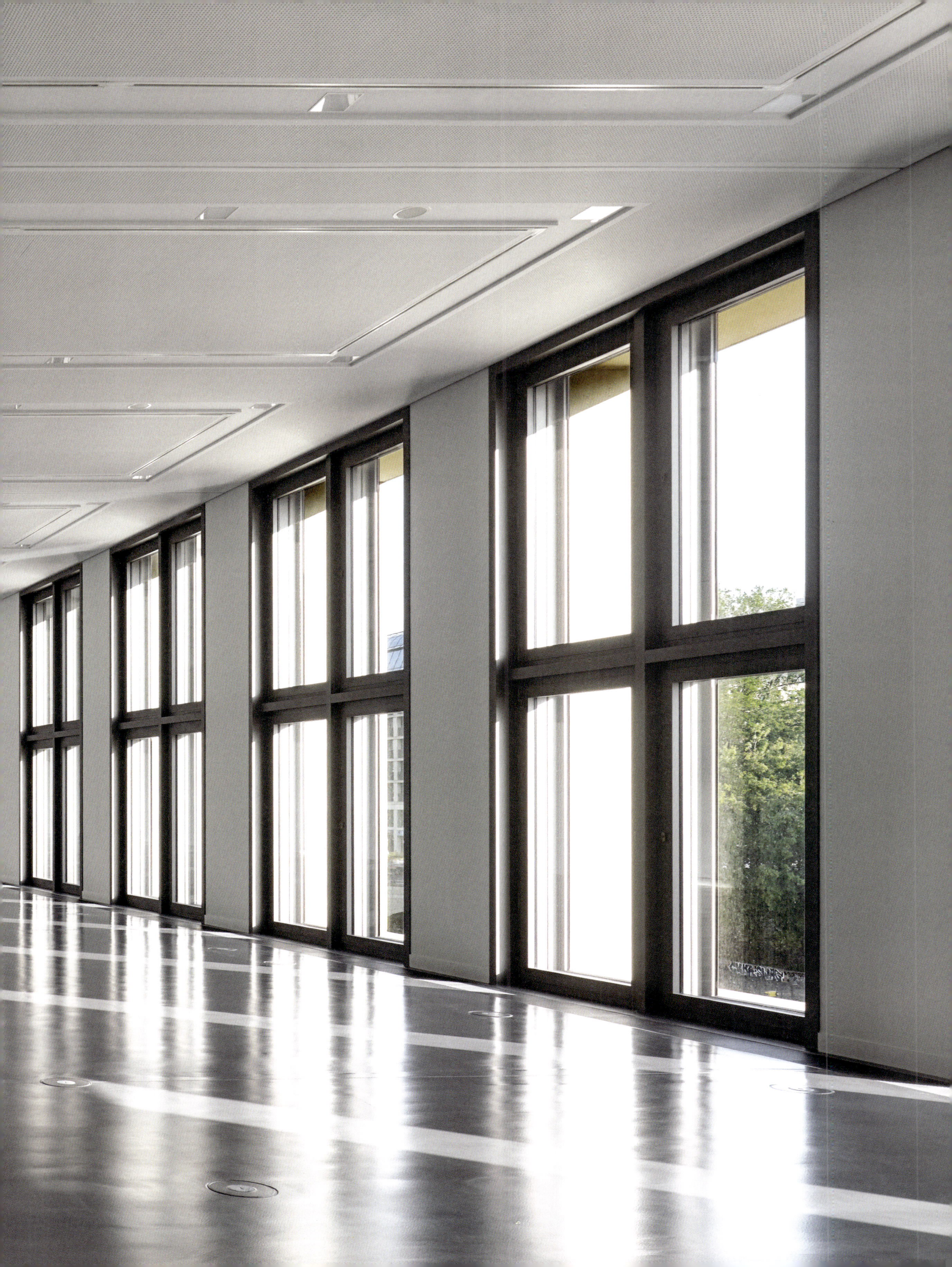

From the famous round bay,
positioned at the southeastern
corner of the building, the view opens
towards the Television Tower and
the Rotes Rathaus (Red City Hall).
Seated here in his study 270 years
ago, Friedrich the Great gazed out
upon a very different world.

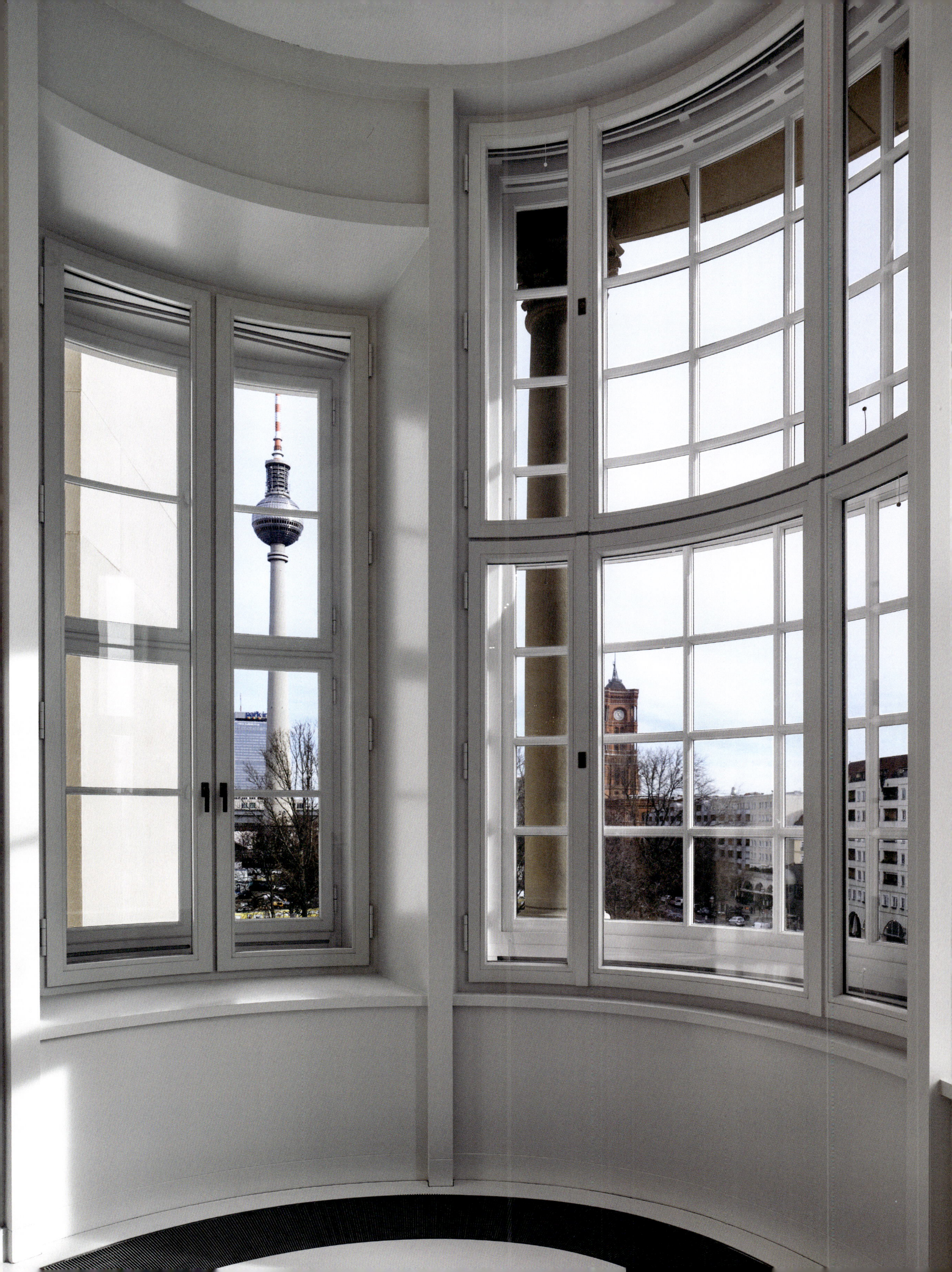

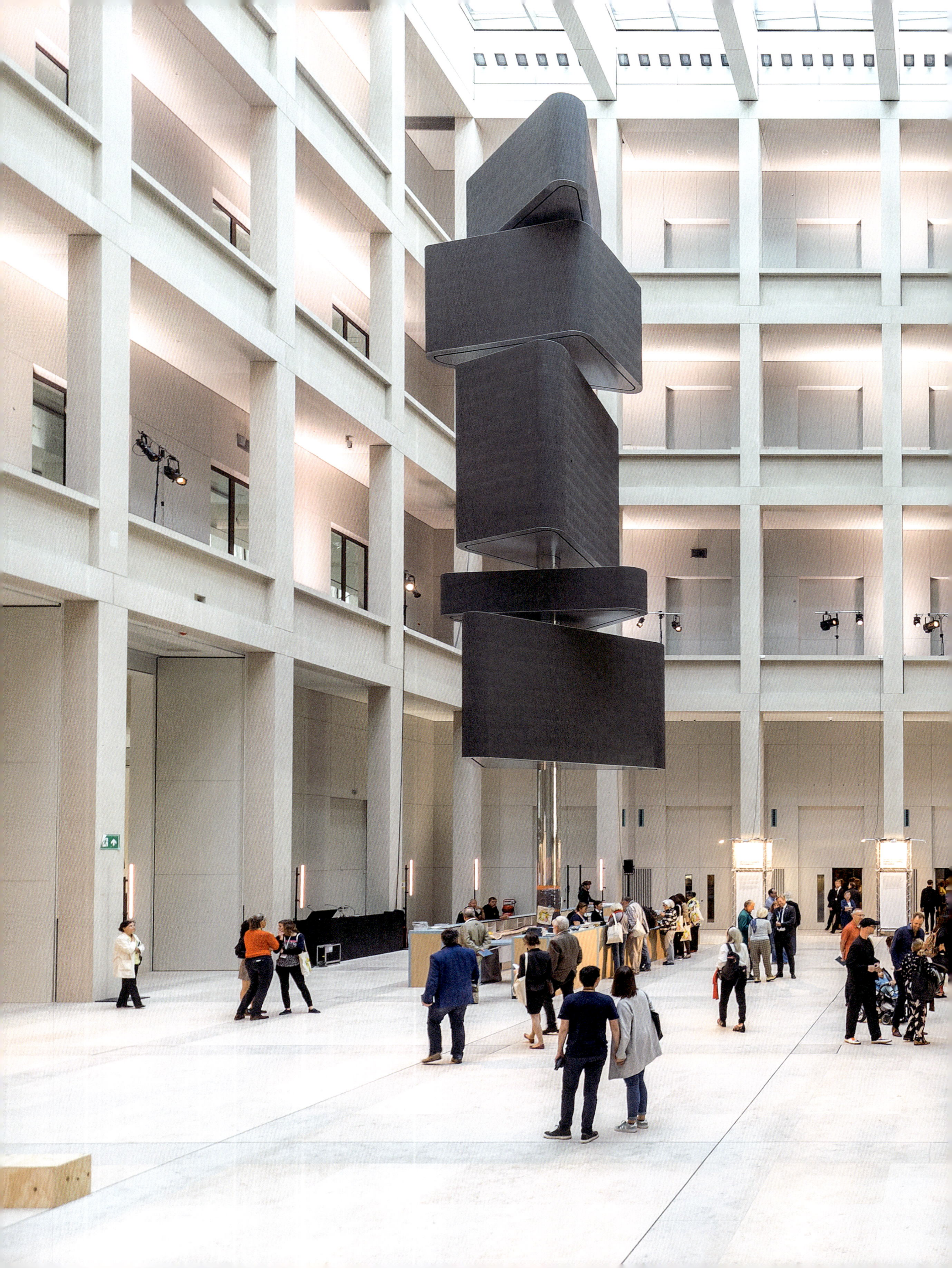

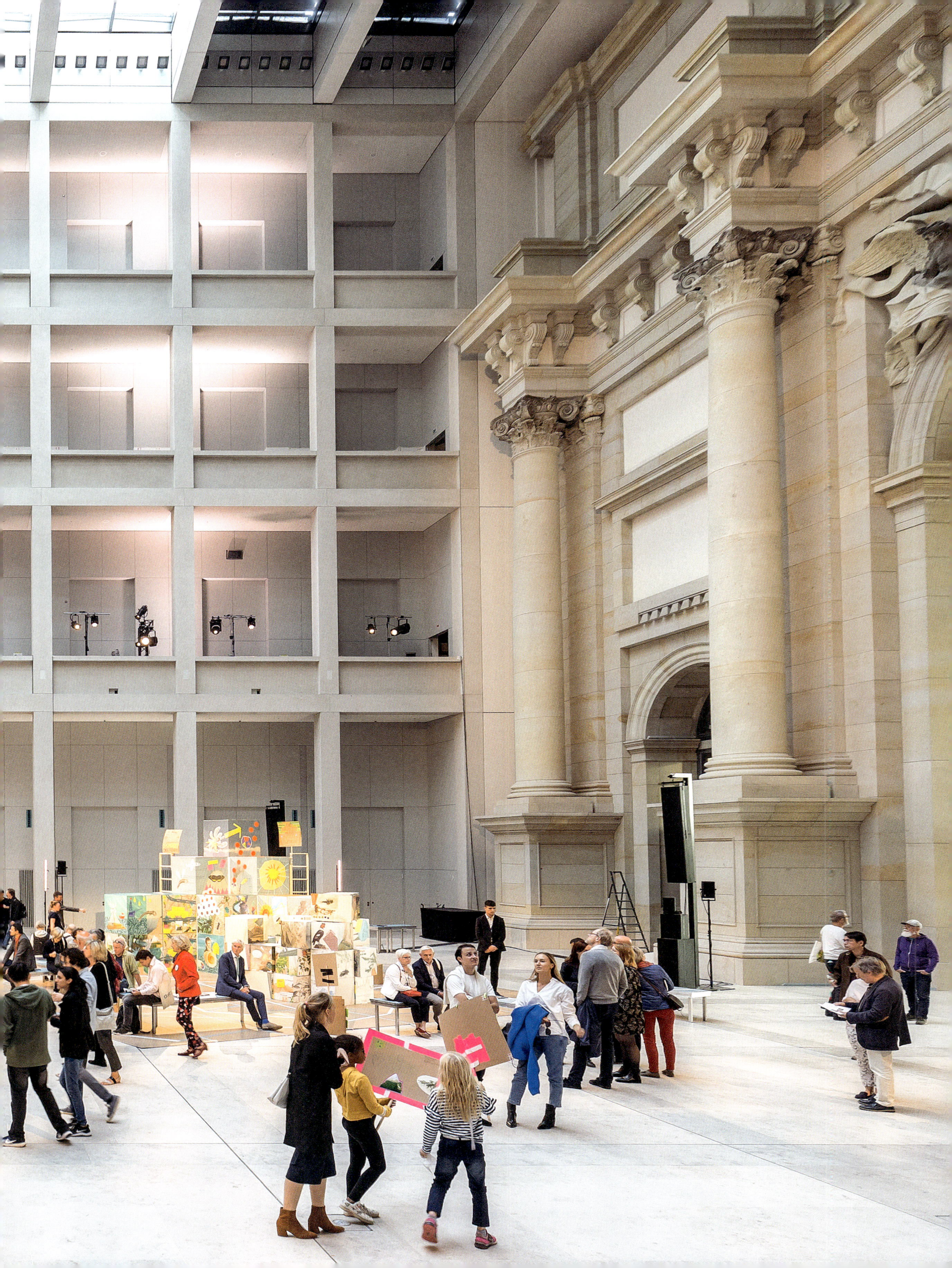

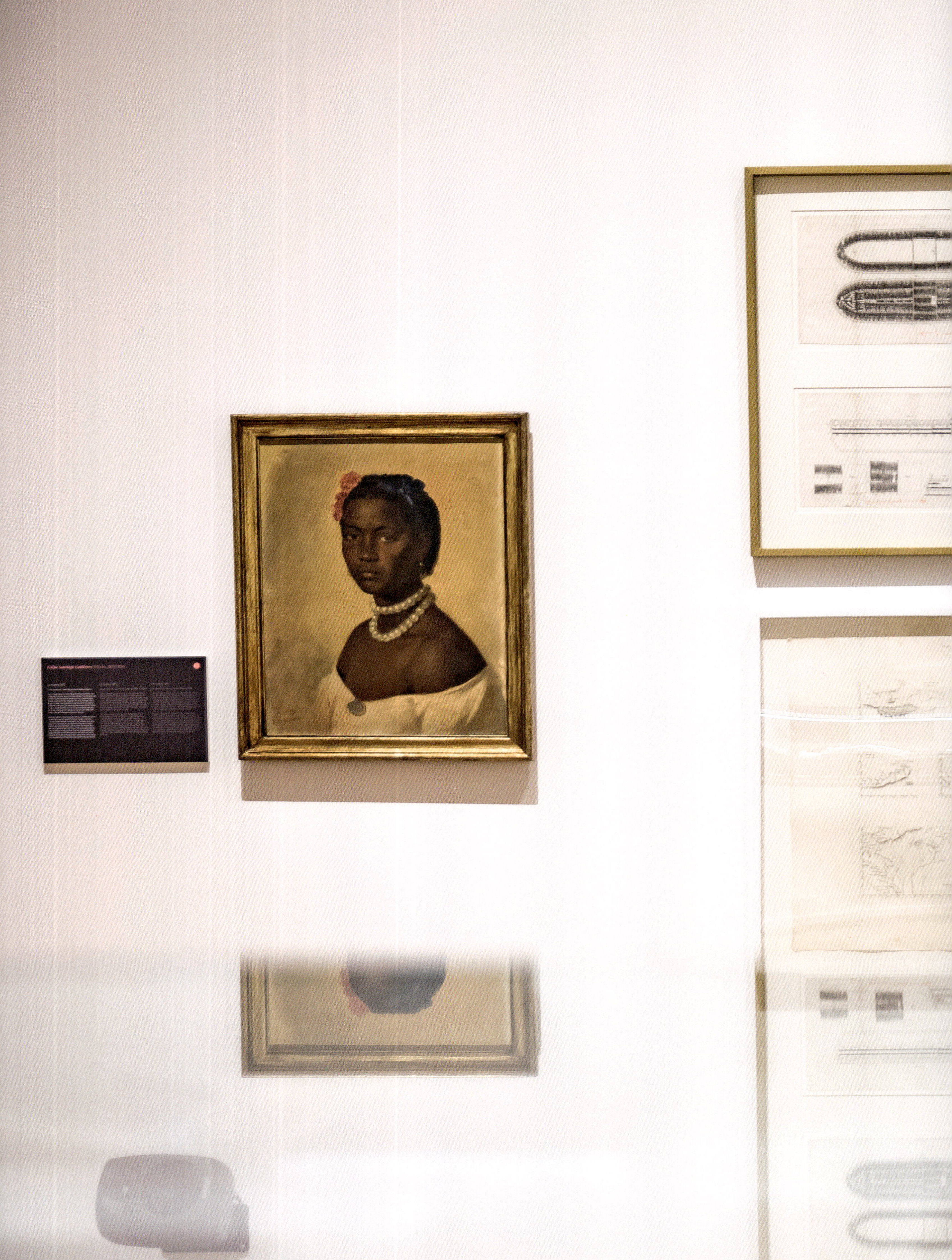

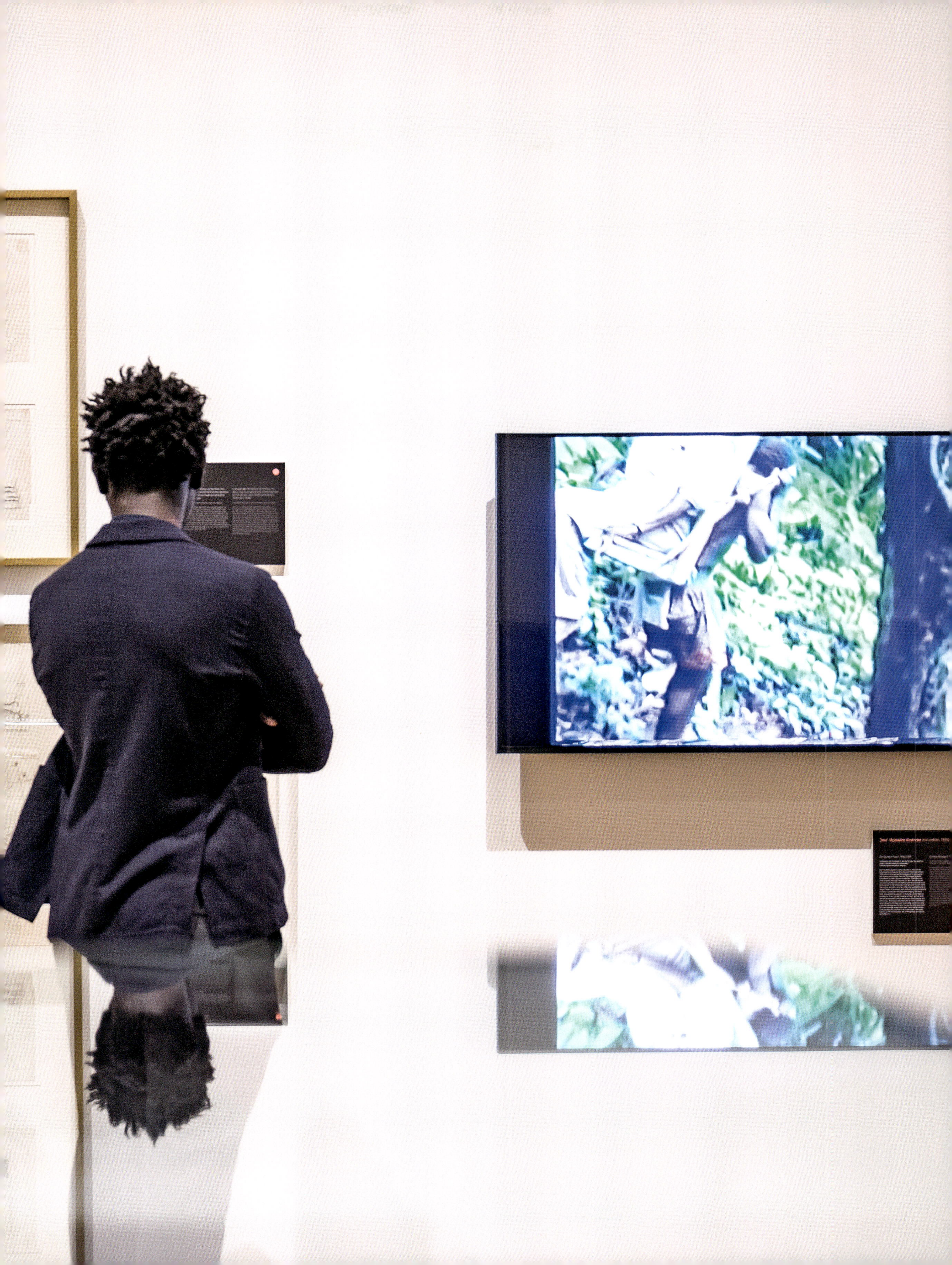

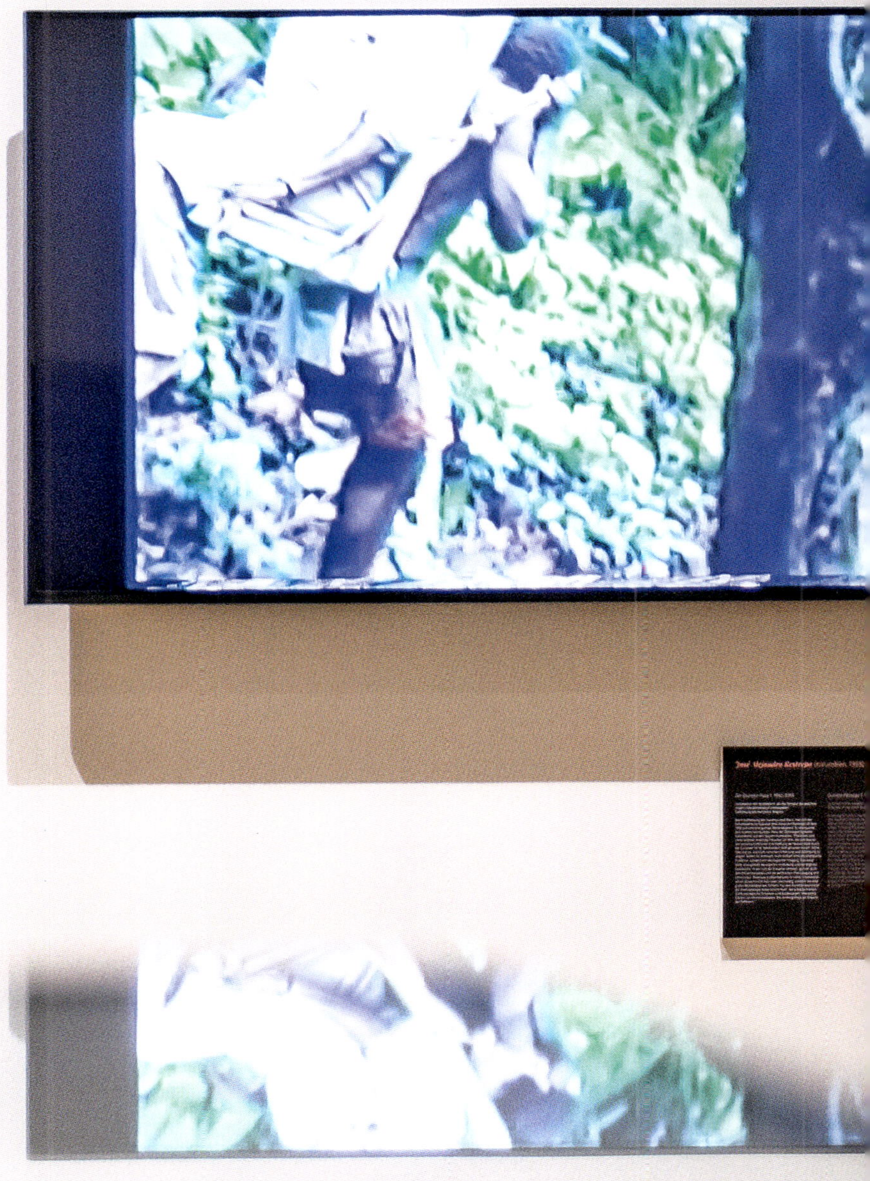

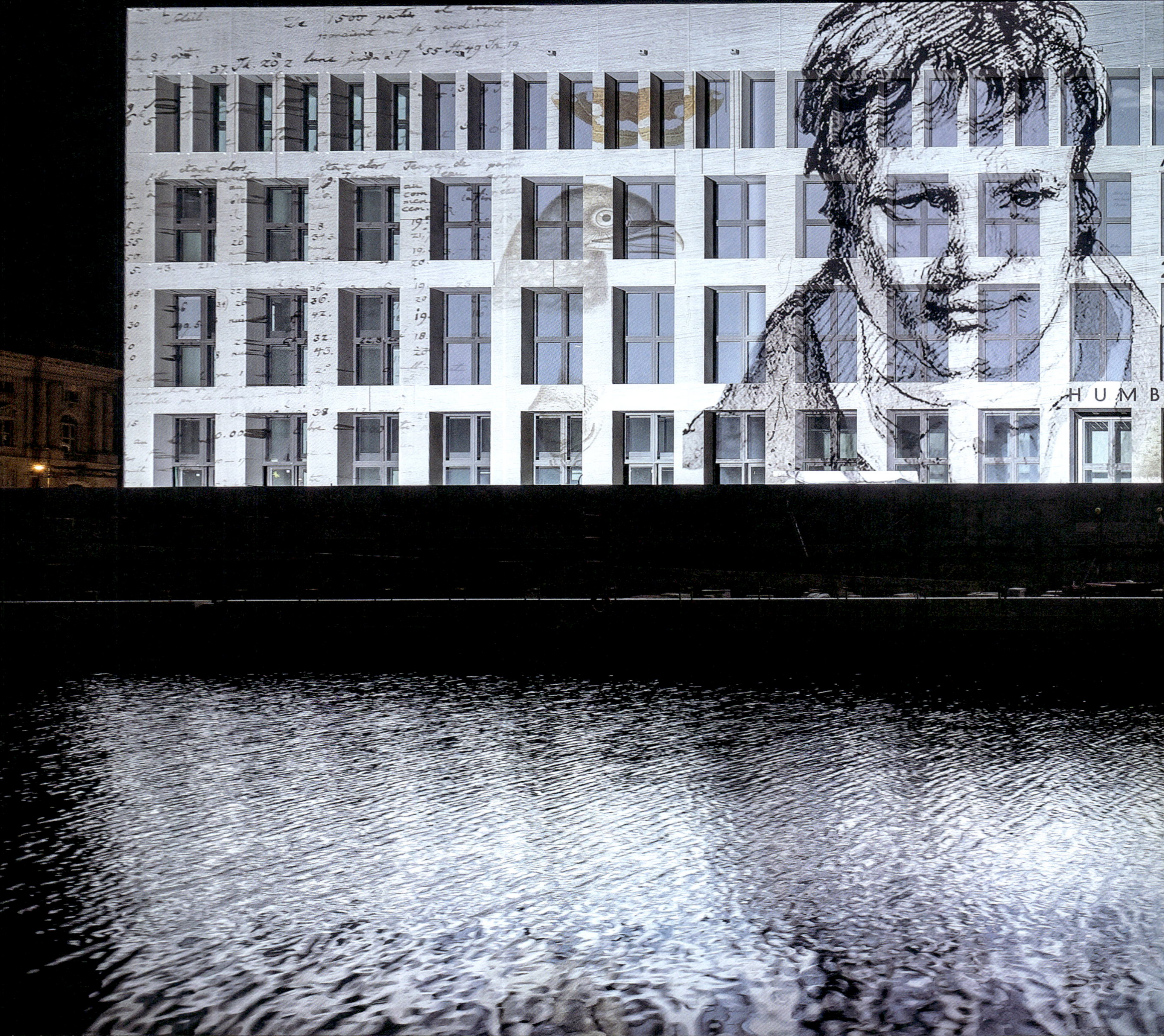
HUMB

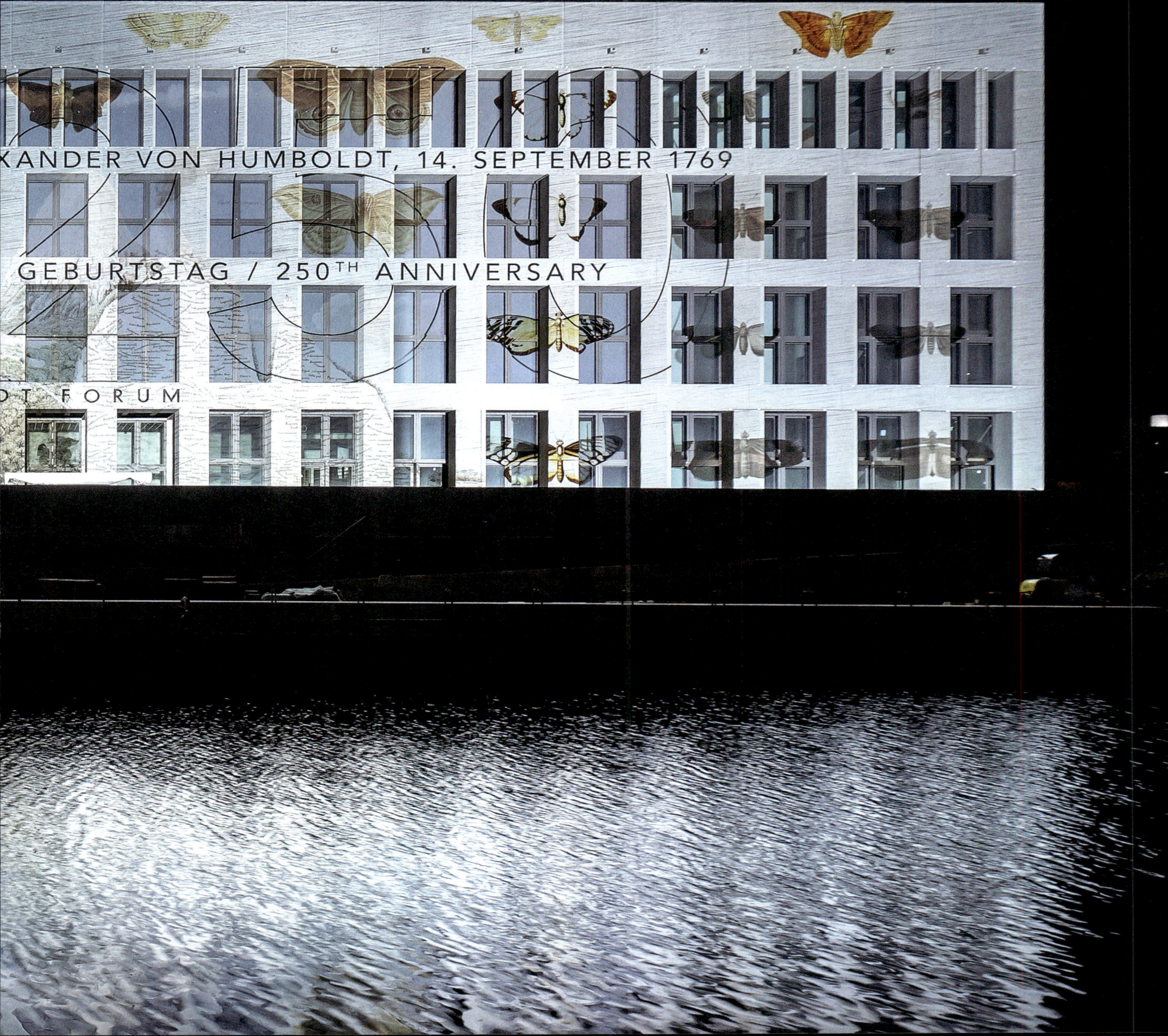
XANDER VON HUMBOLDT, 14. SEPTEMBER 1769
GEBURTSTAG / 250TH ANNIVERSARY
DT FORUM

A Mobile for the Humboldt Forum in the Berlin Palace: The Programme

Hartmut Dorgerloh

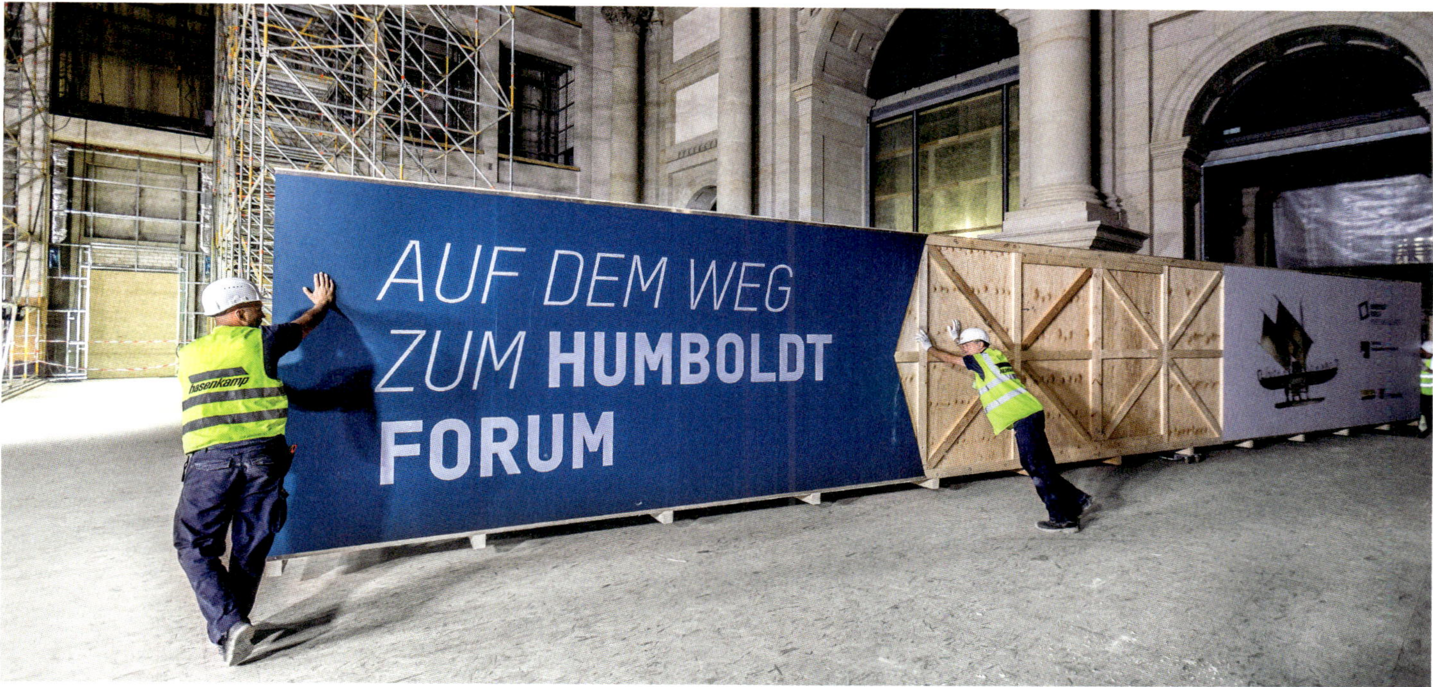

'Only those who know the past have a future' – Wilhelm von Humboldt's fundamental insight is inscribed, figuratively speaking, on the foundation of the new Humboldt Forum.

Not just because the historical stratification of this location on the Spree Island is strikingly perceptible in the reconstructed facade of the former residential palace of the Hohenzollerns. But also because a portion of the non-European objects are returning now to the place that formerly housed the electoral and royal cabinet of artworks and naturalia. These 'rarities' formed the nucleus of the collections of the Berlin museums, including the Völkerkundemuseum (Museum of Ethnology).

Inaugurated here in 1976, on the site of the historical Royal Palace that was demolished after World War II, was the Palast der Republik (Palace of the Republic) – the political and cultural centre of the capital of the German Democratic Republic (GDR, more commonly known as East Germany). In a new way, the Humboldt Forum now embodies the idea of a palace of culture, complete with event venues, bars and restaurants.

These two divergent aspects suffice to make it clear why this historical stratification is such an important element in the programmatic self-conception of the Humboldt Forum: an intensive and unprejudiced attempt to come to terms with the past enables a versatile reimagining of future realities.

The Humboldt Forum reverses the idea of the palace as a royal seat, as a symbol of monarchical authority, of hierarchical distinction into its opposite – both socially as well as politically. Conceived and realized as a forum, it now becomes an open, inviting place of encounter, of cooperation based on equality, of shared experience, of global learning.

Transport and installation in the Humboldt Forum of the Luf boat from the Ethnologisches Museum (Ethnological Museum) in Berlin-Dahlem, 2018

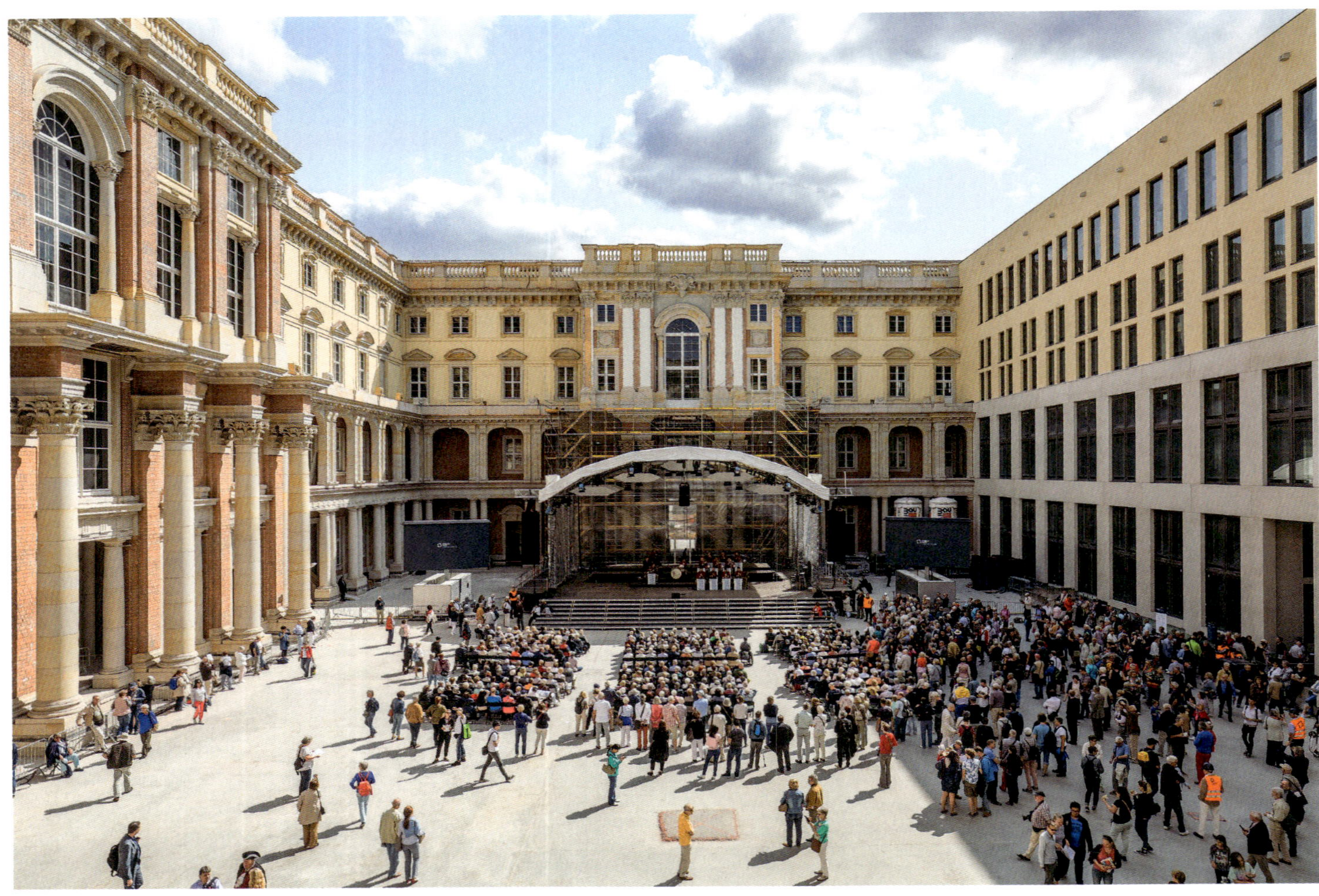

A concert in the Schlüter Courtyard
on the occasion of the last Day of
the Open Construction Site, 2018

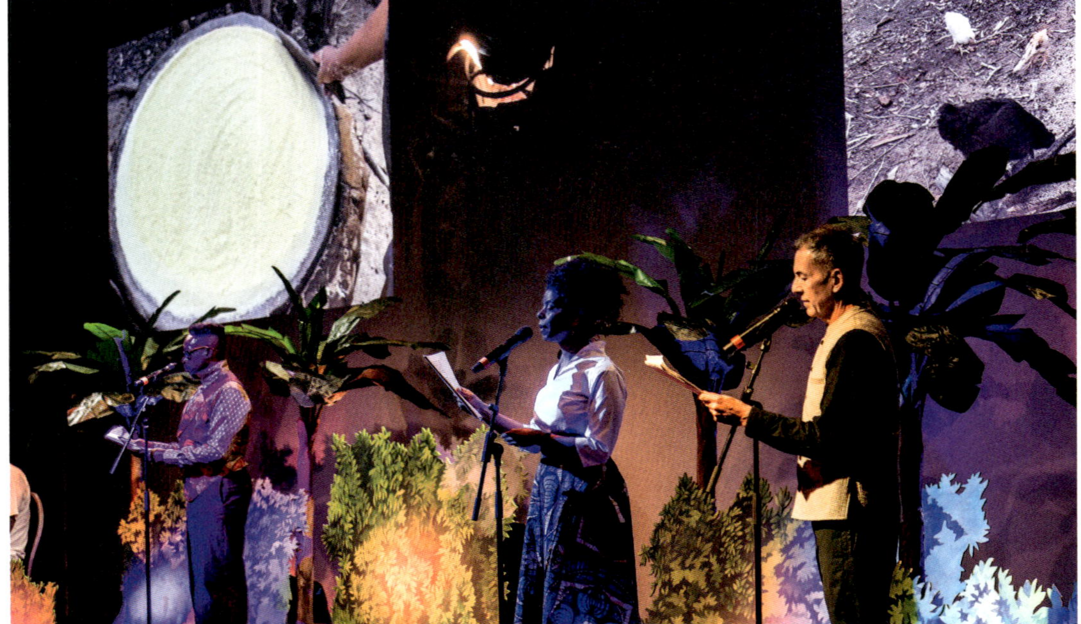

Sobre bogas y remeros (On Bogas
and Rowers): performative lecture
by the group around Mara Viveros
from Bogotá at the Humboldt Forum
on the occasion of Alexander von
Humboldt's 250th birthday, 2019

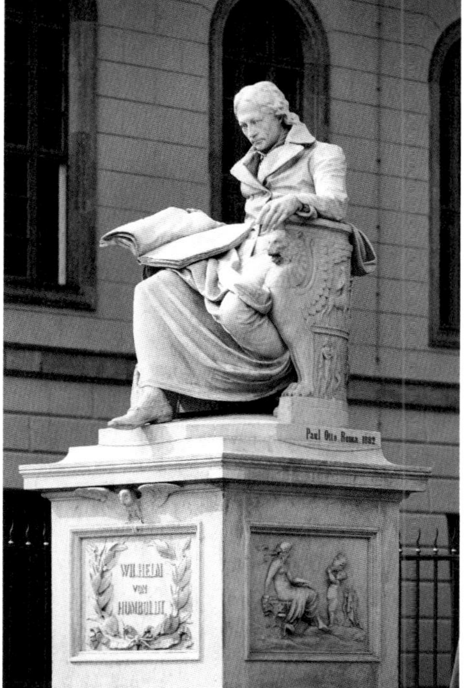

'From its genesis onward, everything strives towards new inter-relatedness!' This essential insight of Alexander von Humboldt's, the second namesake of the Humboldt Forum, shapes all of its activities through the principle of the composite and the modular.

Both topics and institutions will come together here in new, mutually enriching ways: the collections of the Staatliche Museen zu Berlin/ Stiftung Preussischer Kulturbesitz (Berlin State Museums/Prussian Cultural Heritage Foundation) – in the form of the Ethnologisches Museum (Ethnological Museum) and the Museum für Asiatische Kunst (Museum of Asian Art) – will join forces with the exhibitions of the Humboldt Labor of Humboldt-Universität (HUB). The Berlin Exhibition of the Stiftung Stadtmuseum (City Museum of Berlin Foundation), another component of the ensemble, provides an additional perspective through new contexts. Within the wider spectrum of the Humboldt Forum, interdisciplinary exhibitions on scholarship and science encounter presentations of the history of Berlin, of the constitutive characteristics of the city, of the historically evolved collections of non-European art and culture, along with many other collaborative endeavours in temporary and special exhibitions of current relevance. Such exchanges open up astonishing possibilities of interaction, forming new thematic surfaces for friction and adhesion, opportunities for interpenetration, but also differentiation. This conceptually entrenched principle of polyphony and multiperspectivism grounds the potential of the Humboldt Forum and defines its tasks.

Additionally, there are the three components that make the Humboldt Forum a place that remains in constant movement: event programmes (museums and exhibitions), research, and educational activities. As workshops for ideas on equal terms with each other, all three serve to generate impulses in cooperation with many partner institutions, along with creative artists and people working in the cultural field worldwide, setting the most diverse genres and formats into relationship with one another. Coming together here in perpetually new ways are people, topics and formats. In this way, the Humboldt Forum strives to make an independent contribution to the further development of cultural institutions in the twenty-first century.

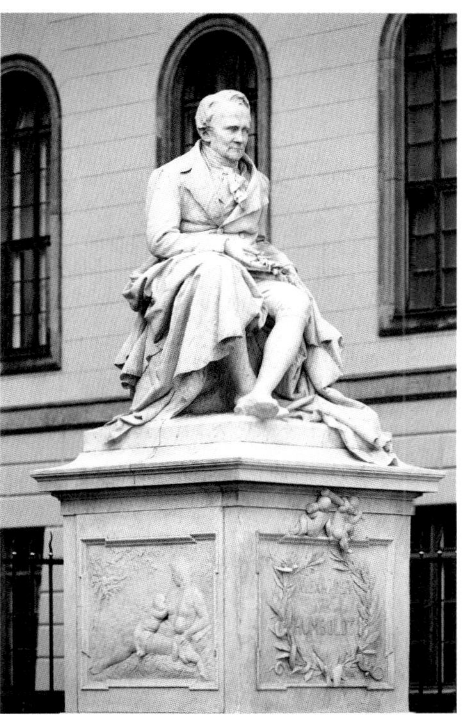

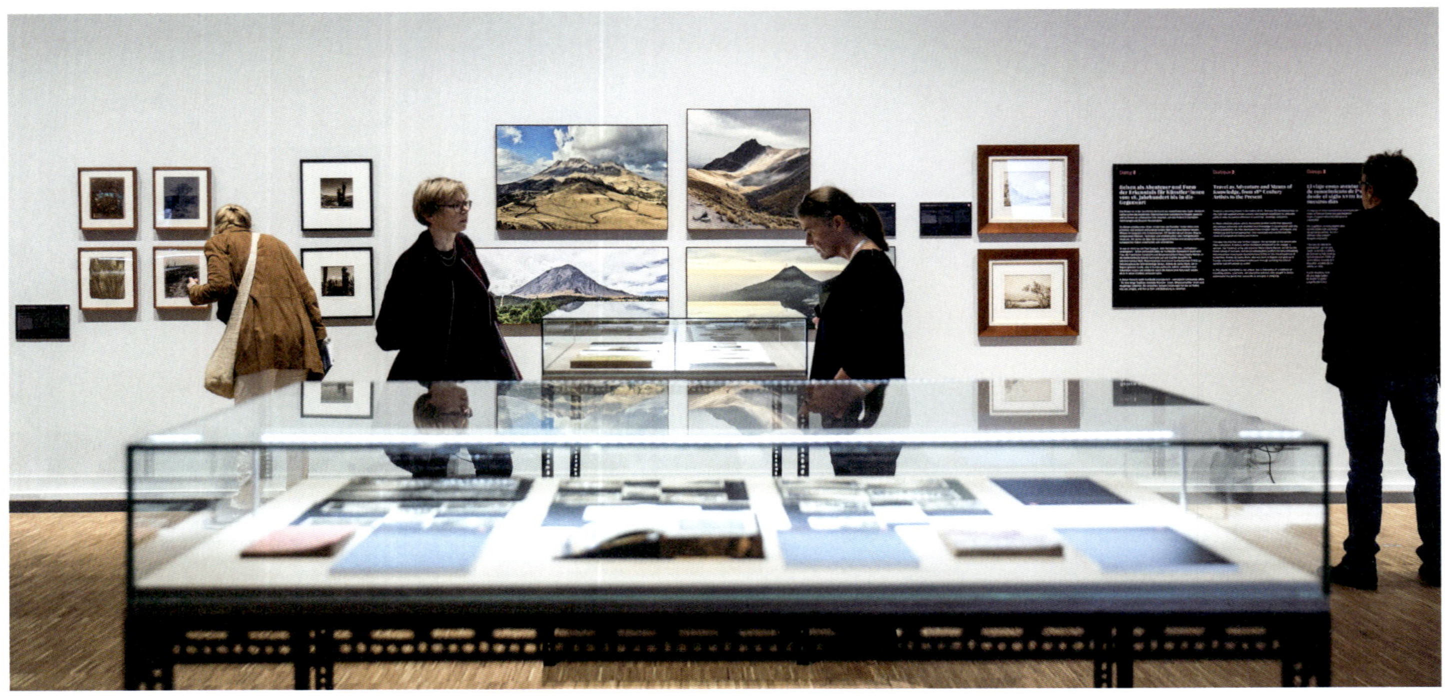

La naturaleza de las cosas (The Naturalness of Things): exhibition at the Humboldt Forum on the occasion of Alexander von Humboldt's 250th birthday, 2019

'Everything is interdependent', as Alexander von Humboldt, one of the great thinkers of relationality, wrote in his travel diary in Mexico in August of 1803.

At the centre of his unquenchable curiosity about manifold places and regions, about historical epochs and cultural forms, was a form of knowledge of life and of the world that interweaves nature and culture with one another – a map on which many different sites and pathways of knowledge and perspectives on the world have been inscribed, hence communicating with one another. Alexander's aspiration to 'connect ideas, to identify concatenations of things' becomes a leitmotiv for the Humboldt Forum, a challenge to contribute to making this 'reticulated, labyrinthine fabric', consisting of cultural styles, habitats, sciences, art forms, political structures and histories, into something visible. The principle of reciprocal relationships operates down to the smallest detail. It can be viewed and understood prismatically, in a multifaceted way.

The vision of the Humboldt Forum is to set processes of thought into motion in various directions as moving, amorphous structures, not unlike a mobile, to supply proposals and impulses for a respectful form of intricate coexistence that promotes peace, thereby making an effective contribution in a rapidly changing multipolar world. In the search for connective differentiations, the Humboldt Forum is conceived as a refuge for ambiguity and multiperspectivism as well as an agent of intercultural and transcultural competencies – a decisive priority here being an appreciation for global diversity.

The courage for contradiction is inherent to the architecture of the building itself – as a sanctuary and a place of debate, the Humboldt Forum becomes a mobile base which nonetheless offers orientation when the focus is broadened to encompass the dynamism of a future world society.

'Thinking and knowledge must always keep pace with one another. Otherwise, knowledge remains fruitless.' – Once again, it is a Humboldt brother, in this case Wilhelm, who points the way forward.

The residency and research programmes, as well as the research and educational offerings of the Humboldt Forum Academy – alongside events and exhibitions – will provide a platform for insecurity in the best sense of the word, a place to challenge one's own position, to listen to other voices, arriving at agreement as well as acknowledging dissent.

The Humboldt Forum is not conceived as a *perpetuum mobile* – on the contrary. It relies on the variably moving synergies from different sides: on involvement on the part of the public, on invitations to forms of cooperation, participation and appropriation, on stimuli from a broad, international public sphere. Here, balance is the decisive factor. When it is achieved, the individual, moving elements form a recognizable three-dimensional structure that is endlessly varied. Let us hope that this aspiration – which is not without its risks – will bear fruit in the coming years. But, as Alexander von Humboldt once declared to King Friedrich Wilhelm IV: 'The difficult never seems impossible to me.'

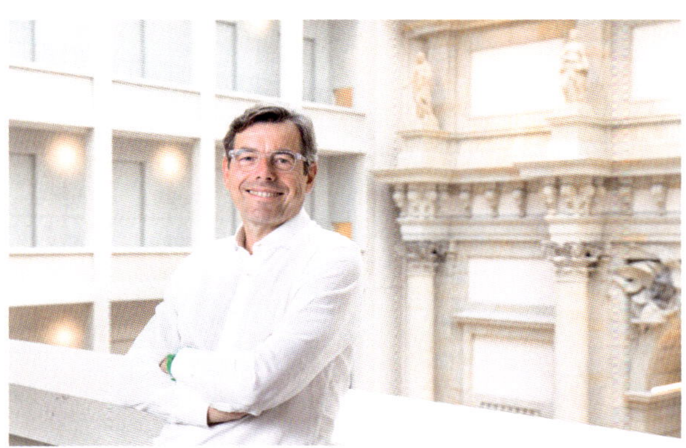

Hartmut Dorgerloh

The Berlin Palace as Urban Architecture

Franco Stella

THE LOST PALACE

Damaged during World War II, the Berliner Schloss (Berlin Palace) was demolished for ideological reasons in 1950 by the rulers of the German Democratic Republic (GDR, more commonly known as East Germany). Throughout its 500-year existence, it had been the most important building in Berlin – whether in socio-political or architectural–urbanistic terms. It was the residence of the prince-electors of Brandenburg (from 1443 until 1701), the Prussian kings (from 1701 until 1870) and the German emperors (from 1871 until 1918); it was the architectural director and leading actor of the city centre, built during the eighteenth and nineteenth centuries.

The Palace consisted of diverse parts of the Renaissance palace, which had been erected successively in the course of 250 years, and of the converted or new parts of the Baroque palace, erected over a period of seventeen years beginning in 1699 according to plans by Andreas Schlüter and later Johann Friedrich Eosander, as well as of the cupola, designed by Friedrich August Stüler in the mid-nineteenth century.

For architects, resolving the conflict between the Renaissance and Baroque elements of the Palace has long been a challenge: their ideal was an architecturally unitary palace with four wings. Schlüter proposed the radical transformation of the old buildings on the Spree riverfront; his successor Eosander, who was open to compromise, would have been satisfied with the demolition of the protruding apothecary wing. About one century later, Schinkel proposed concealing the apothecary wing with a 'wall of trees' so that Schlüter's Palace – 'a monument ... whose dignity and splendour ... rank it among Europe's premier buildings in every respect'[1] – could be perceived as a coherent building. A group of trees stood before the apothecary wing until the destruction of the Palace.

The Spree formerly functioned as the dividing line between the residence of the princely sovereigns and the pre-existing old town across the river, which no longer survives today. All of the important squares and buildings of the centre of Berlin located west of the Spree and still in existence today were oriented towards the Baroque Palace.

The Palace was the starting point, and later the terminus as well, of the monumental boulevard Unter den Linden, lined all the way to the Brandeburger Tor (Brandenburg Gate) with a series of public and private palaces, all constructed on commission from or on the initiative of the royal house. In the course of the nineteenth century, the Lustgarten (Pleasure Garden) on Unter den Linden evolved into the Museumsinsel

[1] Karl Friedrich Schinkel, *Gutachten über die Erhaltung der Statuen auf dem königlichen Schlosse zu Berlin* [Report on the preservation of the statues at the Berlin Royal Palace], 1817.

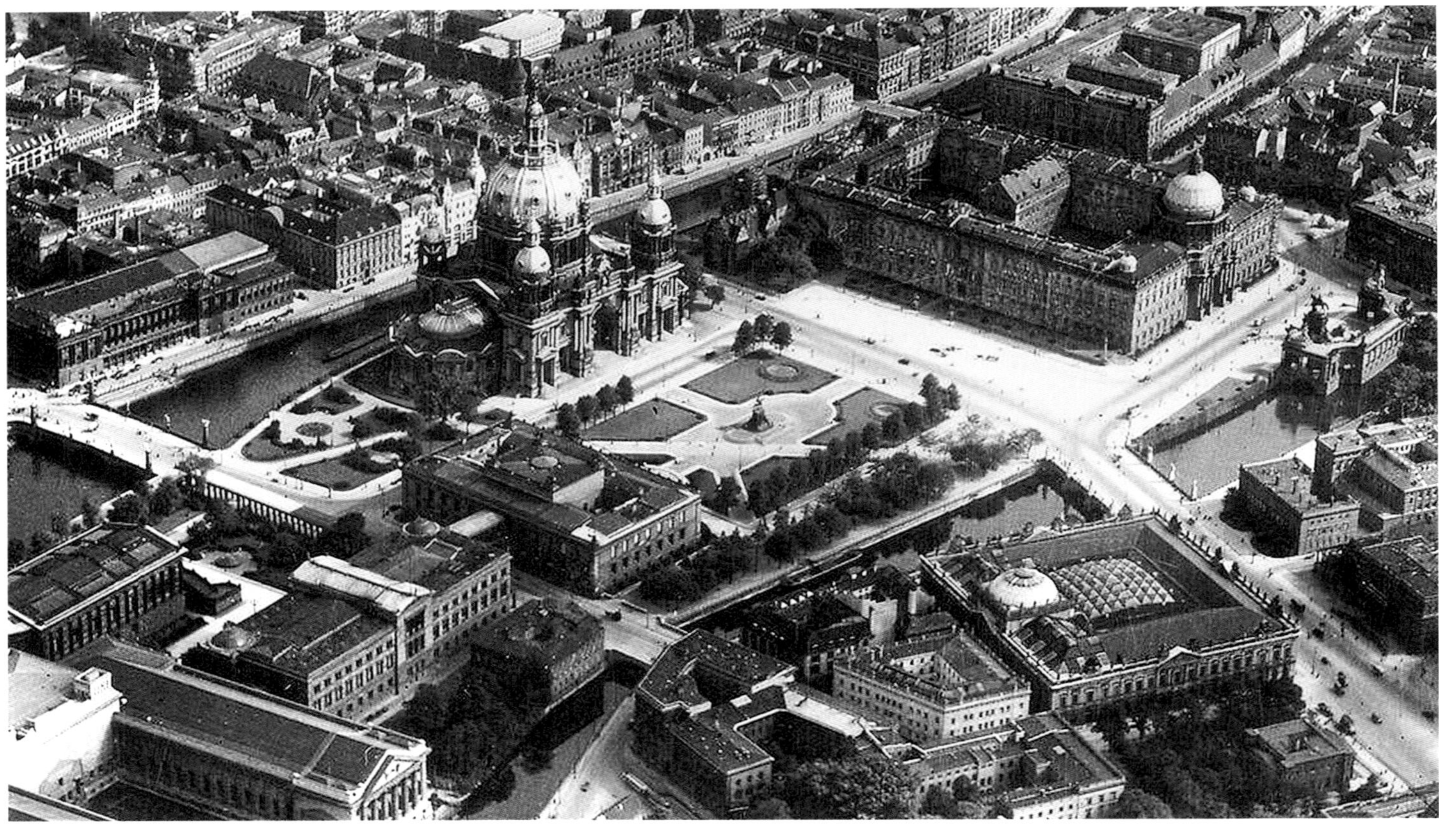

Aerial photograph of the historical
Berlin Palace and surroundings, 1925

(Museum Island). In front of the Palace, an ensemble of symbolically charged buildings related to the military (the Zeughaus or Arsenal), religion (the Berliner Dom or Cathedral), and culture (the Altes Museum or Old Museum) combined with it to form a kind of 'piazza dei quattro poteri' (piazza of the four pillars of the Prussian state). And the monumental Greek colonnade of the Altes Museum had been conceived by Schinkel as the worthy counterpart of the Palace itself.

Disappearing together with the Palace was the comprehensibility of these architectural and urban relationships: the impossibility of experiencing the identity of the centre of Berlin was confirmed by the subsequent use of the former Palace's site as the 'Roter Platz' (Red Square) for political demonstrations, and later for the Palast der Republik (Palace of the Republic).

Manifesting the urban importance of the Baroque Palace were in particular the five open portals and the two inner courtyards, among the largest squares in early eighteenth-century Berlin, to which the portals provided public access.

THE NEW PALACE

The new Palace – the centre of arts and culture named 'Humboldt Forum' – is a unitary Baroque and modern building, with a rectangular plan of 185 by 120 and a height of 30 metres, and with a cupola rising to a height of 70 metres above the western portal. It is the result of a combination of reconstructed and newly constructed buildings.

In 2002 the German Bundestag (Parliament) deliberated the reconstruction of the Baroque parts of the lost Palace, in particular their stereometry and the facades oriented towards the city and the Schlüterhof (Schlüter Courtyard), as well as the contour of the cupola. To the binding reconstruction of these elements, confirmed by the 2007 competition

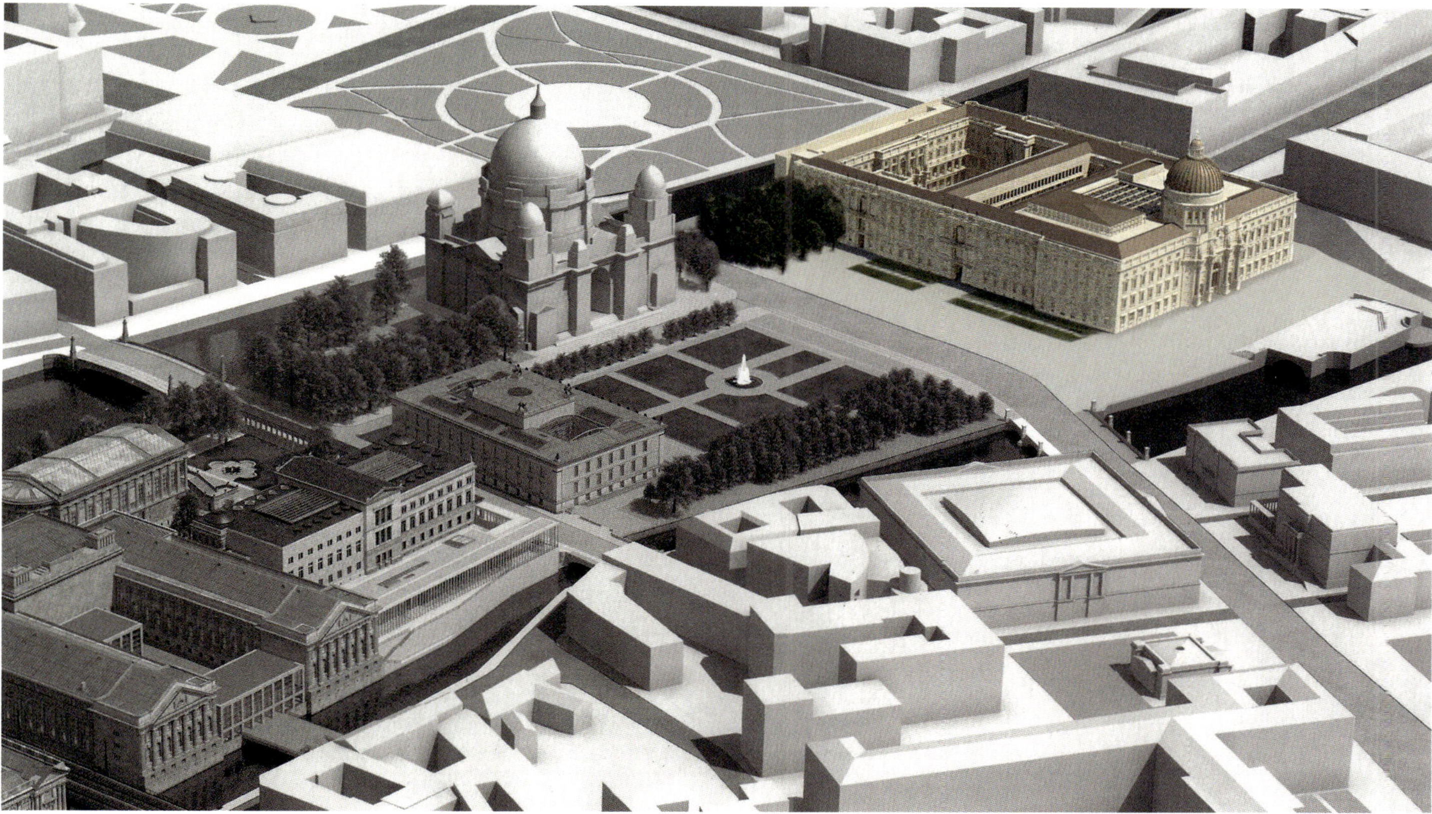

programme, my project adds the optional one of the passage atriums and courtyard facades of the three portals of the former Eosanderhof (Eosander Courtyard), as well as of the original facade of the cupola.

The new construction consists of five distinct elements: the eastern wing facing the river Spree, two linear and two cubic buildings in the area of the former Eosanderhof.

Old and new together form harmonious ensembles recalling the ideal reference figures of the Baroque Berlin Palace: the palazzo, the piazza, the theatre, the town gate. Also, the architectural language is subordinated to the realization of these figures.

The Building as a 'Palace with Four Wings'

Referring to Schlüter's original design, which envisioned a radical transformation of the existing building, the new Palace takes the form of an edifice with four wings. With respect to its position and dimensions, as well as to the architecture of its facade, the new eastern building is designed as the 'fourth wing' of the reconstructed Palace. By virtue of the size and in particular the depth of its window openings (three metres wide, on average six metres tall and 1.30 metres deep), the side facing the Spree recalls the loggia facade of a public building. Due to its retreat from the riverbank, a public square along the Spree is formed for the first time in the history of this place: a new entry portal, cafés and restaurants are located in this modern wing of the Palace.

The Portals as 'City Gates'

Beyond the competition desiderata, all five palace portals, together with their passage atriums – which originally led to two, and now three courtyards – have been completely reconstructed. Moreover, the three

The old Palace (above):
pre-Baroque (yellow) and
Baroque (grey) buildings, the
cupola (dark grey).
The new Palace (below):
the reconstructed (grey and dark
grey) and new (blue) buildings

The old Palace (above):
the axes of public spaces.
The new Palace (below):
the axes of public spaces

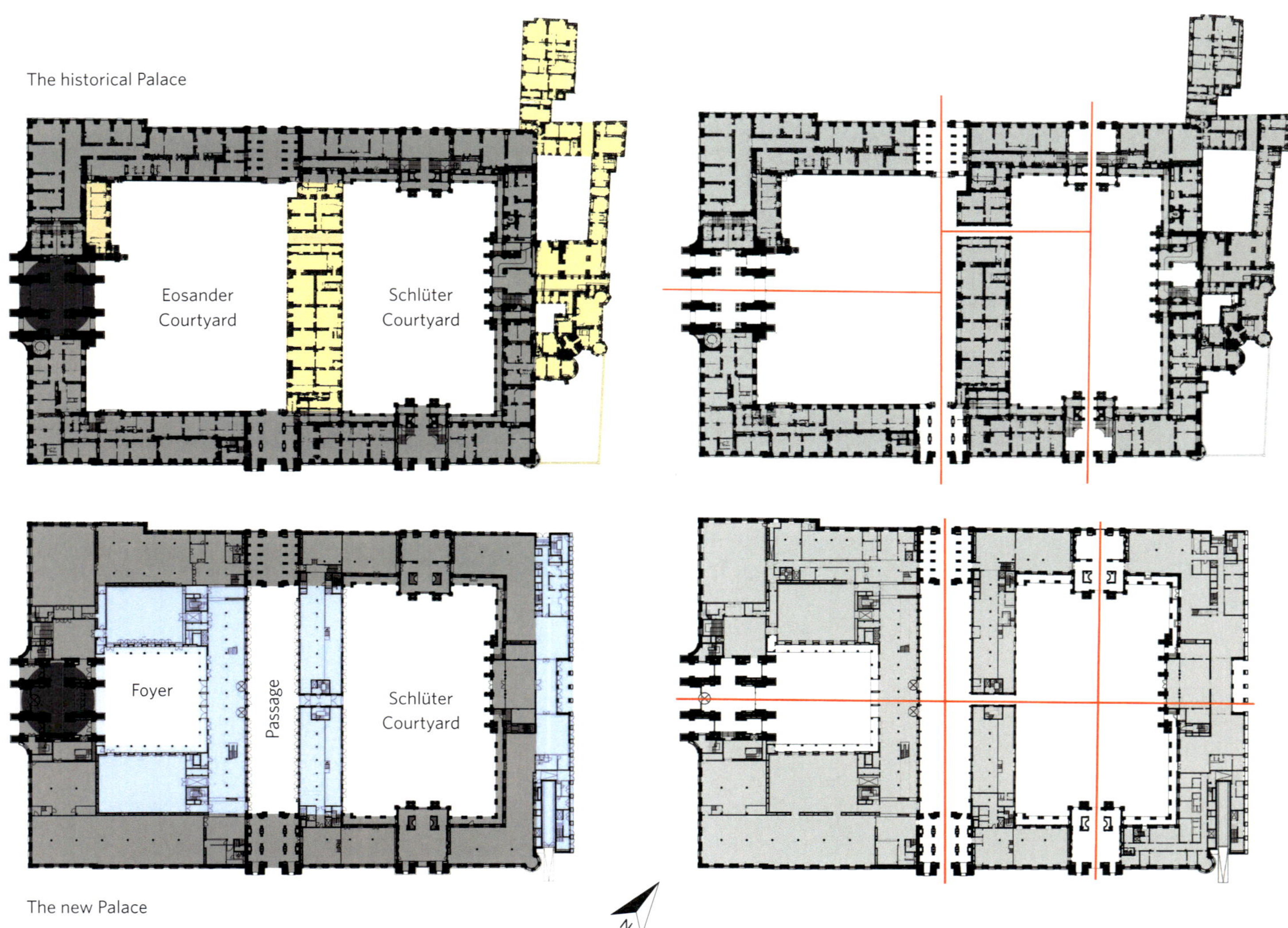

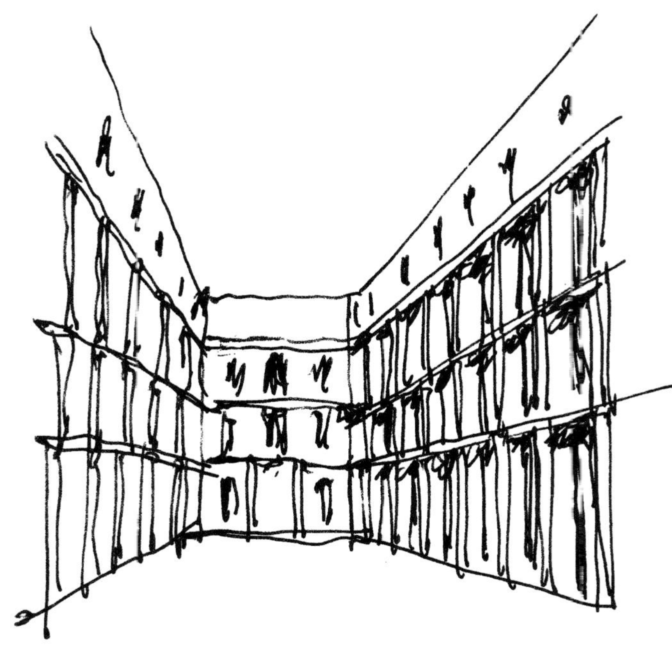

Franco Stella, sketch of
the Palace Passage

portals of the former Eosander Courtyard acquire their original urban
function as 'city gates' – as transitions between public spaces. An
additional portal is situated within the central tract of the new wing on
the Spree.

The Courtyards as 'Piazza'

Within the site of the former Eosander Courtyard two new courtyards
were created, both oriented towards the reconstructed portals: the Palace
Passage between the two opposing portals facing Schlossplatz (Palace
Square) and the Lustgarten, and the glass-roofed courtyard, the Grand
Foyer, with the portal facing Schlossfreiheit (Palace Precinct).

The Schlüter Courtyard as a theatre piazza. The portals and loggias
of the reconstructed Schlüter Courtyard are reminiscent of the elements
of the ideal piazza, as characterized by Leon Battista Alberti and Andrea
Palladio in their treatises. On three sides of the courtyard, which measures
fifty by eighty metres, the wings designed by Schlüter are reconstructed;
on the western side, a modern wing replaces the pre-Baroque 'transverse
building'. Similar to the reconstructed Baroque facades, the two lower
storeys of its facade feature the motif of stone loggias. In this way,
Schlüter's concept of giving this ceremonial courtyard the scenographic
character of a theatre, a suitable place for theatrical or musical
performances, has been adopted and completed. The reconstructed
portals link this courtyard with the squares of the city, opening up views
onto the temple front of the Alte Nationalgalerie (Old National Gallery)
to the north, and the Neuer Marstall (New Stables) to the south. With its
cafés and restaurants, this square becomes an attractive meeting place,
also for the daily life of Berliners.

The Palace Passage as a forum. The public passageway that traverses the
building links the portals that have served as the entrance to and exit from
the Palace. The new facades, adorned by architectural orders of columns,
form a *via colonnata*. The combination of old and new creates a place that
recalls an ancient Roman forum. Like the famous Cortile degli Uffizi in
Florence, this place is simultaneously a courtyard within a building and a
piazza in the middle of the city.

Behind identical facades, however, are wholly different spaces and
utilizations: situated on one side is the stair hall that extends over all
storeys; on the other, the ground floor with café and museum shop, and
above, mezzanine storeys for administration offices. The suggestive view
of the Altes Museum's colonnade through the northern portal, and of the

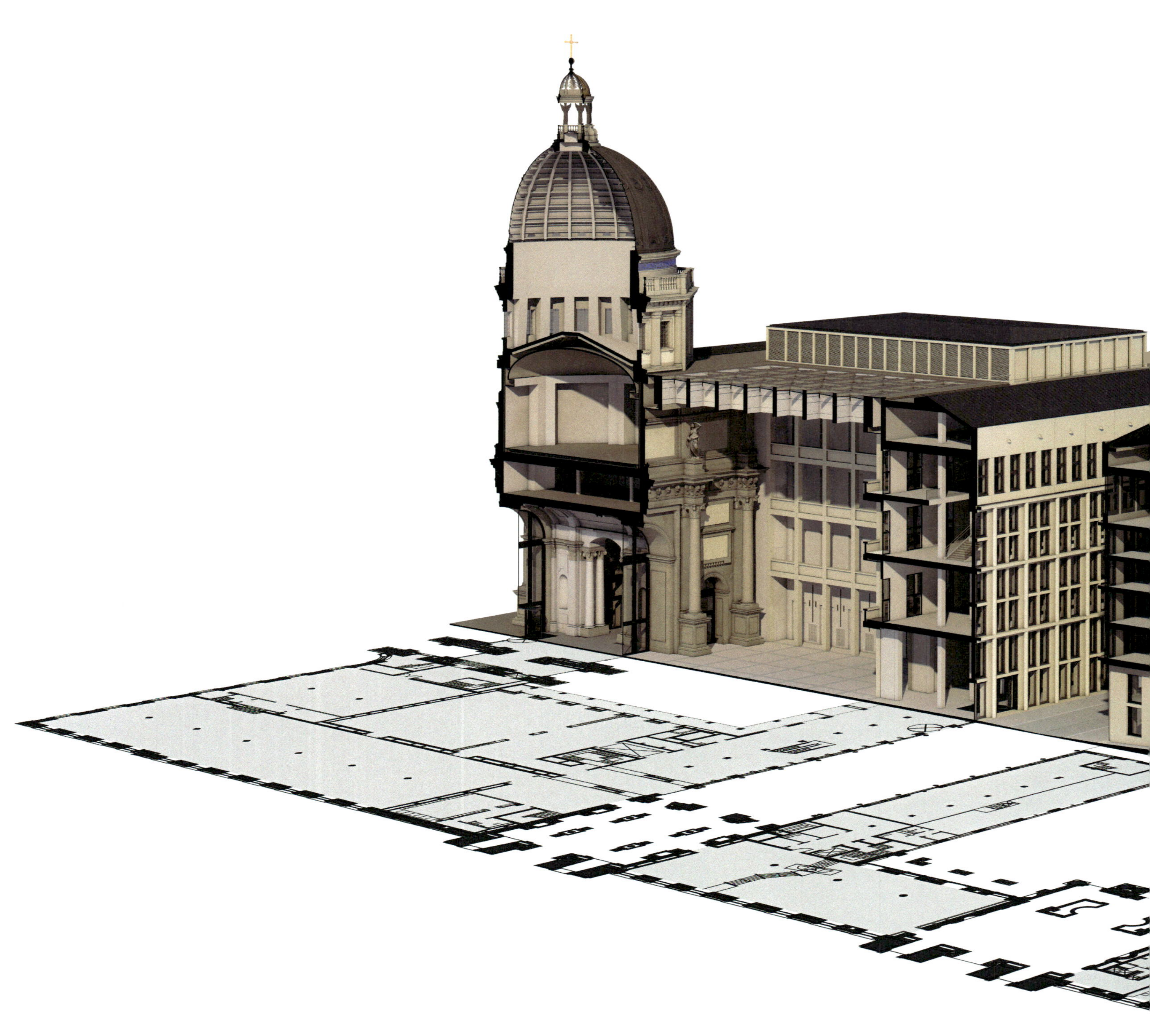

Perspective section of
the entire building

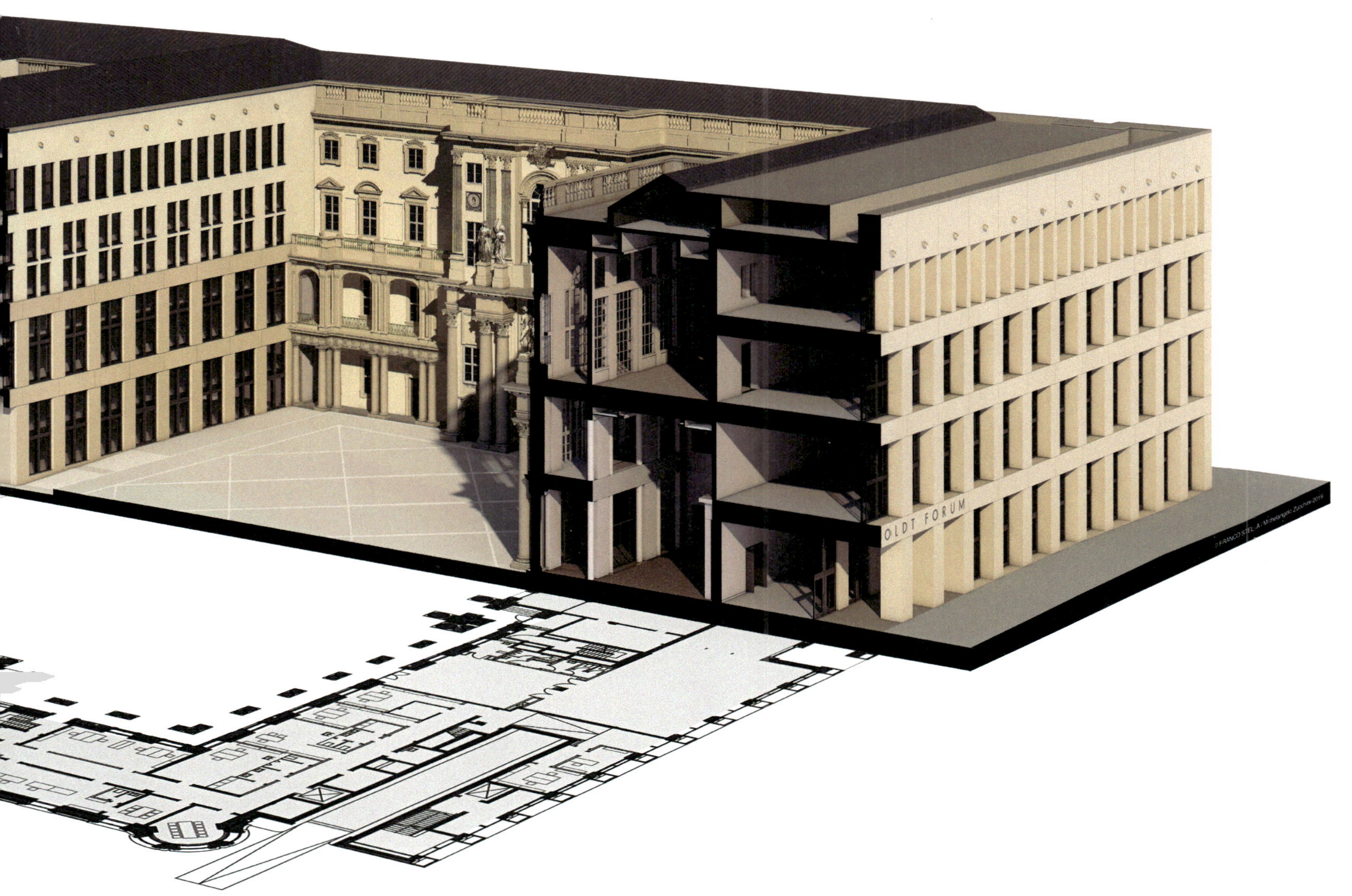

OLDT FORUM

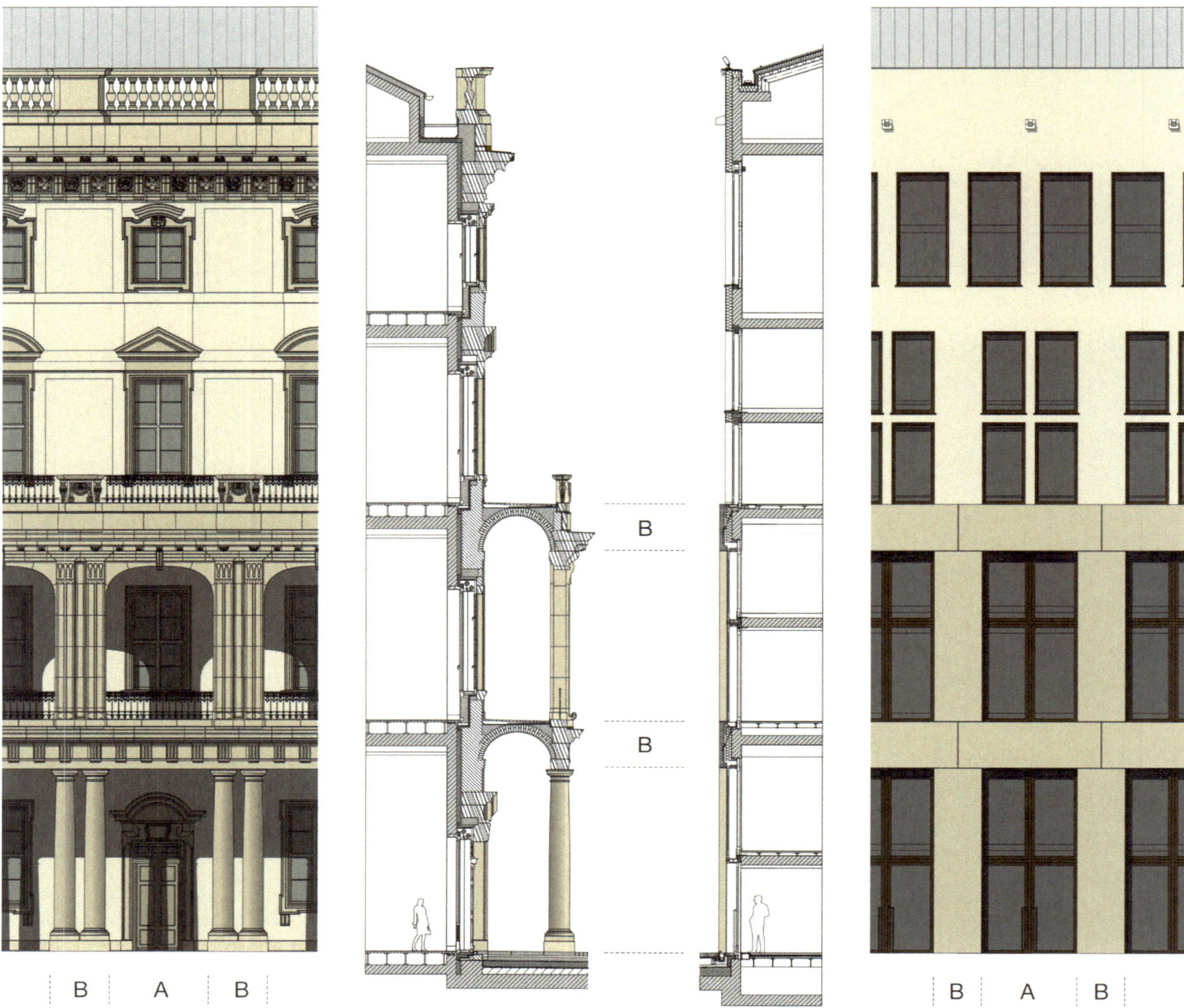

Schlüter Courtyard:
comparison of the proportions
of the old and new facades

axis of Breite Strasse through the southern portal, display the relationship
between the city and the palace.

The Grand Foyer as a theatre. The Grand Foyer, a reception and event
hall, is a cube whose sides measure thirty metres with a glass roof divided
by steel cassettes. Impressive on the western side is the great portal that
Eosander designed in the early eighteenth century based on the Roman
triumphal arches of Constantine and Septimus Severus. On the other
three sides are the open loggias of the new cubic buildings. The interplay
between old and new gives this space the character of a theater: the
reconstructed portal represents the *scenae frons* (stage wall) – comparable
to that of Palladio's Teatro Olimpico in Vicenza – and the new loggias evoke
the spectator galleries.

The Facades Made of Walls and Columns

The facades of both reconstructed and new elements are made of walls
and columns, often combined with one another, each with its own original
and traditional function: the masonry wall assumes the task of the actual
construction; the columns provide for the dignity of the building and are an
ornament of the city.

The Baroque facade is a powerful, three-layered wall system whose
thickness is comparable to that of the former Palace. A massive,
65-centimetre-thick, self-supporting brick wall with integrated elements

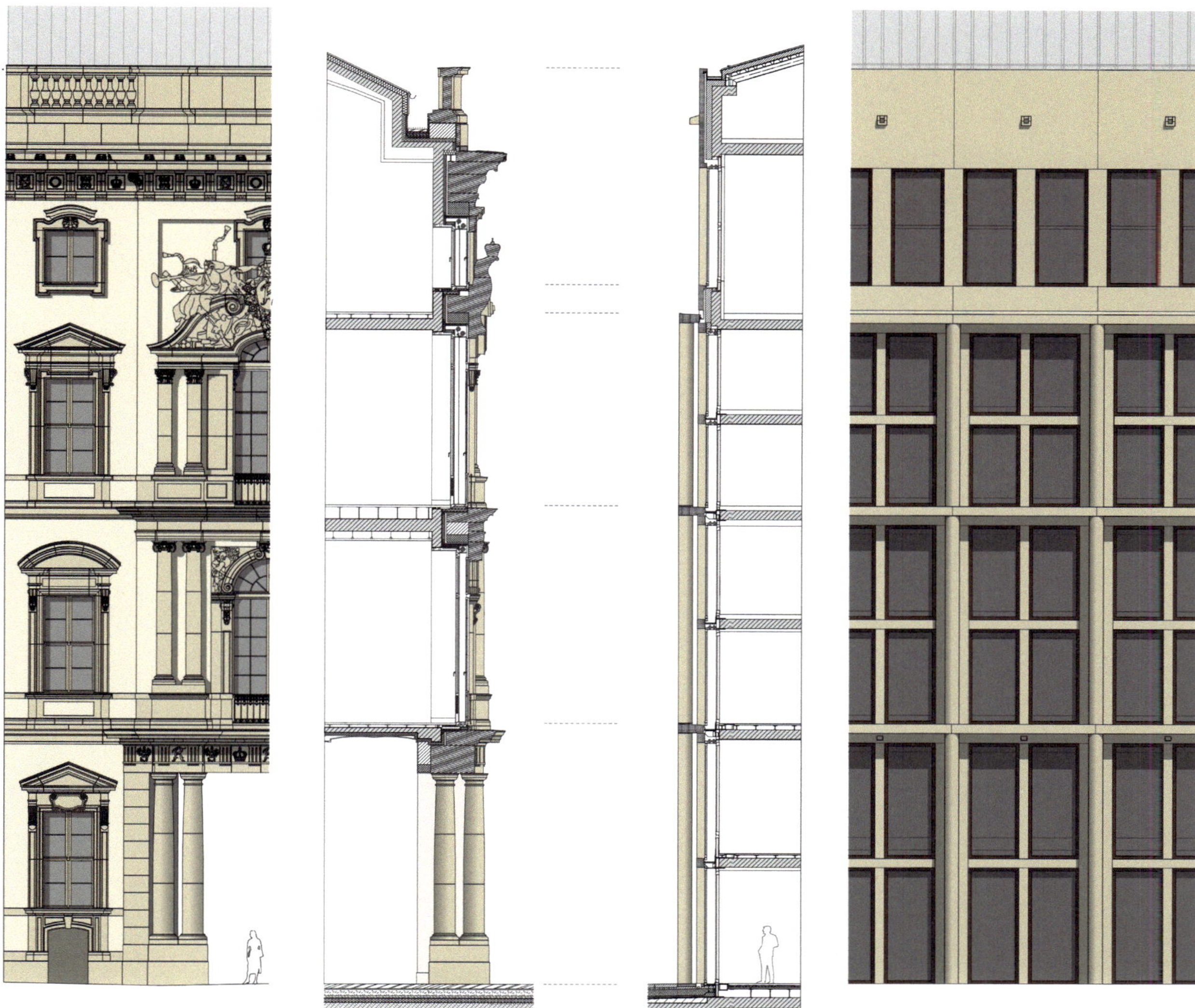

Palace Passage:
comparison of the proportions
of the old and new facades

in natural stone is connected flexibly with the inner reinforced concrete wall, measuring thirty to fifty centimetres in thickness; between them is a mineral core insulation, twelve centimetres in thickness. Each individual sandstone piece is oriented by its historical format and material; the brick walls are plastered and painted ivory-yellow.

The modern facade also consists of three layers: the supporting reinforced concrete wall, the core insulation, and the outer layer, fifteen centimetres in thickness, of artificial stone; the columns and architraves are prefabricated monolithic elements, which consist of a mixture of white cement and fine-grained sandstone.

The Berlin Palace as Humboldt Forum

The arts and culture centre, dedicated to the Humboldt brothers, accommodated in the new Palace, is conceived as 'a meeting place for the cultures of the world', in particular for those outside Europe.

Of the altogether 40 000 square metres of usable floor space, about 30 000 square metres will be devoted to exhibitions, and about 10 000 to public uses of common urban importance. The interior spaces have been designed and equipped with the most modern technologies in relation to their specific functional and symbolic purpose.

Located on the ground floor are spaces for common public utilizations: entry lobby and staircase hall, the Grand Foyer and the multifunctional

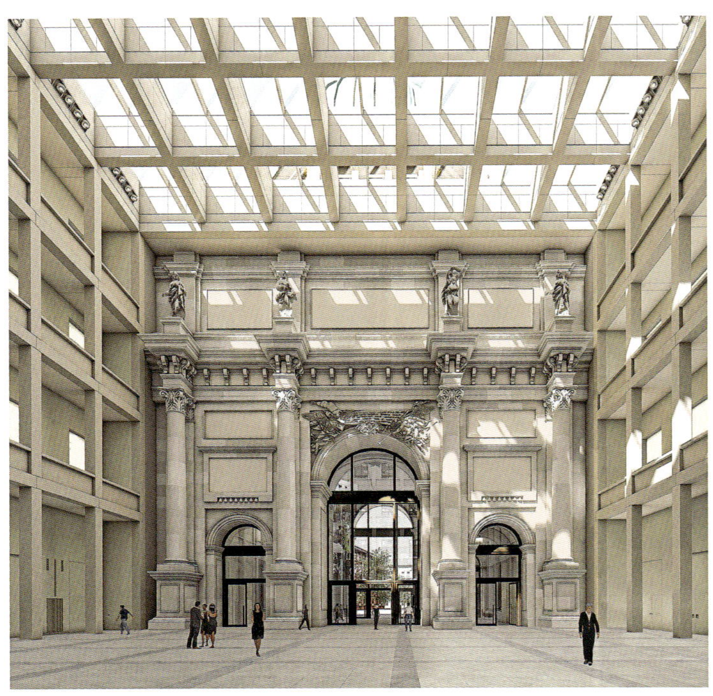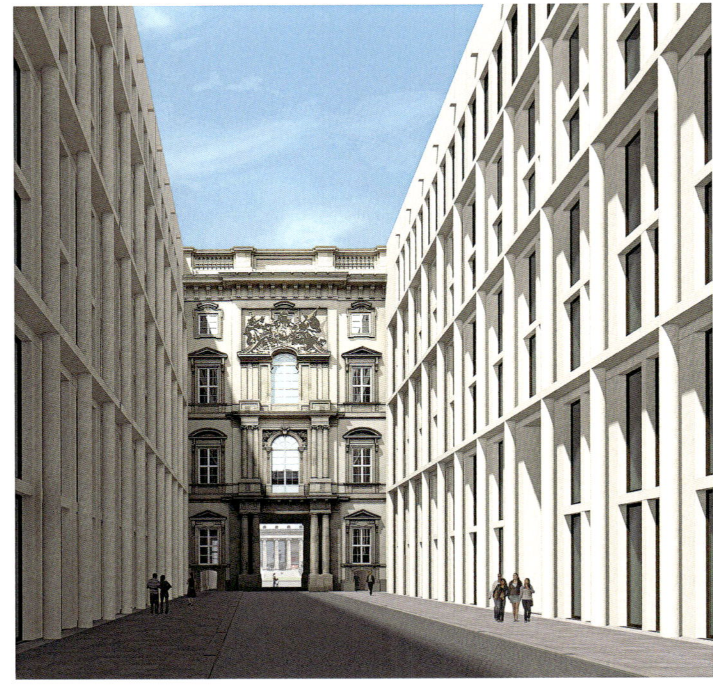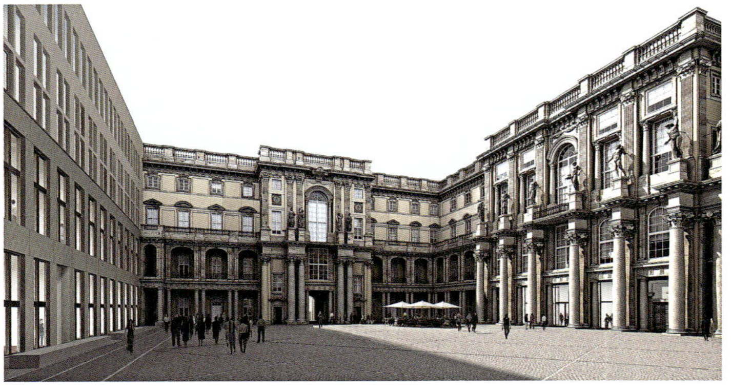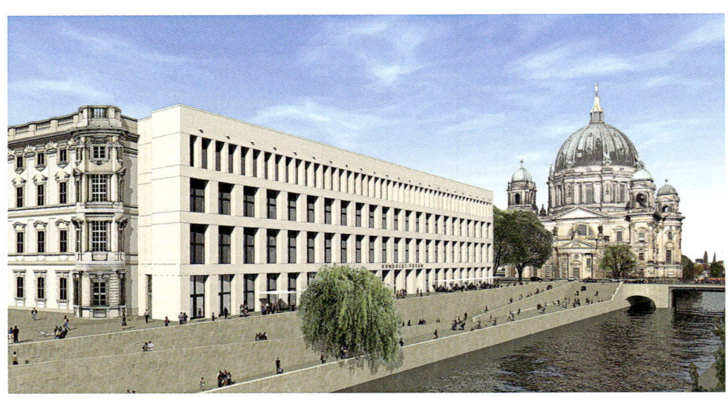

The three interior squares and the square facing the Spree: the Grand Foyer (upper left), the Palace Passage (upper right), the Schlüter Courtyard (lower left), and the Spree Terrace (lower right)

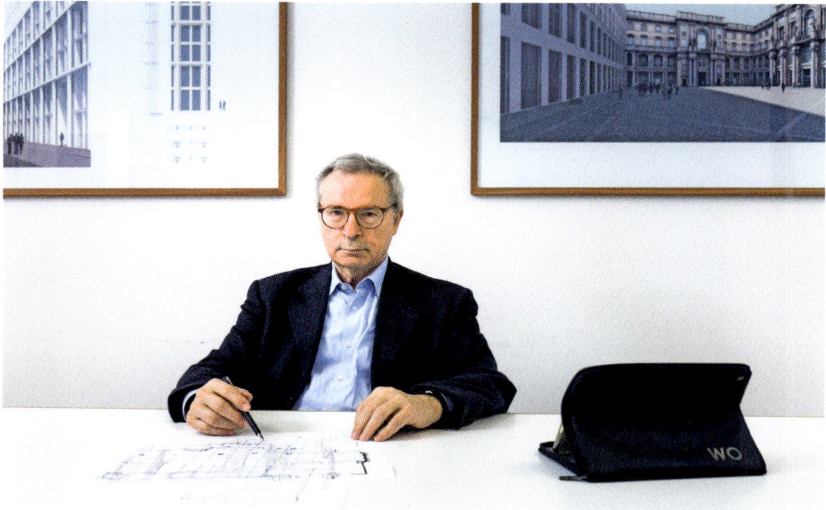

Franco Stella

room, halls for temporary exhibitions, the sculpture hall, the museum of the history of the site, book shops, cafés and restaurants.

On the first upper storey there is a special museum devoted to Berlin, the exhibition and meeting spaces of the Humboldt-Universität, and the Humboldt Academy; on the second and third upper storeys respectively the collections of the Ethnologisches Museum (Ethnological Museum) and the Museum für Asiatische Kunst (Museum of Asian Art). The arrangement of the supporting structure does not exclude the future reconstruction of spaces of particular historical importance.

Found in one section of the basement level, measuring about 1500 square metres, are the publicly accessible remains of the palace cellar with an exhibition of archaeological finds. The remaining areas of the basement level, which encompass the entire building site, as well as the entire attic storey, altogether 16 000 square metres, are available for the technical equipment of the palace.

The Berlin Palace as City Centre

The reconstruction of the volumes and the facades of the Baroque Berlin Palace makes the relationships between the most important places and buildings at the centre of Berlin perceptible and comprehensible once again. The open portals link the squares around the Palace and its inner courtyards with one another to form a grandiose public space at the heart of Berlin.

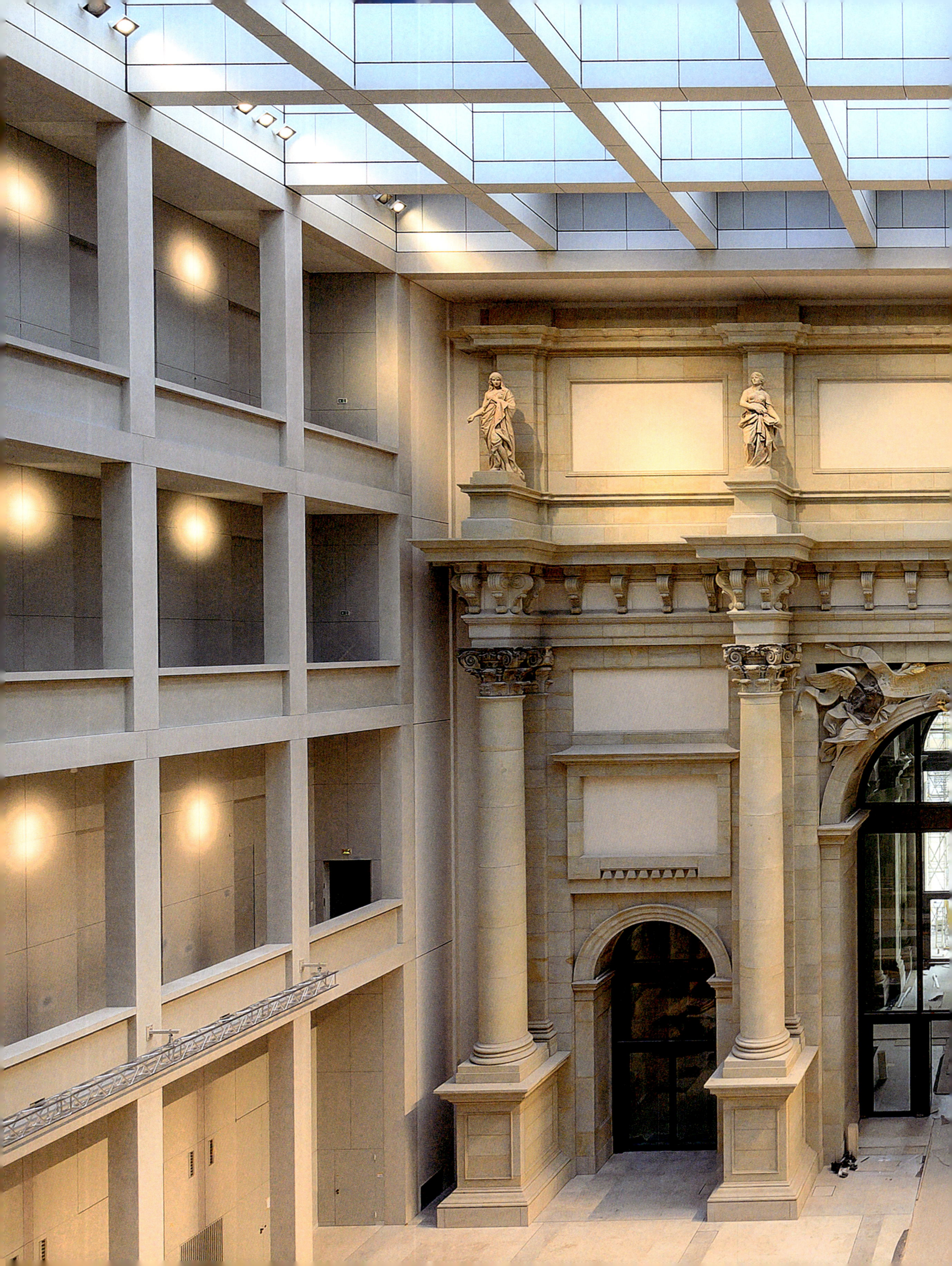

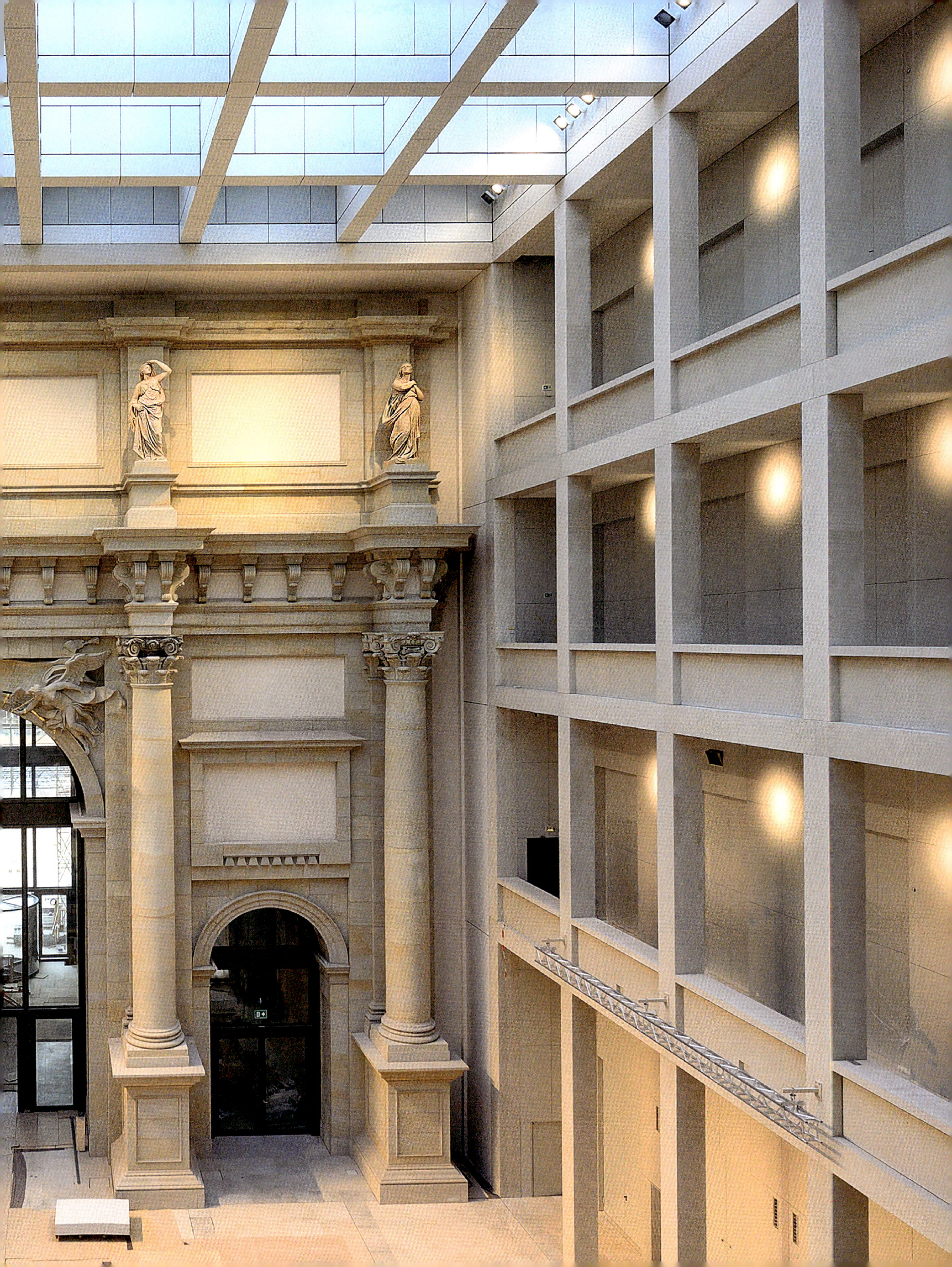

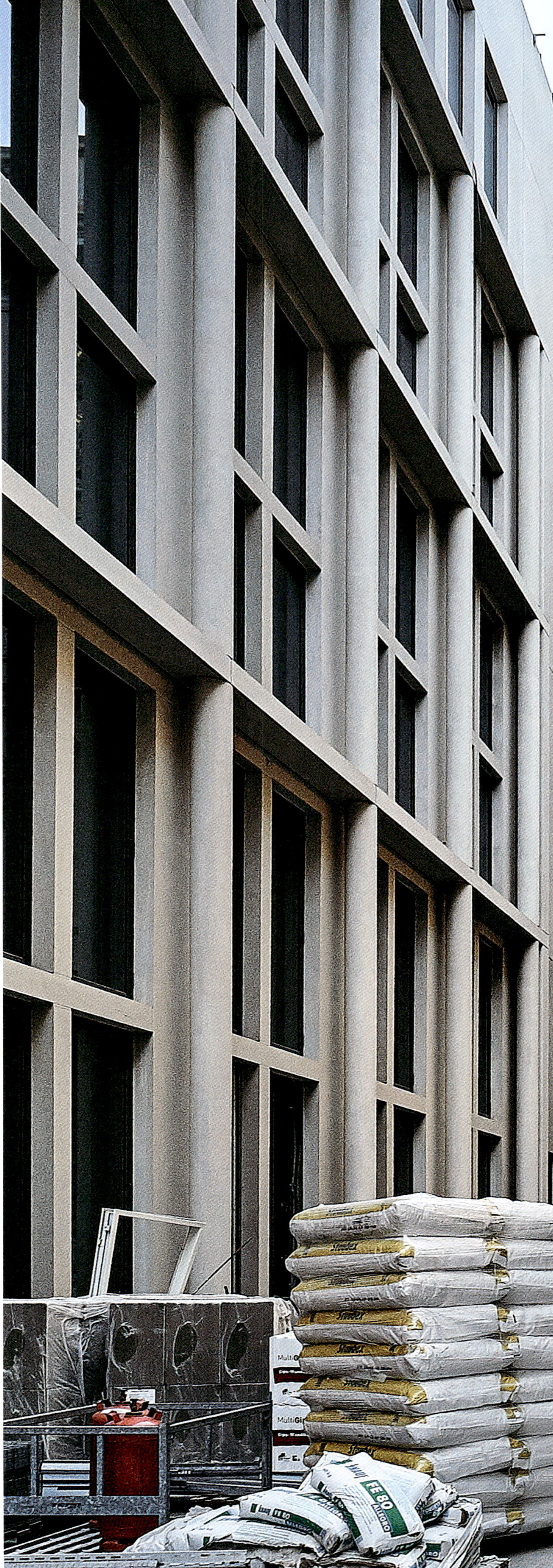

Fig. pp. 52–53:
The Humboldt Forum in the Berlin
Palace receives guests in the Grand
Foyer, which is dominated by the
reconstructed interior of Portal 3.
Johann Friedrich Eosander based its
design on the Arch of Constantine in
Rome. The architect Franco Stella set
it in a hall with accessible galleries,
as though in an opera house, citing
Andrea Palladio's Teatro Olimpico
in his hometown of Vicenza.

Among the spectacular new
inventions produced by the architect
Franco Stella is the Passage, which
traverses the entire building, its fronts
characterized by the reconstructed
inner portals of the former great
palace courtyard, seen here with
a view through Portal 4 showing
Schinkel's Altes Museum. The Palace
Passage is open day and night.

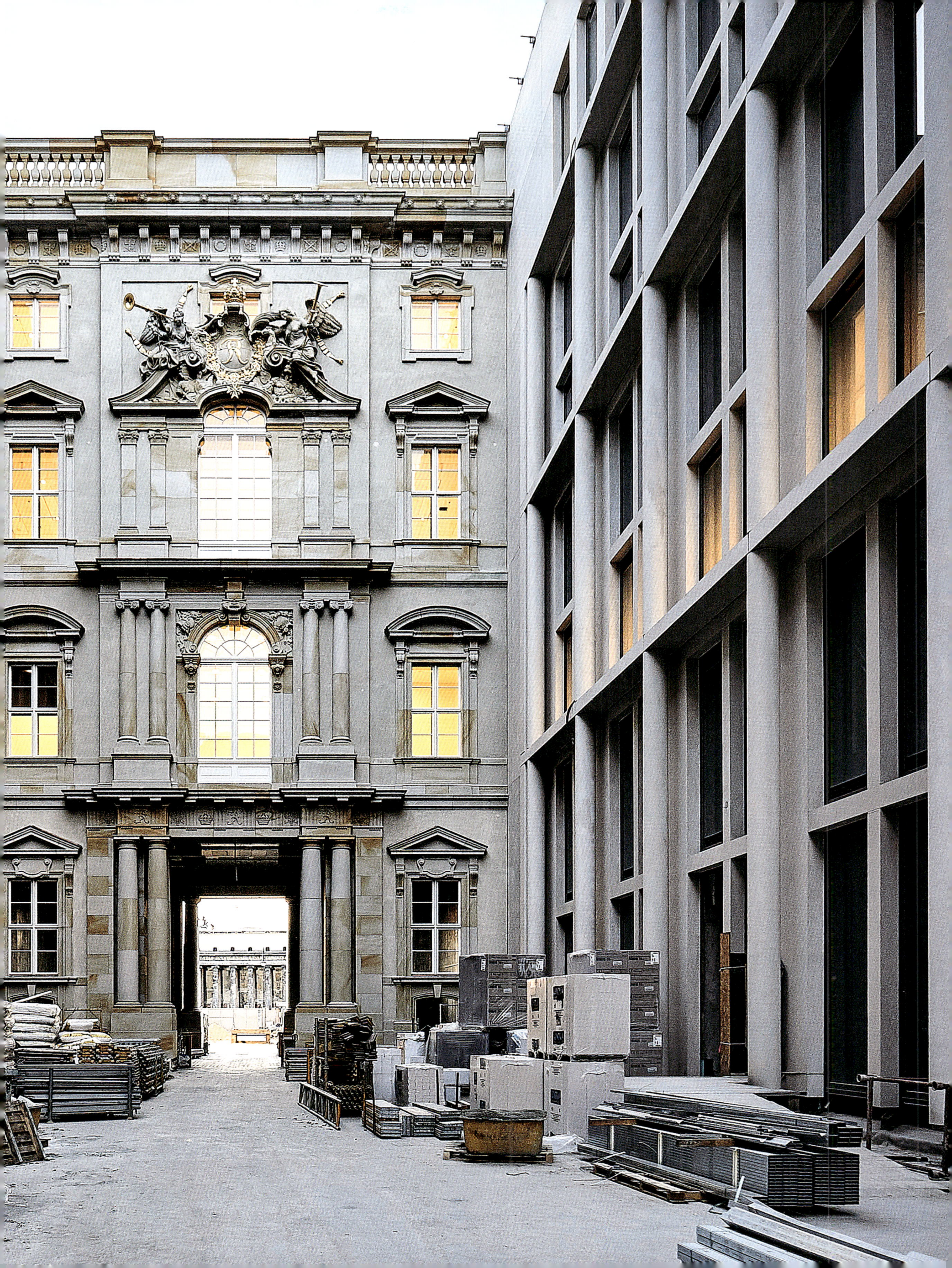

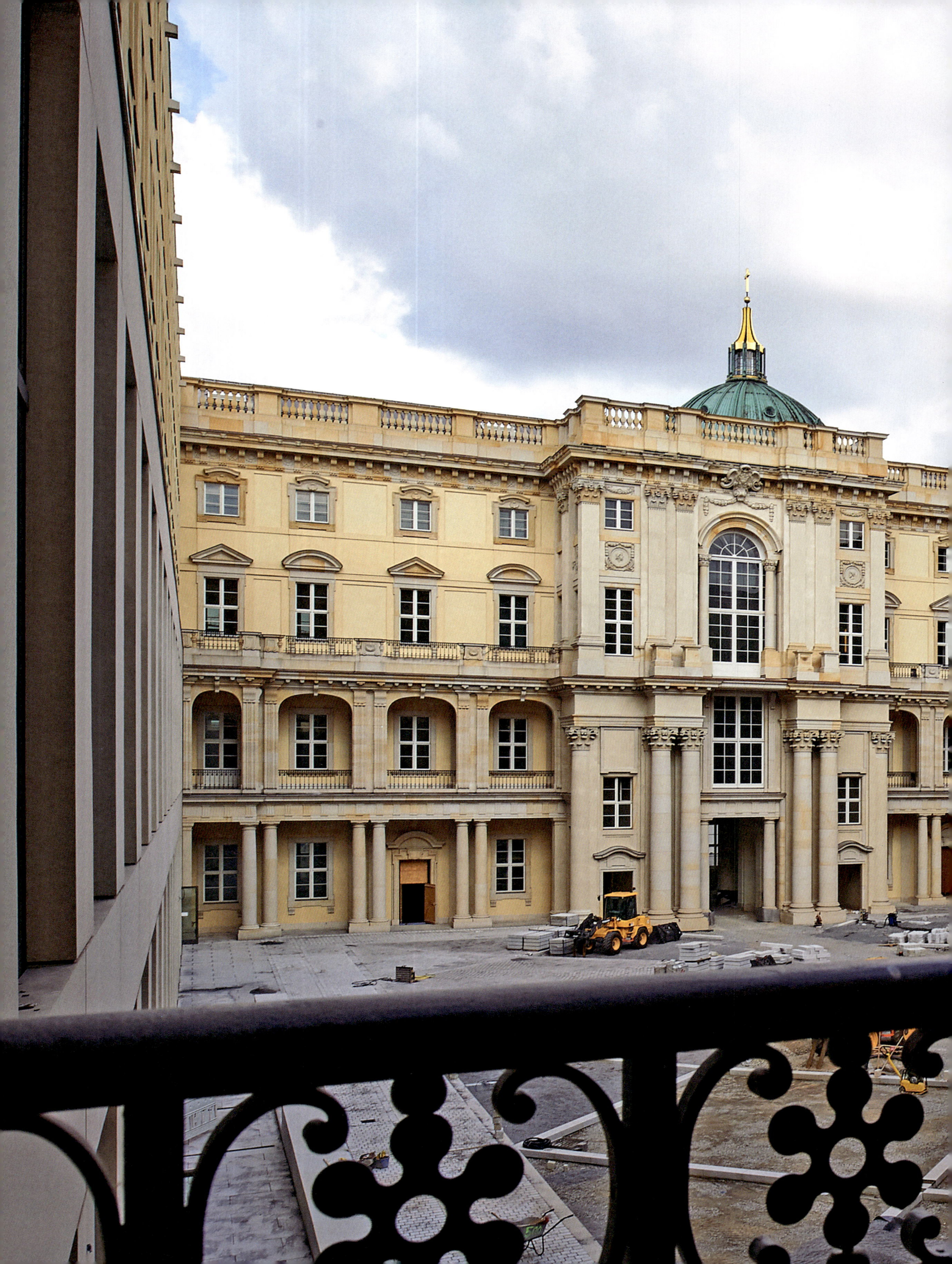

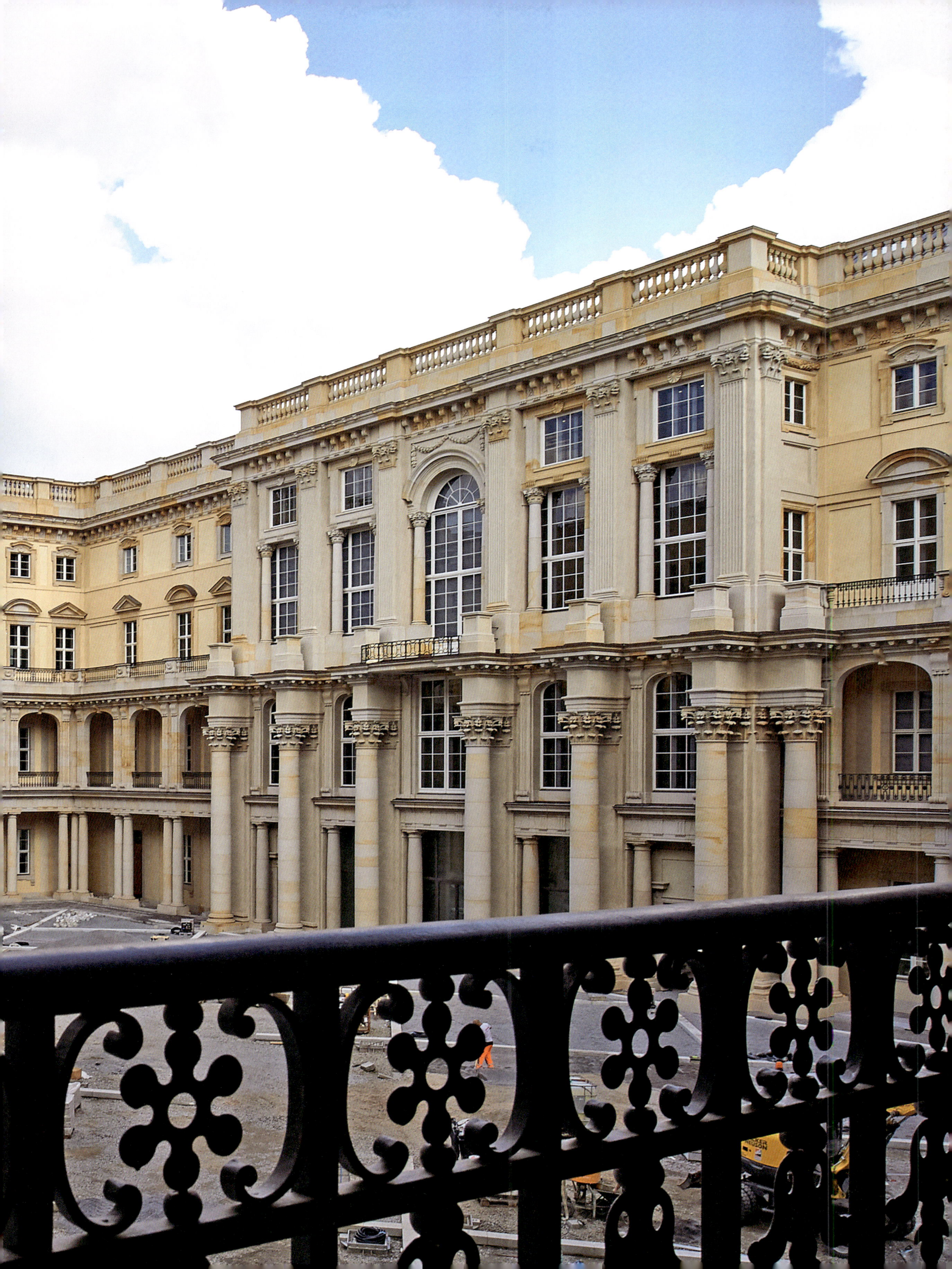

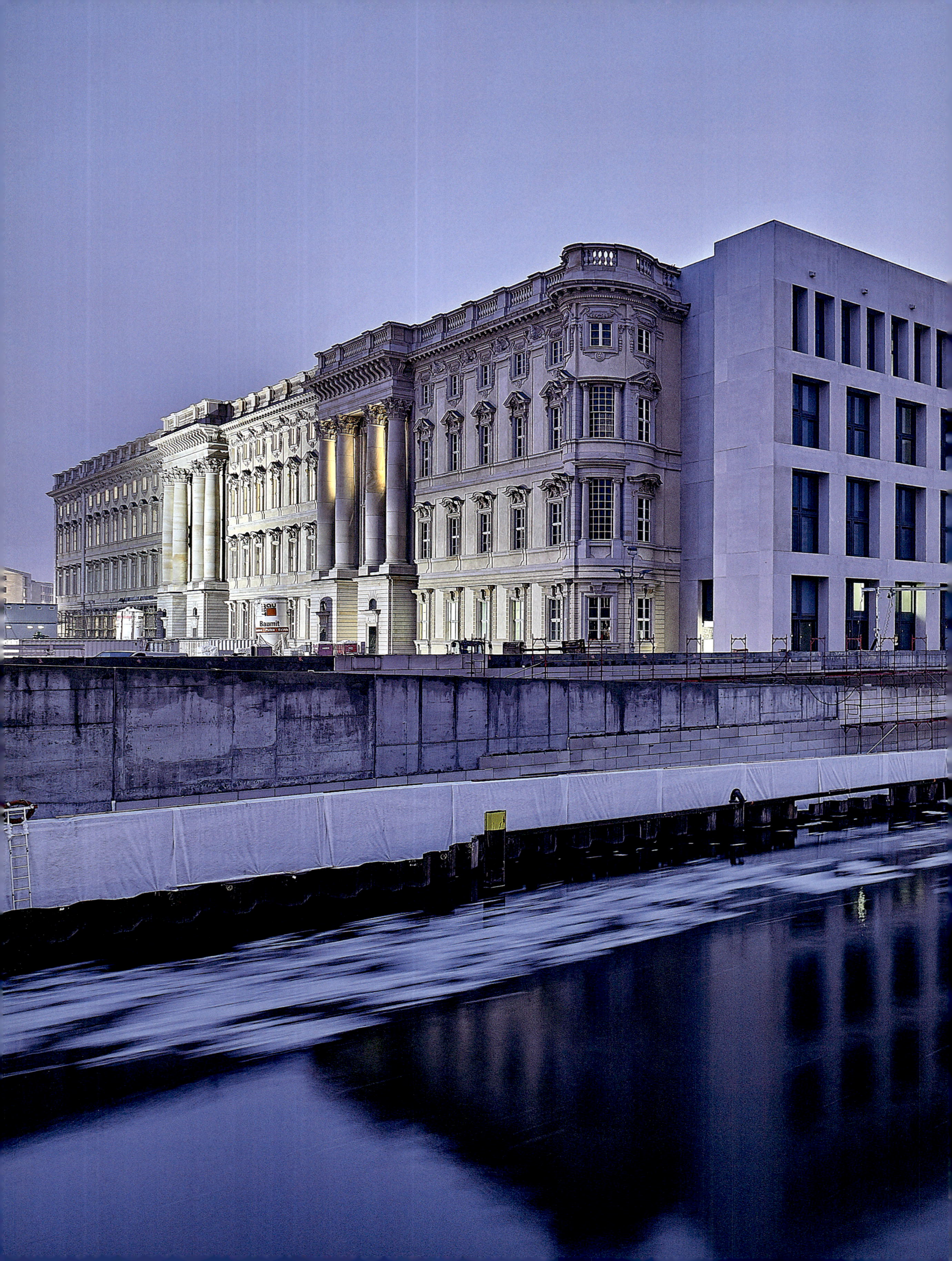

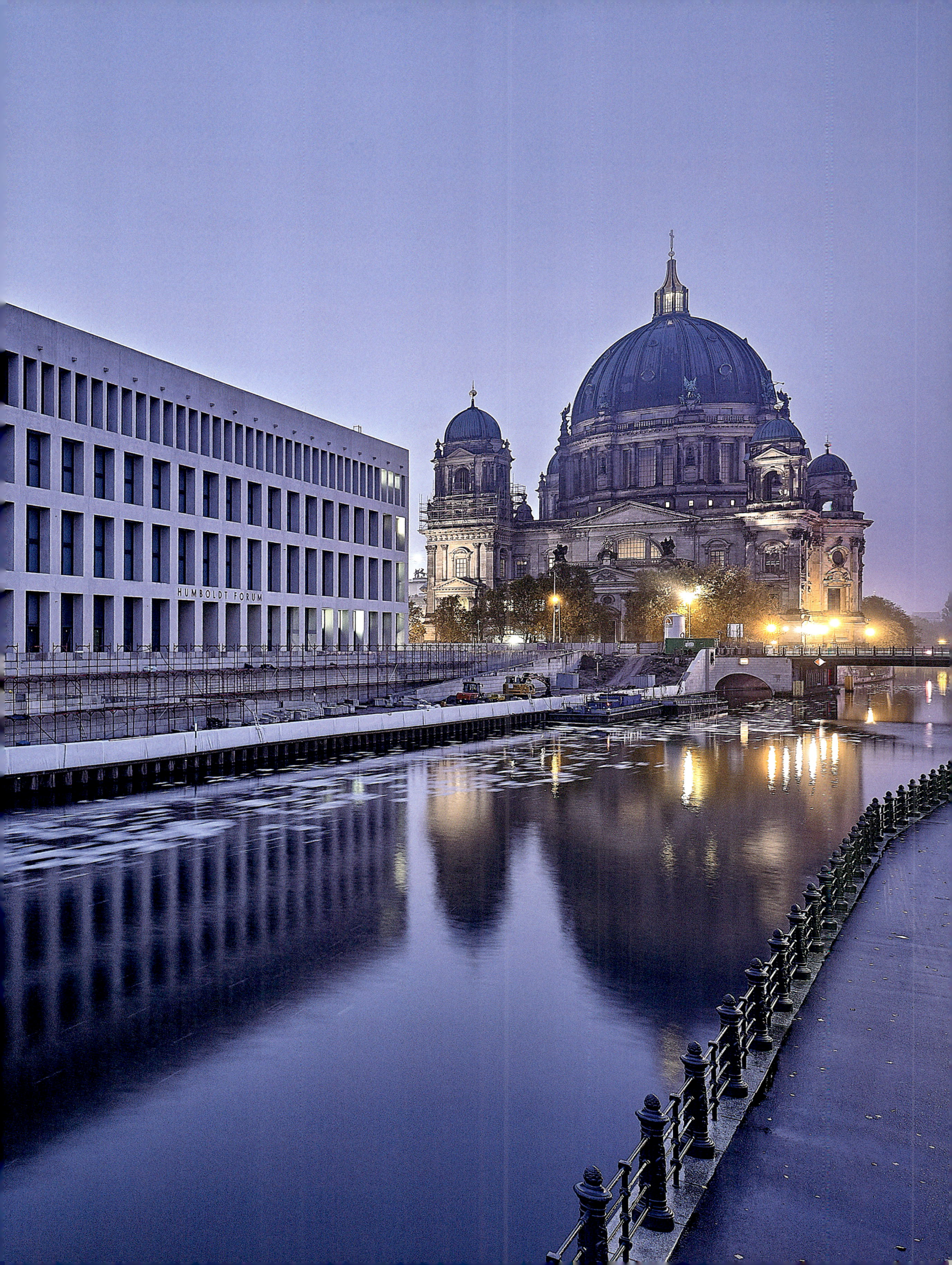
HUMBOLDT FORUM

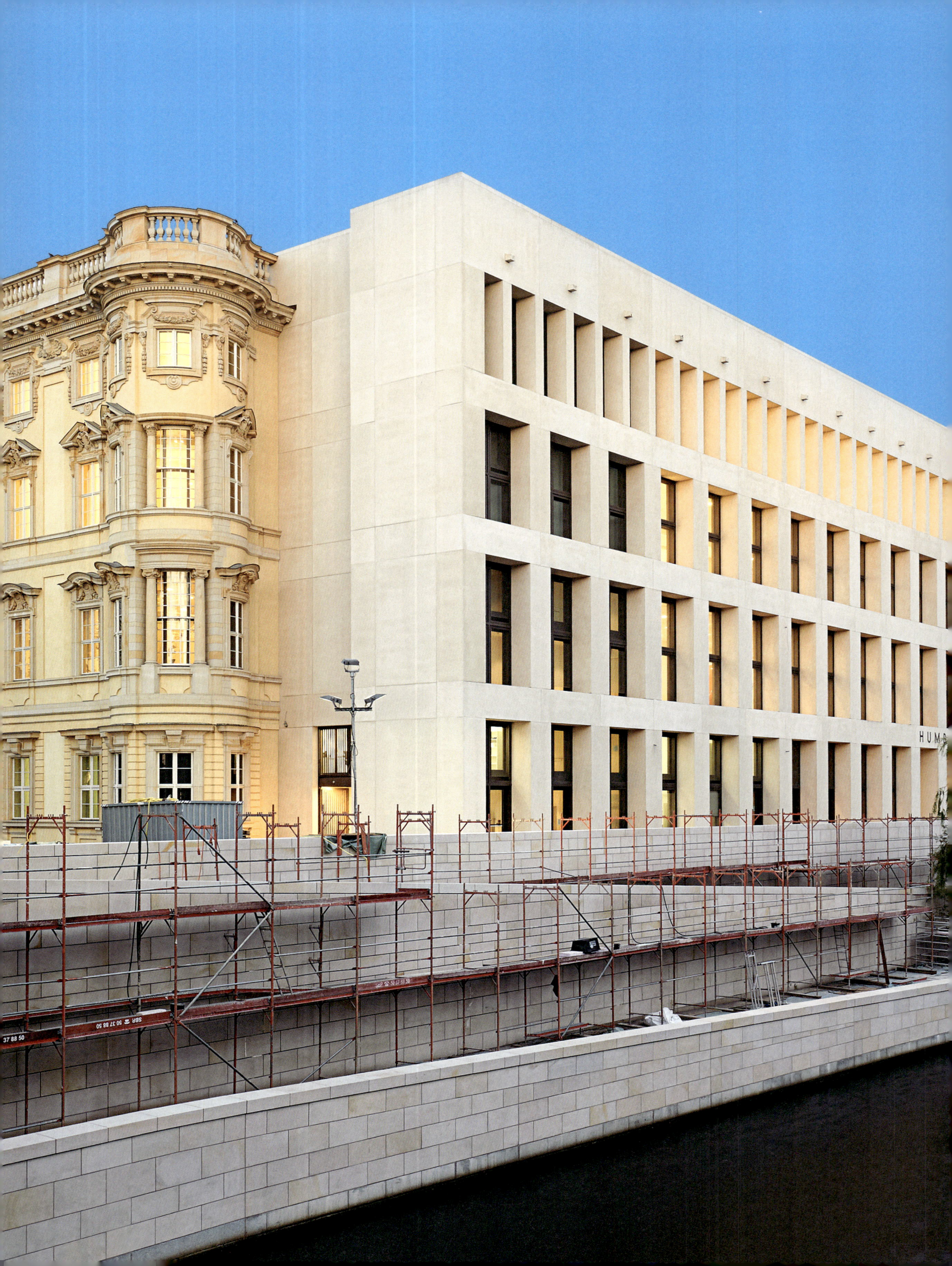

HUM
37 88 50
SBR 50 37 88 50

Fig. pp. 56–57:
The Schlüter Courtyard too is a
public town square in the interior
of the building. Reconstructed
on three sides are the Baroque
interior facades that served as ideal
backdrops for the ceremonies of
the royal court – today, just as in
the mid-19th century, it invites the
citizenry of the city to linger and
relax.

Fig. pp. 58–59:
At the southeastern corner of
the building, reconstructed
Baroque collides forcefully with
uncompromising modernism.
A second look, however, reveals
that when it comes to storey
heights and wall divisions, the
gridded facade actually takes up
the 'architectural grammar' of the
historic facade on Schlossplatz.

The rounded bay at the southwest
corner is the sole structural element
that serves as a reminder of the
pre-Baroque Renaissance palace
that was 'modernized' (so to speak)
by Schlüter for his royal patron. The
undecorated southern shoulder of the
modern east wing displays humility
and a reverence for the Baroque.

With its rounded columns and plain
cross-members above storey-height
mullions, the contemporary facade
that runs along the long side of the
Passage – a public space that runs
through the entire building – conveys
a convincing sense of spatiality. As a
'via colonnata', it opens up to the city
via the two reconstructed Portals 2
and 4.

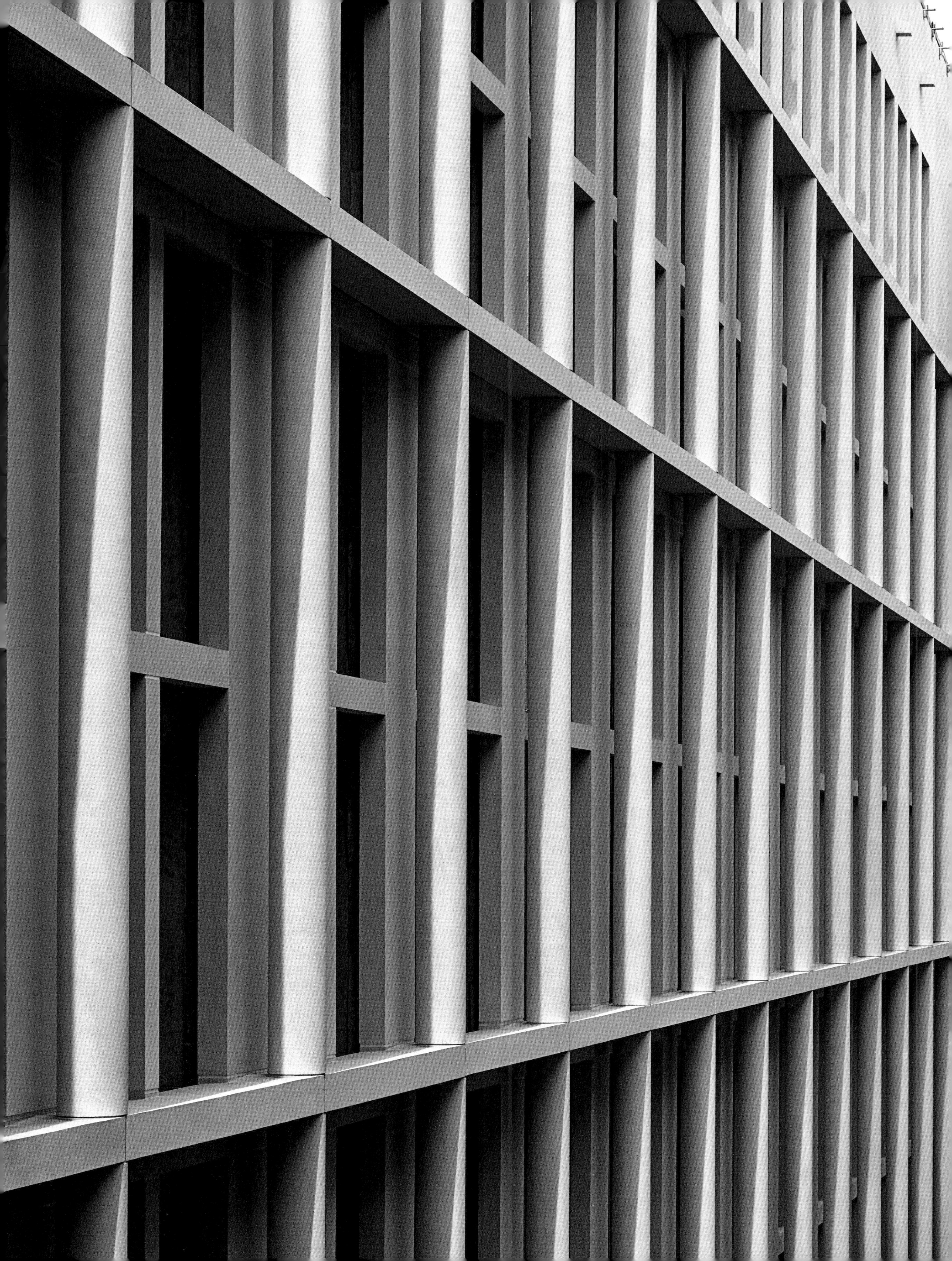

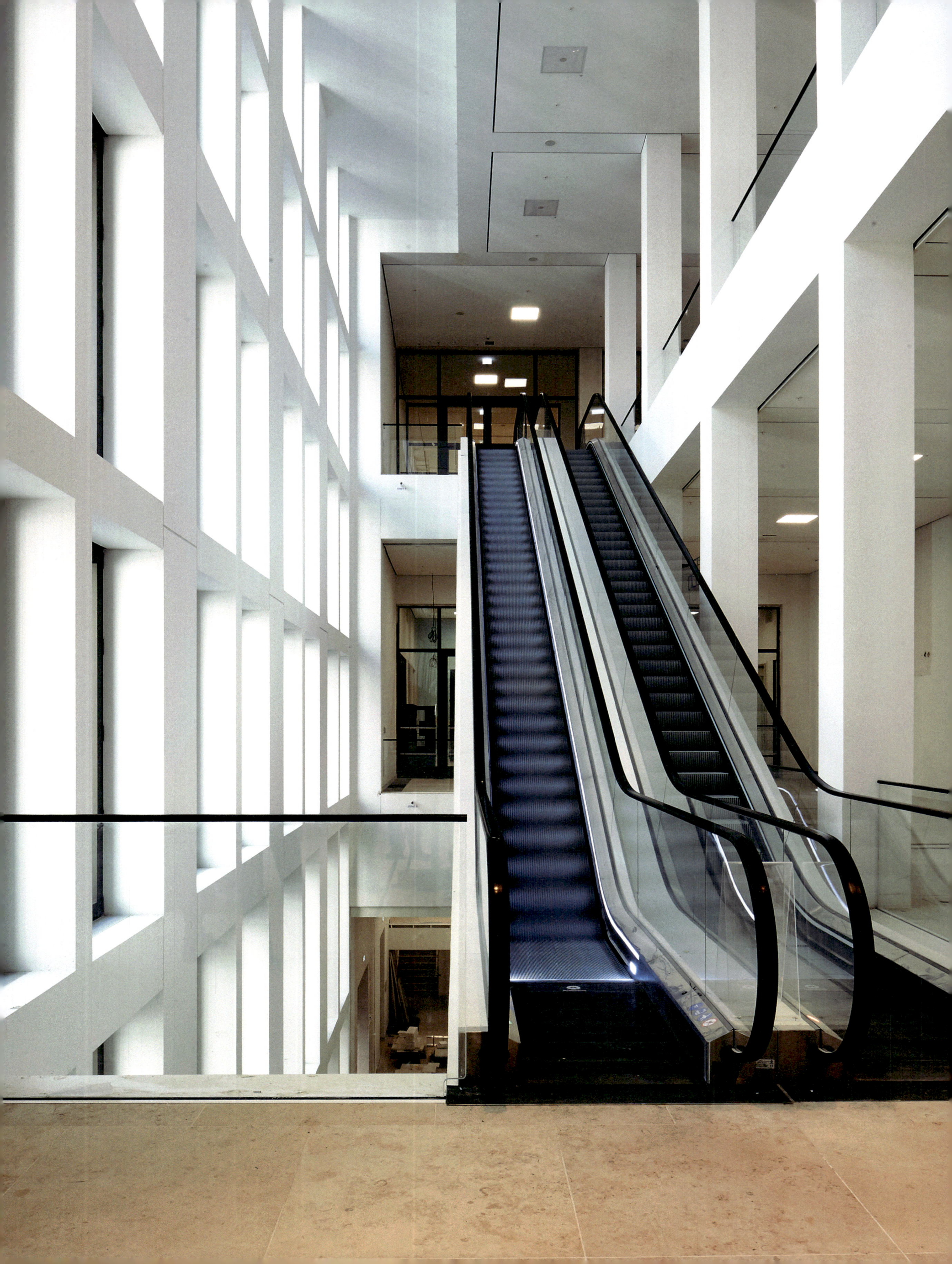

The open staircase in the western transverse wing along the interior Passage extends through the entire height of the building. Before the user-friendly escalator on the north side could be implemented, powers of persuasion on the part of the client were required to win over the architect.

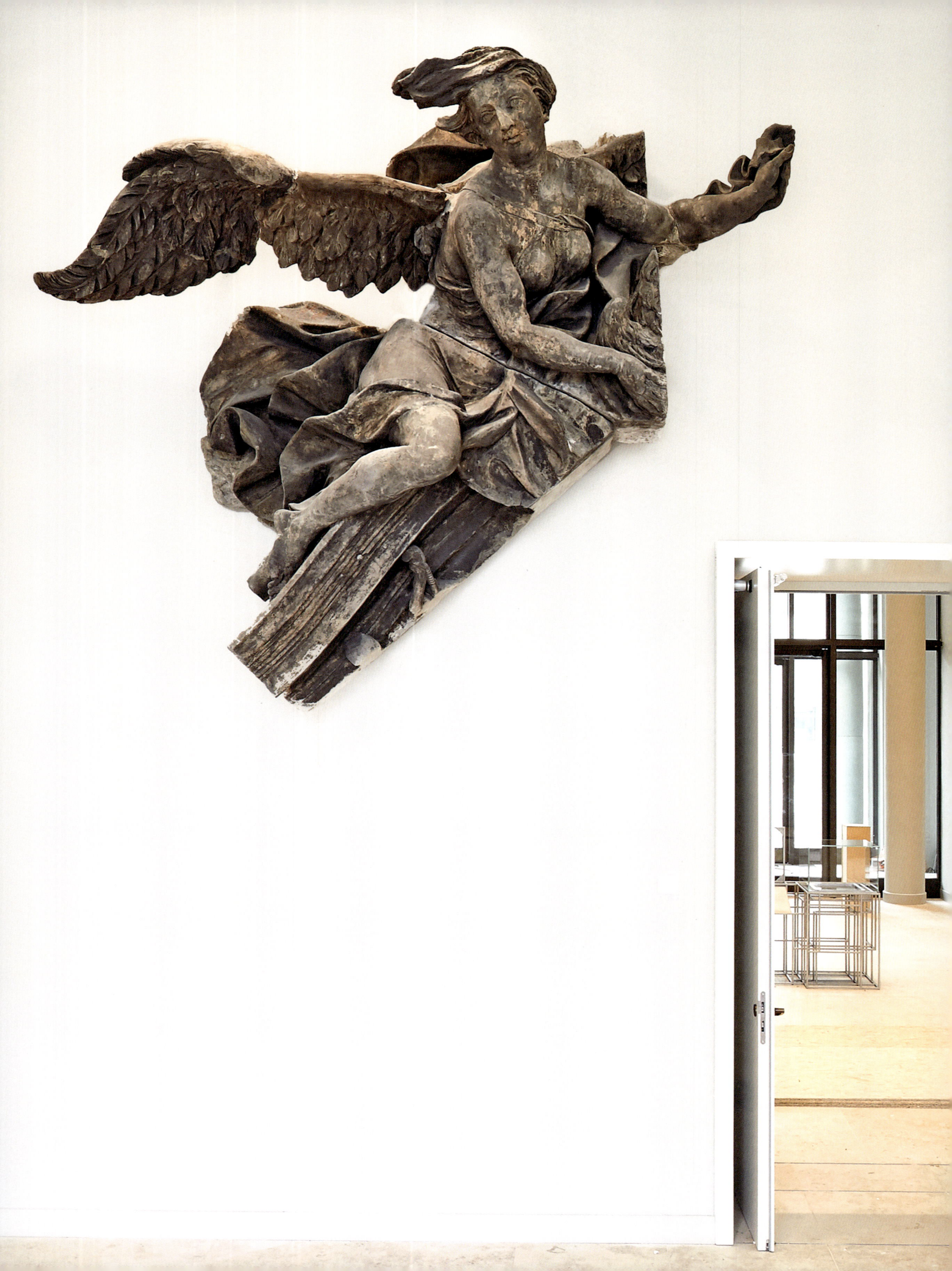

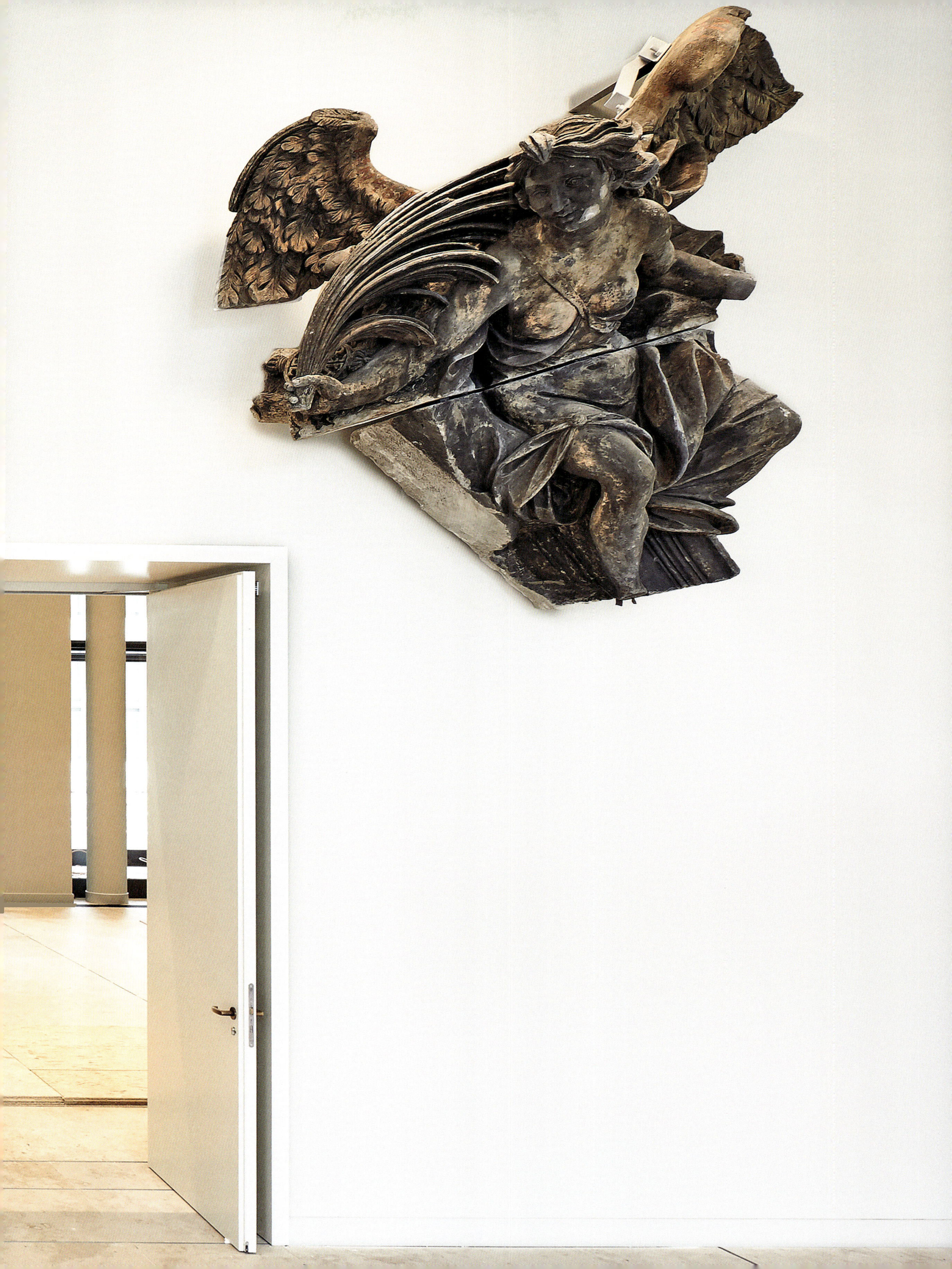

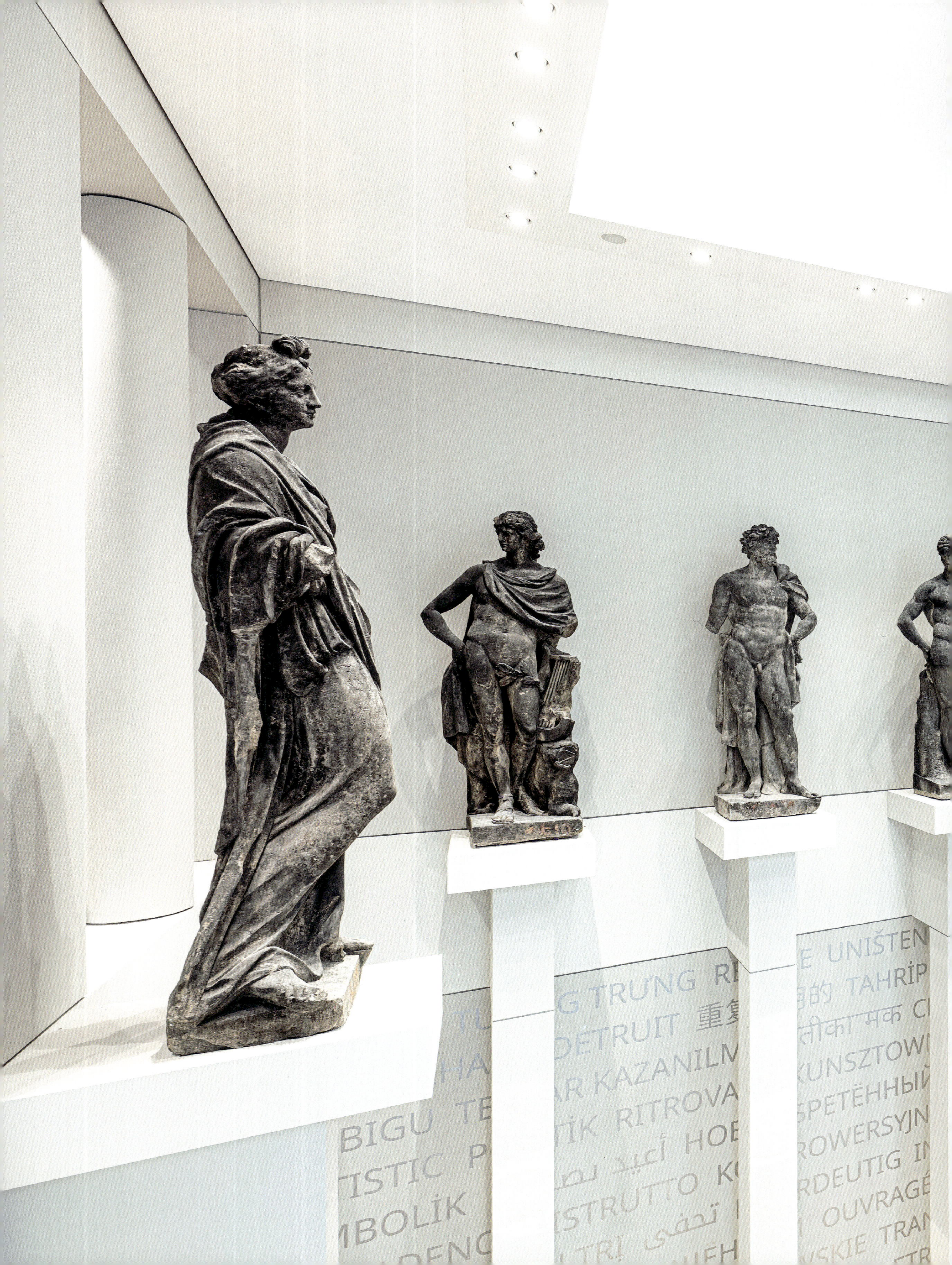
TU   G TRƯNG RE   E UNIŠTEN
HA   DÉTRUIT 重復   的 TAHRİP
BIGU TE   AR KAZANILM   KUNSZTOWI
TISTIC P   TİK RITROVA   SPETËHHЫ
عيد صا HOE   ROWERSYJN
MBOLİK   STRUTTO KO   RDEUTIG IN
تحفى DENG   TRI   OUVRAGÉ
ЧЁН   WSKIE TRAN

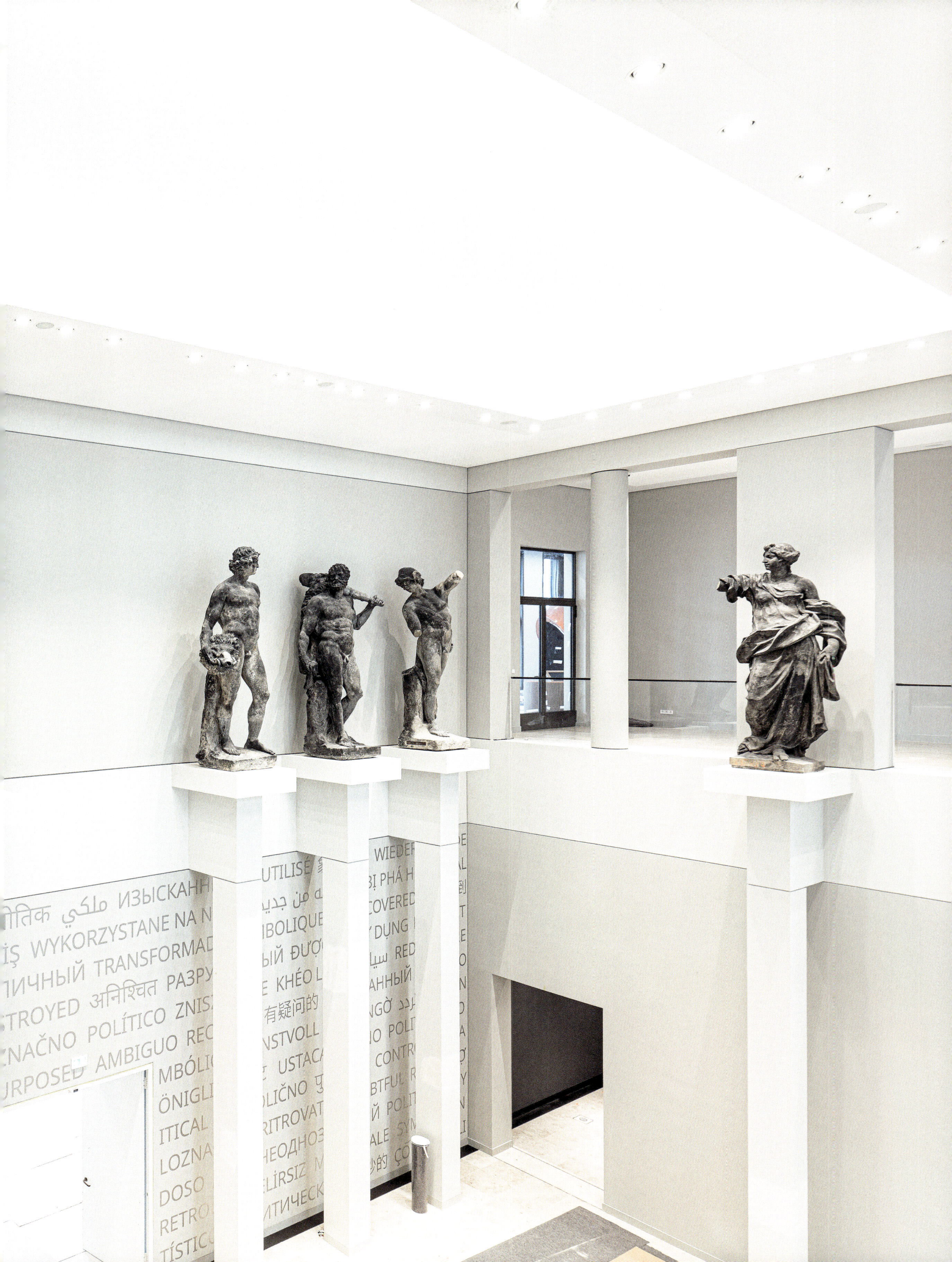
IŞ WYKORZYSTANE NA N
ИЧНЫЙ TRANSFORMAD
STROYED अनिश्चित РАЗРУ
NAČNO POLÍTICO ZNISZ
URPOSED AMBIGUO REC
MBÓLIC
ÖNIGLI
ITICAL
LOZNA
DOSO
RETRO
TÍSTIC
UTILISÉ
BOLIQUE
WIEDER
BỊ PHÁ H
Y DỤNG
KHÉO L
NGỜ
POLIČNO
RITROVAT
НЕОДНОЗ
ĔLİRSİZ M
ATNYECK
COVERED
RED
АННЫЙ
NSTVOLL
USTACA
CONTR
BTFUL R
Й POLI
ALE SYM
少的 ÇO
有疑问的

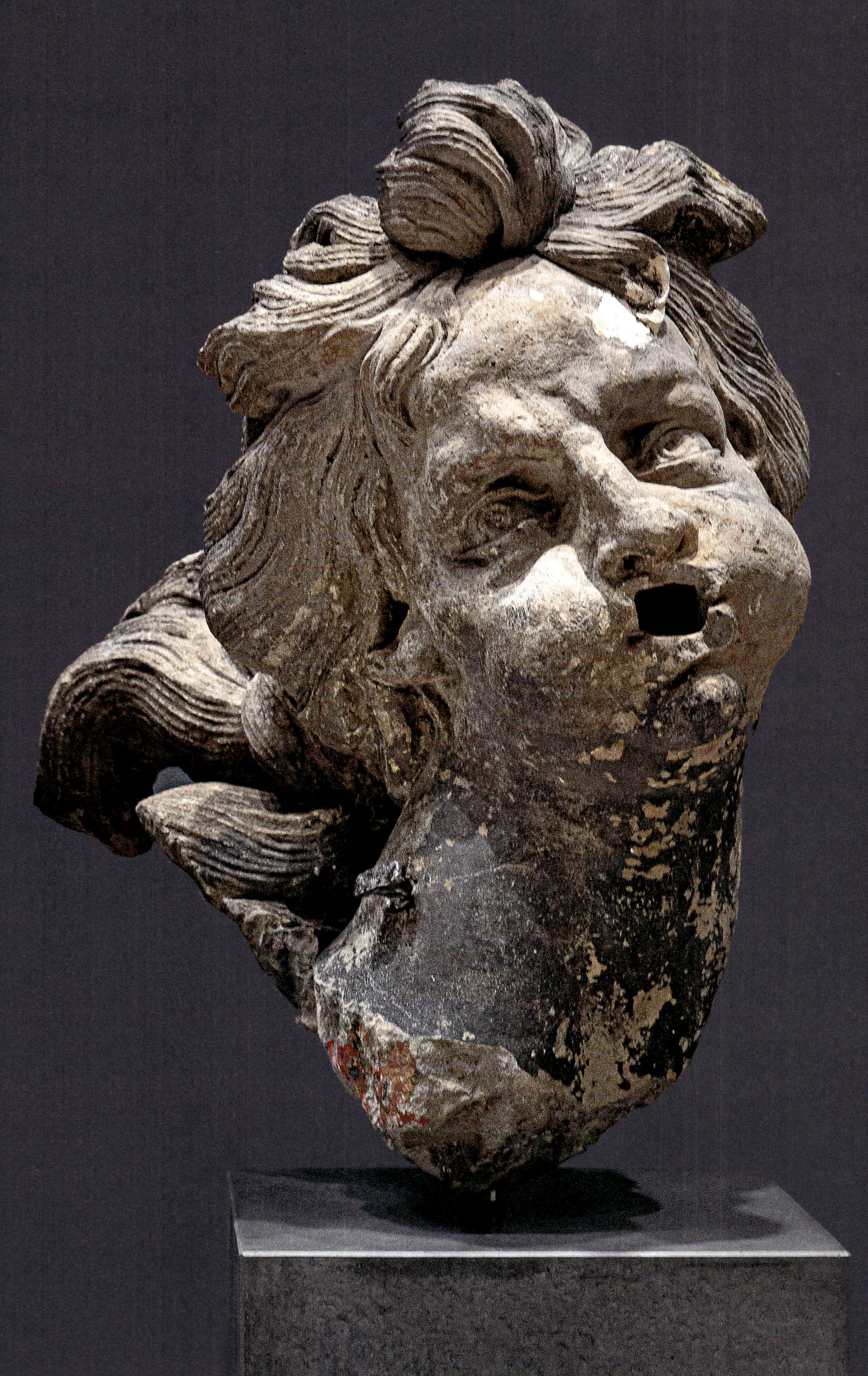

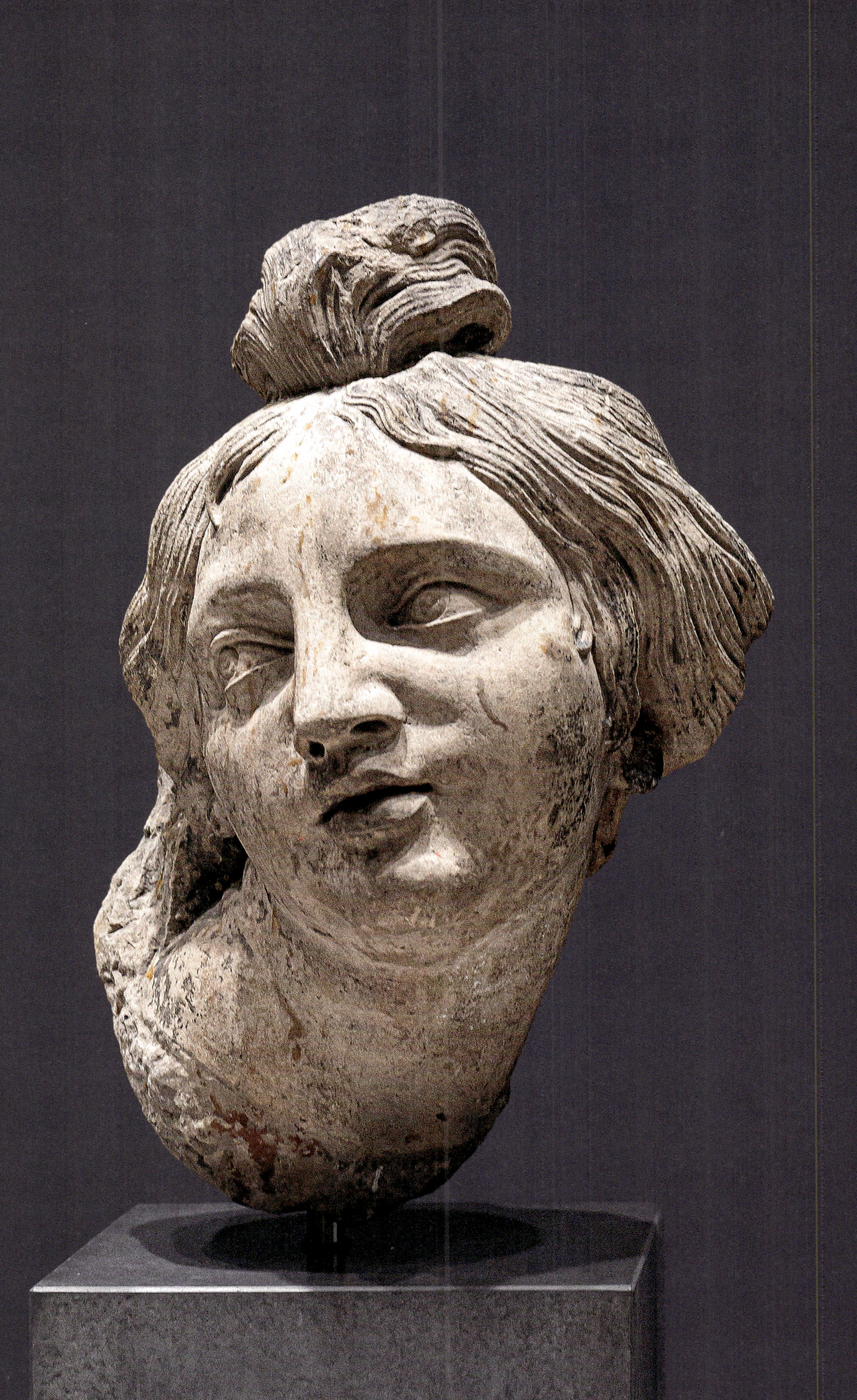

From Architectural Competition
to Realization

*An Excursus by
Manfred Rettig*

After the inauguration of the Palast der Republik (Palace of the Republic) in 1976, I travelled with a group of fellow students of the Technische Universität Berlin (Technical University of Berlin) to the eastern part of the city to view this masterwork of socialist architecture. I never suspected that many years later I would assume supervisory functions in the area of construction work, both regarding the technical treatment of the building as well as for the Humboldt Forum in the transformed Berlin Palace up until my retirement in 2016.

The history of the Palace of the Republic is a topic for another time. But I do want to mention that the removal of the sprayed asbestos from the building was urgently necessary. In the 1990s, moreover, I had a number of meetings with Heinz Graffunder, the building's chief architect, in which he did not challenge the necessity of removing the asbestos. We were both aware that this would mean stripping the building down to its shell. But I never experienced the political interference that has often been imputed.

From 2001 until 2009 I headed the Bundesbaugesellschaft Berlin mbH (BBB, Federal Construction Company), which was responsible for construction for the German Bundestag (Parliament) and the Bundeskanzleramt (Federal Chancellery). On the achievement of the functionality of the buildings, this successful and efficient GmbH was phased out at the behest of the responsible politicians. This meant losing an opportunity to deploy the highly experienced BBB, with its well-coordinated team of technicians, businesspeople and legal experts, for other difficult, large-scale projects such as the BER Airport or the Humboldt Forum.

For the Humboldt Forum a foundation under private law was established which is responsible for the project as the owner and awarding authority. In 2009, having been appointed a member of the founding board and speaker of the foundation, I worked with a small team to get things up and running. Besides establishing contacts with the federal ministries and the Berlin Senate, future institutional users, the contracting federal office and development associations and donors, I regarded it as my principal task in the initial stage to examine the winning design from the architectural competition to see whether it could be realized smoothly. It soon became evident that the architect Franco Stella was a decidedly creative, cooperative and agreeable contractual partner, and that we could carry the project forward expeditiously and with the necessary functionality.

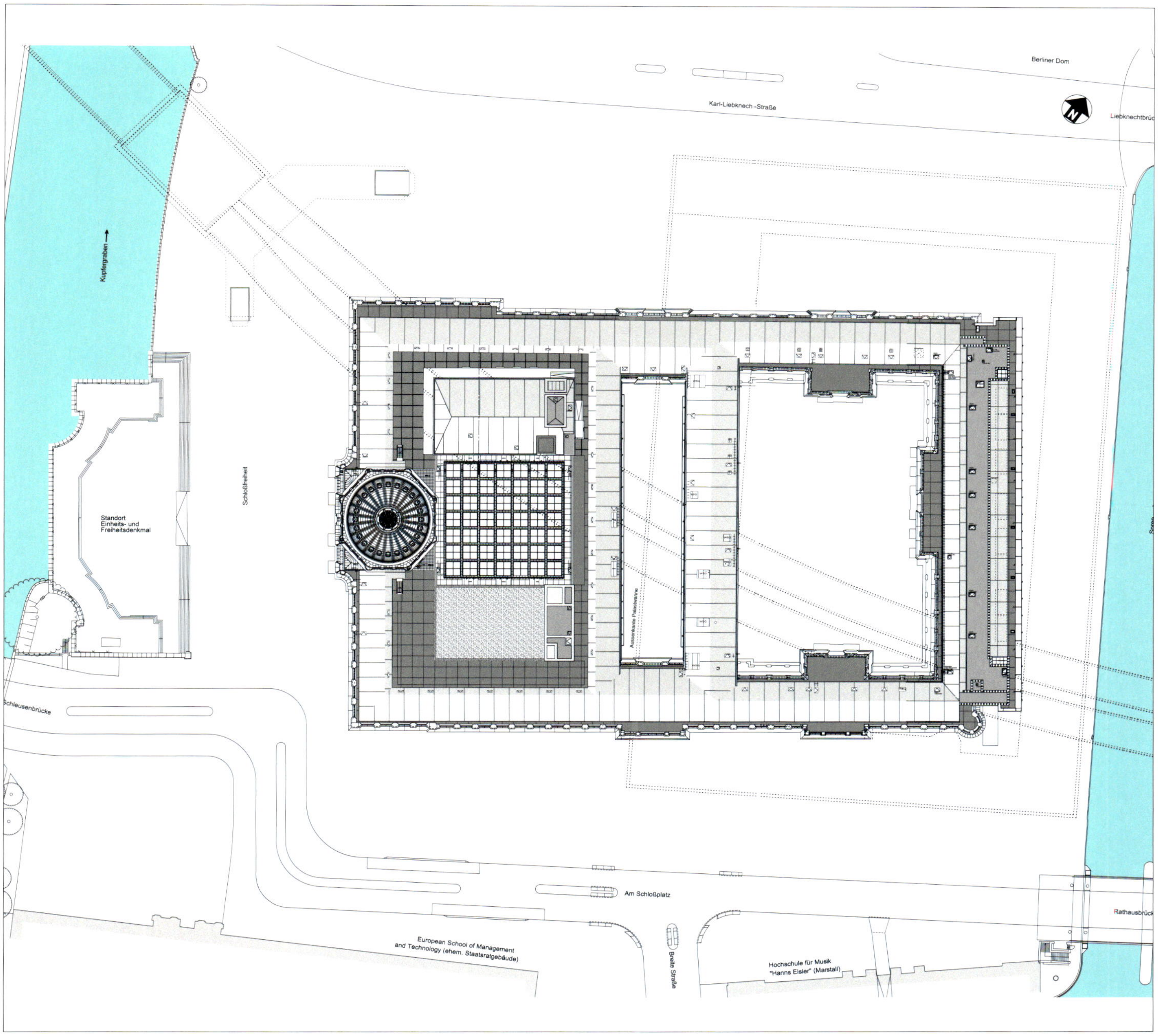

When we first met, Stella's design envisioned only a partial basement. The technical centre had not yet been planned, and the decision to do without a subterranean garage had not yet been taken. Moreover, the handling of the existing archaeological remains was still unresolved. It was perfectly clear, on the other hand, that the projected date of completion in 2014, established by the then current construction minister and his undersecretary, was utterly unrealistic. It was evident to me that in order to avoid the prospect of a future building scandal, the project would need to be given a solid basis.

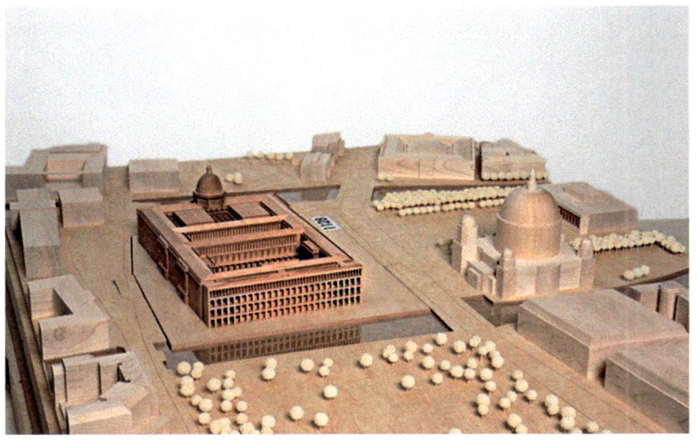

Site plan of the design showing the course of the underground tunnel of the U5 line beneath the Humboldt Forum in the Berlin Palace

Model of Franco Stella's design, 2008

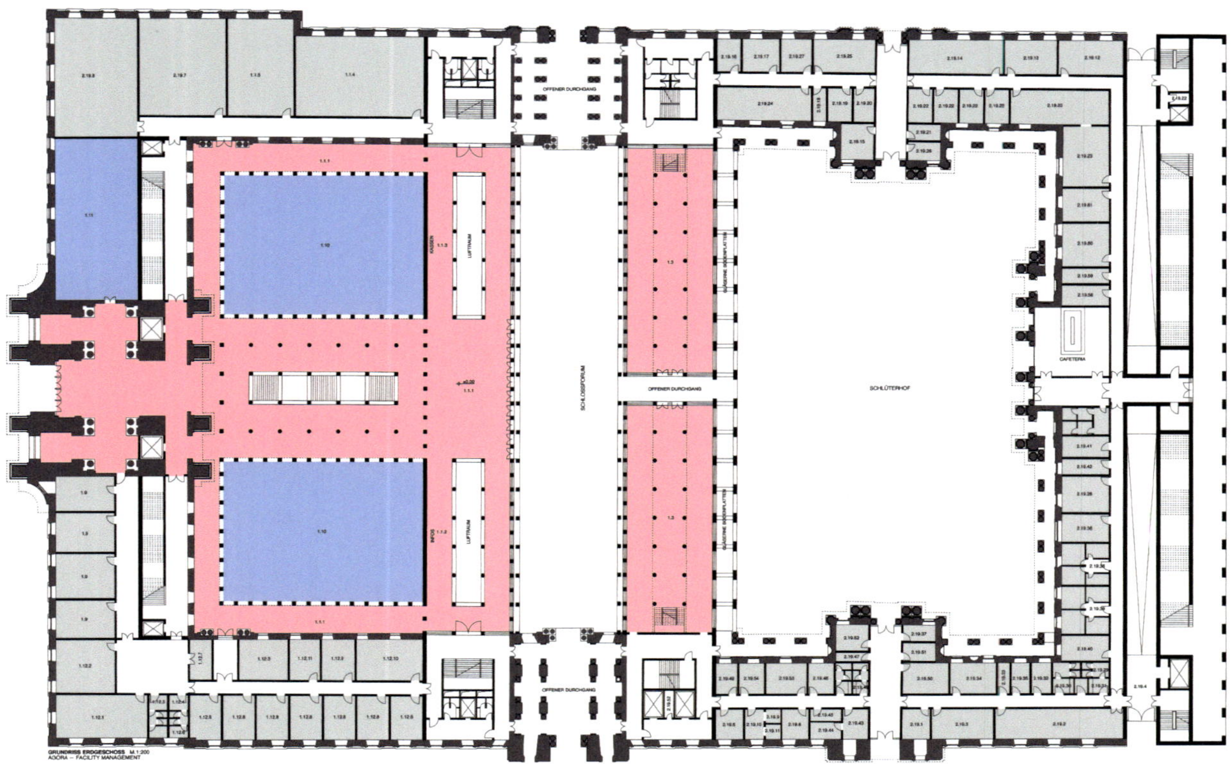

Floor plan of the ground floor in
the competition draft – with the
reconstructed Baroque interior
facades of the Great Courtyard and
the Belvedere wing to the east

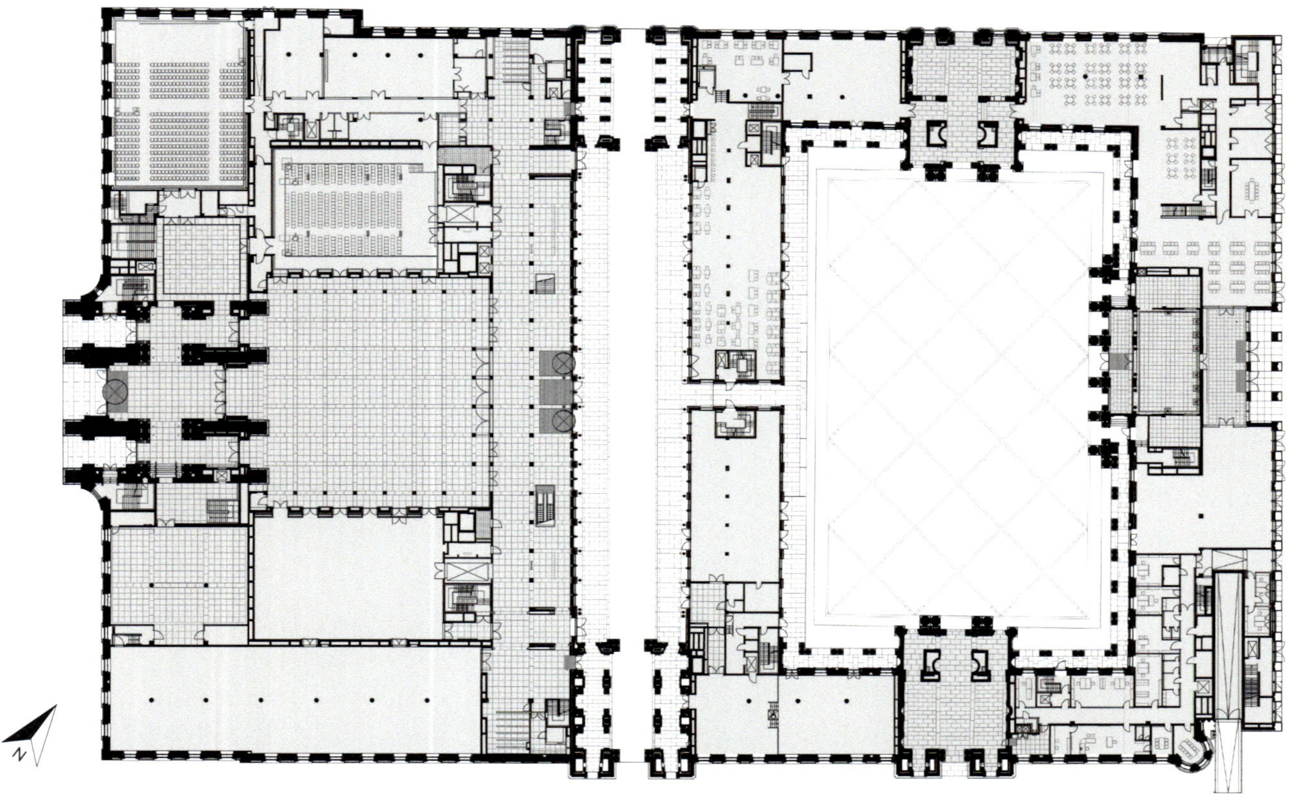

Floor plan of the ground floor in the
design planning stage

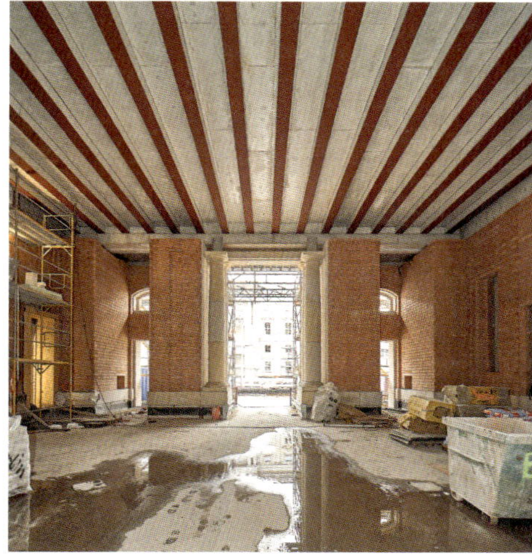

View into the passageway
of Portal 1, 2018

The worst thing that can befall a major project is a change in the intended utilization after the completion of the design planning. To avoid this, I conducted discussions with each user about the requisite functionality. Addressed during these intensive exchanges as well were supposedly ancillary questions concerning cloakrooms, toilet facilities and kitchenettes. More important, however, were questions of access and circulation and the positioning of major event and exhibition spaces within the building.

Without clarifying these aspects, it is impossible to plan the building technology. At the Humboldt Forum as it exists today, the building has a full basement level, and the technical systems accommodated there for the most part service only the ground floor and first upper storey, while the technically equipped attic storey serves the second and third upper storeys.

Access and Circulation

The surfaces surrounding the Humboldt Forum were not integrated into the competition assignment. Berlin had waited far too long to announce a competition for the outside spaces. In the absence of such an overall plan, the Berlin authorities made decisions concerning street layouts and cable routing that would prove critical in the course of the project. It was only after, on our recommendation, the Association of Arts and Culture of the German Economy at the Federation of German Industries (BDI) in conjunction with the Förderverein Berliner Schloss (Association Berliner Schloss e.V.) had organized a student landscape planning competition that Berlin began organizing the official competition. This made early coordination between Franco Stella and the landscape planners impossible. Subsequently, cable routing had to be altered at considerable expense. Other design optimizations, for example the return of the Neptune Fountain to Schlossplatz, are difficult to realize.

Moreover, it is my view that the political decision to locate the Freedom and Unity Monument on the west side of the reconstructed Palace reopens the issue of the main entrance.

When arriving from the boulevard Unter den Linden, visitors to the city will view the monument before entering the Humboldt Forum via Portal 3. In his competition design, however, Franco Stella assumed that the main entrance to the Humboldt Forum would be from the side of the Lustgarten (Pleasure Garden) via Portal 4 and would open onto the passage he had planned there. From his perspective, Portal 3, with its cupola, had only a subordinate role to play regarding public access. But Stella responded to the a tered outdoor planning by seizing it as an opportunity and using it to develop a markedly improved entrance situation.

Archaeology

Due to its extensive technical infrastructure, the building has a full basement level. This necessitated decisions concerning the handling of archaeological finds. The original planning envisioned a walkable glass surface in the domed Portal 3 which would have provided a limited view of the foundation of the historical palace. For me, it was clear that such a window was inadequate compensation for the disposal of the extensive archaeological remains of the Berlin Palace. I therefore proposed to the curator of archaeological monuments that a portion of the excavations be made accessible to the public. This concept was developed further in conjunction with the architect. The location of this accessible basement to the south of Portal 3 is ideal. The location of the exhibition on the history of the site on the ground floor, above the archaeological basement and directly behind the Freedom and Unity Monument, was unfortunately abandoned during the subsequent planning process.

Floorplans

During the early planning phase, I enacted an imagined walking tour of the building together with the project participants. This exercise revealed the need for essential adjustments, in part for the sake of users. Particularly notable was the displacement of the conference halls from the area of the

Design drawings, exterior views
of the reconstructed palace, west
(above) and south side (middle)
and west-east section through the
transverse wings (below)

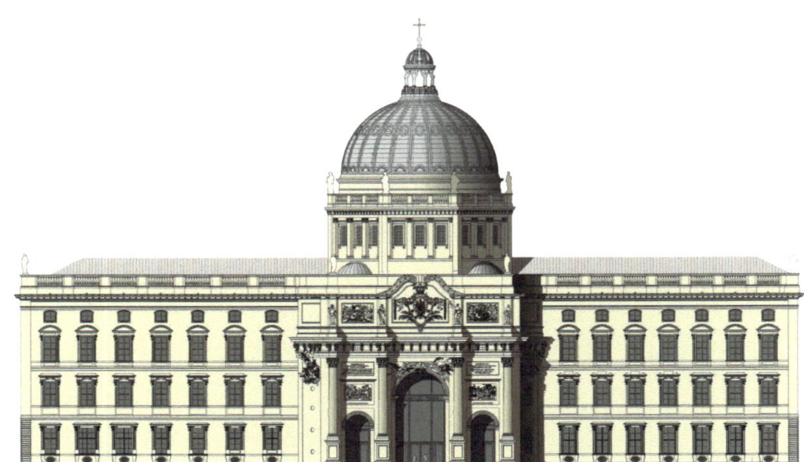

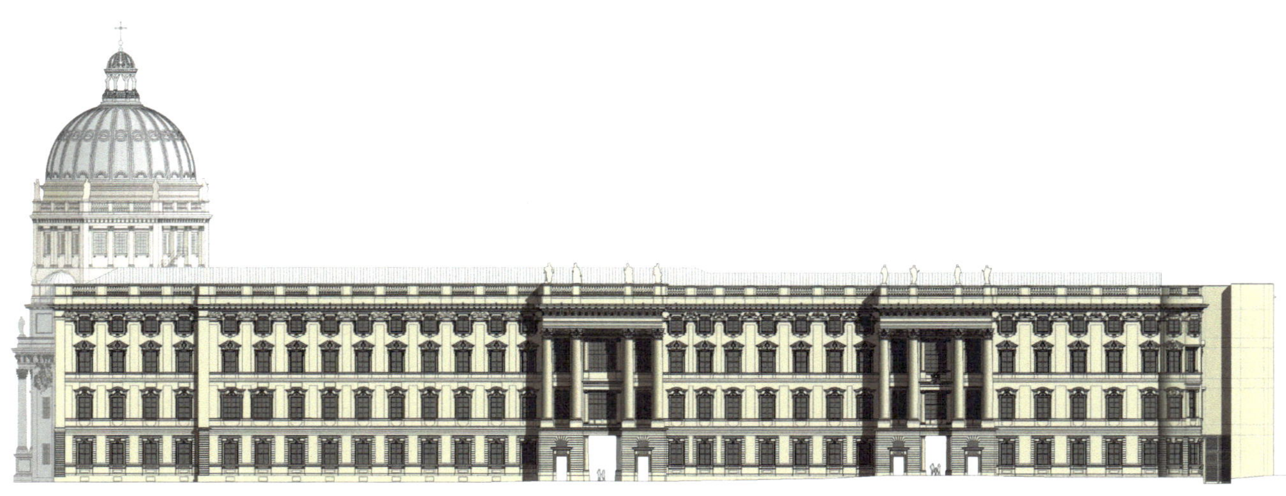

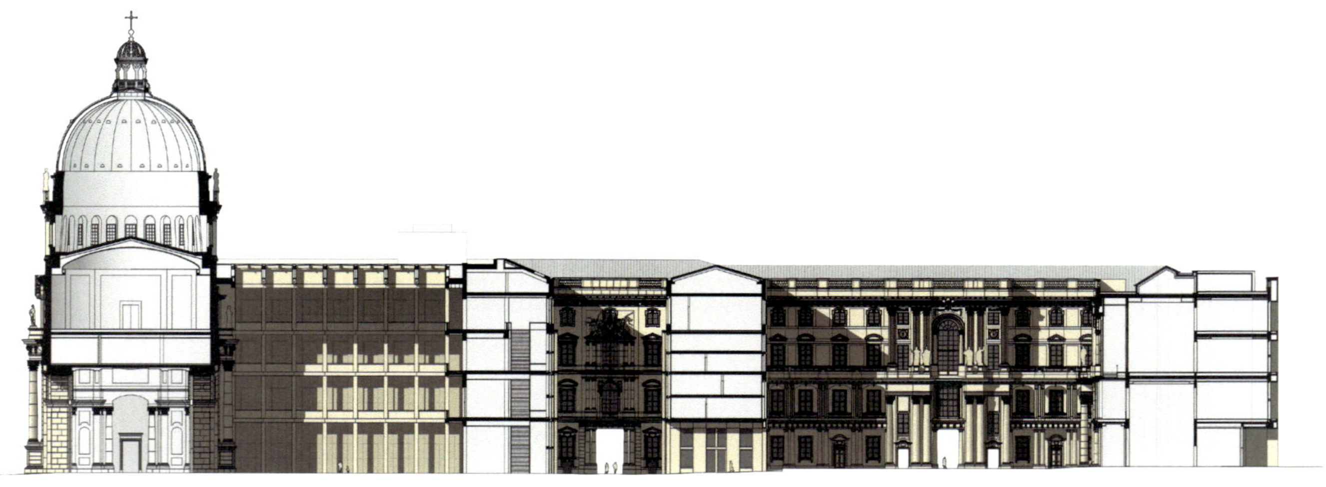

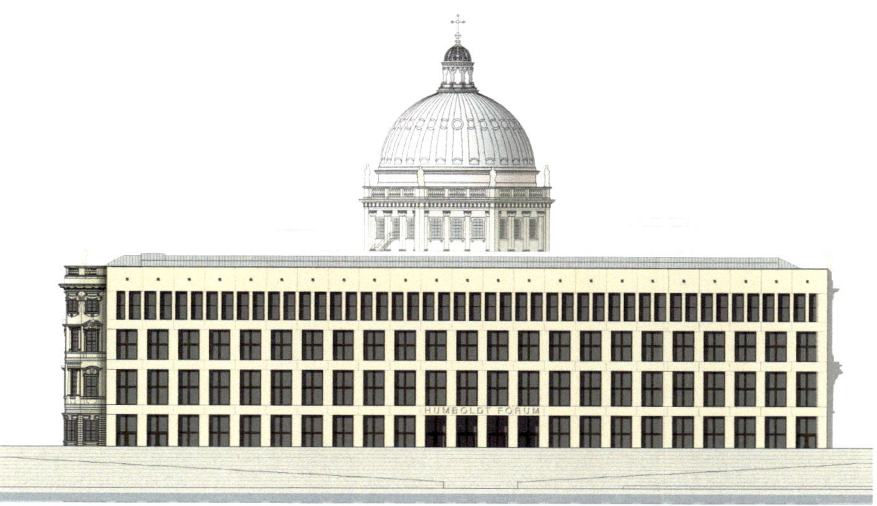

Design drawings, exterior views
of the reconstructed palace,
east (above) and north side (middle)
and north-south section trough the
Passage (below)

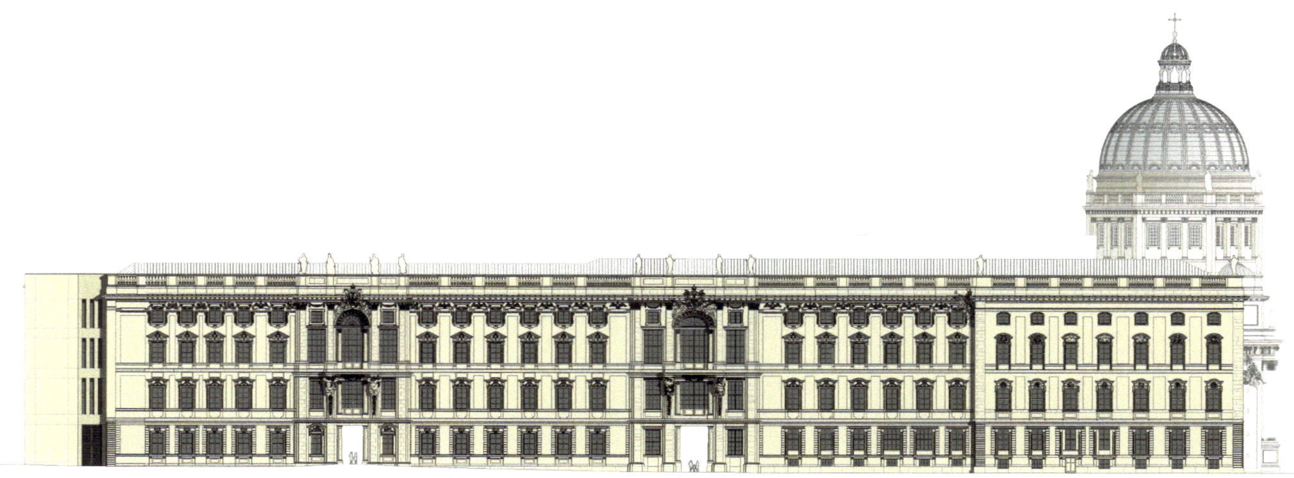

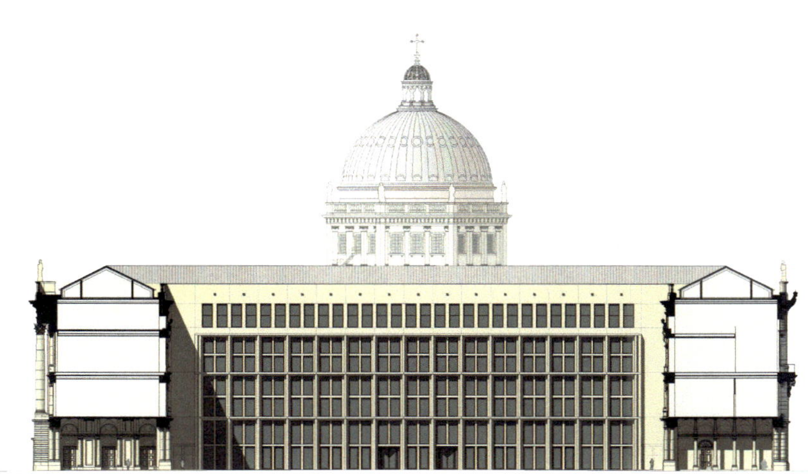

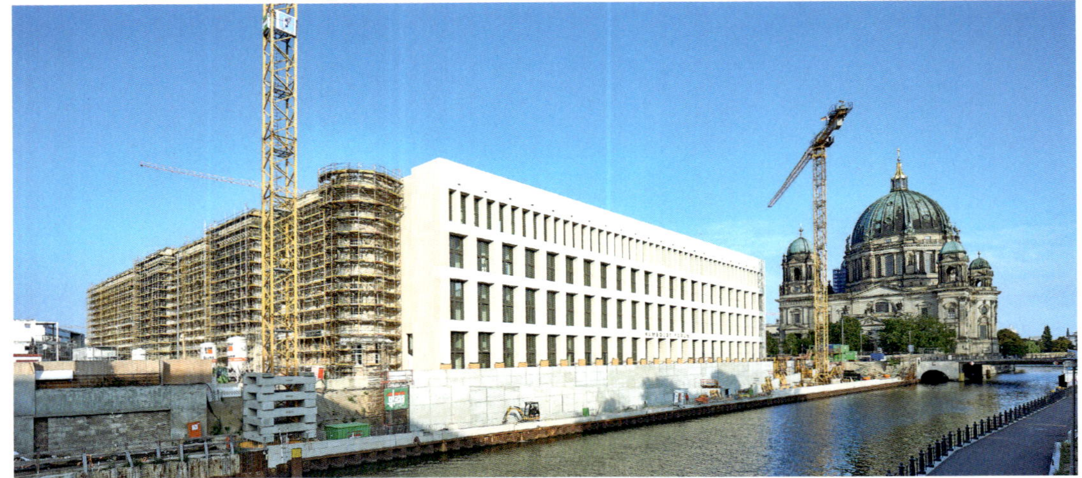

present entrance hall to the western part of the building, and the relocation of the South Sea boats from the east side of the building into the cubes in the area of the entrance hall.

Furthermore, the proposal of the Federal State of Berlin to accommodate its Zentral- und Landesbibliothek (Central State Library) in the first upper storey was subjected to intensified planning with regard to feasibility. In my view, it was important to offer visitors convincing attractions that would encourage them to perceive the building vertically, and not just through the ground floor. To the chagrin of the architect, this also meant the construction of escalators in the upper storeys. Based on the experience of the construction of the roof restaurant of the Reichstag building, I called attention early on to the need for such a restaurant in the Humboldt Forum.

It would take us too far here to enumerate all of the changes that were adopted. Suffice it to say that after completion of this evaluation of the competition design, we arrived at a reliable planning status on the basis of which technical planning could proceed.

Palace Workshop

When I began my work with the Foundation, the projected reconstruction of the Palace facades was often referred to in the media in a derogatory fashion as a mock-up or stage scenery. For the sake of the credibility of the endeavour as a whole it therefore became vital to create a basis for the facade reconstructions that would receive recognition from experts. At a closed conference with international participation, specialists developed ten theses that would need to be considered in planning the reconstruction. Recommended for the Berlin Palace was, among other things, the establishment of a palace workshop.

My knowledge of the property situation in Berlin enabled me to locate a suitable building with all due speed. It proved more difficult to find the right director. After a number of interviews, I finally hired the highly qualified sculptor Bertold Just. Within the briefest possible period of time, he organized the workshop's structural operations. He also set up the

Palace Workshop as a publicly accessible information source. It is especially tragic that this wonderful man did not live to experience the completion of the palace facades.

Förderverein Berliner Schloss e.V.

Several associations of friends (Fördervereine) with diverse focal centres have devoted their energies to the reconstruction of the Berlin Palace. The greatest impact was certainly achieved by the Förderverein Berliner Schloss (Association Berliner Schloss e.V.) with its incomparable promoter, Wilhelm von Boddien. Again and again, sceptics have called into question the success of the Association on various levels and have sought to hinder its activities. Today, its success speaks for itself, and the envisaged donation goal has nearly been reached. Additionally, the Association was able to raise funds for options going beyond the original budget framework. I have always linked these special donations with achieving a balance between the task of collecting donations for reconstructing the historical facade and the responsibility for achieving a coherent building that would be seen by an international public. How embarrassing it would have been, for example, to have erected a palace reconstruction with a cupola that was a mere shell structure.

Collaboration with the association of friends, the Förderverein, was also important for public perception. At the same time, I consistently sought to avoid any supervisory role over this independent entity by the Foundation, the Stiftung Humboldt Forum. Only in this way could the Association work in an independent and successful way. The Foundation had only limited resources at its disposal for public relations activities. This made cooperation with the Association Berliner Schloss e.V. even more indispensable.

Public Outreach

With major building projects, political decision-making and the inception of construction activity are separated as a rule by an extended planning phase. To avoid having the public surprised

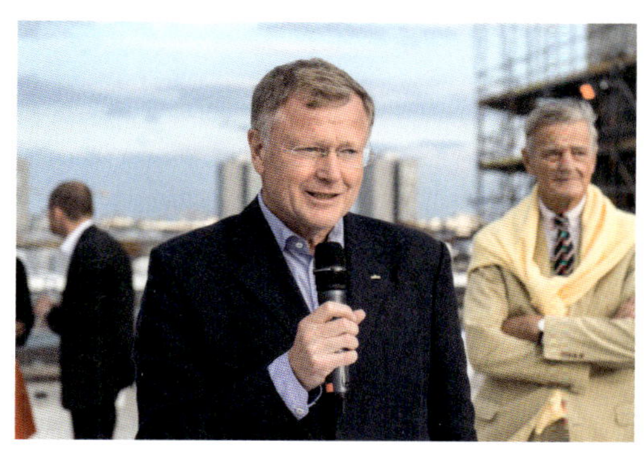

Manfred Rettig, behind him Jens Odewald

by the sudden inauguration of building activities, as with the project Stuttgart 21, we organized public forums from the start. The response was impressive. Prior to each decision concerning implementation, interested individuals could express their views after lectures by experts that were followed by podium discussions. These exchanges were often helpful to the subsequent planning process.

Taking place annually, in addition, were the Tage der offenen Baustelle (Days of the Open Construction Site) – the first took place on the day of the ground-breaking ceremony. On these days, thousands of people flocked to the construction site. Early on, this led to a sense of identification with the project.

Exhibitions in Germany and abroad supplemented the public relations outreach for the Humboldt Forum. All events were also designed to elicit donations for the historical facade. To this end, numerous books and pamphlets were published as well.

Risks and Solutions

I will never forget the general assembly of the des Association Berliner Schloss e.V. in the year 2010. More than 500 members and donors gathered in the spaces of the Rotes Rathaus (Red City Hall) in Berlin-Mitte (Berlin Centre). In a closed-door meeting, the German Cabinet had just decided to postpone the project of the Humboldt Forum in the Berlin Palace until further notice. This resolution was celebrated by our adversaries as the demise of the project. At this event, I regarded it as especially crucial that the existing level of civic commitment not be dissipated. Now, the original, politically motivated adoption of an unrealistic timetable worked to my advantage. Although the design planning did not yet exist, millions of euros were already available for use in the federal budget, to which we had access as the Humboldt Forum Foundation. Moreover, Berlin had already begun constructing the Number 5 underground line, which runs diagonally underneath the Humboldt Forum. For our building measures, a later beginning would have meant considerable extra costs, since we would have had to build

over the underground tunnel with a kind of bridge structure. For this reason, I proposed beginning with what I called advance measures. This wording was unobjectionable and met with general approval. We were able to carry out the initial percussion boring for the foundation. This was the decisive breakthrough for the launching of construction work.

Despite intensive coordination work with future users, I was unable to prevent costly, time-consuming and to some extent major changes in utilization: the Federal State of Berlin discarded completed plans, which had already cost millions, for its Zentral- und Landesbibliothek (Central State Library). Moreover, the federal authorities altered the design of the Ethnologisches Museum (Ethnological Museum) several times, and the founding directorate was given permission to develop, once again, overall proposals for the functions that would occupy the Humboldt Forum.

All of these changes had a considerable impact on the building technology, and hence on the construction workflow. It is in particular thanks to the Humboldt Forum Foundation, the federal building authorities and the planners that the Humboldt Forum was nonetheless completed with such speed.

Now, the directive of the German Bundestag to create a place for dialogue between cultures must be substantively implemented. In the future, a global conversation will take place here. Civic commitment in the form of associations, federations and organizations (NGOs) is prepared to contribute to the Humboldt Forum in the Berlin Palace, which can now become a cultural centre for world peace.

How It All Came to Pass: The Debate about Reconstruction

Wilhelm von Boddien

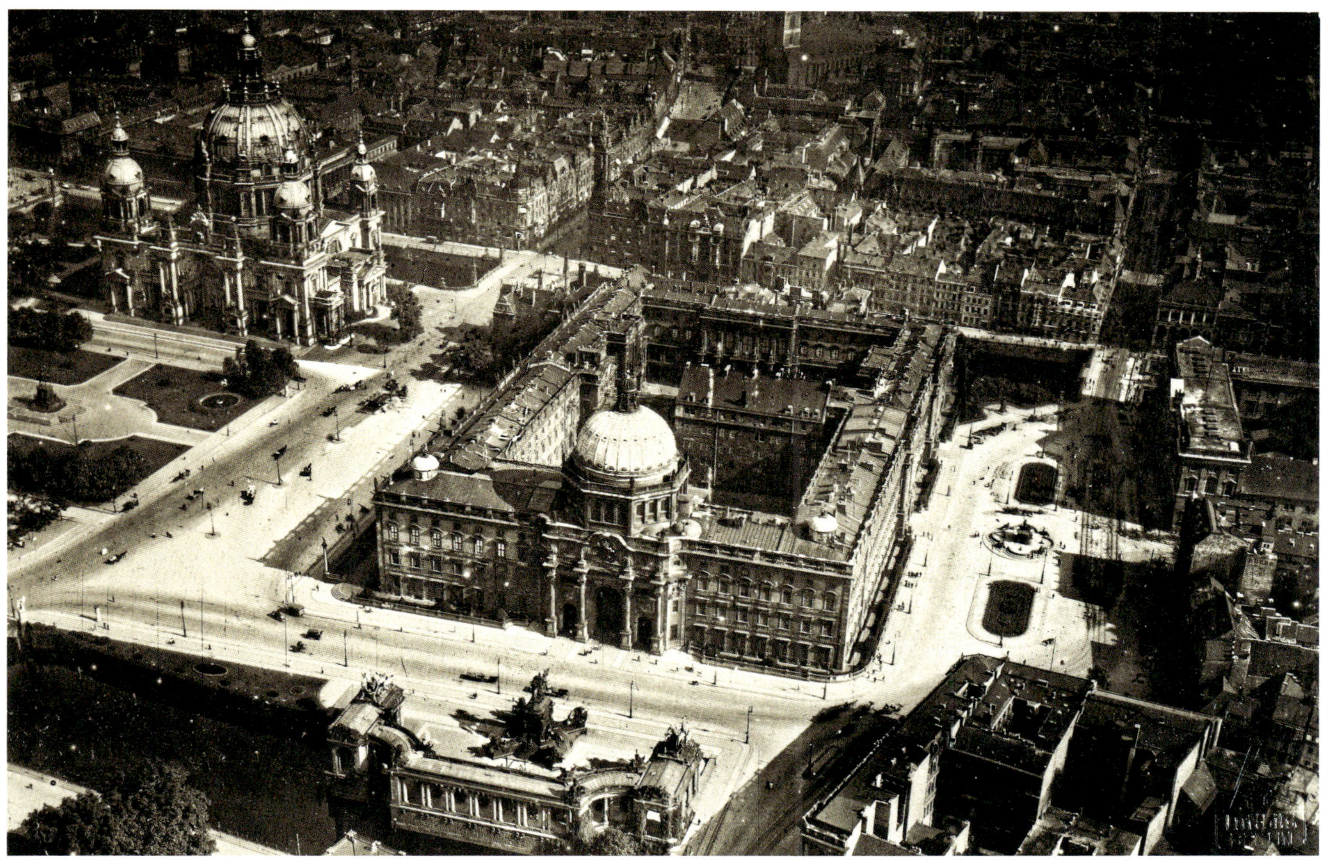

The Berlin Palace at the end of the splendid boulevard known as Unter den Linden was the city's heart, it was the centre of gravity and nucleus of crystallization for all architecture in the vicinity.

In *Abschied von Preussen* (Farewell to Prussia; 1991), Wolf Jobst Siedler writes: 'The Palace was not in Berlin; Berlin was the Palace.'

The image of the Berlin Palace, continuously reshaped and enlarged up into the eighteenth century, emblematizes the evolution of Berlin into a metropolis, into the German capital. It was the city's pivotal secular building, and Berlin grew around it like the annual rings of a tree around its core. Oriented towards the look of the Palace were the major historical buildings still in existence today, all designed by the best Prussian architects, among them the Zeughaus (Arsenal), the Neo-Baroque Cathedral, the buildings on Museum Island, the Staatsoper (Opera), the University, the churches and the Schauspielhaus (originally a theatre, now a concert hall) on Gendarmenmarkt, and all the way to the Brandenburg Gate. All were engaged in intensive dialogue with the Palace. Together, they formed a world-class architectural ensemble that was extolled in histories of art as 'Berlin's Gesamtkunstwerk' (synthesis of the arts), and was known affectionately by the people of Berlin as 'Athens on the Spree'.

Concerning the importance of the Berlin Palace, Karl Friedrich Schinkel remarked:

'The Palace is widely regarded as a monument ..., one whose dignity and splendour ... rank it among Europe's premier buildings in every respect. As a monument of this kind, it is inviolable, and it is the duty of the state at the very least to preserve it in its present condition for posterity – at the very least! –

Aerial view of the Berlin Palace
from the southwest, 1919

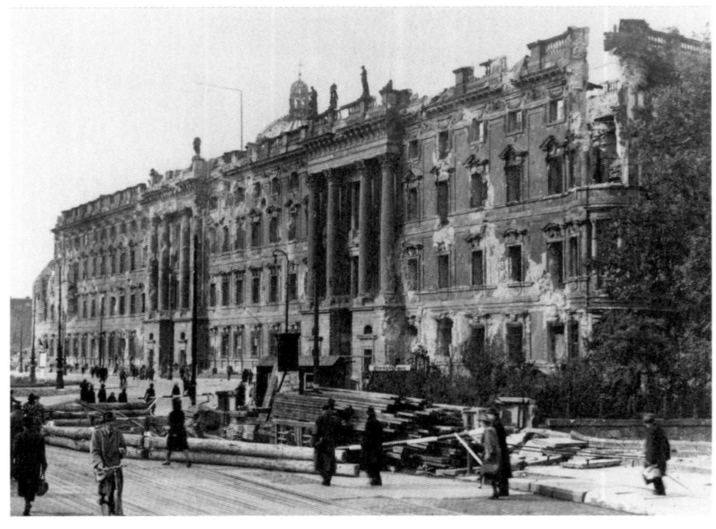

Ruins of the Palace at the end
of World War II, 1945

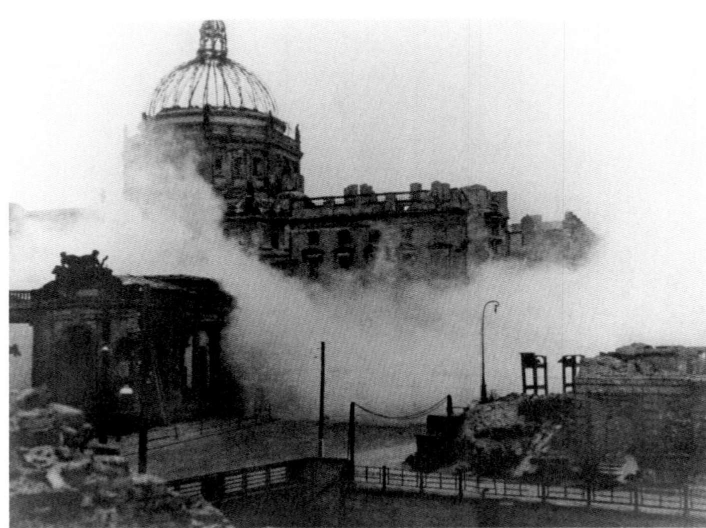

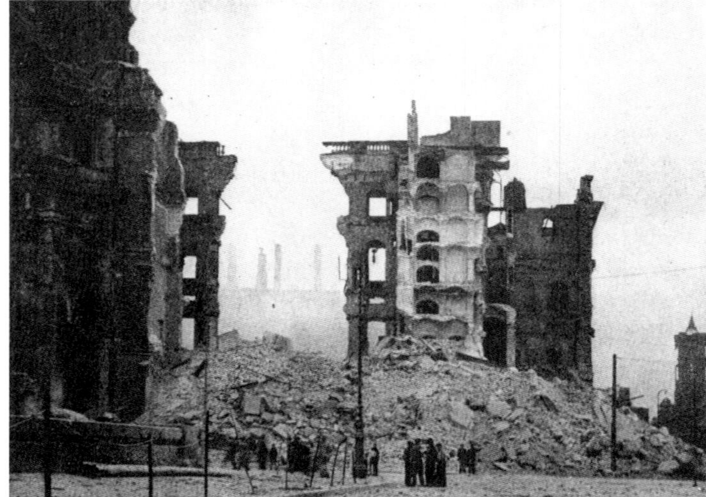

The Berlin Palace, demolition of
the west and south sides facing
Schlossplatz/corner of
Schlossfreiheit, 1950

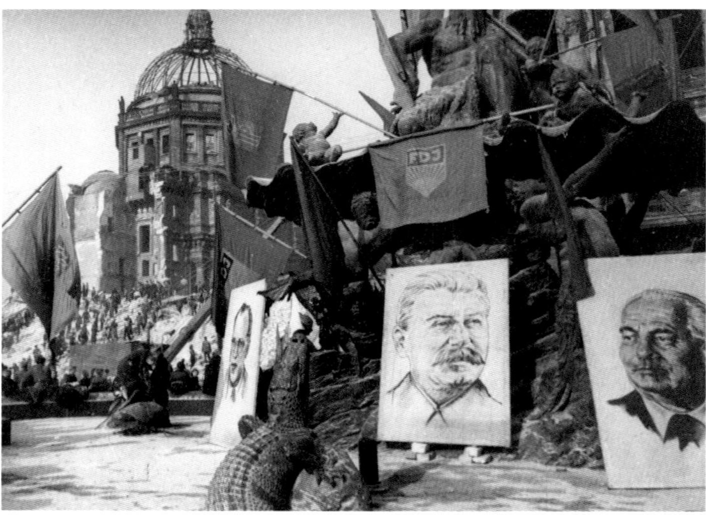

The Free German Youth performing
'voluntary building shifts' during
the clearing of the ruins of the
demolished palace. In the foreground, banners and portraits of
Otto Grotewohl, Josef Stalin and
Wilhelm Pieck (from left) at the
Neptune Fountain, 1950

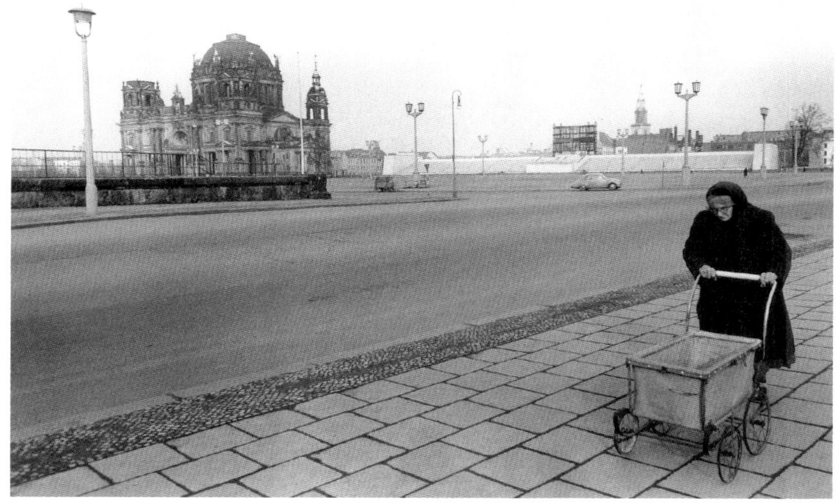

*... Architecturally, our own era must acknowledge with humility the talent of our
great artist and countryman Schlüter, and commend what this master achieved.'*

In February of 1945, late in World War II, the enormous building sustained
severe damage, and during fires that lasted for four days was gutted
almost entirely. Nonetheless, considerable architectural substance
survived, as compared for example with Schloss Charlottenburg, already
destroyed in 1943, whose heavy wartime damage is no longer visible to
the eye. But the Berlin Palace fell victim to political caprice. In 1950, Walter
Ulbricht, Secretary-General of the Socialist Unity Party of Germany (SED)
and the highest authority in the German Democratic Republic (GDR, more
commonly known as East Germany), decreed that the Palace be razed to
create space for a gigantic parade ground. The decision triggered vigorous
protest worldwide:

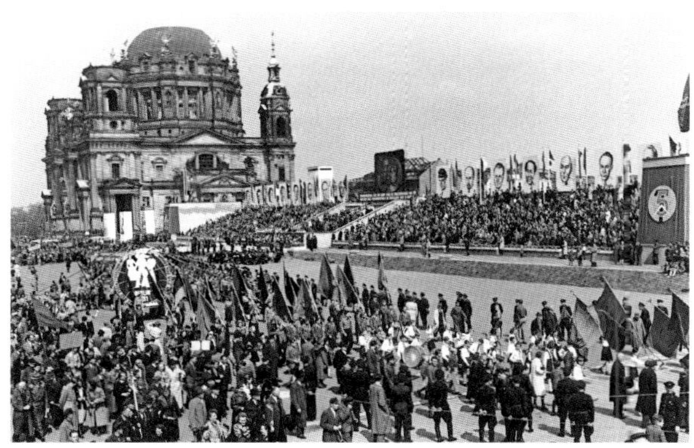

'The demolition of the palace means the collapse of old Berlin as a whole.'
(Margarete Kühn, who rescued Schloss Charlottenburg)

*'What is happening here is cold-blooded murder. We will need to give the city a
new name!'* (Walter Stengel, Director of the Märkisches Museum, Berlin)

*'Evidently, the ruling powers of the moment in eastern Berlin perceive the Palace
mainly as a political manifestation. To them, its architecture is apparently
reminiscent of the "clang of clashing steel shields, the blasting of martial
trumpets". Clearly, these sounds are perceived as the jarring noises of a cult of
royalty which has long since ceased to exist. They have irritated the sensitive
eardrums of the current potentates, and must be silenced. They prefer listening
to their own noises on the parade grounds they are laying out on the site of
the demolished Palace. This desolate square to will one day be a monument –
a monument to irreverence, small-mindedness and intellectual poverty.'*
(Ragnar Josephson, *Svenska Dagbladet*)

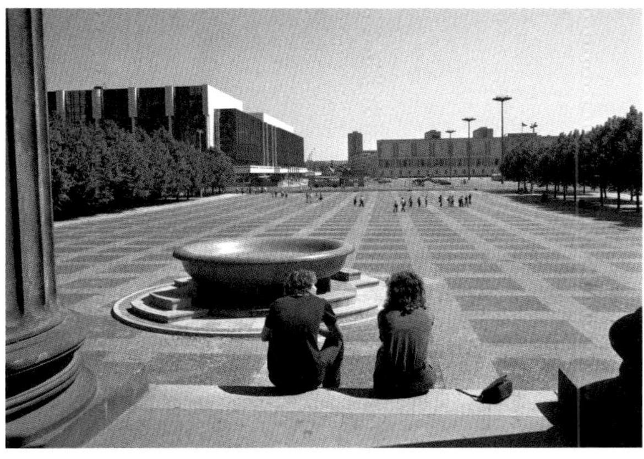

But protest proved ineffective, and in May of 1951, the enormous parade
grounds on the site of the now razed Palace were inaugurated with a mass
demonstration. Ever since, the city has suffered from phantom pain at this
location.

    Meanwhile, the most important historical buildings of the city centre,
all oriented architecturally towards the Palace, were reconstructed by the
GDR, but they now lacked any point of reference in the parade grounds
or the Palast der Republik (Palace of the Republic). The Berlin Palace was

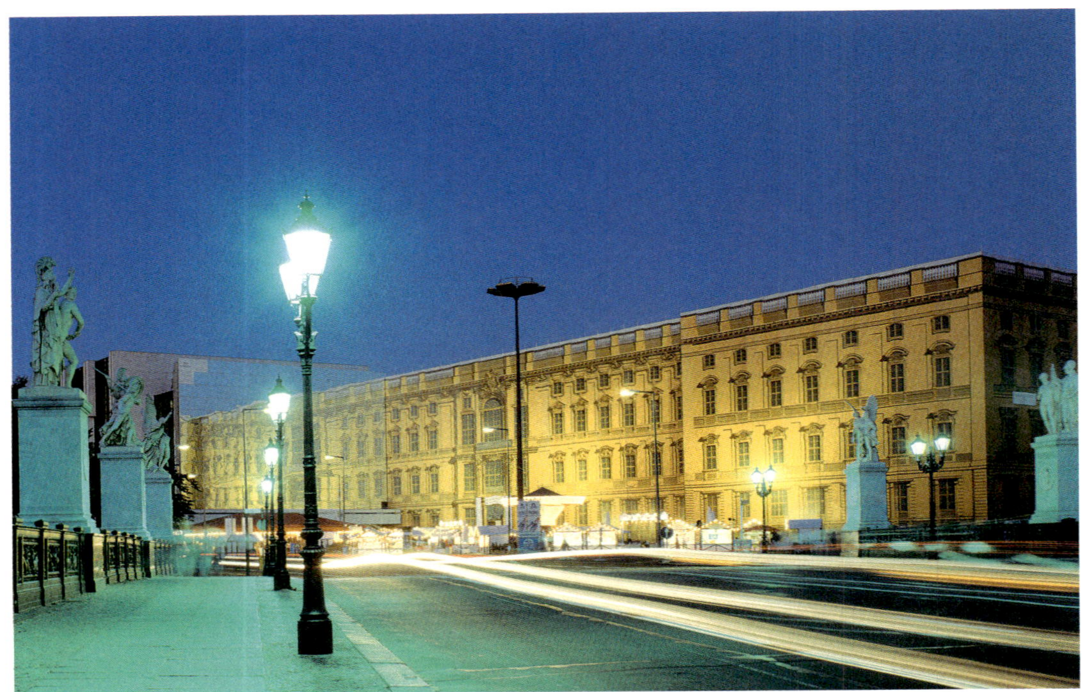

The Palace simulation, consisting of a painted tarpaulin and gigantic scaffolding, 1993. A mirror installed in front of the simulation created an optical extension of the simulation, concealing the Palace of the Republic behind it.

soon forgotten, and the old heart of the Berlin was reshaped by the GDR and its state buildings.

The reconstruction of the Palace can be traced back to an initiative launched in 1993 by the Förderverein Berliner Schloss (Association Berliner Schloss e.V.), which created a sensation at that time by erecting a one-to-one scale simulation of the Palace at its original location – funded exclusively by private resources. The Association was established for this purpose by myself along with seven other friends, and was hence a tiny citizen's initiative. We thus intervened in plans for the future design of the site, for which the Federal Government and the Berlin Senate had announced the Spree Island Competition: a master plan for the future development of the island was to have been adopted as early as 1994. Participating were more than 1000 architects and urban planners. The results of the competition were to be endowed with the force of law. Afterward the reconstruction of the Palace would no longer be conceivable.

In 1993–94, these circumstances represented the outward occasion for the decision on the part of the Association to rescue the Palace from oblivion by erecting a one-to-one scale simulation on the former site. The simulation consisted of an enormous scaffolding for the three-dimensional painted palace facades, created in France by the Parisian artist Catherine Feff, who specializes in large-scale paintings in the finest tromp l'œil manner. Through this gesture, we sought to inject the idea of a reconstruction into the emerging architectural debate.

The sceptical response, but also the ridicule in the media, from representatives of the architectural profession, from art historians and conservators of historical monuments, was acrimonious: does it really make sense to rebuild a structure that had already been completely destroyed? Wouldn't that be retrograde, an expression of yearning for some eternal yesterday? Contemporary buildings, it was argued, should rely upon the expressive forms of democracy. A palace would be inconsistent with modern times, and only a king can live in one (Stefan Heym). Moreover, the Palace of the Republic still stood on the site of the former Palace.

Through the simulation, however, the Palace re-emerged emphatically within collective memory. Growing numbers of people were enthusiastic

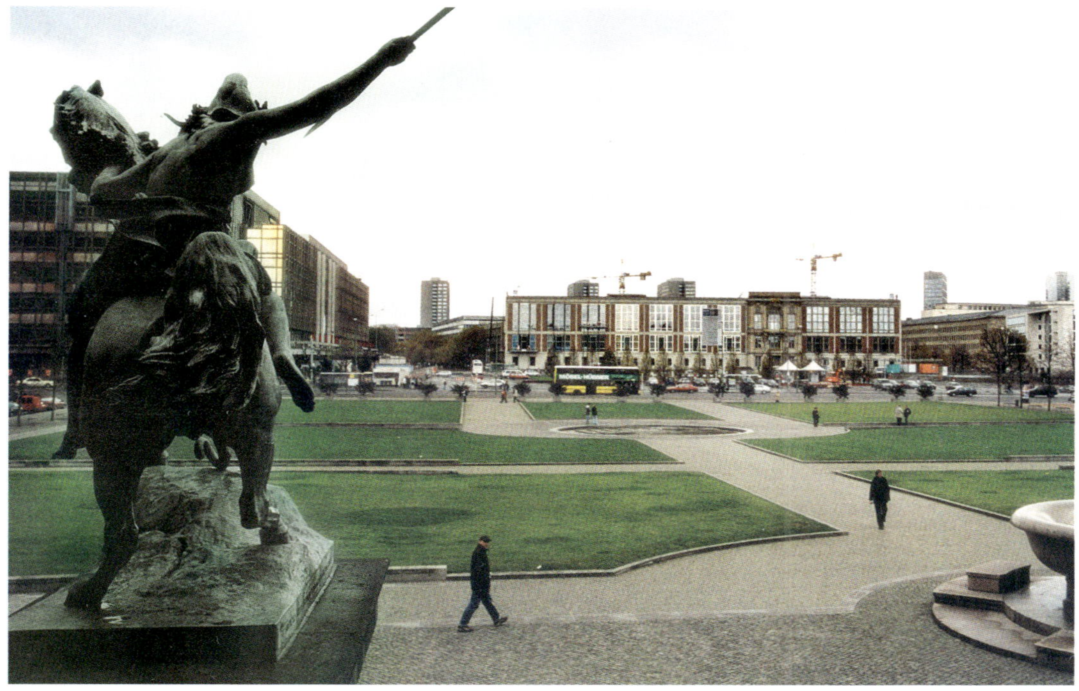

View from the colonnade of the Altes Museum towards the Palace of the Republic and the former State Council Building, 2006

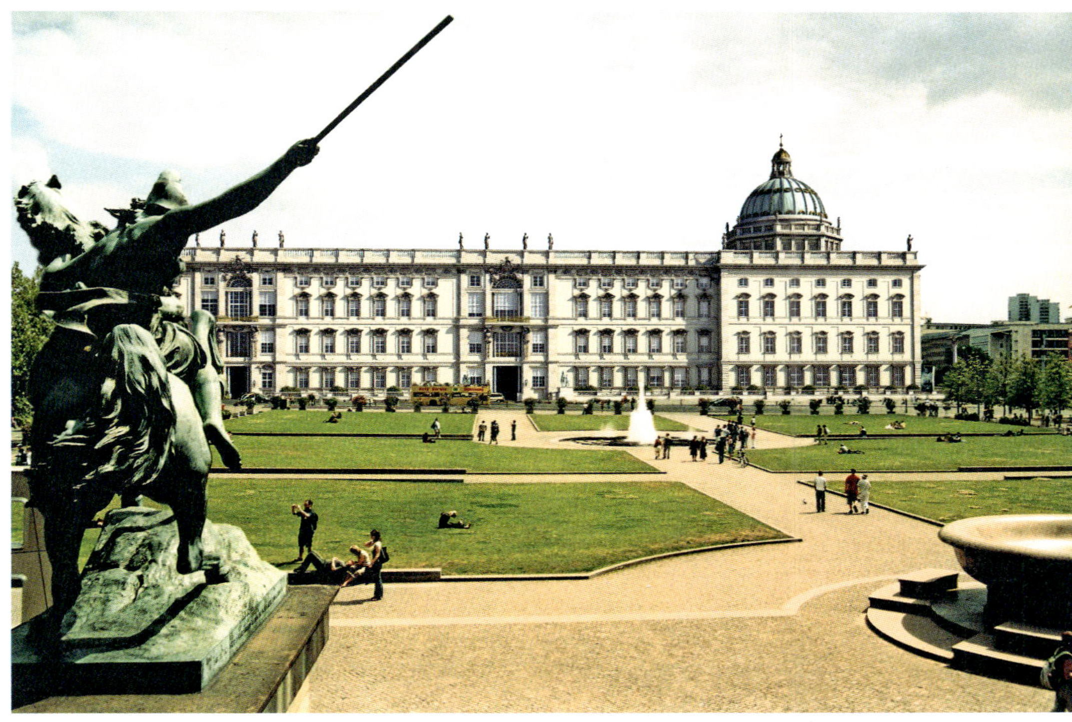

The same perspective with a virtual simulation of the reconstructed Berlin Palace

about reconstruction, and in the end, astonishingly, it came to occupy a position of equal standing in the Spree Island Competition: all three designs selected for prizes by the jury envisioned structures with the same dimensions as the Palace at its original location. Without the palace simulation, with its potent powers of suggestion, such a result would likely have been inconceivable. Although nothing but a mock-up, the simulation restored the old fabric of the city, one still familiar to many people. 'Once again, Berlin now looks as though nothing else has ever been there!' (Marianne von Weizsäcker)

Our sole concern was rehabilitating the historical ensemble of the centre of Berlin, and not the Palace as a solitary building. Things would have been very different had the Palace stood instead at Alexanderplatz or Potsdamer Platz, where the demolition frenzy that followed World War II

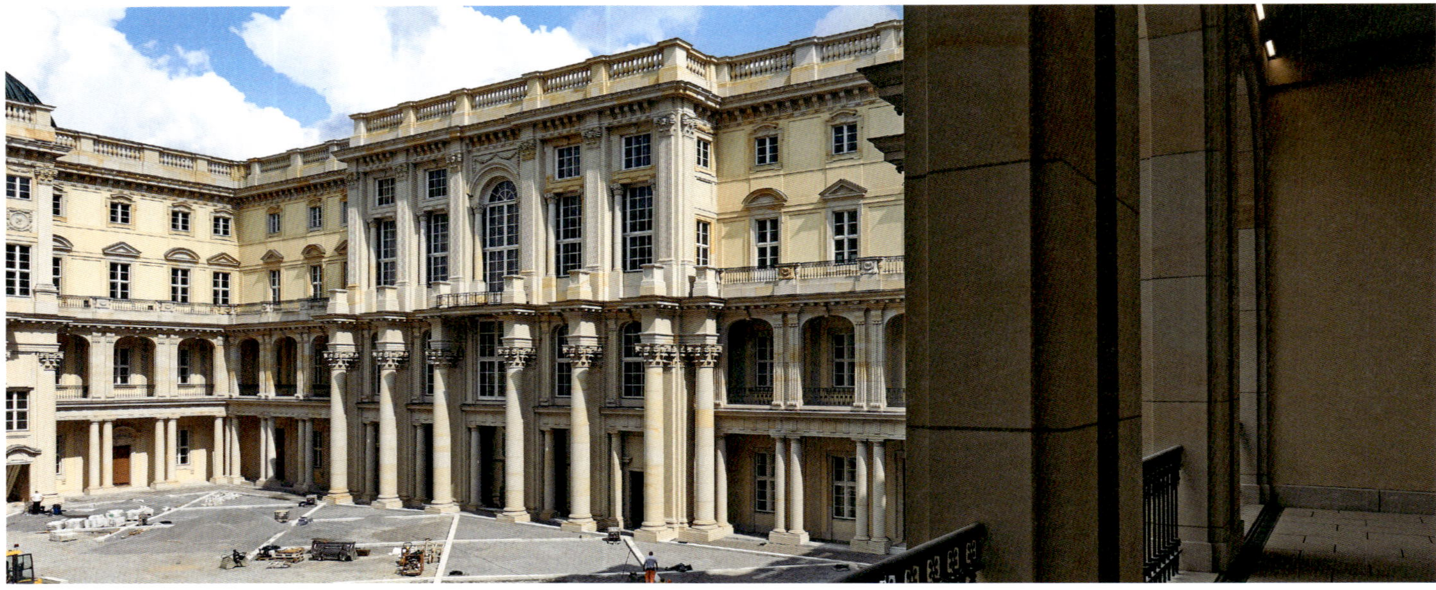

The Schlüter Courtyard, view
towards the northeast, 2020

created a tabula rasa: a reconstruction in such modern settings would have been pointless. There the gigantic Baroque building would have been a disruptive element – not unlike the architectural impact of the Palace of the Republic within the opulent historical ensemble at Berlin's heart.

The simulation was followed by a highly contentious debate that lasted eight long years, devoted to the question of whether the Palace should be rebuilt, and whether the removal of the Palace of the Republic would not constitute a crime as grave as the razing of the Berlin Palace had itself once been. In arguments for a reconstruction, prominent exponents of architectural modernism perceived a presumptuous infringement on their putative prerogatives as the sole authorities in architectural matters. In their eyes, a decision for reconstruction – in the face of their objections – would be nothing less than sacrilegious, the victory of 'retro'. I myself received the honorary title of 'palace ghost' or 'head of the palace forgery gang'.

Later, following the final decision by the German Bundestag (Parliament) for a reconstruction of the palace exterior, some of these people unhesitatingly registered grave allegations against me with the public prosecutor's office of Berlin. Ultimately, these proceedings were dropped 'on account of proved innocence'. None of which was exactly a picnic, especially for my wife and family, all of whom however – like our friends – stood by me steadfastly.

A key point of the counter-arguments at the time was the absence of any utilization concept. Proposals for using the Palace for political functions (as a building for the Federal States or the Foreign Office) or commercial uses (a hotel, gastronomy, event centre, shops) lacked majority support. The opponents of reconstruction sought to put planning on ice indefinitely by exploiting the rationale: 'No planned utilization, no palace – or: 'Form follows function'.

All of this changed abruptly in 2000, when Professor Dr. Klaus-Dieter Lehmann, then serving as President of the Stiftung Preussischer Kulturbesitz (Prussian Cultural Heritage Foundation), developed the idea of the Humboldt Forum – suddenly, there was broad public consensus. For the first time, the anti-palace camp found itself on the defensive.

In 2001, the Federal Government and the Berlin Senate appointed an 'International Expert Commission on the Historical Centre of Berlin' under the chairmanship of the Austrian Dr. Hannes Swoboda. In April of 2002, after a year of work, the commission's recommendation to the German

Bundestag was for a reconstruction of the palace exterior in conjunction with a modern interior (which received a narrow majority), together with the concept of the Humboldt Forum (which received a large majority).

On 4 July 2002, the German Bundestag voted with a nearly two-thirds majority – through a rare rollcall vote, and with suspension of party discipline – to approve this basic concept, and determined that three Baroque facades of the historical Palace along with the three facades by Andreas Schlüter in the small courtyard were to be rebuilt. The eastern facade facing the Spree as well as the western facade of the Schlüter Courtyard were to be modern in design, thereby giving visual expression to the destruction of the historical Palace. In light of the 'new-tech economic downturn', the Bundestag initially adopted a moratorium of several years.

In 2007, the Building Ministry organized an international architectural competition on the basis of the Bundestag resolution. In a two-stage competition that concluded in November of 2008, the design of the Italian architect Franco Stella was so persuasive that it emerged as the victor, with a unanimous vote of fifteen to zero.

In the end, the Berlin Palace was rebuilt – not exactly as it was, but instead in a way that is adapted to our own time. Externally, it is as beautiful as formerly, and has once again become Berlin's premier building. The conjunction with the idea of the Humboldt Forum is optimal, but also an extraordinary challenge to the conceptions of subsequent users.

The familiar image of Berlin has now been restored. The architectural ensemble of the historical centre has once again been made whole, and the historical buildings facing the Lustgarten (Pleasure Garden) and along the eastern side of the boulevard Unter den Linden have reacquired their dignity. The cityscape has been healed. Through the reconstruction, Berlin again becomes the beloved 'Athens on the Spree'. We now have a counterpoint to the austere modern districts that later arose on a massive scale. Berlin has once again become architecturally exciting.

At its centre, the city had been surrendered almost entirely to modern post-war architecture. During the years following wartime destruction, the city annihilated itself to an extraordinary degree: the damage from the bombing raids was now multiplied several times. An example is the demolition of the Fischerkiez (Fishermen's Village) on Spree Island, which dated in part from the late Middle Ages. It had survived the war unscathed. Rising now in its place was a row of standardized slab high-rises, which today still form a soulless ensemble. The urban layout has been altered in many places, with formerly renowned neighbourhoods becoming unrecognizable even on city maps.

With the rebuilding of the Berlin Palace, Berlin has rediscovered itself. The reconstructed Palace has rehabilitated the distorted image of the centre of Berlin brought about by its demolition.

Here, as in other European metropolises, modernism will henceforth be obliged to confront urban history, to measure itself against historical architecture, to contend with it – or else risk becoming boring. Berlin has now returned to the family of Europe's major historical cities. The Palace will reconcile the citizenry with the rebuilding of their city.

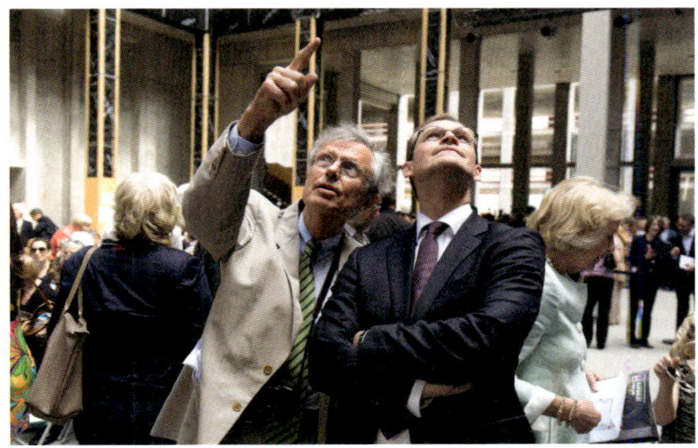

Wilhelm von Boddien (left) with
Michael Müller

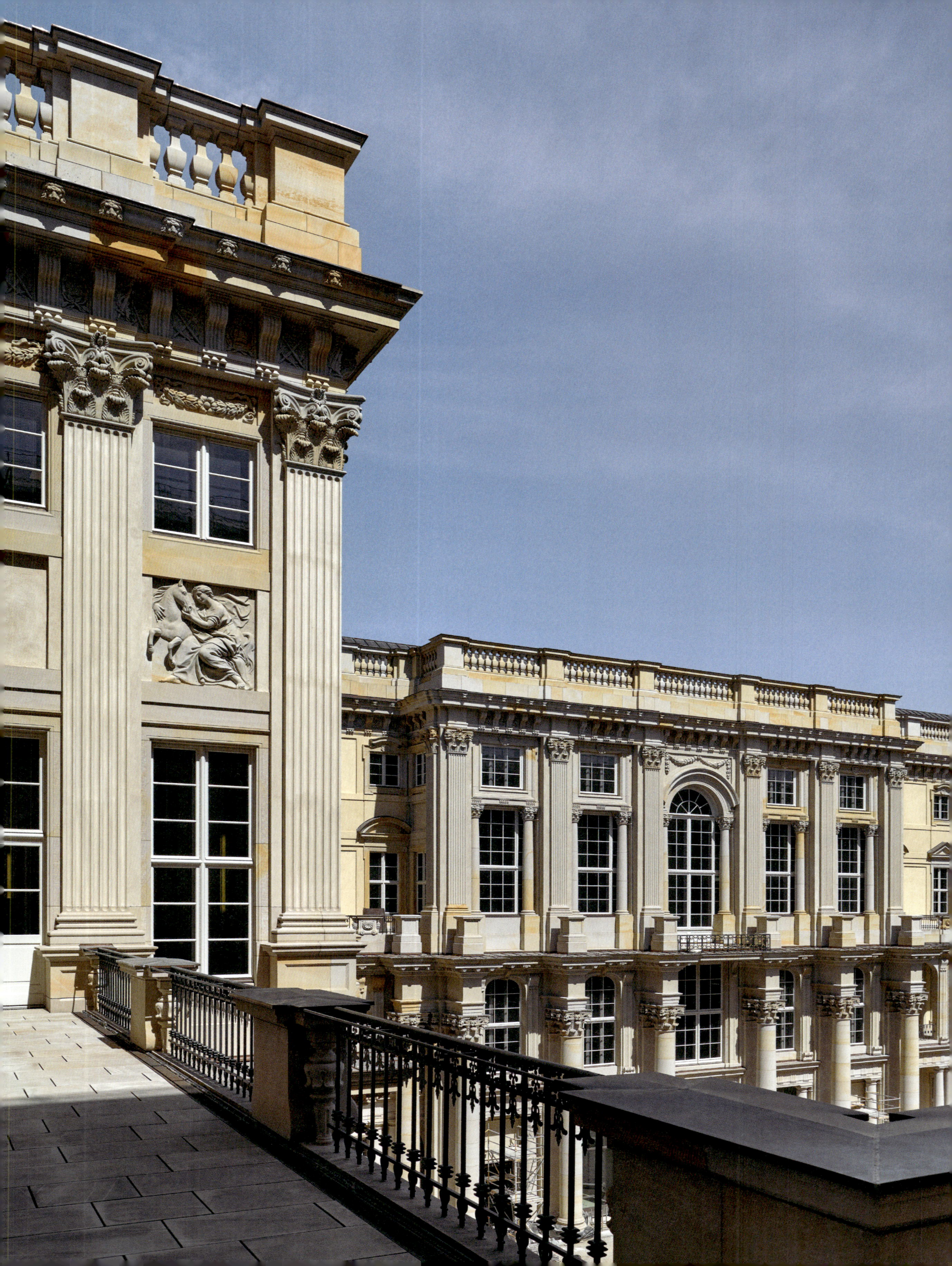

In the Schlüter Courtyard, formerly
the focus of ceremonial life at the
royal court, the three Baroque
facades have been faithfully
reconstructed. Missing in the image
are only the monumental sandstone
sculptures on the column pedestals in
front of the central portal.

Fig. p. 90:
The corner cartouche positioned
along the Lustgarten facade alongside
Portal 4: eight meters in height and
weighing 56 tons, it is composed of
19 sandstone blocks. Goddesses of
fame hold a decorative frame bearing
the initials of the king, surmounted by
the head of Minerva, the goddess of
wisdom and of war.

Fig. p. 91:
The reconstruction of the Baroque
Court Portal 2 integrates war-
damaged but nonetheless original
genius figures by Andreas Schlüter
into the sculptural design of the
upper terminus of the portal, as seen
here in a photograph from the Palace
Workshop

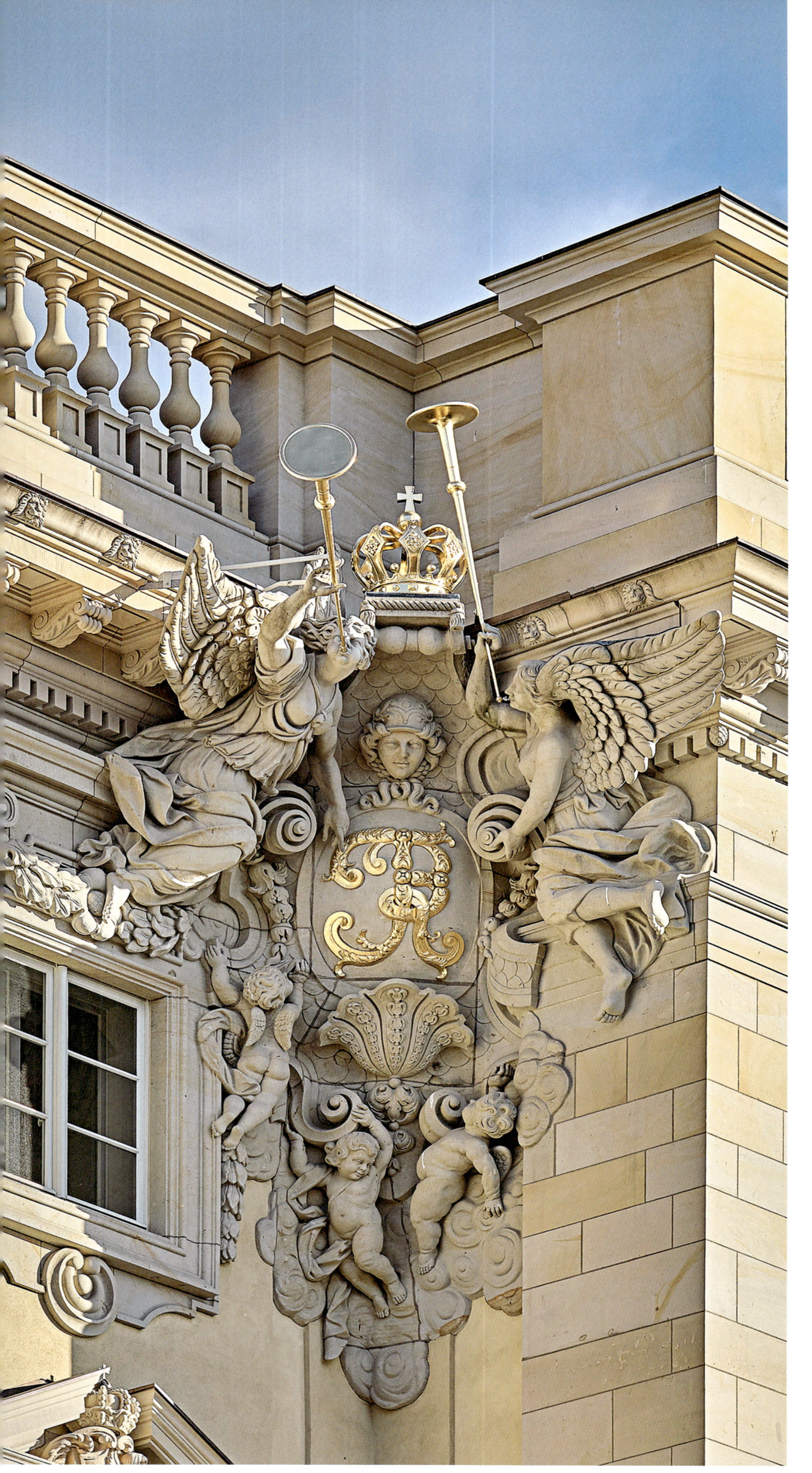

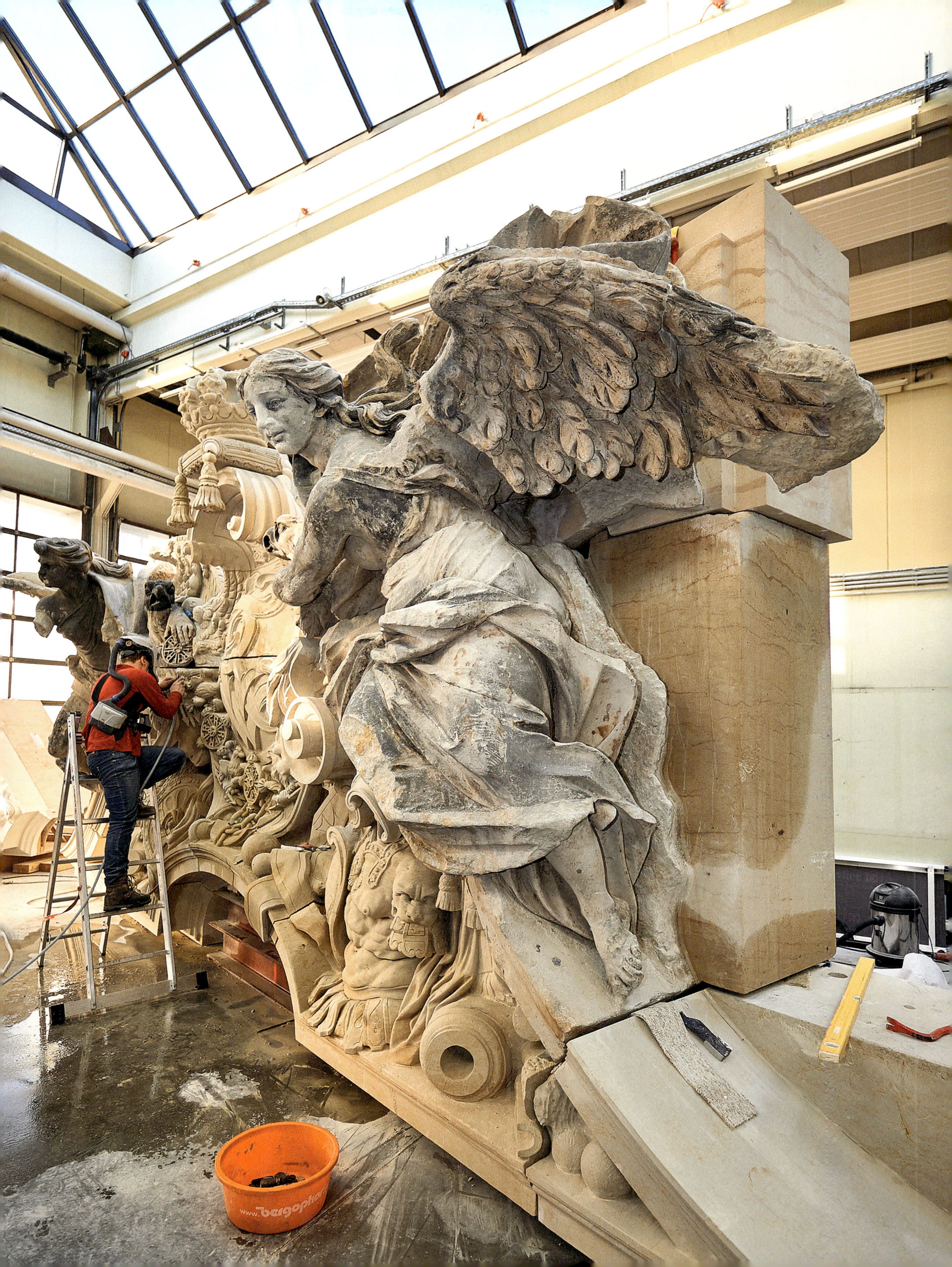

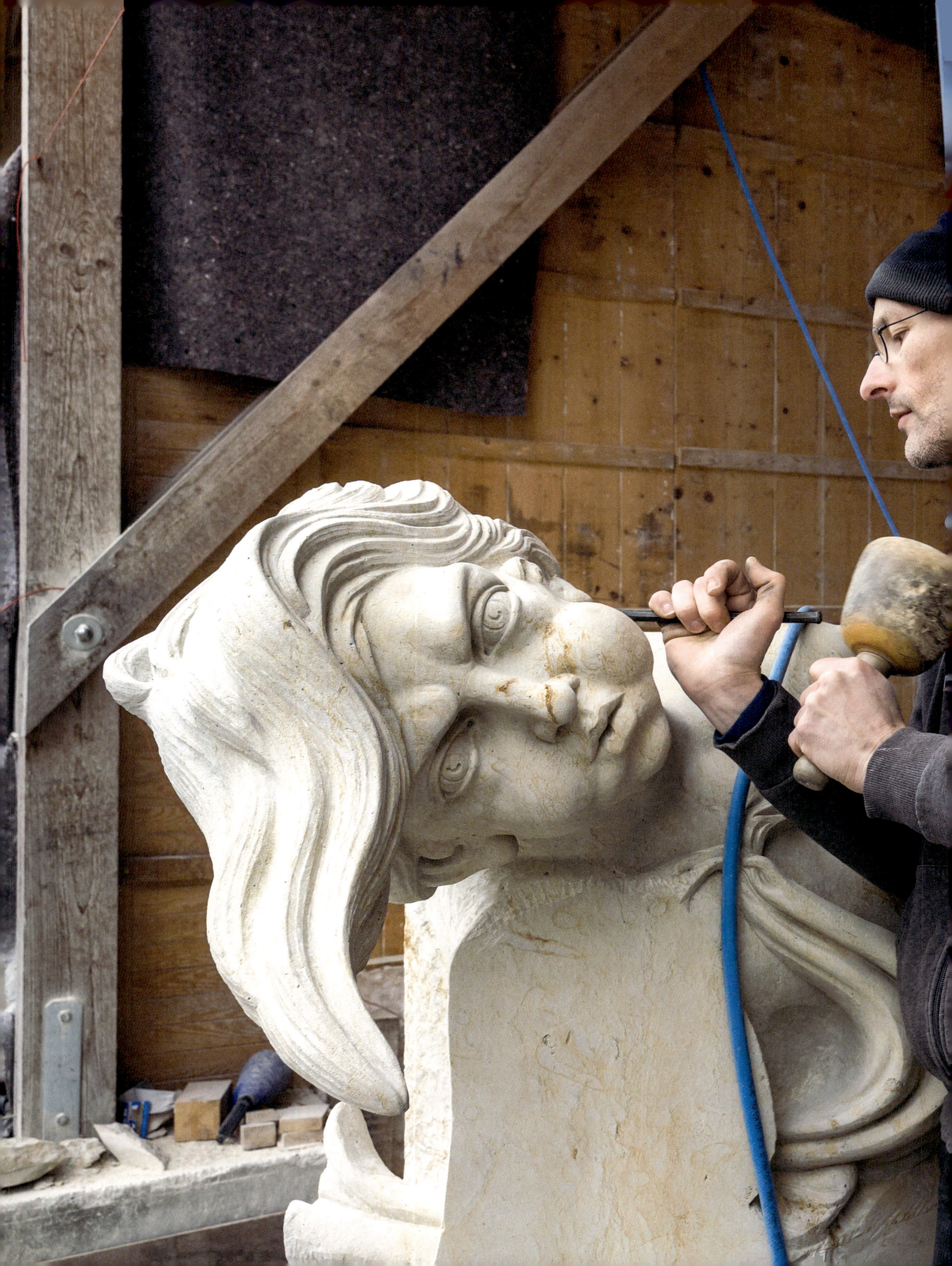

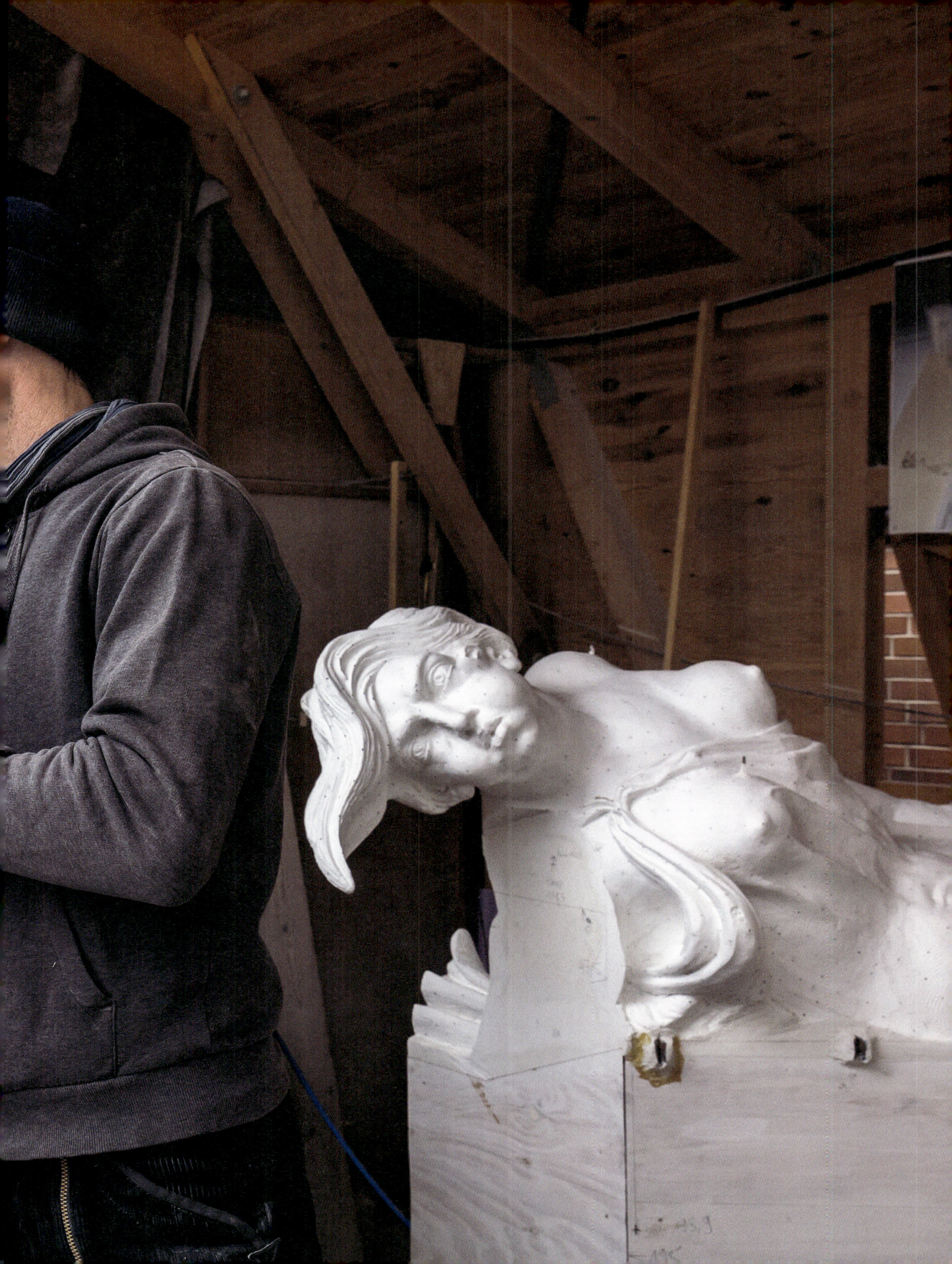

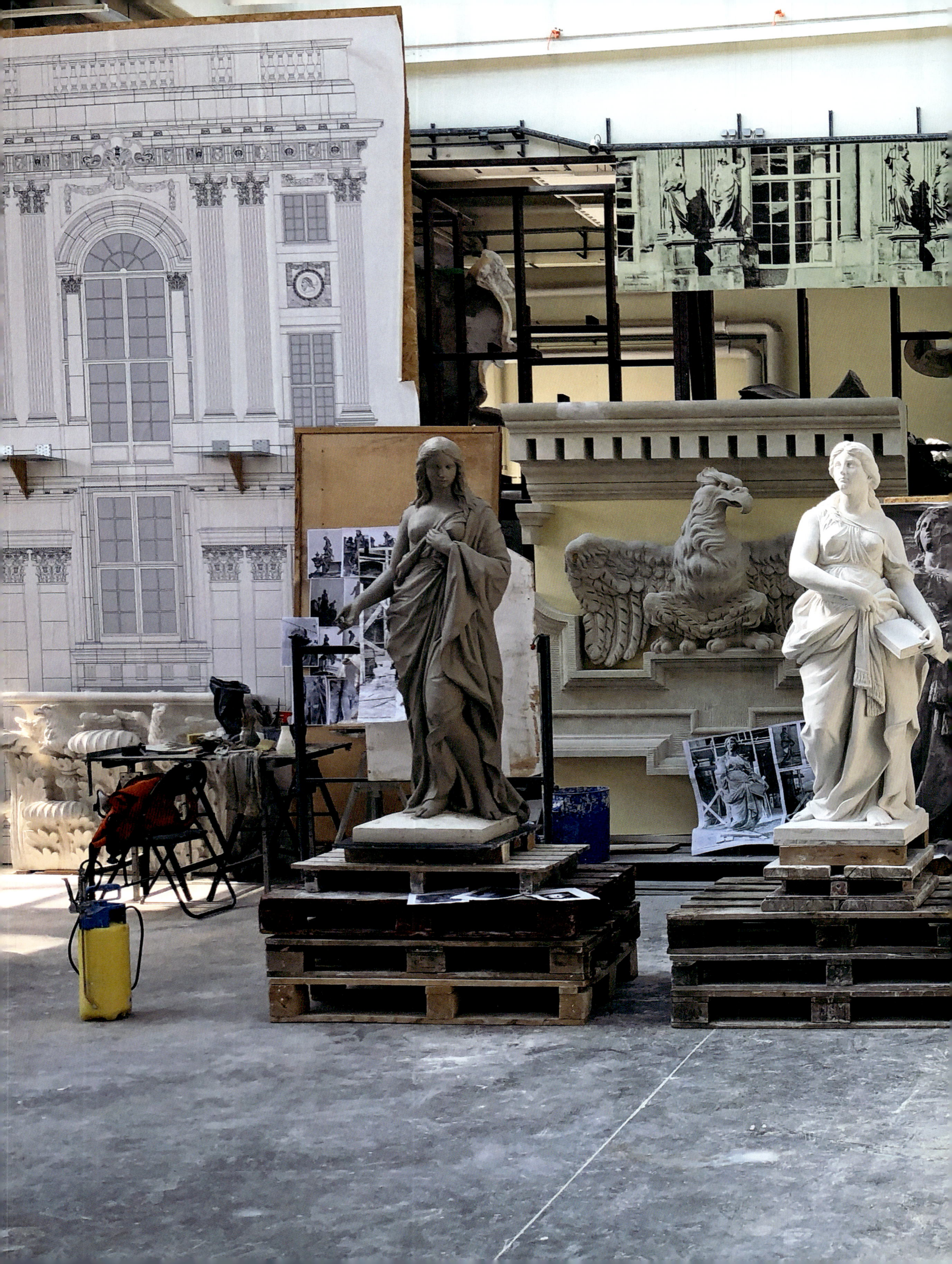

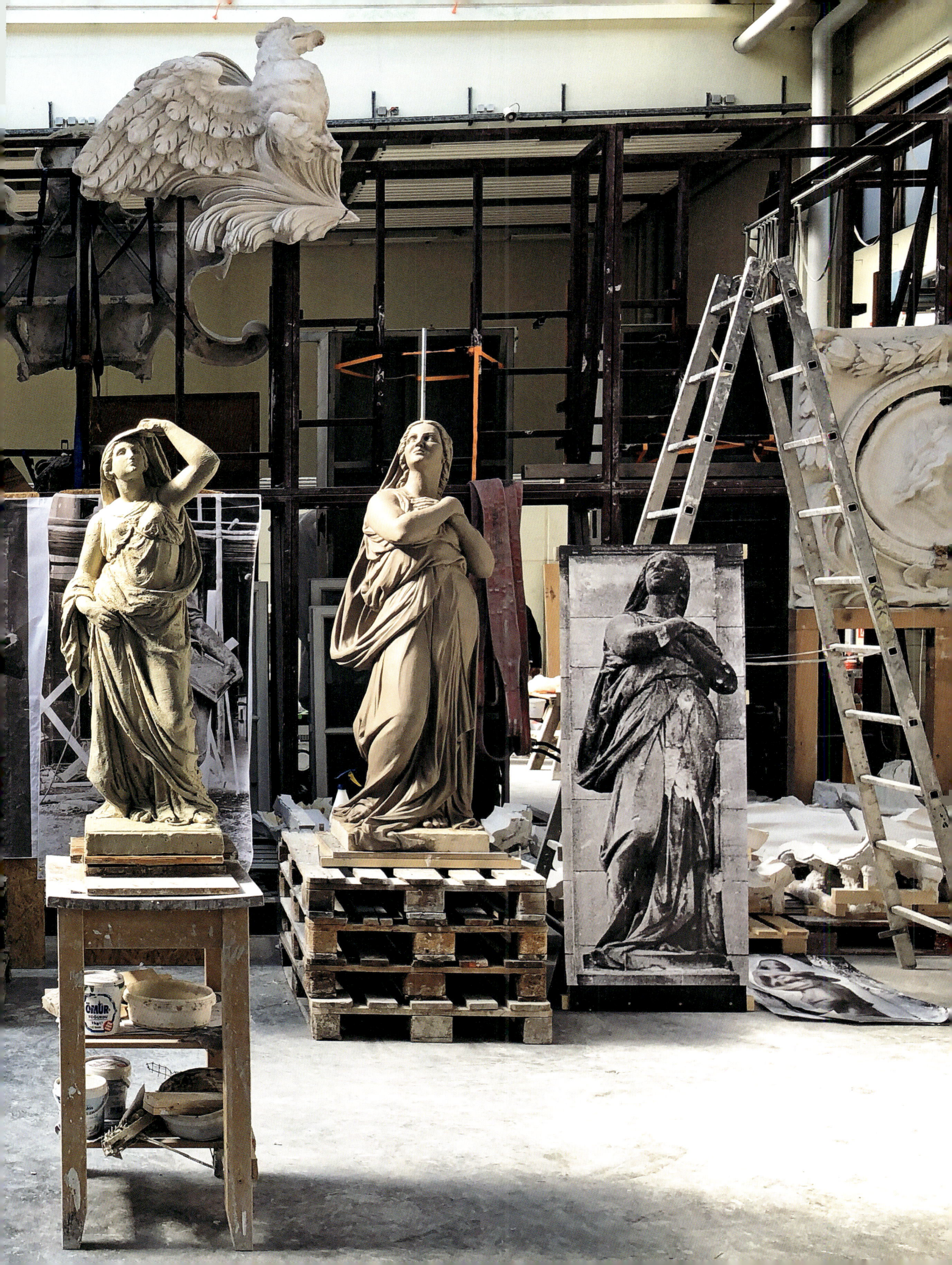

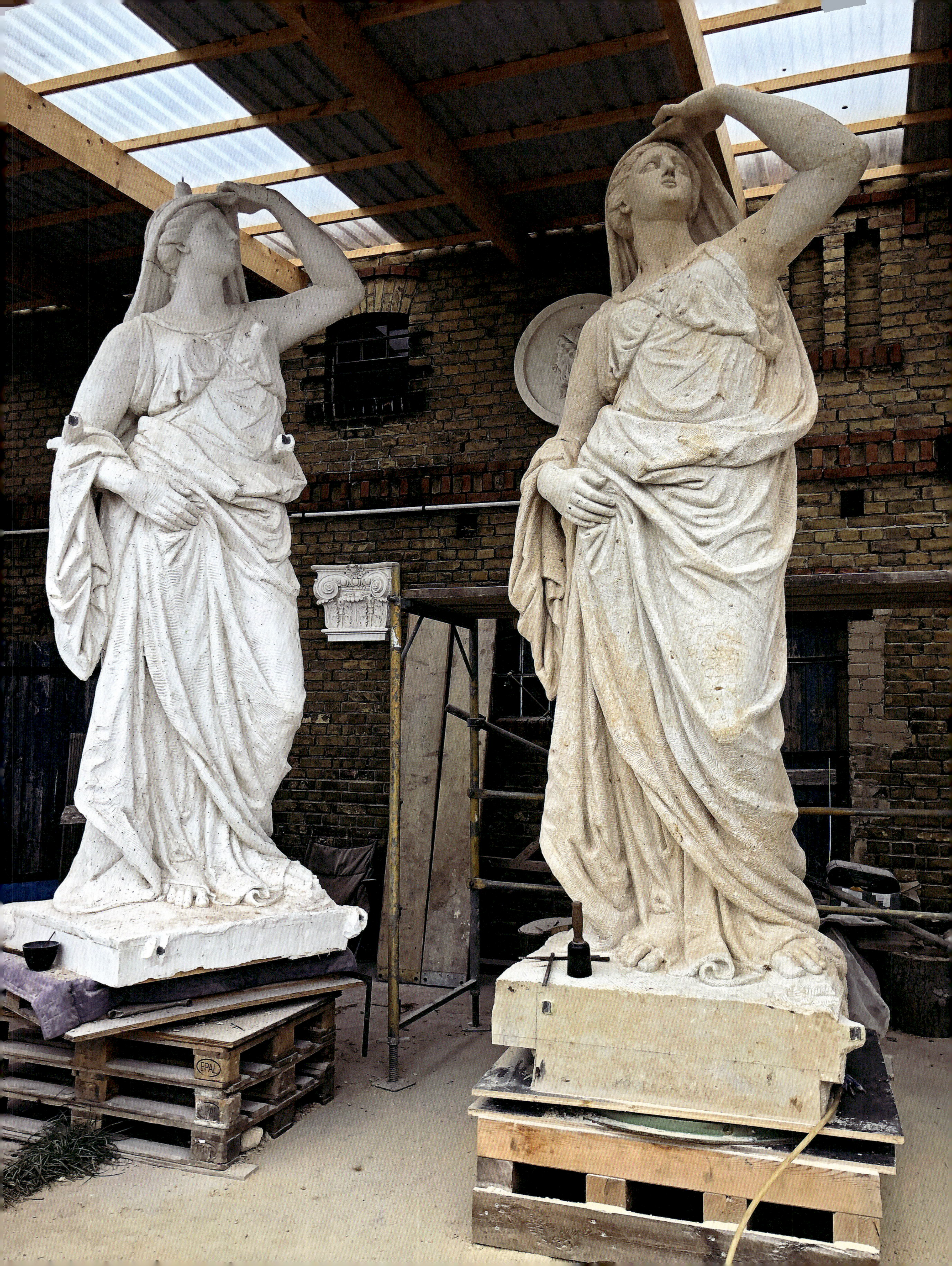

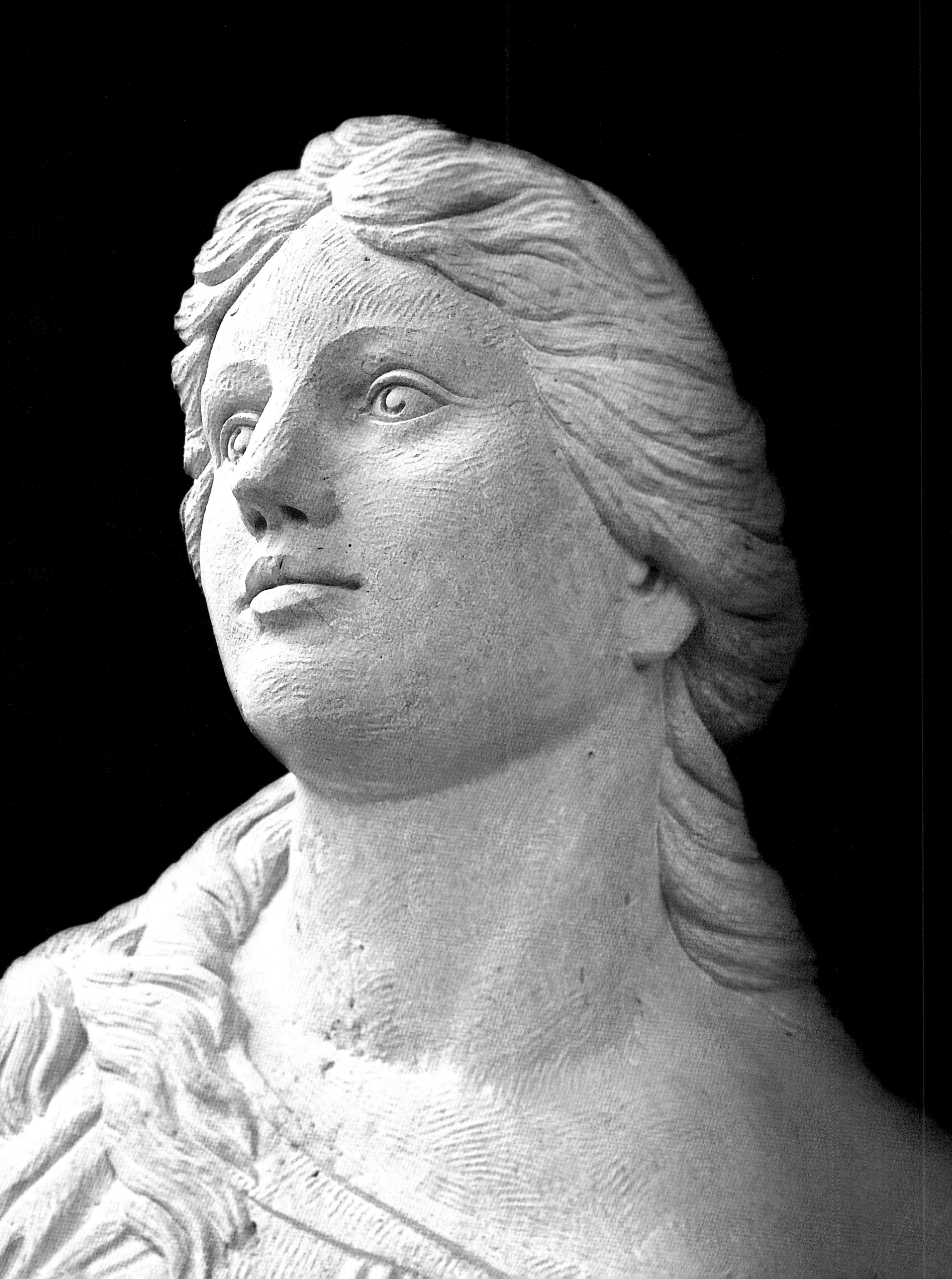

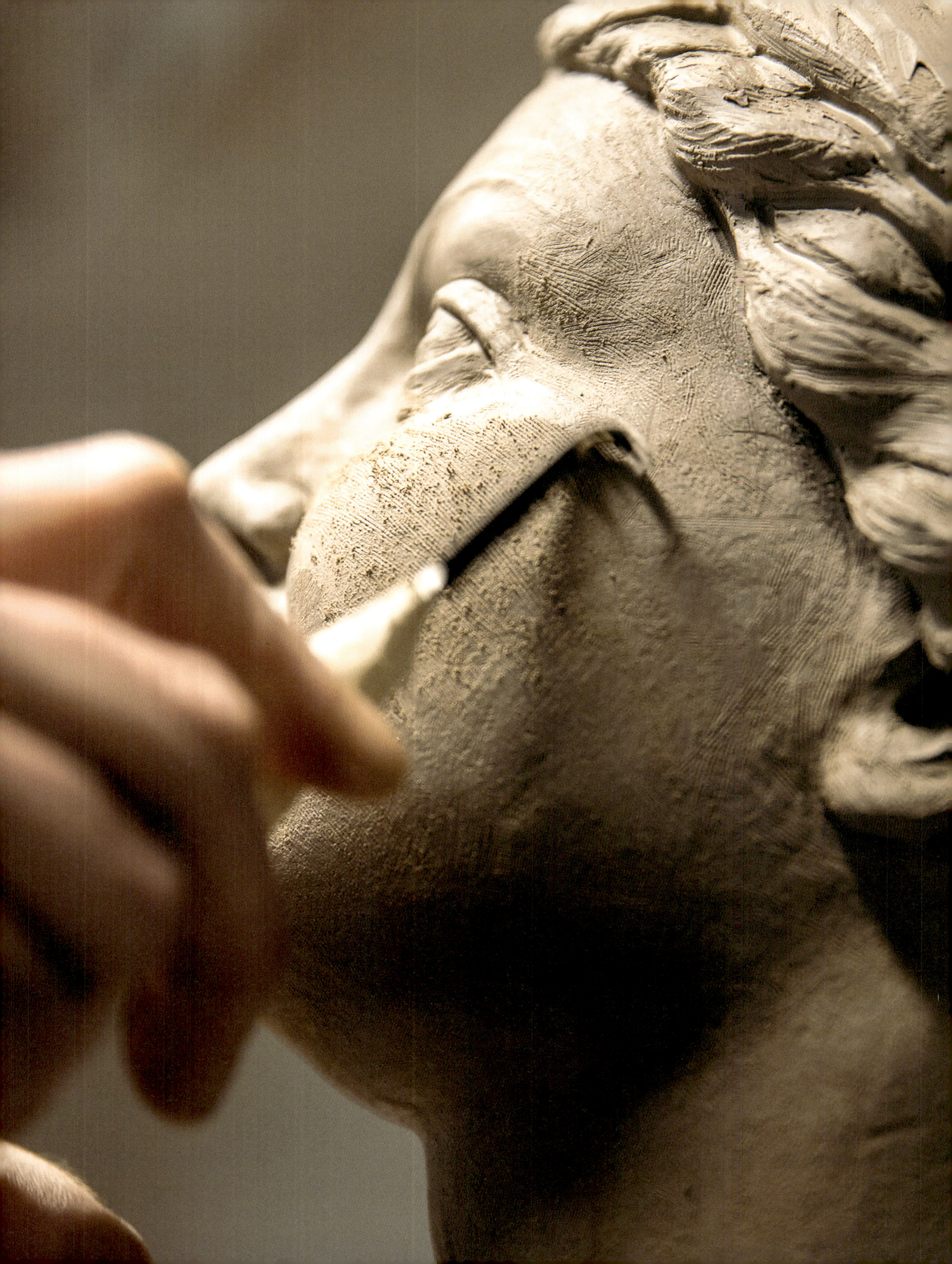

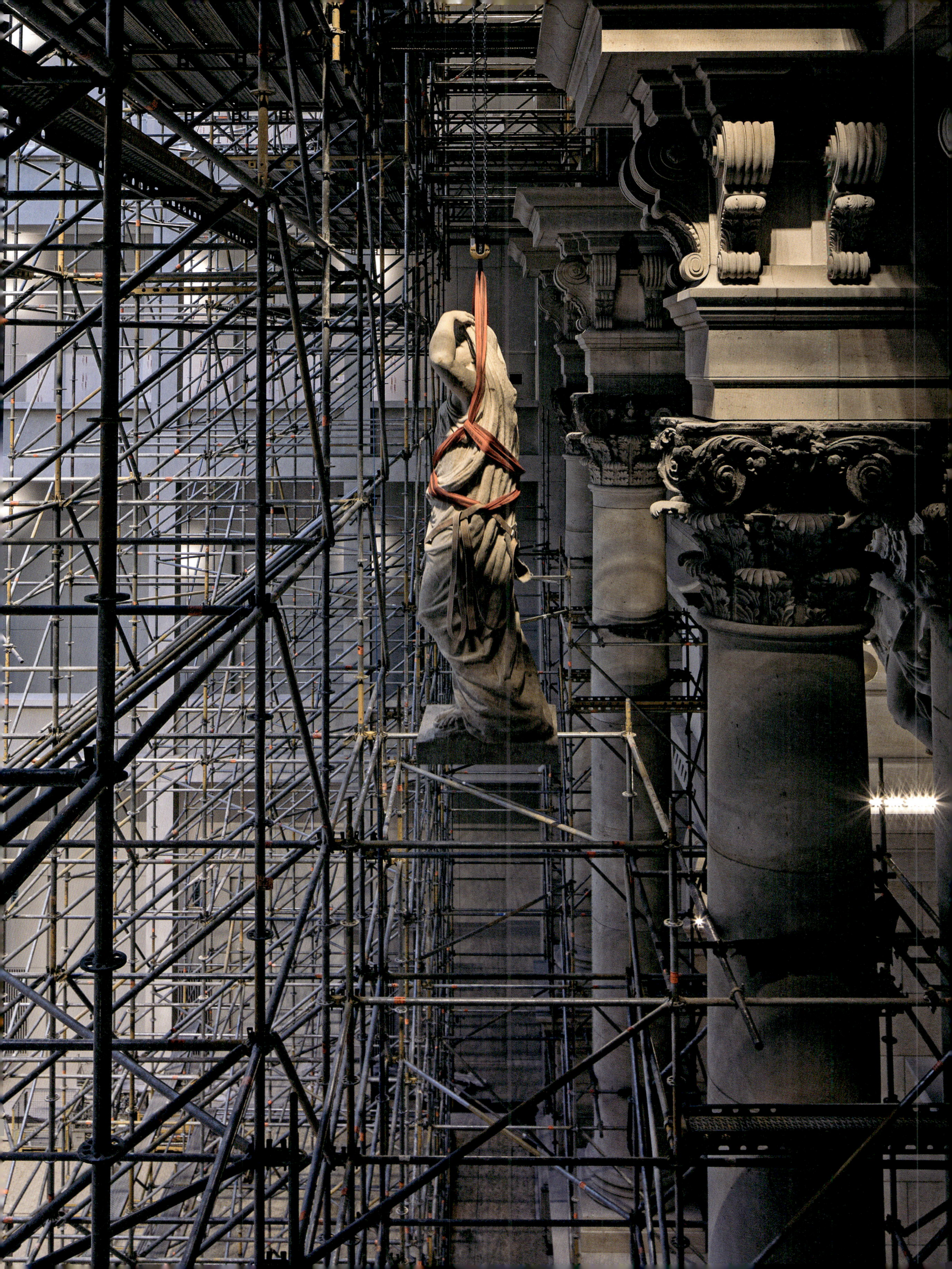

Fig. pp. 92-93:
Working with chisel and wooden
mallet, the sculptor Steffen Werner
works from a plaster model, visible
to his right, to create a sandstone
sculpture for the large cartouche
above Portal 3.

Fig. pp. 94-95:
The four colossal figures for interior
Portal 3 in the Grand Foyer represent
the three Christian virtues of Faith,
Love and Hope, and also Prayer.
Visible here in the Palace Workshop
in front of historical photographs are
the clay models and a plaster model
on a scale of 1:2.

Fig. p. 96:
The sandstone figure of Hope being
carved based on a 1:1 plaster model
seen on the left.

Fig. p. 97:
The face of the figure personifying
Love still clearly displays chisel marks
on its sandstone surface.

Figs. pp. 98-99:
This image captures a moment of
modelling work on the clay model of
Prayer. The image on the right shows
Hope suspended on the scaffolding
on the column pedestal of Interior
Portal 3.

Antinous was regarded as 'the most
beautiful youth in Greece'. Alongside
the gods of the classical world, this
newly created sandstone copy adorns
the large central portal of the Schlüter
Courtyard. At the Day of the Open
Construction Site in 2017, the public
was offered a preview of this figure.

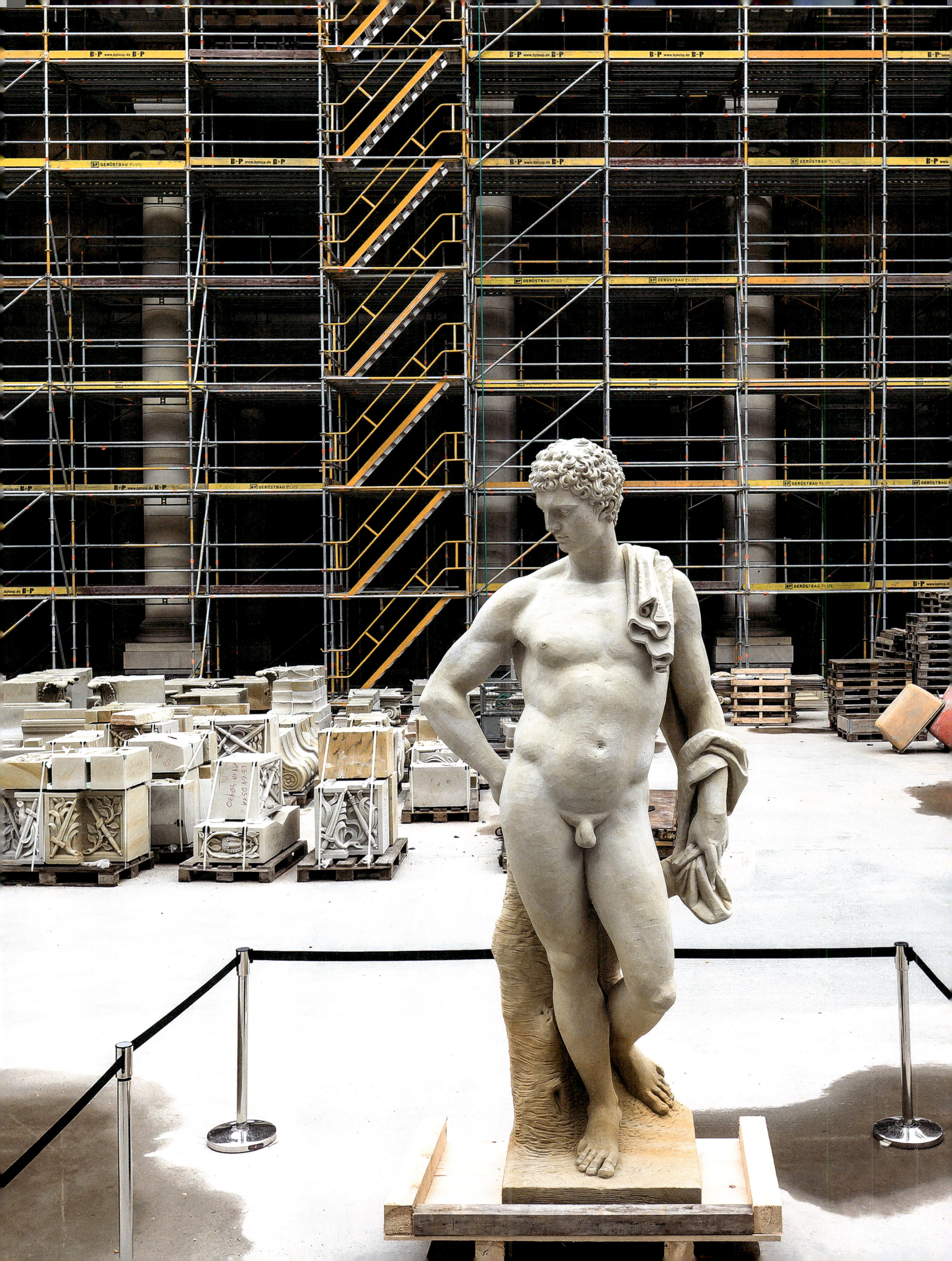

A sandstone element with a cherub
for the large corner cartouche on
the facade facing the Lustgarten is
'shifted' at the building site, which
is to say: mounted with a crane at
a height of about 33 meters. The
massively heavy stone block will not
be visible after installation, and will
sit on the 60-centimeter-thick brick
wall in front of the reinforced steel
structure.

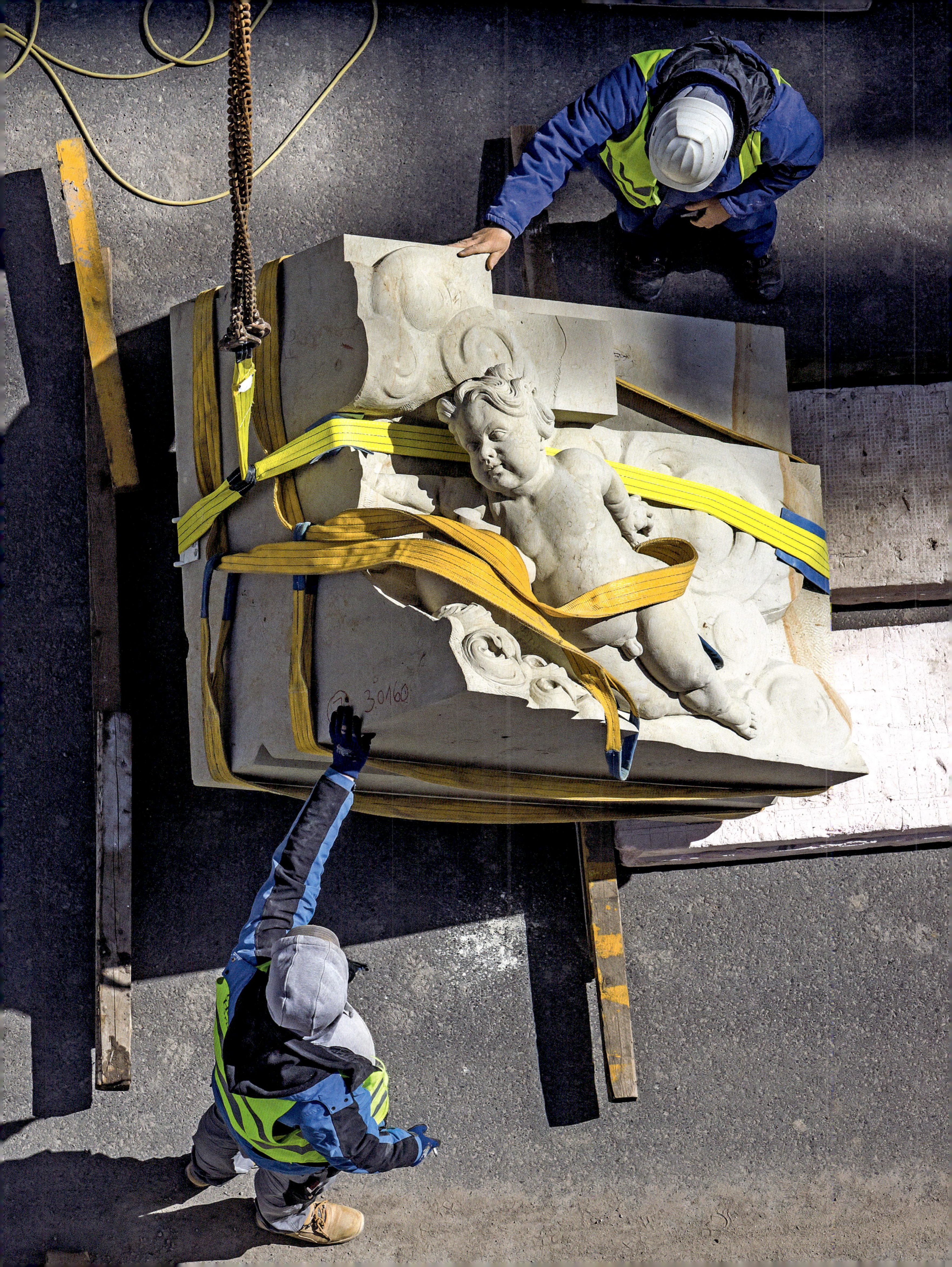

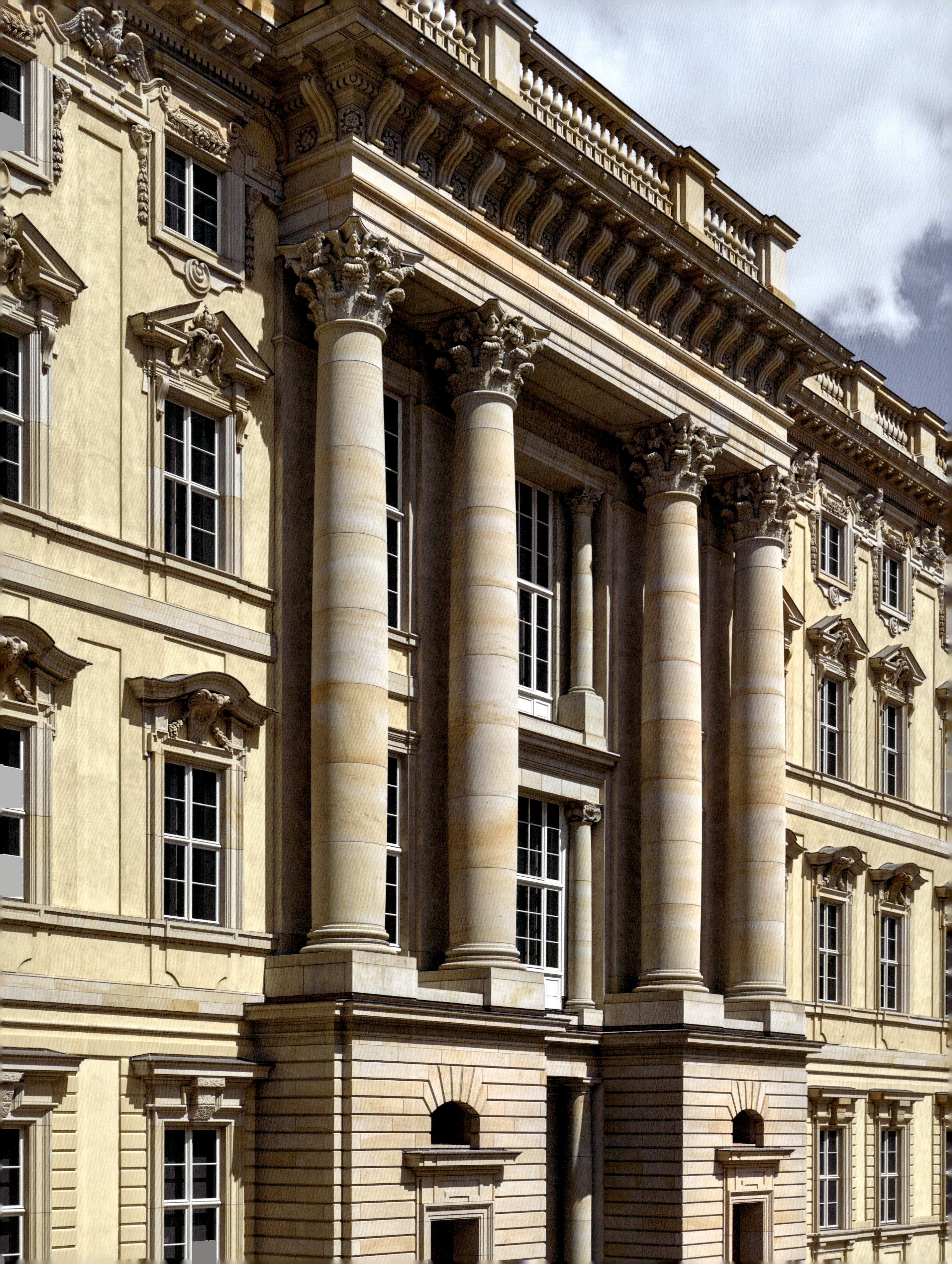

Here at Portal 2, the facade on
Schlossplatz (Palace Square) is
characterized by massive Corinthian
columns, which carry the architrave
above to the full height of the facade
and into the mezzanine. On the
interior, Schlüter positioned the Doric,
Ionic and Corinthian orders one
above the other, a practice regarded
as one of his distinctive features.

The historic rounded bay, which
once offered a view of the former
Lange Brücke (Long Bridge), today
Rathausbrücke (City Hall Bridge),
once contained the work chamber
of Friedrich II. Its realization was
made possible – diverging from the
architect's competition design –
thanks to a generous single donation.

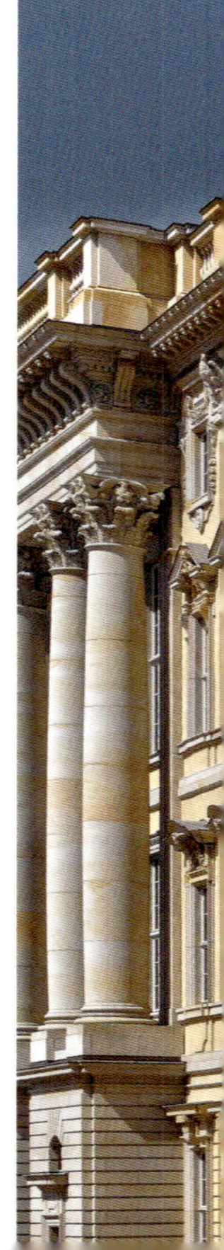

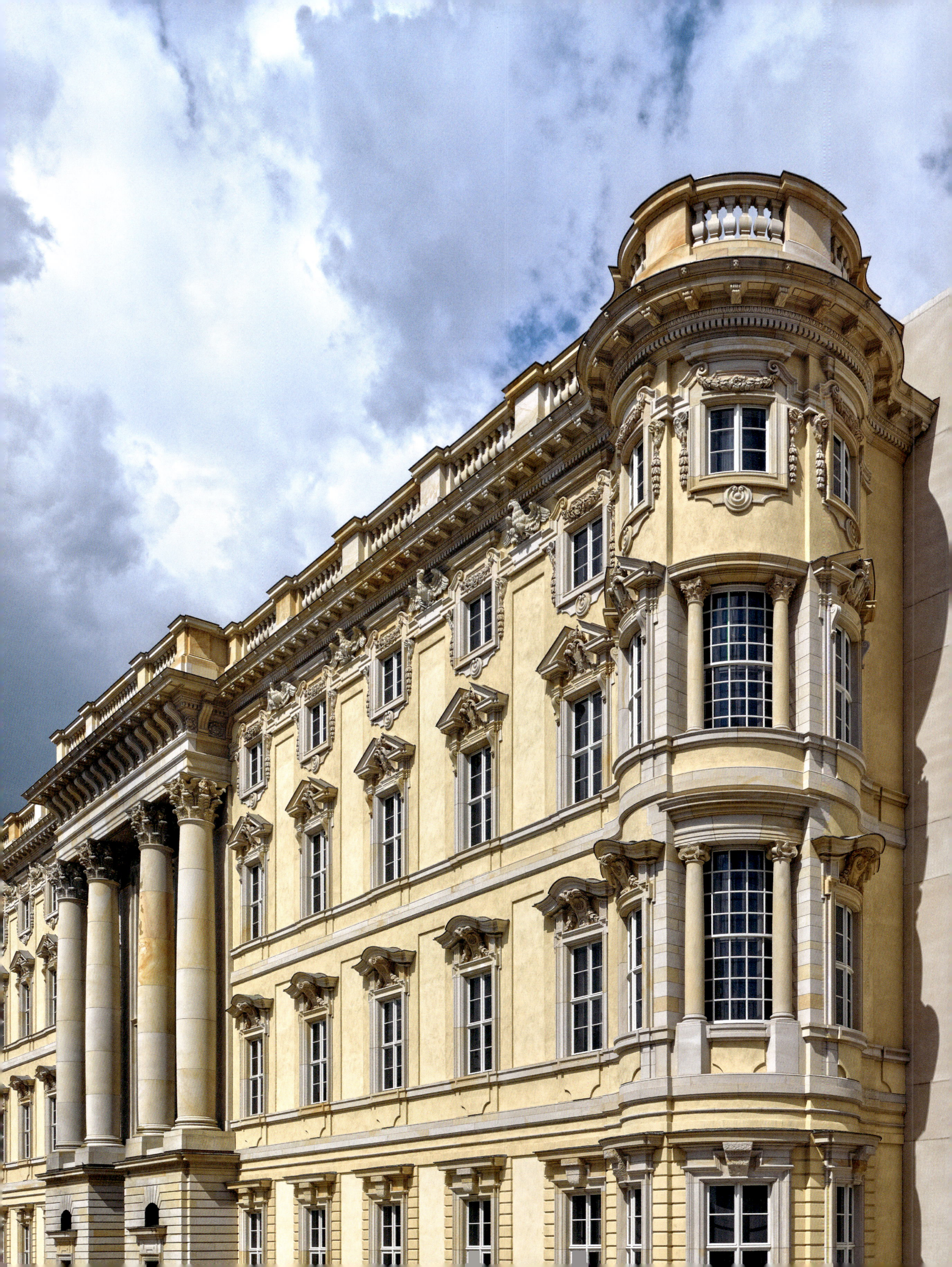

On the Building History of the Berlin Palace

Bernhard Wolter

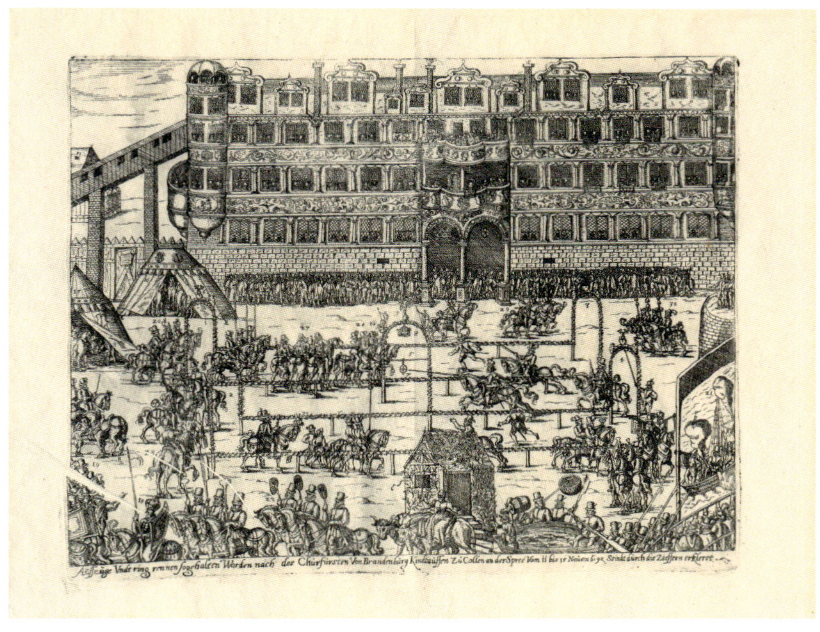

The tournament grounds at the
Electoral Palace, engraving, 1592

Until its destruction at the end of World War II, the Berlin Palace evolved
over a period of more than 500 years to become the urbanistic heart and
architectural point of reference of the surrounding centre of Berlin. This
was true of the view from the boulevard Unter den Linden as well as the
view from the open staircase designed in 1825 by Karl Friedrich Schinkel
for the Altes Museum (Old Museum) looking on the facade of the Palace
facing the Lustgarten (Pleasure Garden).

The construction of the Palace was a continuous process of extensions,
alterations and additions by the prince-electors of Brandenburg, the
Prussian kings and the German emperors. In art-historical terms, the most
important restructuring was carried out by the architect and sculptor
Andreas Schlüter. He is the author of the Baroque transformation of the
Palace in the early eighteenth century.

The Era of the Prince-Electors

On 31 July 1443, Elector Friedrich II 'Irontooth' (1440–1470) laid the
foundation stone for a new palace building on the Cölln side of the river
Spree, whose shell structure was completed in 1448. For his residence,
he chose the little double-town of Berlin–Cölln, then the most important
town in the Margravate of Brandenburg, although it was a rather
insignificant locale within the Holy Roman Empire. In the form of the
'Grünen Hut' (green hat), an element of the Cölln town wall was integrated
into the complex which survived until it was destroyed in 1950. The Elector
moved into the new Palace in spring of 1451.

The extensions ordered by Elector Joachim II (1535–1571), the
modifications carried out by Elector Johann Georg (1571–1598) and
the additions commissioned by Elector Joachim Friedrich (1598–1608)
shaped the appearance of the Palace until Schlüter's remodelling. They
already encompassed the outer palace courtyard, whose dimensions were
later enlarged by Johann Friedrich Eosander beginning in 1707.

Initially, however, work was interrupted by the Thirty Years' War. The
architects Johann Gregor Memhardt and Johann Arnold Nering initiated
the first Baroque modifications during the era of the Great Elector Friedrich
Wilhelm (1640–1688). However, the Elector's priority was the newly
created Lustgarten (Pleasure Garden), laid out in accordance with Dutch
models.

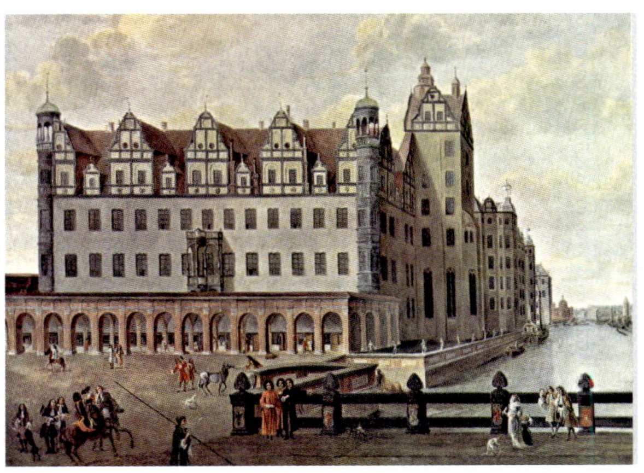

View of the Berlin Palace from
Lange Brücke (Long Bridge),
painting, c. 1690

The Royal Palace

Prince-Elector Friedrich III (1688/1701–1713) found himself obliged to emphasize his new royal dignity as Friedrich I, King 'in' Prussia, and hence the political significance and prestige of his fragmented state within feudal Europe. He therefore had the electoral residence transformed into a Baroque royal palace according to plans by Andreas Schlüter, who had already worked on the Berlin Zeughaus (Arsenal) and, as court sculptor, had created the equestrian monument to the Great Elector on the Lange Brücke (Long Bridge).

Schlüter encased the Renaissance building in a new Baroque facade based on Italian models. Even before completion of the conversion plans in 1706, his triumph was cut short abruptly by the disaster of the Münzturm (Mint Tower). Shortly before its completion, the striking tower, which rose to 108 metres in height, began leaning dangerously to one side, and ultimately had to be removed. Schlüter subsequently forfeited his position as palace building director, and Johann Friedrich Eosander, called von Göthe, took over his post.

Friedrich Wilhelm I (1713–1740), the 'Soldier King', severely pruned his father's royal household. His austerity measures drove away the majority of Berlin's architects and artists. The construction of the Palace was completed by 1716 under the supervision of Martin Heinrich Böhme in accordance with the existing plans; the plan for a palace cupola, however, was abandoned for the time being.

Subsequent Prussian kings shifted their architectural ambitions to the creation of new suites of rooms in the Palace. Friedrich II, 'the Great' (1740–1786) and Friedrich Wilhelm II (1786–1797) installed their own apartments there, although they preferred to reside in other palaces, as did Friedrich Wilhelm III (1797–1840). Other contributing master builders include Carl von Gontard, Carl Gotthard Langhans, Friedrich Wilhelm von Erdmannsdorff and Karl Friedrich Schinkel. Their interior decorations were among the most successful creations of Neo-Classicism.

Under Friedrich Wilhelm IV (1840–1861) the first important change in the exterior of the Palace since its extension by Johann Friedrich Eosander was achieved between 1845 and 1853 in the form of the construction of the palace cupola. The preliminary design is the work of Schinkel, and the final version was carried out in a modified form by his student Friedrich August Stüler.

The German Empire and the Subsequent Period

Emperor Wilhelm I (1861/1871–1888) had the facades of the inner transverse wing redesigned in the Neo-Renaissance style. His grandson – Emperor Wilhelm II (1888–1918) – planned further alterations and extensions to the Palace, in particular the radical reconstruction of the western wing with the state rooms and the extension of the Weisser Saal (White Hall). Another focus was the installation of bathrooms, telephones and a modern heating system.

World War I put an end to this work before it could be completed. Up until the destruction of the Palace, the projecting northwestern wall of the Eosander Courtyard displayed the extension of the White Hall. Adjustments to the courtyard facade together with the Eosander Portal up to the southwestern corner were never carried out.

During the Weimar Republic, the Kunstgewerbemuseum (Museum of Decorative Arts) moved into the abandoned building, becoming its most important user, known as the Palace Museum. Accommodated here

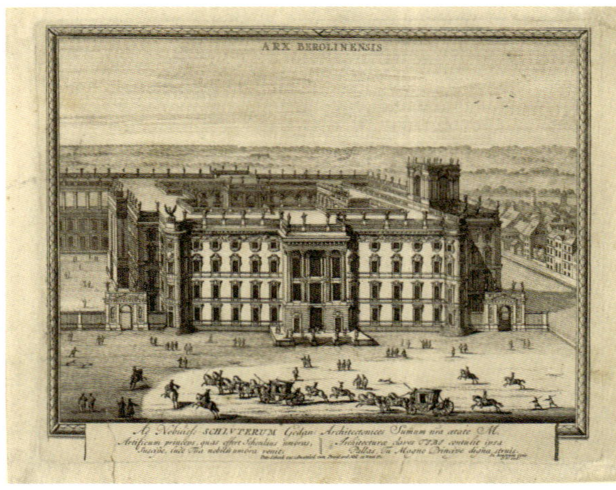

'Arx Berolinensis': perspective view of the Palace, probably after a model by Andreas Schlüter, 1699. Etching by Pieter Schenk, 1702

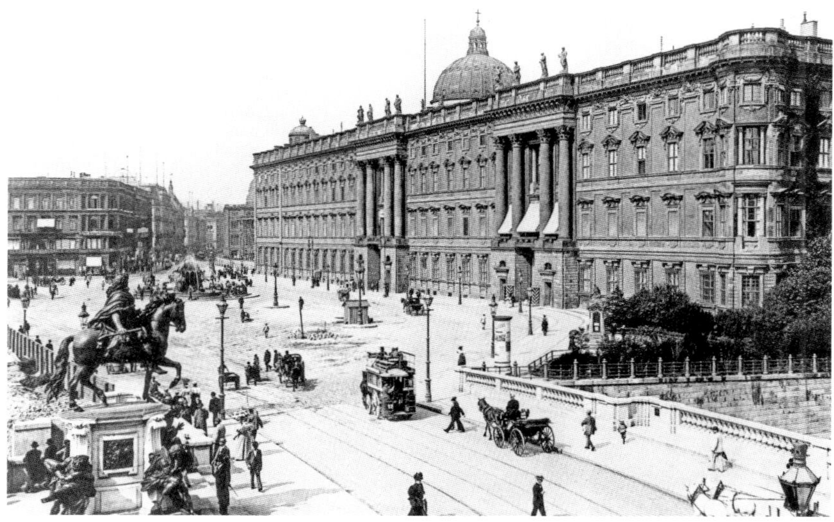

View of the south facade of
the Palace with the equestrian
monument of the Great Elector
on Lange Brücke, 1896

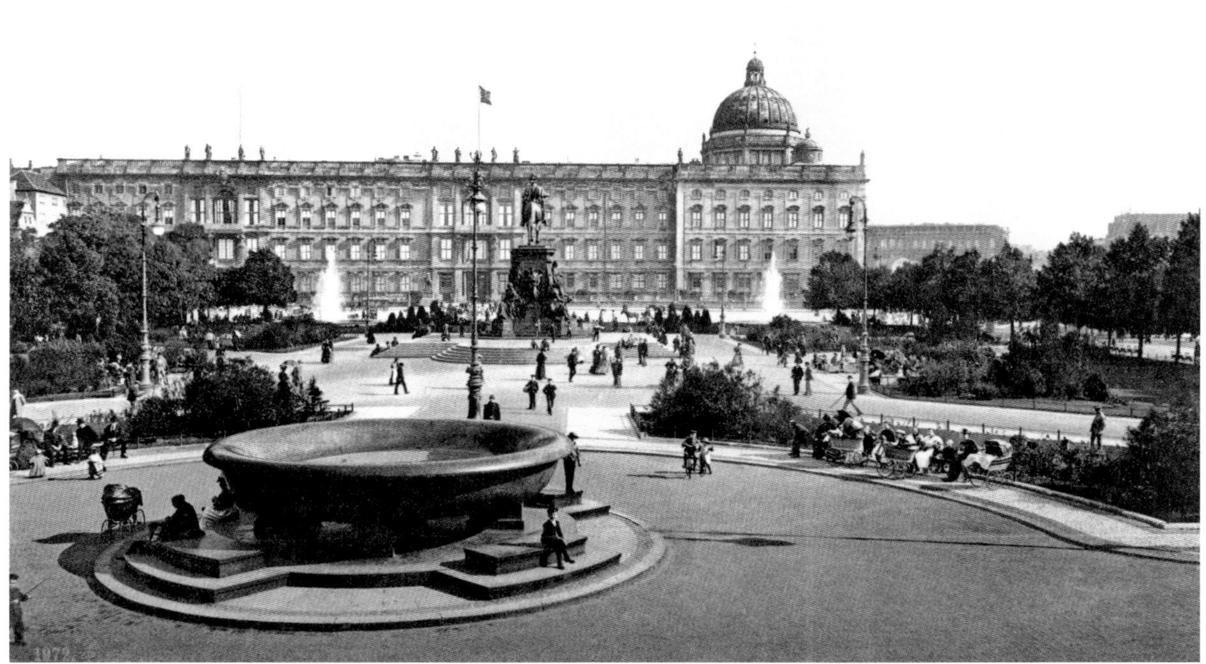

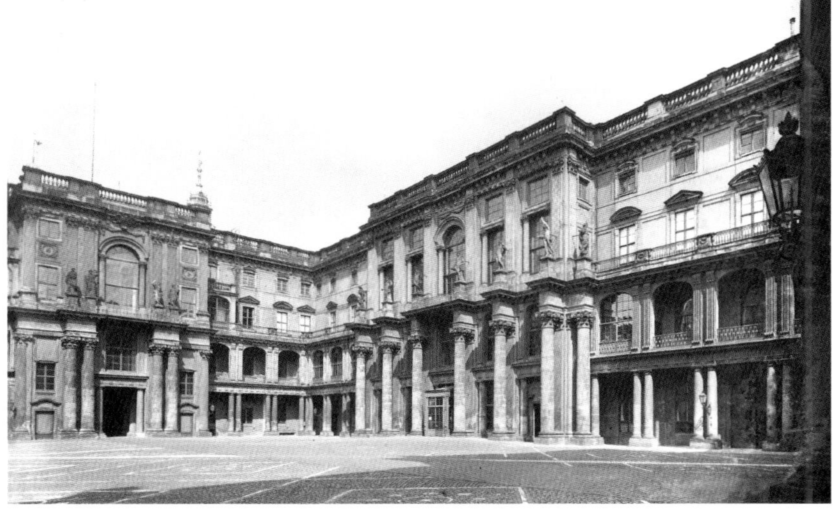

View from the staircase of
the Altes Museum across the
Lustgarten (Pleasure Garden)
towards the Palace, 1898

View of the Schlüter Courtyard,
c. 1930

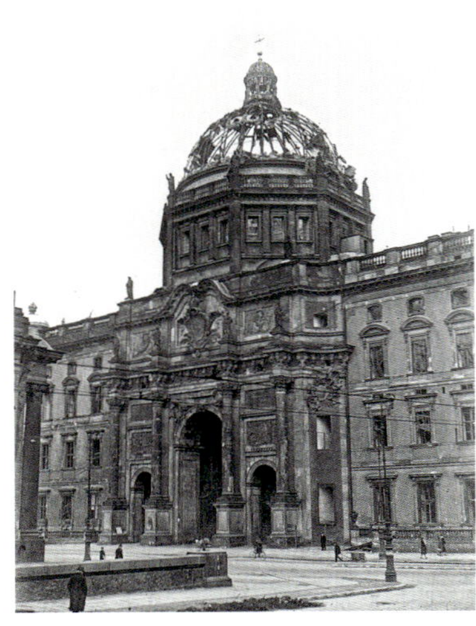
The west facade of the Palace
after World War II, 1945

alongside it were many other institutions, among them research institutes and foundations and parts of the university, which suffered from space shortages, along with a day centre for young woman scholars. In spring of 1945, towards the end of World War II, the building was badly damaged in a bombing raid and almost completely gutted. Nevertheless, soon after the end of the war the surviving rooms could be used for exhibitions, among them a show devoted to the urban development plans for the rebuilding of Berlin by the architect Hans Scharoun in 1946.

At least for a while, the politically motivated demolition of the Palace on orders from Walter Ulbricht (Chairman of the Council of State of the German Democratic Republic (GDR, more commonly known as East Germany) and head of the Socialist Unity Party of Germany) on 7 September 1950 concluded the history of the Berlin Palace.

Der Palast der Republik (Palace of the Republic)

At first, the vacated terrain was used as a festival and parade square for the mass demonstrations of East Germany. Among numerous plans for the upgrading of East Berlin as the capital of East Germany were proposals for high-rises in the style of the Stalinist showpieces in Warsaw and Moscow. However, these were never realized.

It was not until more than twenty years after the demolition of the Berlin Palace that construction work was initiated on the Palast der Republik (Palace of the Republic), built to serve as the seat of the Volkskammer (People's Legislative Chamber, the East German parliament), but also to accommodate concert halls and a cultural centre. The design was the work of Heinz Graffunder, the chief architect and head of the design collective. The Palace of the Republic was inaugurated on 23 April 1976. Apart from serving as the seat of the Volkskammer, this large building also served as a setting for numerous popular events, and its theatre and numerous restaurants and bars gave it the character of a 'Volkshaus', a house of the people, remaining for many visitors a source of happy memories up to the present. On 23 August 1990, the first freely elected Volkskammer, meeting in the Palace of the Republic, approved the unification treaty between the German Democratic Republic and the Federal Republic of Germany.

Following protests by employees due to the health hazard caused by asbestos, the Ministerrat der DDR (Council of Ministers of the GDR) decided to close the Palace of the Republic even before the end of the GDR. After the building was stripped down to its shell to free it of asbestos

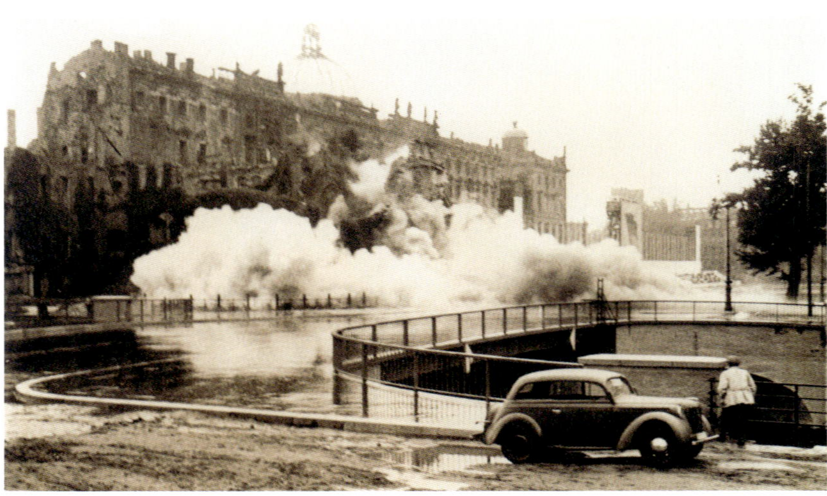
Demolition of the Apothecary Wing
of the Berlin Palace, 1950

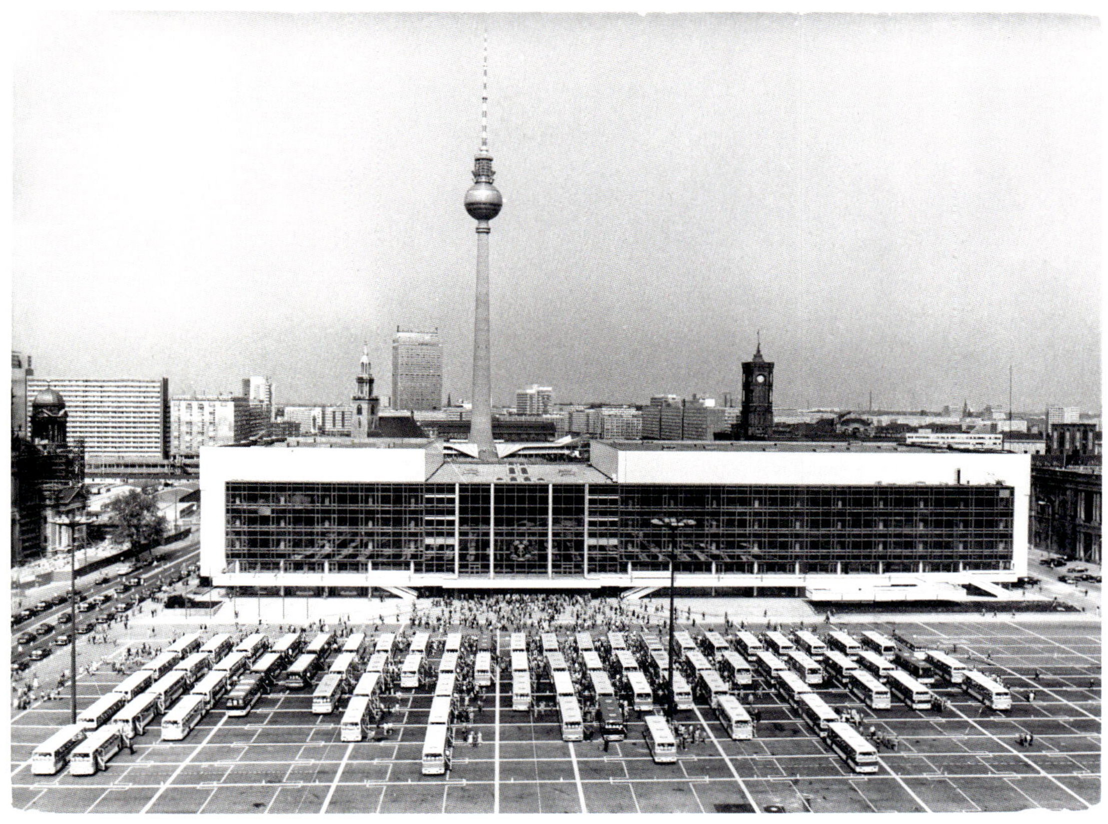

The Palace of the Republic, with the Marienkirche (St Mary's Church) in the background, the Television Tower and the Rotes Rathaus (Red City Hall) (from the left)

contamination, the German Bundestag decided to demolish the entire structure, a task that was completed only in 2008.

Early on the technically compelling reasons for the closing and demolition of the Palace of the Republic were overlaid by the debate about the Berlin Palace. In 1993–94, together with York Stuhlemmer, Wilhelm von Boddien – who initiated the association of friends Förderverein Berliner Schloss e.V. (Association Berliner Schloss e.V.) – called public attention to the idea of reconstructing the Berlin Palace in a highly dramatic fashion by means of a one-to-one scale simulation of the palace facade.

The gutted shell of Palace of the Republic offered artists and event managers an extraordinary backdrop for a variety of performances and event concepts. These ranged from the annual conference of a management consultancy firm all the way to the flooding of the building in order to navigate boats among the steel girders. In another spectacular art action, large letters spelling out the word ZWEIFEL (DOUBT) were installed on the roof of the building.

All of this serves as another reminder of just how charged with meaning the location of the Humboldt Forum in the Berlin Palace actually is – and serves simultaneously as an incentive and a challenge to create a commensurately fascinating and stimulating programme.

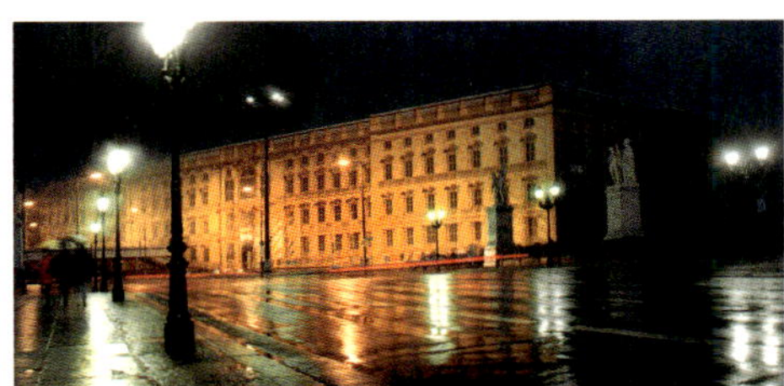

Simulation of the Palace facades, 1993

The Palace of the Republic:
A German Place of Memory

*An Excursus by
Judith Prokasky*

It consumed vast quantities of foreign exchange and precious labour power, was expensive to maintain, and was soon in need of renovations. It was observed by the secret state-security force, and visitors were selected according to their loyalty to the state. It was ridiculed as the 'lamp store' and the 'ballast of the Republic' – yet the Palast der Republik (Palace of the Republic) was a success story just the same, boasting an incredible seventy million visitors in just fourteen years on its dainty 22 329 square metres of floor area. Even after its closure and eventual demolition, the Palace of the Republic lives on in various senses – despite the fact that the state that erected it perished thirty years ago.

The phenomenon is explicable: like the predecessor building, the Palace of the Republic was built propaganda. Whereas the Baroque expansion of the Berlin Palace under Prince-Elector Friedrich III once demonstrated the royal ambitions of the Hohenzollern dynasty, the Palace of the Republic asserted that East Germany (the German Democratic Republic, GDR) was a modern, broad-minded, cosmopolitan and democratic state. In both instances, skilful marketing bore fruit, just as in the fairy tale about the emperor's new clothes: the Elector created a kingdom; Erich Honecker the illusion of the better Germany.

How did he do it? After two decades of discussions about a representative high-rise for the party elite, Honecker decided to build a 'Volkspalast' (people's palace) on the site of the former Berlin Palace: a palace for all, so to speak, through which East Germany would finally realize what Karl Liebknecht had proclaimed at the Berlin Palace during the Revolution of 1918 – or so claimed the head of government at the roofing ceremony that took place on 18 November 1974. Under the direction of Heinz Graffunder, the architects of the Palace of the Republic anchored it urbanistically in the new centre of East Berlin: the building constituted a sort of *point de vue* of the boulevard Unter den Linden, respecting the heights of neighbouring buildings, its glass foyer linking the western and eastern urban environment and creating, together with the Marx-Engels-Forum and the Neptune Fountain, an axis that led towards the TV Tower.

Tempting people to enter the building – alongside trendy design and artistic variety – were thirteen restaurants and

Bird's eye view of the city centre of
East Berlin with the Berlin Cathedral
and the Palace of the Republic, 1985

View into the foyer of the Palace of
the Republic with the *Glass Flower*
by Reginald Richter and Richard
Wilhelm, behind it the Palace Gallery

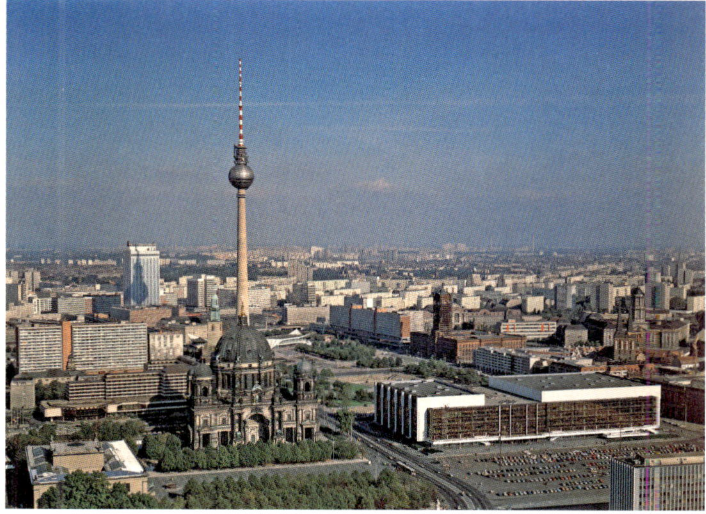

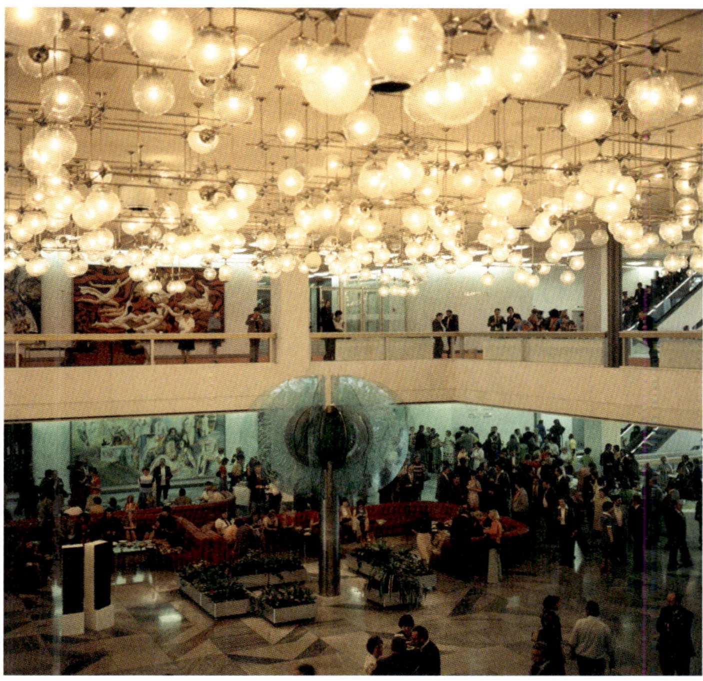

cafés, a discotheque, a bowling alley, and finally a variegated programme consisting of rock, pop, classical music, dances, lectures and theatre. Most of the guest performers were national favourites, plus occasional international stars such as Harry Belafonte. And there was a legendary appearance by the provocative West German rock musician Udo Lindenberg in 1983 in the framework of the festival *Rock for Peace* in front of a carefully selected audience of 4200.

By presenting itself at the same time as a political place – with the Volkskammer (People's Legislative Chamber), during state visits and receptions, party conventions and congresses, and not least of all during parades on Republic Day – it conveyed the bond between the government and the people. As the East German historian Stefan Wolle remarked in retrospect, this claim had feet of clay: 'This staged production of a *happy and contented people at places of gaiety* functioned because the background actors were prevented from exiting.'

On 7 October 1989, when party and government leaders and their guests celebrated the fortieth anniversary of the GDR on Republic Day, the voices outside calling for reform were growing louder. Not long afterward, the Berlin Wall was toppled, and in March of 1990 the first freely elected Volkskammer gathered in the Palace of the Republic – the same body that would assemble there on 23 August 1990 in order to resolve that would join the Federal Republic of Germany.

And this concludes the East German history of the Palace of the Republic, which was closed on 19 September 1990 as a consequence of its high level of contamination with sprayed asbestos. Its future seemed as open-ended as the collaborative shaping of a reunited Germany. The subsequent years became an era of missed opportunities, for the will to engage in genuine exchange and to initiate common new departures was absent among so many on both sides. In 2002, on the recommendation of an International Expert Commission on the Centre of Berlin, the German Bundestag resolved to erect the Humboldt Forum based to a large extent on the appearance of the former Berlin Palace – and hence to 'remove' the Palace of the Republic.

By virtue of the initiative *Zwischenpalastnutzung* (interim palace use), which ran from 2003 until 2005, productions, performances, concerts, interventions and exhibitions taking place in the now gutted shell structure revived perspectives for the location's mult farious possibilities. A resolution stipulating the building's demolition was ultimately adopted on 19 January 2006. Since then, the Palace of the Republic – and in particular the monumental sculpture 'Glass Flower' that once embellished the foyer – have become coded as insignias of East German identity. Fuelled by politicians, interest groups and journalists, an appreciation of the 'Flower' has often been equated with a recognition of the East German experience. Meanwhile, it is being stored in a museum depot – emblematically?

Indisputably, the Palace of the Republic is a key site of memory, a symbol cally charged point of reference for society at large. It is hence the intention of the Humboldt Forum Foundation in the Berlin Palace to do justice to its significance – one particular focus of the foundation's activities is in the field of the 'history of the site'.

The Planning of the Facade Reconstruction

York Stuhlemmer

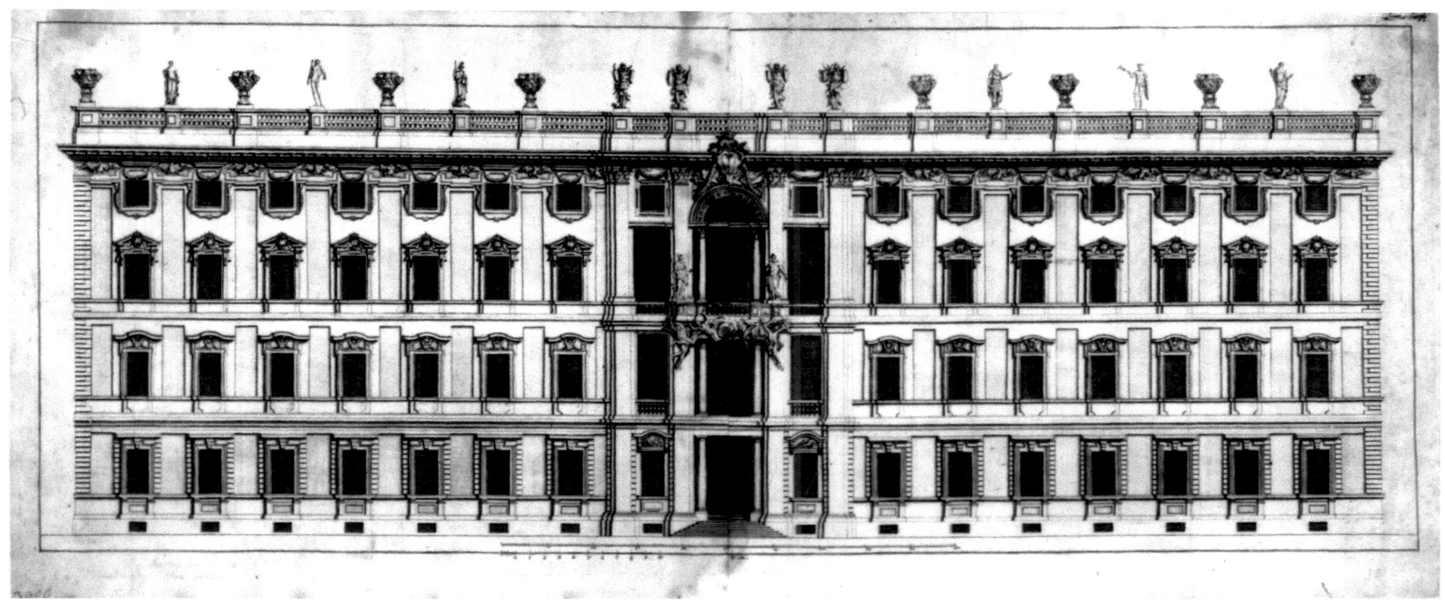

No building plans for the Berlin Palace exist that could have been simply copied and applied to the building site. All of the plans prepared by Andreas Schlüter and his successors from the construction period between 1698 and 1716 are presumed to have been lost, and even if they had survived, they would not have been precise enough for the current reconstruction undertaking.

All of the plans and drawings for the Baroque Palace that was demolished in 1950–51 had to be developed as floor plans, sections, views and details, and were hence constituted for the first time in an architectural–constructional context. To this end, archives, storage depots and museums were searched for documents and fragments. These diverse sources had to be evaluated and rendered usable for the sake of reconstruction planning.

The earliest representations – among them the travel sketches of Christoph Pitzler (c. 1701–1704), the presentation engravings of Paul Decker and Wilhelm Heckenauer (c. 1703), as well as those of Jean Baptiste Broebes (c. 1733), and two drawings of Portal 3 dating from 1707 and 1713, which have been attributed to Louis Remy de la Fosse – document either idealized views or individual parts of the building, and the specifications they provide are often somewhat vague. The situation is similar with more recent drawings, among them a series of floor plans dating from 1794 and a set of extraordinarily detailed floor plans from around 1840 (these, however, provide dimensions only for the rooms, not the facades). From the year 1876 we have Reinhold Persius's one-to-ten scale measurements for a window axis facing the Schlossgarten (Palace Garden). The most recent plans prior to the Palace's destruction date from the late 1930s and served as layout plans in the context of repairs to the facade carried out by the firm of Zeidler & Wimmel. Finally, during the demolition major parts of the building were measured and sketched by what was referred to as the Wissenschaftliches Aktiv (scientific unit) under the direction of Gerhard Strauss. These were carried out for the sake of a possible reconstruction at a different site.

Taken together, these drawings, with their disparate degrees of detail and levels of quality, represent a kind of auxiliary or 'fill-in text' that lacks dimensional coherence and is for the most part characterized by contradictory information.

The Lustgarten (Pleasure Garden) facade of the Berlin Palace, engraving by Paul Decker the Elder after Andreas Schlüter, 1703. Strongly idealized facade elevation; it proved possible to verify the dimensions and positioning of individual structural members of the historical buildings and to adopt them for reconstruction planning.

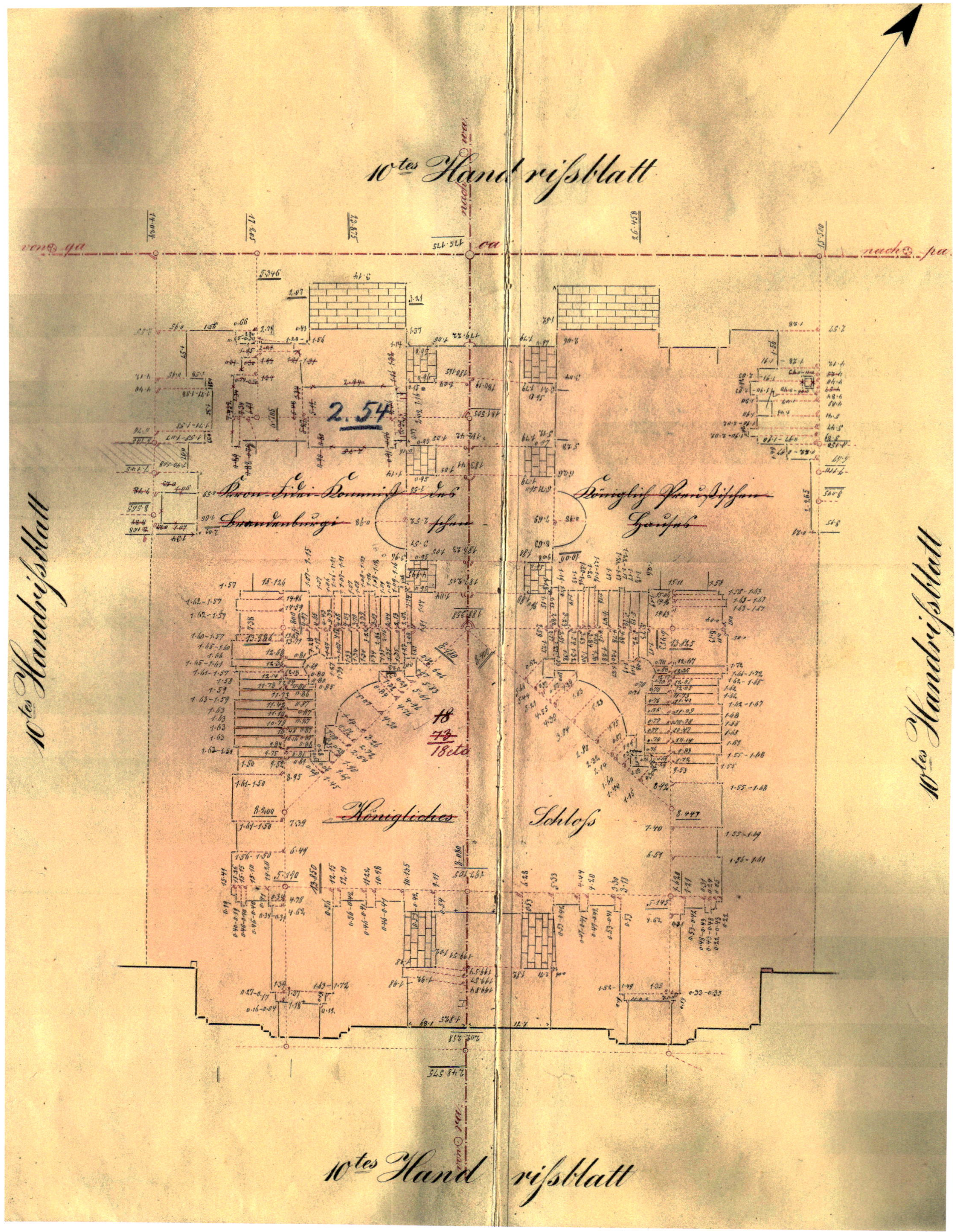

10tes Handrißblatt
10tes Handrißblatt
10tes Handrißblatt
10tes Handrißblatt
von ga
nach pa
2.54
Königliches Schloß

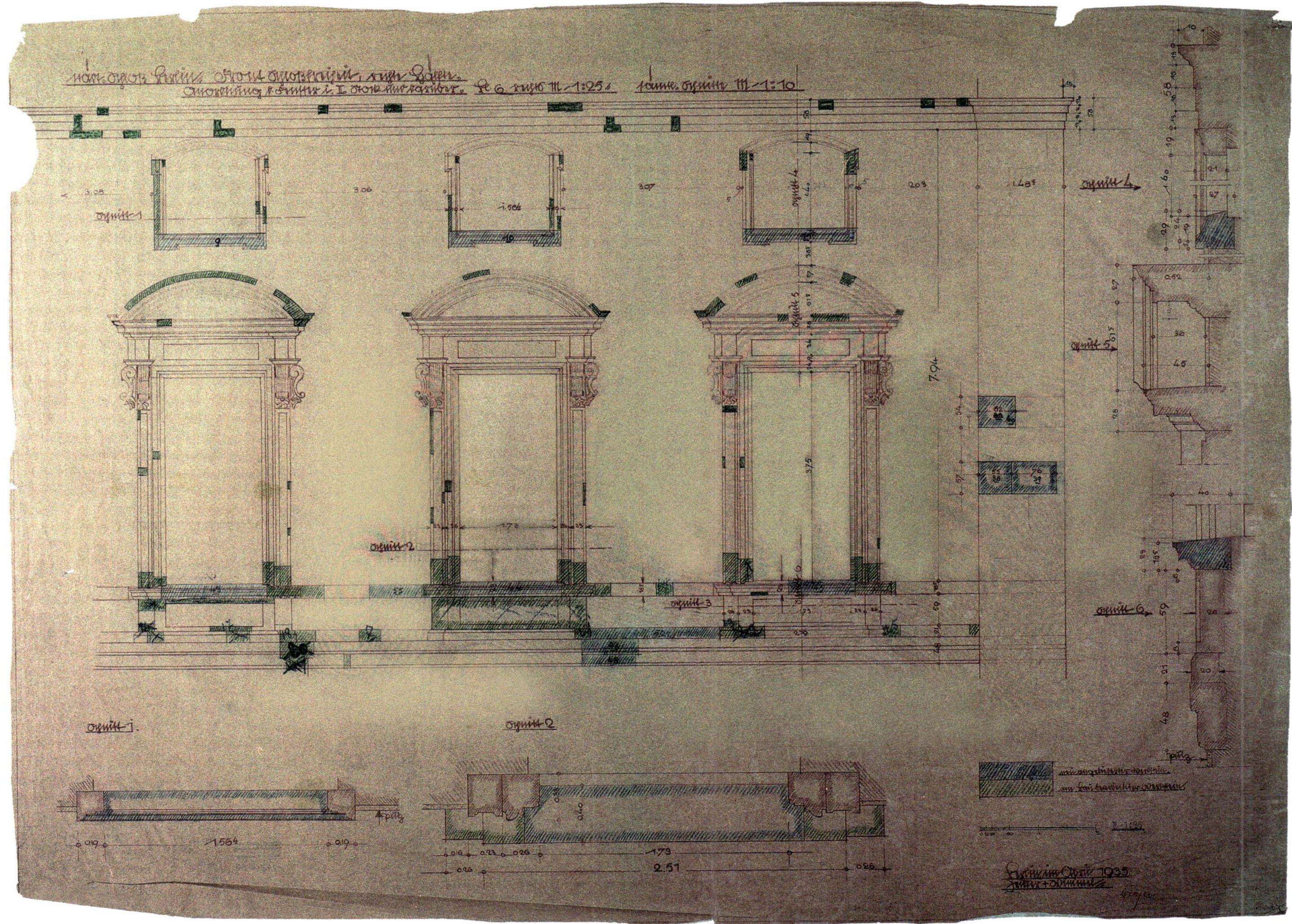

It turns out that the only integrated measurements of the Palace are
the hand sketches from the new survey measurements of the capital
and residential city of Berlin carried out from 1876 on. These remarkably
precise plans do not, however, document the facade details, instead
providing precise specifications of the outer lines of the base of the
building, which was surveyed for fiscal purposes. On this basis, it became
possible to accurately determine the outer lines of the ground plan of the
Palace within its urban setting right down to the centimetre, with all of its
deformations and angle deviations. Where there were basement spaces,
these measurements could be confirmed when the basement was exposed
by archaeological excavations.

There were, however, no comparably consistent specifications for
the divisions of the window axes and the height of the facades at the
recessed sections and the portals. For this reason, the various dimensions
of the exterior and courtyard facades were determined by means of
photogrammetry. In collaboration with the department of photogrammetry
and cartography of the Institute of Geodesy and Geoinformation Science
at the Technische Universität Berlin (Technical University of Berlin), the
specific measurement points needed to determine the dimensions for the
preparation of the reconstruction drawings were calculated. The basis for
these were Meydenbauer's survey photographs. These images, captured
on large glass plates measuring forty by forty centimetres, document
the Palace all-round, including courtyards and passageways as well as

Hand drawing, new measurements
of the capital and residence city of
Berlin, Portal 1, c. 1876

Drawing by the firm of Zeidler &
Wimmel, 1935. The stonemasonry
firm of Zeidler & Wimmel was hired
to carry out repairs to the sandstone
elements of the facade. Prepared for
this purpose were simple overviews
on which the intended repair
measures were plotted.

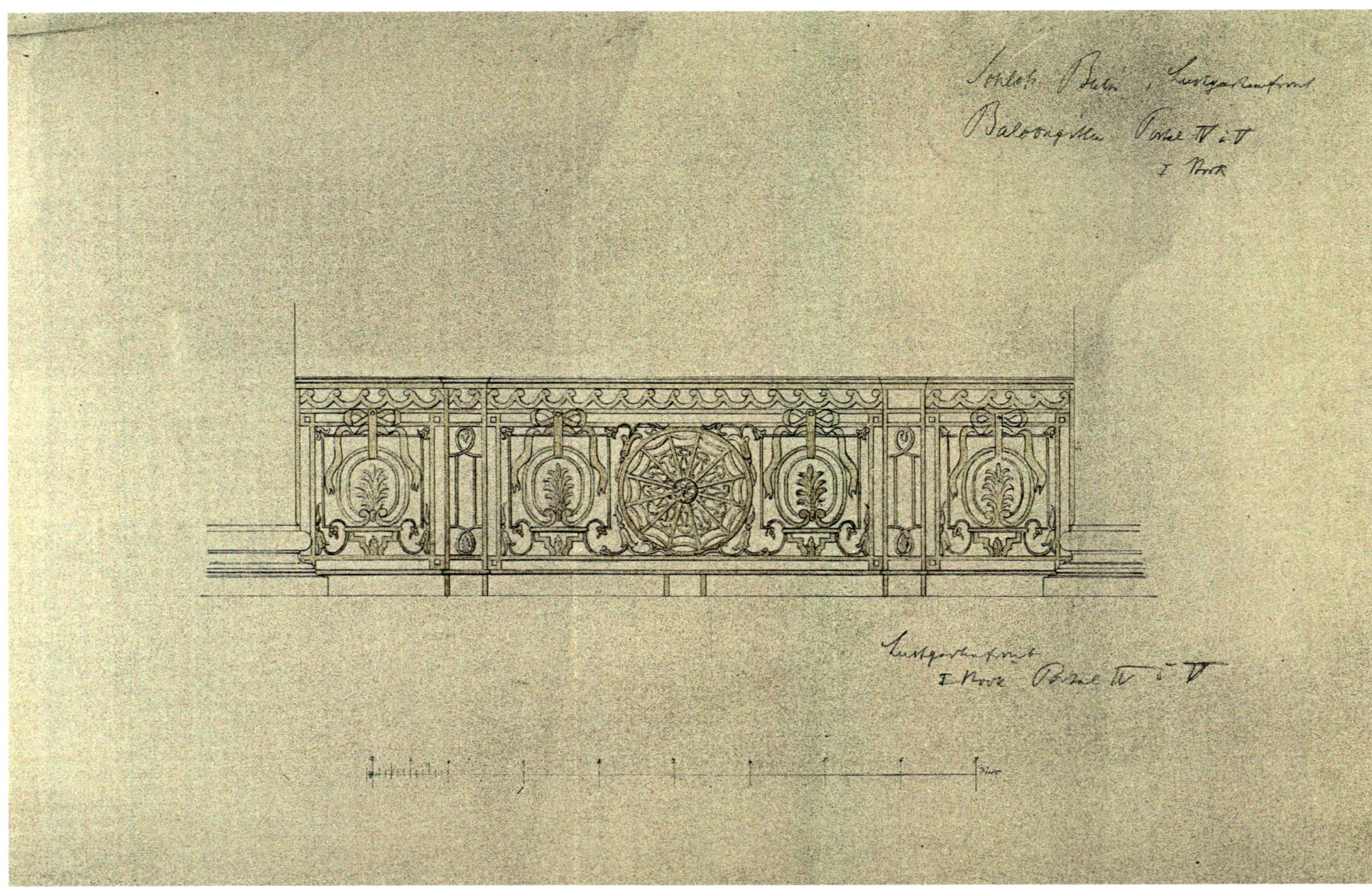

Hand-drawn design for a balcony
grating on the north side of the Palace

important interior rooms. The collection encompasses about seventy
images of external and courtyard facades in a brilliant resolution.

By means of photogrammetric rectification of the images, which were
produced from 1885 on, it became possible to determine both the recessed
areas between the window axes on the north, south and east sides, as
well as the window axes on the west side and the elevations of individual
subdividing elements and to represent them in a simple coordinate system.
The position of the Schlüter Courtyard was determined by means of aerial
photographs depicting both the exterior and the courtyard facades. The
photographic reconstruction made it possible to determine key features of
the main subdivisions of the facade as a whole – recessed areas, window
axes, the avant corps of the portals and the main cornice – with great
accuracy for selected facade levels, but it was not possible to determine
details, in particular those with curvatures.

Based on this information, the three-dimensional features of the
facades, with all of their architectural and sculptural details, were
reconstructed by means of the calculated main measurements and
additional comprehensive planning resources.

It was here that historical image documentation emerged as the most
important source, since it provided direct renderings of lost architectural
features. Relevant here are the earliest photographs, beginning around
1855, which come from the estate of Eduard Gärtner, the above-mentioned
images from the survey archives, all the way to the photographic
documentation compiled by Eva Kemlein and Kurt Reutti during the
demolition. Thousands of photographs serve to document the Palace
exterior as well as the courtyards virtually without gaps. Recognizable in
photographs, some of them taken from facade scaffolding, are numerous

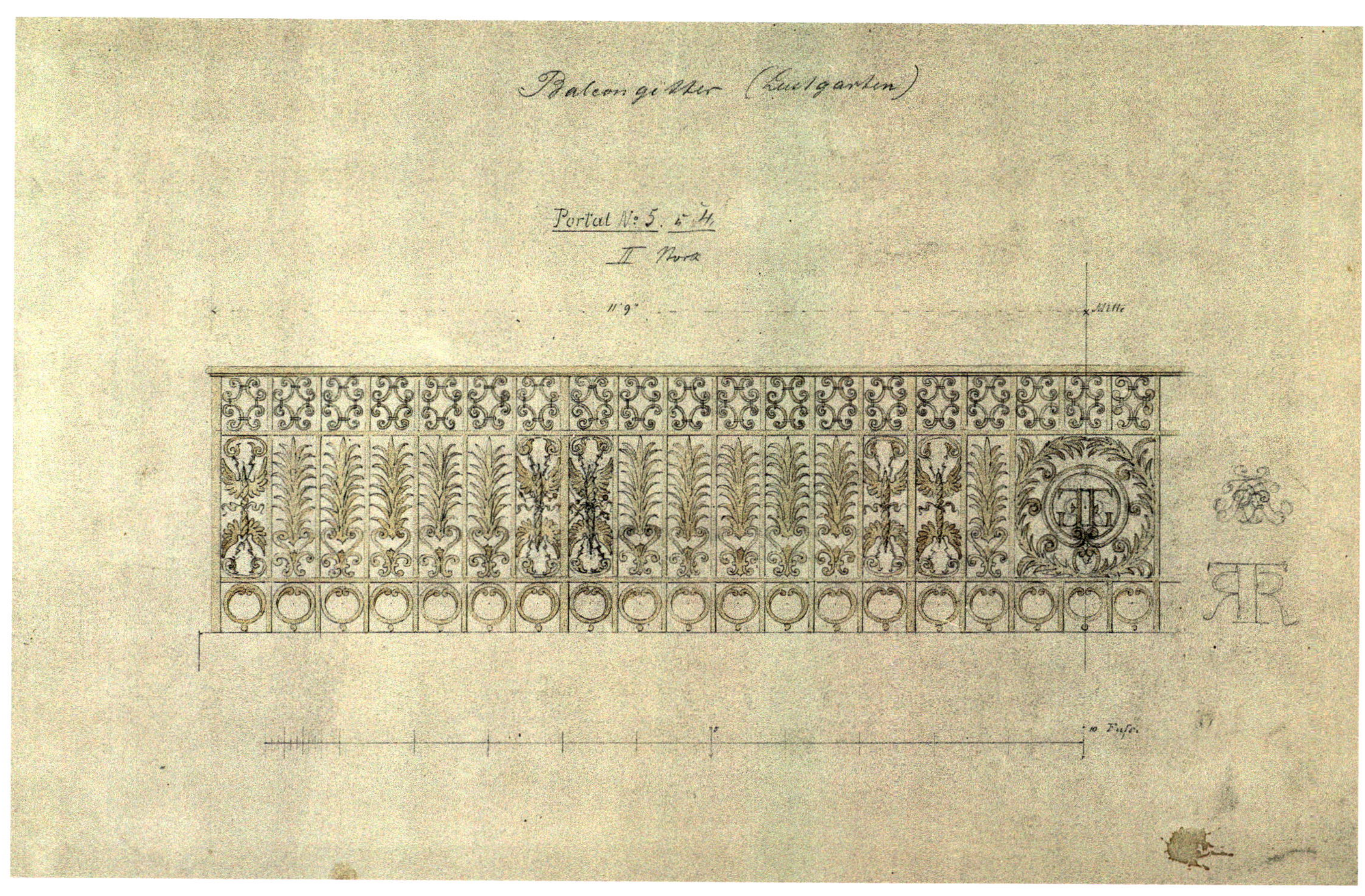

Hand-drawn design for a balcony grating on the north side of the Palace

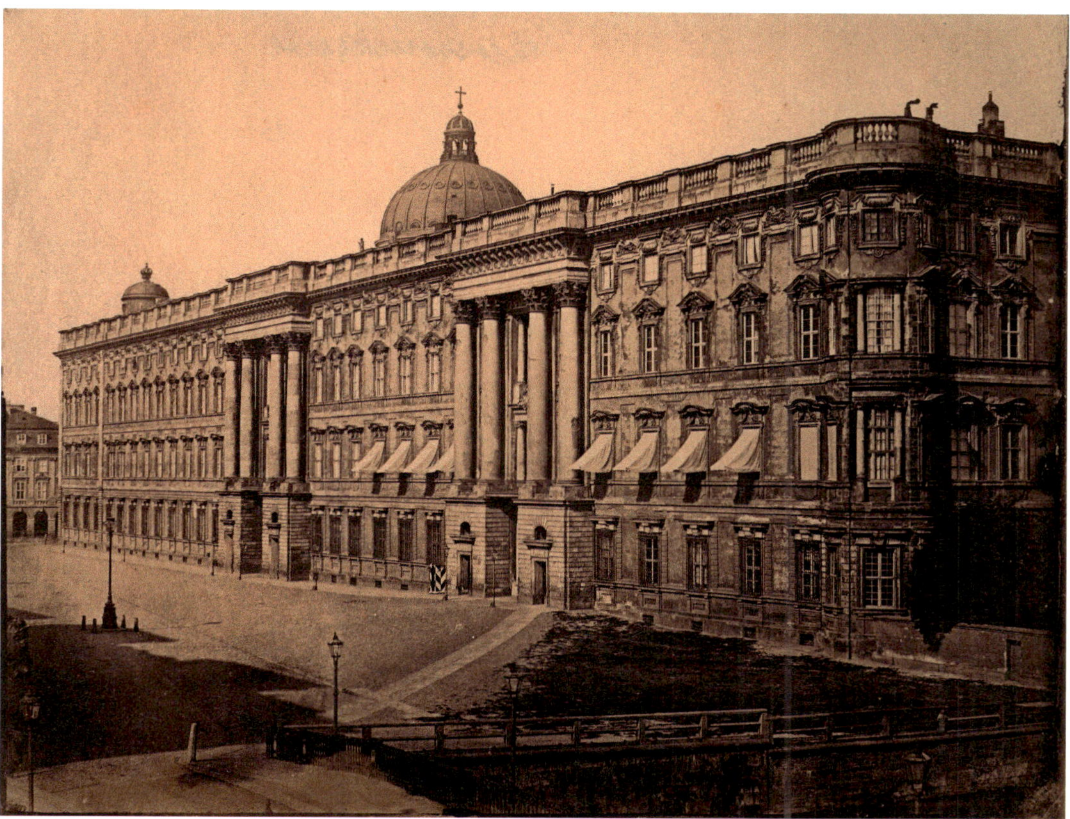

The Berlin Palace from the southeast, c. 1855

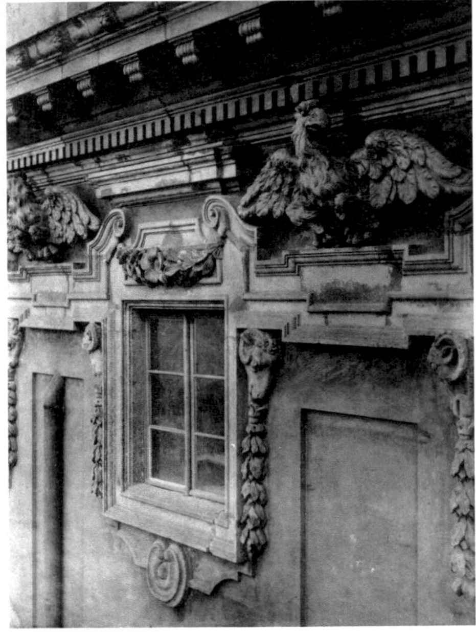

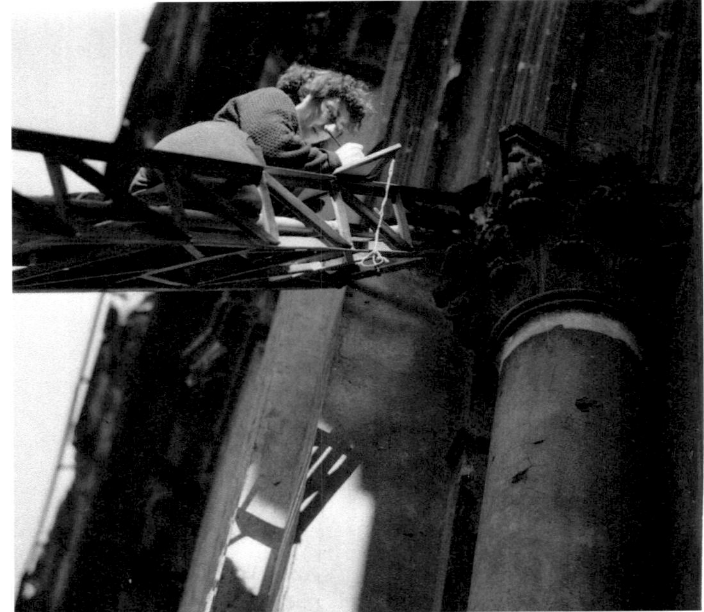

Mezzanine, north side of the Palace.
The extraordinarily good quality of
this photograph displays all of the
details of the profiles and facade
ornamentation.

Schlüter Courtyard, Portal 1,
photographic documentation of
the Palace prior to demolition,
Eva Kemlein, 1950

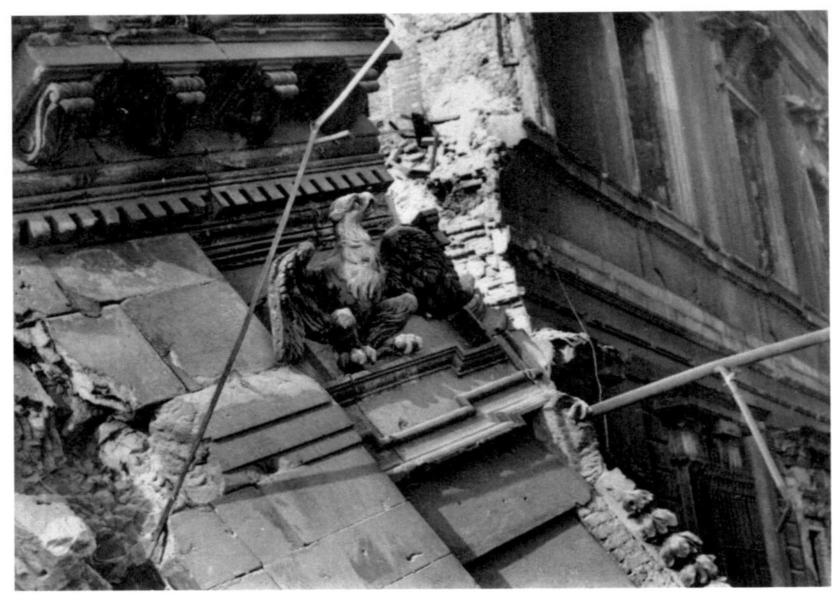

Southwestern corner of the Palace
with fallen eagle from the mezzanine,
photographic documentation of
the Palace prior to demolition, 1950

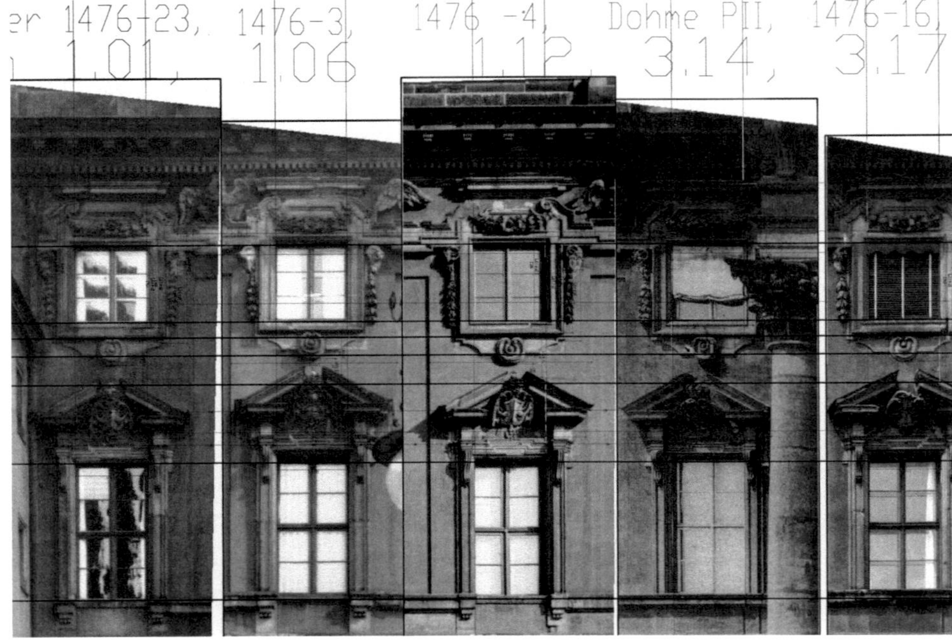

Parade storey windows. Juxtaposition
of numerous photographic details
with the aim of assessing the sizes
and elevations of the structural
members of various facade sections

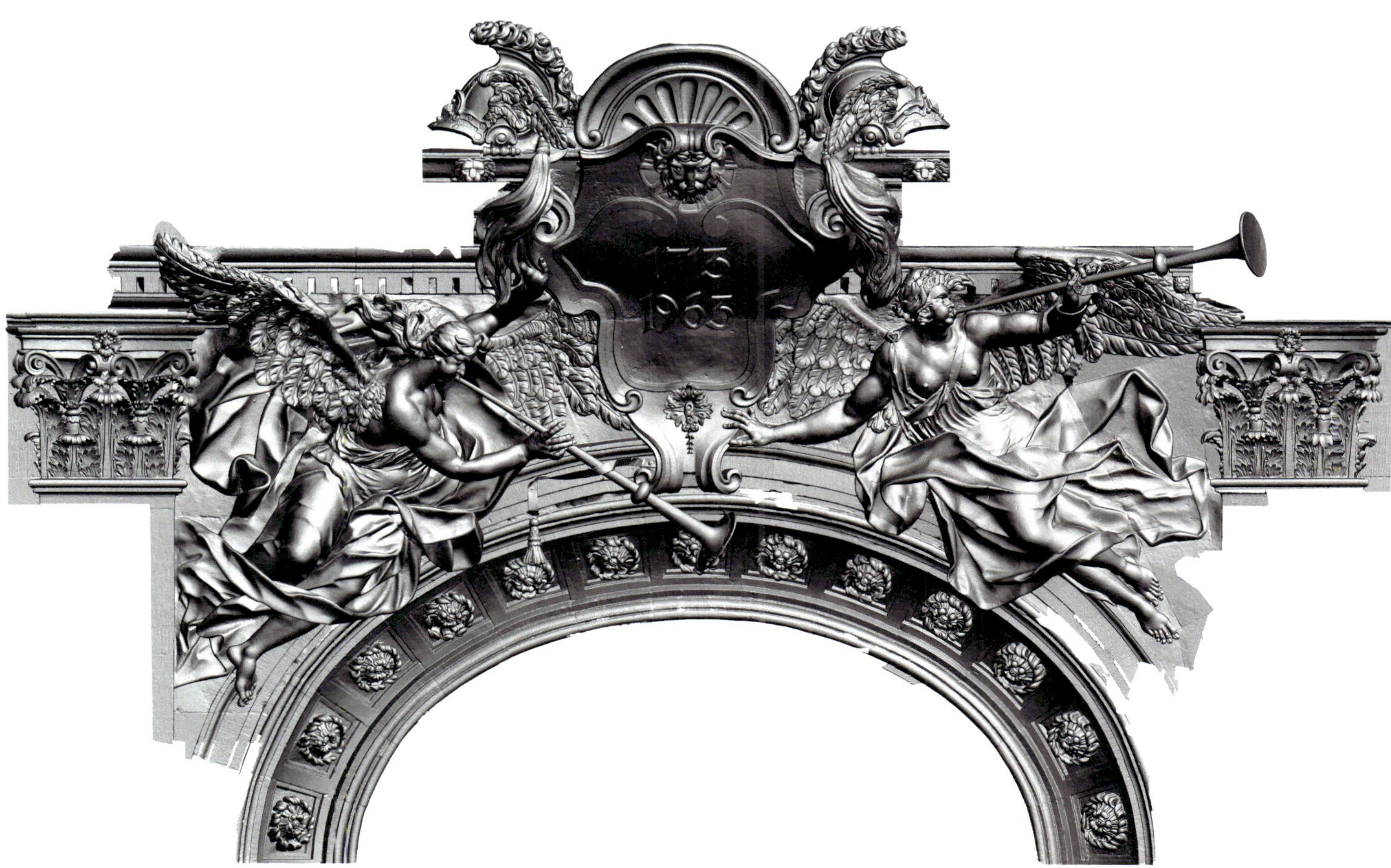

architectural as well as sculptural details, and in a few instances the measurements were determined by means of rectification of single images. Specifications concerning the depths of architectural elements can even be derived from the cast of the shadows. Visible evidence of material differences – as seen for example in photographs of rubble – also served as a resource for reconstruction planning. Along breaklines, for example, it became possible to distinguish between sections in sandstone and brick. In particular in the Schlüter Courtyard, complex disjunctions between levels, for example cornices and recessed areas as well as articulating elements such as fluted pilasters in the upper levels of the portal, were executed in brickwork. The colossal columns at the corners of Portals 1 and 5 consisted of brickwork built out from the wall surfaces, and only the bases and capitals were executed in sandstone.

Surviving fragments are deemed to be the most precise models for reconstructions. In the case of the Berlin Palace, however, virtually none have survived. Of the altogether 2000 pieces (exterior and interior) originally recovered by the Wissenschaftliches Aktiv (scientific unit), only approximately 150 fragments are known today to be from the exterior and courtyard facades of the Palace. Among them are the original sculptural spolia (herm pilasters, serliana, Corinthian capitals of the small order of columns and the pilaster capitals) of Portal 4, called the Liebknecht Portal, erected in 1963; the herm pilasters of Portal 5; eight colossal figures from the Schlüter Courtyard; the figural crests from two portals from the Eosander Courtyard; sculptural fragments from Portals 1 and 3 (colossal capitals, Genius from the inner portal); as well as a few architectural elements from the recessed sections of the facades and the Schlüter Courtyard (including a balcony slab). Then there are the graphic measurements by the well-known architectural historian Goerd Peschken,

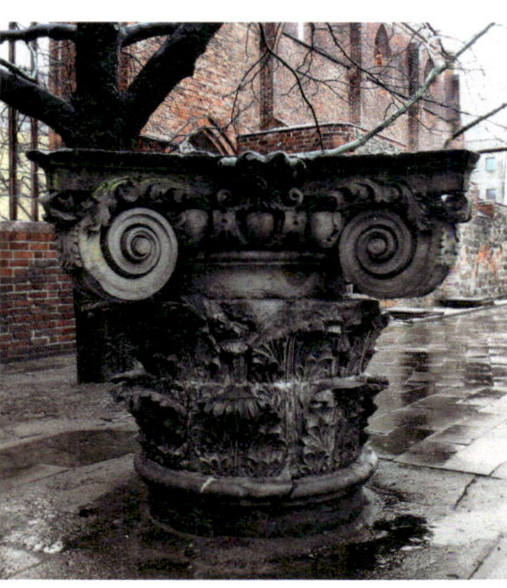

Visualization of the Liebknecht Portal of the former Staatsratsgebäude (State Council Building) of East Germany, erected in 1963 as an approximate reconstruction of Portal 4 of the Palace. Mounted in place of the eagle in the East German era were the years 1713-1963. The scan shown here facilitated the production of a 3-D print on a 1:1 scale.

Fragment of a colossal capital from Portal 3. Following the demolition of the Palace, parts of the capitals were deposited in the ruins of the Klosterkirche (Monastery Church) and in the urban environment in the vicinity of the Märkisches Museum. They have now been reintegrated into the courtyard side of Portal 3.

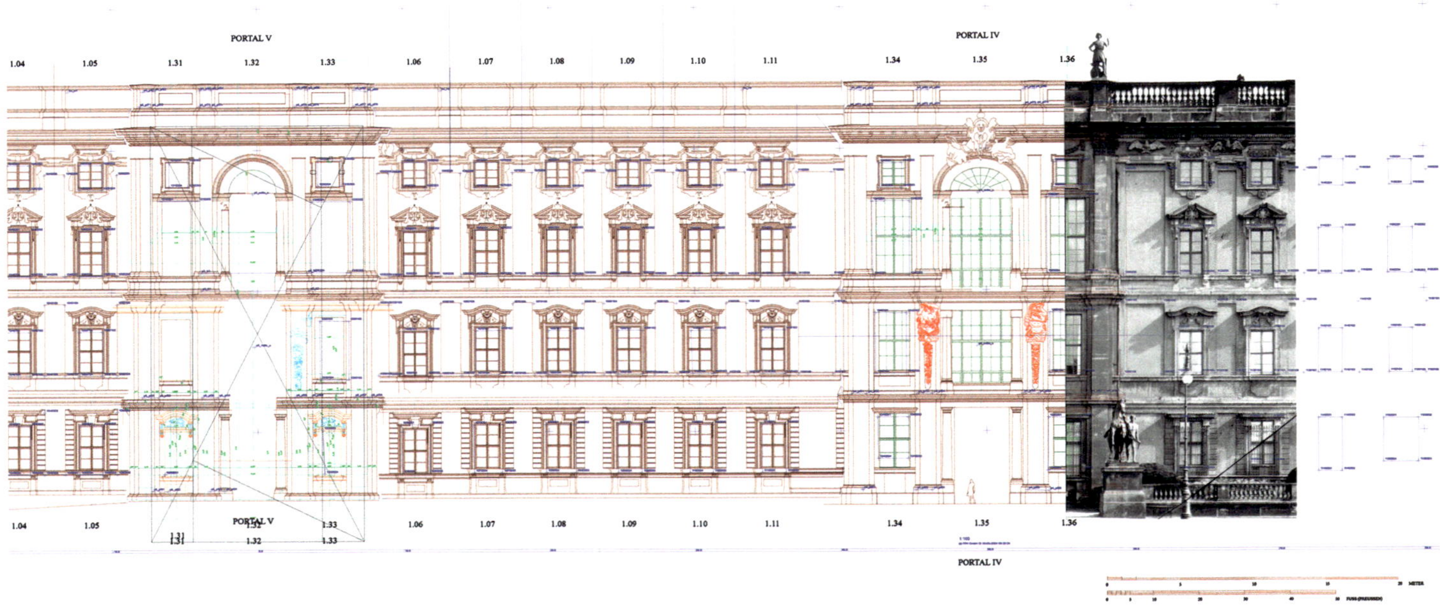

Elevation of the north facade of the Palace with Portals 4 and 5, reconstruction planning office of Stuhlemmer architects. On a previously determined facade plane, control points were calculated (right) to facilitate the positioning of structural members in reconstruction planning.

Profiles of the cornice and window jambs with dimensions, based on the analysis of plans and photographs; drawing by the office of Stuhlemmer architects. Various sources were used for the reconstruction, among them the 'Persius measurements' of 1878, repair plans by the firm of Zeidler & Wimmel from the 1930s, and building measurements made by the Wissenschaftliches Aktiv (scientific unit) in 1950.

which he prepared between 1964 and 1966 from fragments, some of which have since become lost, and published together with his own facade reconstructions in the multivolume work *Das königliche Schloss zu Berlin* (The Berlin Royal Palace), which appeared beginning in 1992.

Fragments were integrated into the rebuilt Portal 5, Portal 3 (inside) and Portal 6, thus documenting the precision of the reconstruction, but also the history of loss.

Since virtually all of the architectural members were lost, they had to be reconstructed in the absence of one-to-one models. In order to arrive at the right decision for a given form or proportion when confronted with contradictory or absent data, reconstruction planning proceeded in the spirit of the original construction period. Appraised as a sort of common denominator, as a corrective measure, were classical architectural treatises or analogous buildings dating from the historical construction era. Examples include the architectural doctrines of François Blondel (*Cours d'architecture*, 1675, 1683) and Charles Philippe Dieussart (*Theatrum Architecturae Civilis*, 1679, 1697), as well as Leonhard Christoph Sturm and Nicolai Goldmann's *Vollständige Anweisung zu der Civil-Bau-Kunst* (Comprehensive Instruction on the Art of Civil Construction, 1696).

Published in these works were the columnar orders (from Vignola, Scamozzi, Palladio), as well as the window orders and the proportions of rooms and staircases. The representations and descriptions of the individual profiles were precisely rendered and measured for subsequent use. Certain structural members are therefore applied in identical forms at various locations, and can hence be reconstructed in this context. Decisive for the reconstruction of the Berlin Palace was the identification of the doctrines, of the 'recipe book' that had guided Schlüter or Eosander in the design of a given component. It was possible to verify the dimensions of Portal 3, for example, which corresponded exactly to the classical orders given by Vignola. Moreover, it was possible to establish a set of clear proportions which ordered the widths and heights of the arches in a certain relationship.

In order to do justice to the historical dimensions, our planning measures used the Rhenish–Prussian Fuss (foot) and Zoll (inch). This

Berliner Schloss, Zusammenstell. Aufmaße Fenstergewände

Persius — Aufmaß 1878	Ergebnis Foto- und Plananalyse — Stuhlemmer Architekten	Sonstige

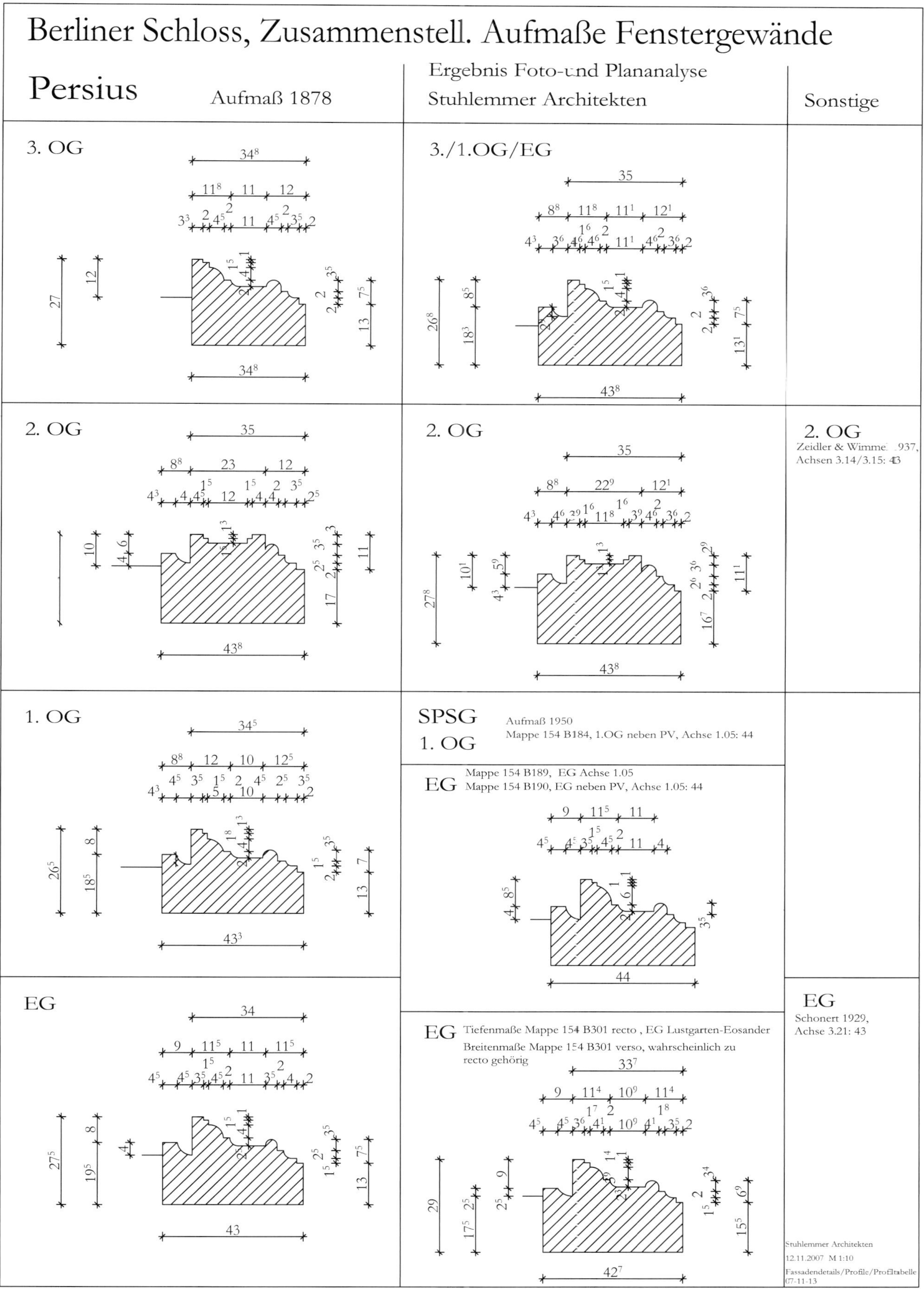

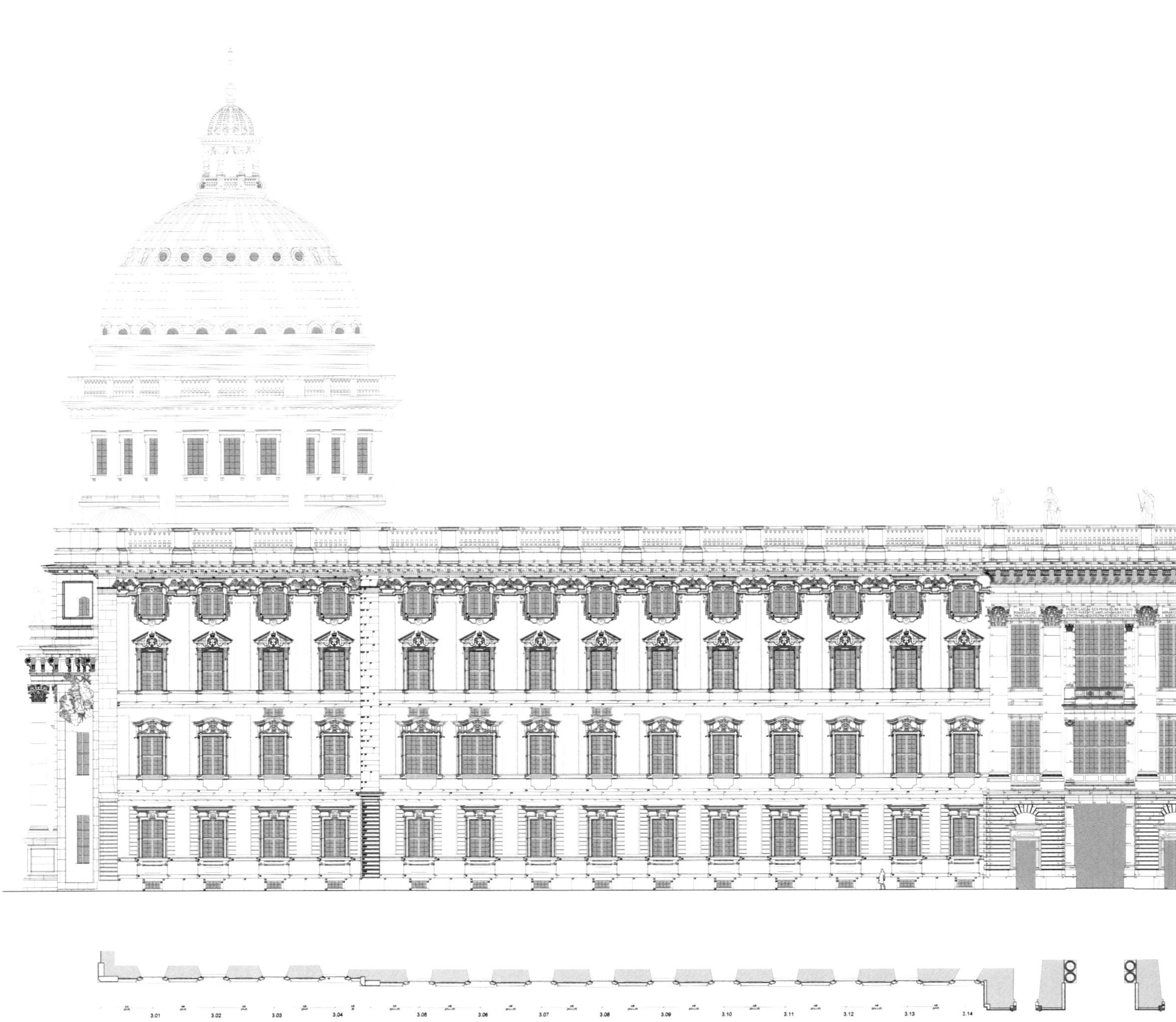

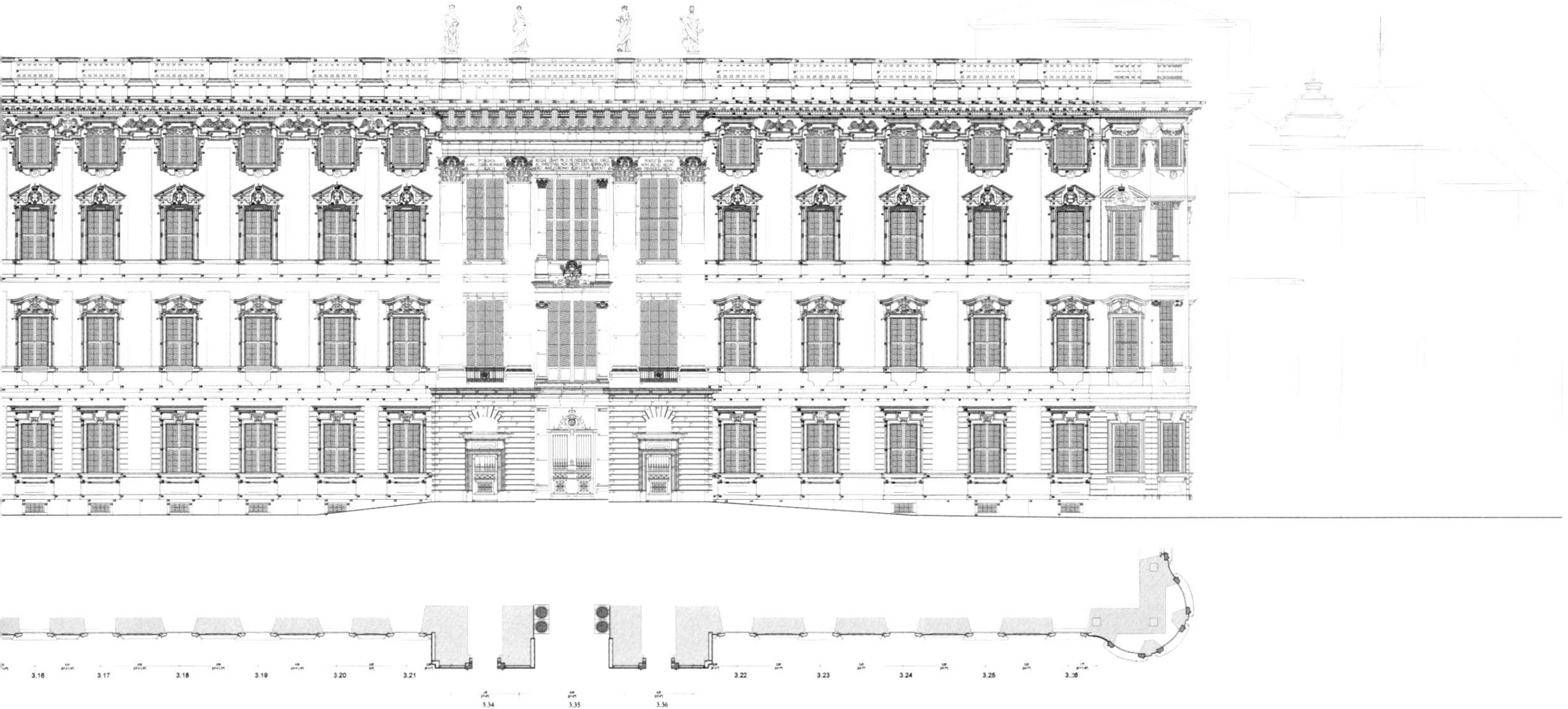

Facade elevation of the
Berlin Palace, south side.
Reconstruction planning by
the office of Stuhlemmer
architects. The axis distances
between the windows vary
as a result of the previous
Renaissance building that
was reshaped by Andreas
Schlüter.

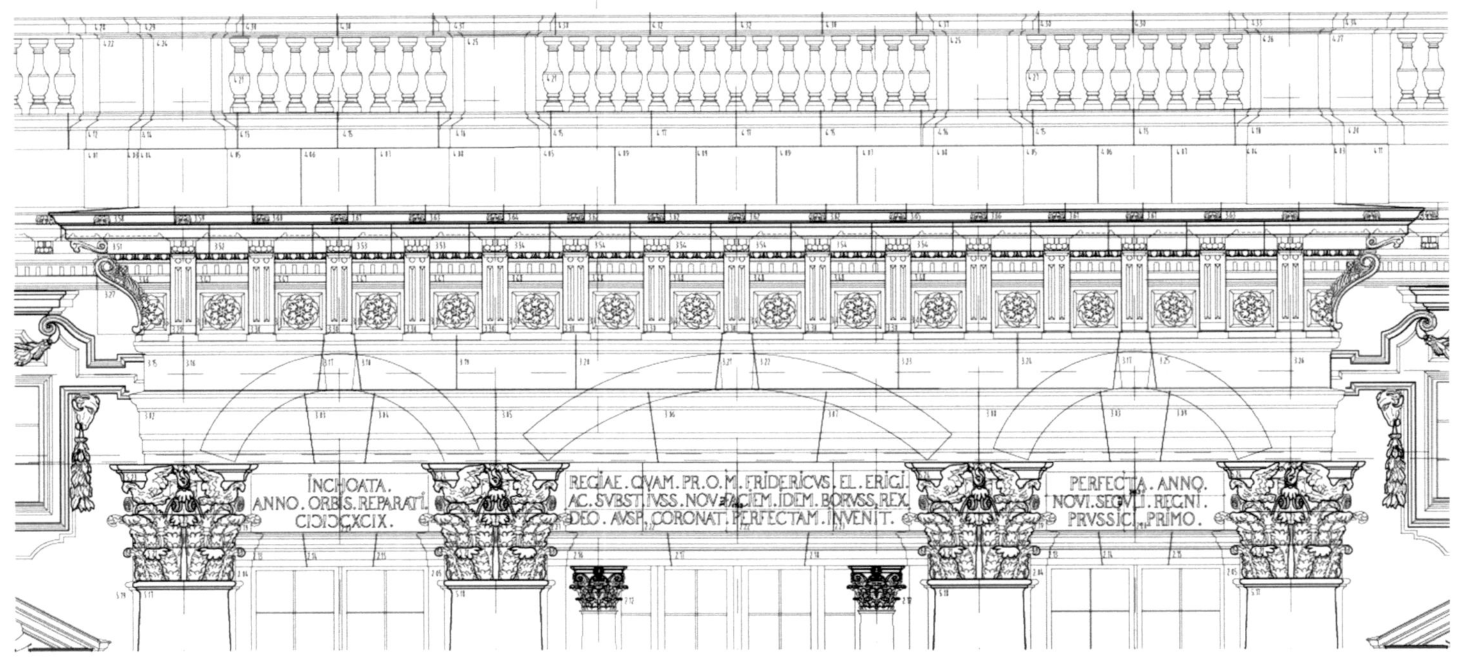

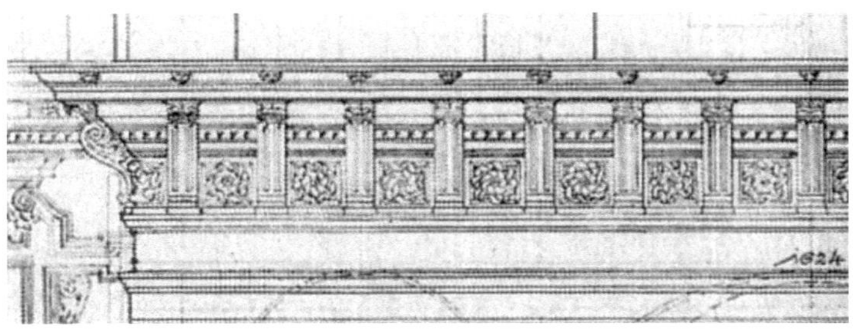

Portal 1, entablature with attic above colossal columns, reconstruction planning by the office of Stuhlemmer architects. Planned in the drawing as well are the stone arches with their keystones, arranged behind the entablature.

Portal 1, measurements by Erich Schonert, 1929

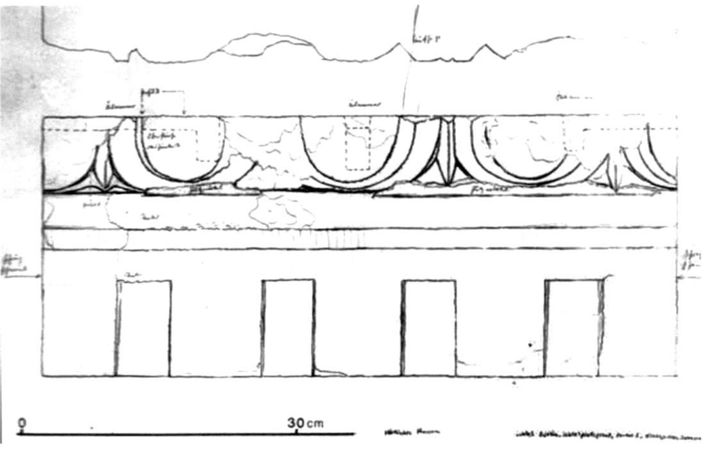

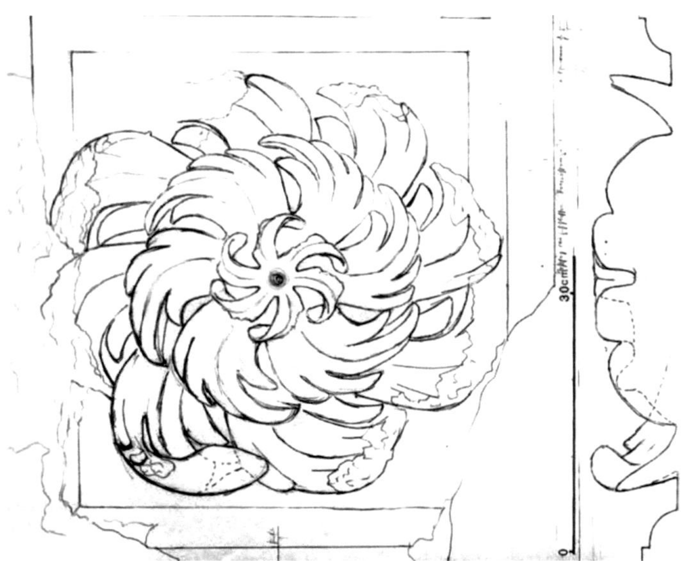

Egg and dart with tooth frieze and metope, measurements by Goerd Peschken, 1964

made it possible to avoid rounding errors which could have led, in detail, to false profile calculations. Accordingly, we arrived at dimensions of not 2.5, but instead 2.6 centimetres (corresponding to one inch), and not 31, but instead 31.4 centimetres (corresponding to one foot). In centimetres, according to modern maintenance measurements, the clear window dimensions amounted to widths of between 1.54 and 1.58 meters and heights of between 3.13 and 3.17 meters. Only conversion into feet and inches results in the rational dimensions of 5 by 10 feet, corresponding to 1.569 x 3.139 meters. Again and again in the course of our work, we realized that with minimal corrections of centimetre or millimetre specifications this conversion often resulted in consistent values in feet and inches. The rounded balusters of the Lustgarten attic in a one-to-ten measurement from about 1900, adding up individual measurements, measure 133.5 centimetres, and in the one-to-fifty repair drawings by Zeidler & Wimmel, 134 centimetres. The corresponding value in inches equals 133.4 centimetres (which corresponds to 4 feet, 3 inches).

In order to accurately reconstruct the form world of these Baroque architectural members and sculptural elements while respecting special features, specifically in the context of Berlin Baroque, we studied the few surviving analogous buildings, among them the Zeughaus (the Arsenal, with its fantastic helmets, warrior heads, architectural members, bronze inscriptions), the equestrian statue of the Great Elector, the splendid coffins of King Friedrich I and Queen Sophie Charlotte in the Berlin Cathedral, and the tomb art of the Schlüter Era (among other things, the Monument for Daniel Männlich in St Nicolas' Church or Nikolaikirche, 1700), profile shapes, decorative strokes and the surfaces of various feigned materials (feathers, fabrics, foliage, etc.), and adopted them for the reconstruction.

Our aim was to allow history to become legible in the reconstruction. To some extent, Schlüter was obliged to respond to the irregularities of the predecessor building and to adapt his idealized design to them – as documented by vedute. Historically documented deviations, beginning with a non-orthogonal ground plan, a slightly trapezoidal Schlüter Courtyard, and continuing with irregularities with regard to the intervals between window axes and columns, all the way to differences in elevation, for example on opposite facades, were reproduced and made binding for the reconstruction. All details of the facades needed to be precisely planned so that dimensions and designs were perfectly coordinated. Prepared altogether were approximately 3000 plans and detailed drawings, which served as the basis for the execution of the sandstone and plaster surfaces and as the basis for sculptural work for the entire outer shell and the Schlüter Courtyard.

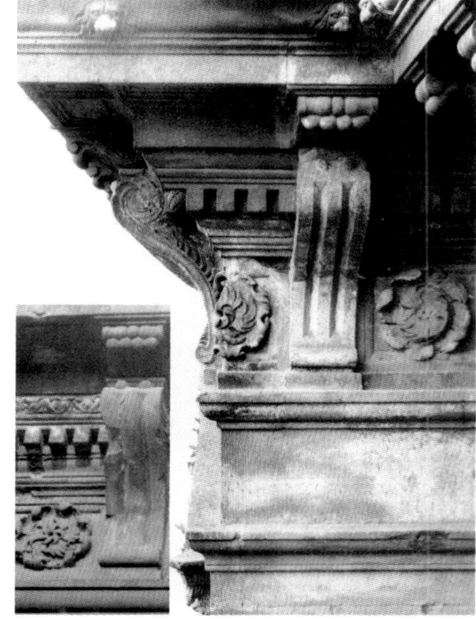

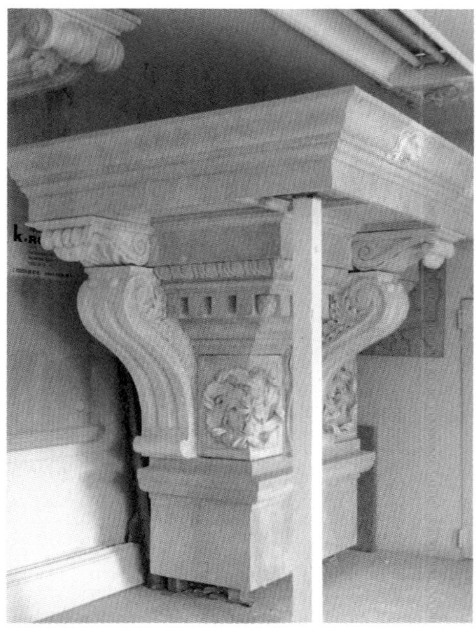

Main cornice of Portals 1 and 2 with metope, photo from 1950

Portal 1, entablature with details of consoles and rosettes, model by Frank Kösler and the Rogge firm based on the planning of the office of Stuhlemmer architects

A Modern Building behind Historical Facades
Hans-Dieter Hegner

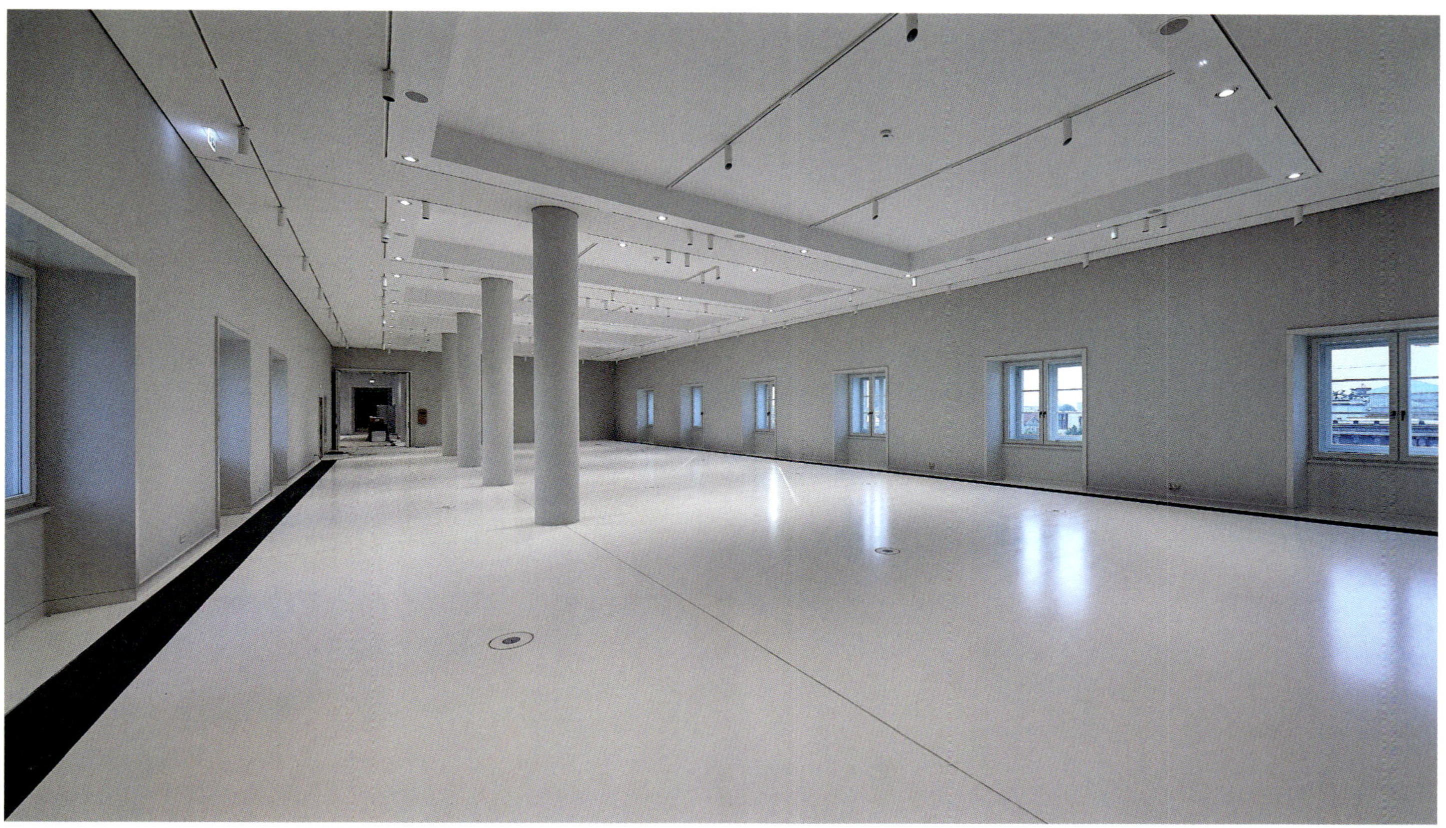

The new Humboldt Forum building, with its historically accurate appearance, is oriented towards the layout and the height of the Berlin Palace immediately before its destruction and hence fits in perfectly (according to expert opinion) with the architectural ensembles found in the immediate vicinity. The building occupies a ground area measuring somewhat more than 20 000 square metres and has a total floor space of nearly 100 000 square metres.

Organization and Utilization

Regarding use, the new building is strongly horizontal in organization. The second and third upper storeys accommodate the two museums (the Ethnologisches Museum or Ethnological Museum and the Museum für Asiatische Kunst or Museum of Asian Art), which belong to the Staatliche Museen zu Berlin (Berlin State Museums), on 18 000 square metres of surface area. The galleries, measuring about five to fifteen metres in height, offer an optimal setting for spacious exhibition design. The first upper storey will be used mainly by the Federal State of Berlin. Presented here on a surface measuring 4000 square metres will be the exhibition Berlin Global. At the same time, this level will also be used by the the newly inaugurated Humboldt Laboratory of Humboldt-Universität (1000 square metres). The ground floor contains the spacious foyer and accommodates areas that are usable for highly diverse functions. Available here are large surfaces for special exhibitions and two halls for conferences, concerts, performances and lectures. Altogether, an additional 10 000 square metres are available here. Also located on the ground floor is the permanent exhibition on the history of the site. It includes what can be called an archaeological window (to the 'Schlosskeller' or palace basement), which occupies an area measuring 1800 square metres in the lower level. Vertical access is offered in

Exhibition area of the Museum für Asiatische Kunst (Museum of Asian Art), 3rd upper storey

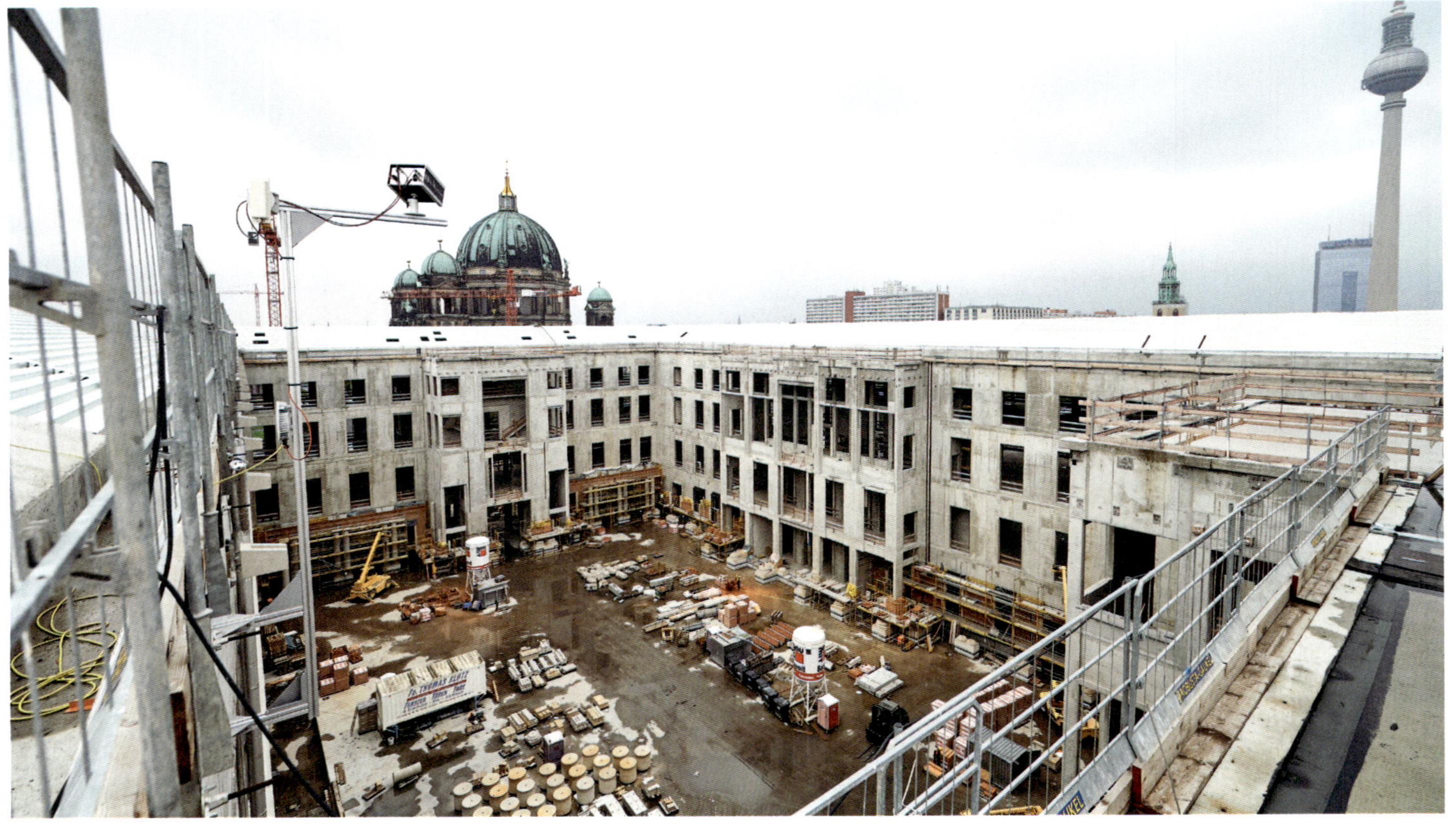

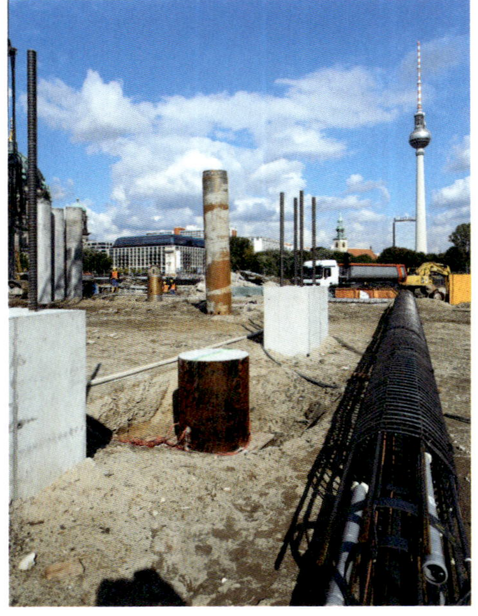

During construction: view of
the Schlüter Courtyard towards
the northeast, 2015

During excavation work:
reinforcement cages for the
large diameter bored piles, 2012

particular via the main staircase. In addition to many staircases, there are also 28 elevators and six escalators.

The Shell Construction

The new building is a monolithic reinforced concrete structure with curtain facades. The historical facade is self-supporting and is decoupled from the reinforced concrete supporting structure within. The resulting spaces are expansive, bright and multifunctional. The ceilings cover spans of between eight and 24 metres. The spacious foyer, which replaces the large former palace courtyard, has a span of about 34 metres and a height of about 31 metres and terminates with horizontal glazing. By virtue of modern reinforced concrete ceilings, whose loadbearing capacity could be increased fourfold in comparison to the former Palace, their surface load is now 10 kN/m². The cavity floors were constructed on top of the reinforced concrete ceilings. Large display cases and the showcases, up to three metres in height, are positioned on the ceiling slabs, while the remaining exhibition architecture is assembled on the cavity flooring. Vital installations have been inserted into the floor cavities, including the air intake system and power and media supply lines.

The building rests on concrete foundation piles that measure up to forty metres in depth. Work on the foundation had to take into account the tunnel excavation of the U5 underground line, then under construction, which runs diagonally beneath the building at approximately 23 metres below ground level. At its deepest point, the basement lies 8.5 metres below ground level. Used in the construction were altogether 100 000 cubic metres of concrete and 20 000 tons of steel.

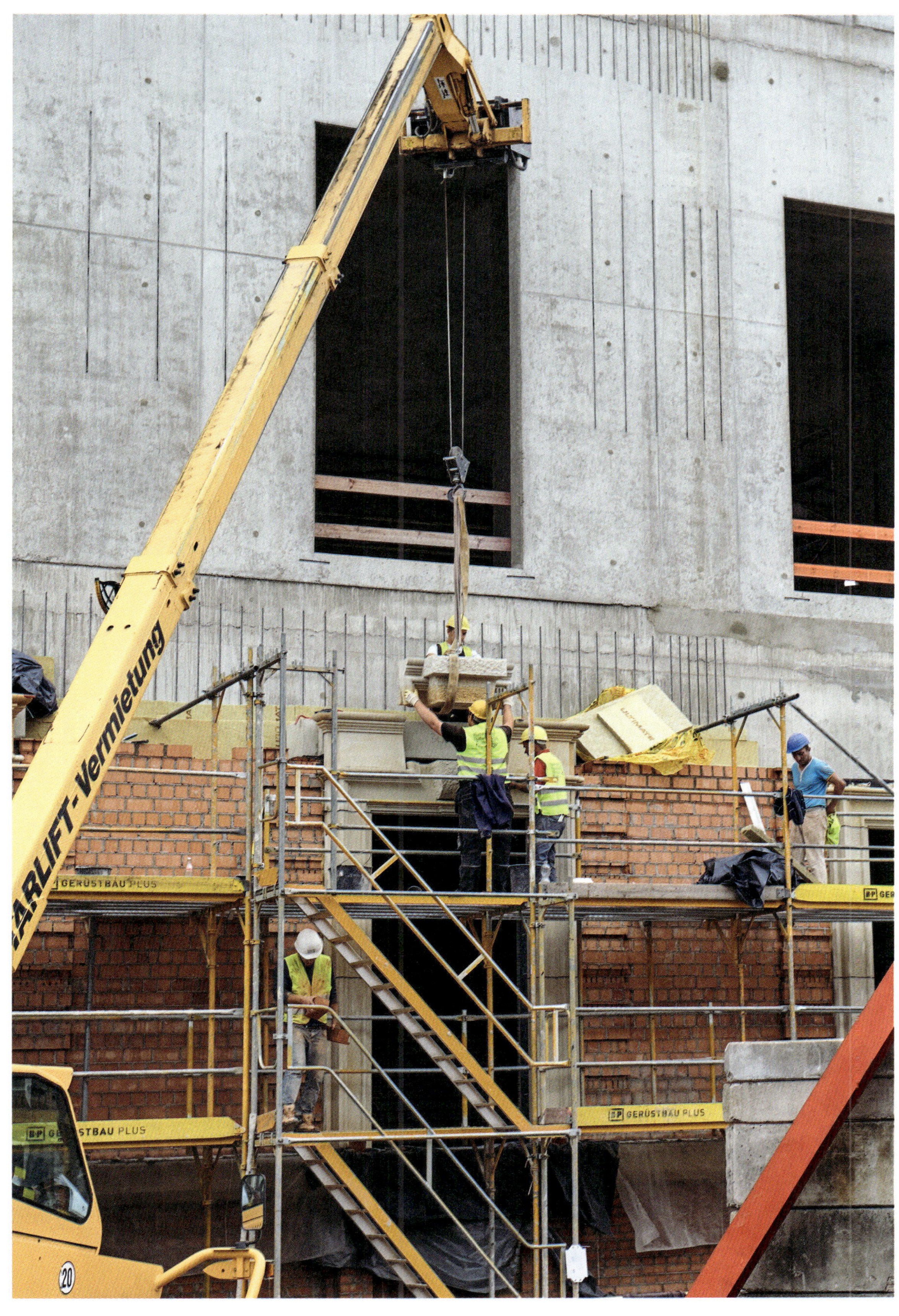

Assembly of the keystones on
the window jambs, 2015

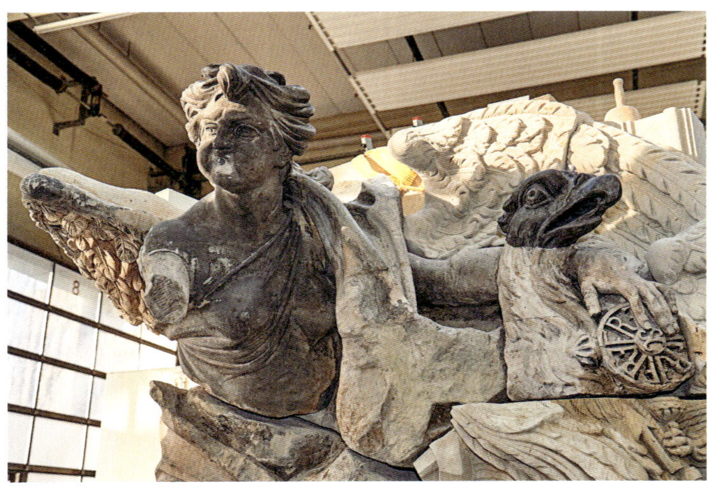

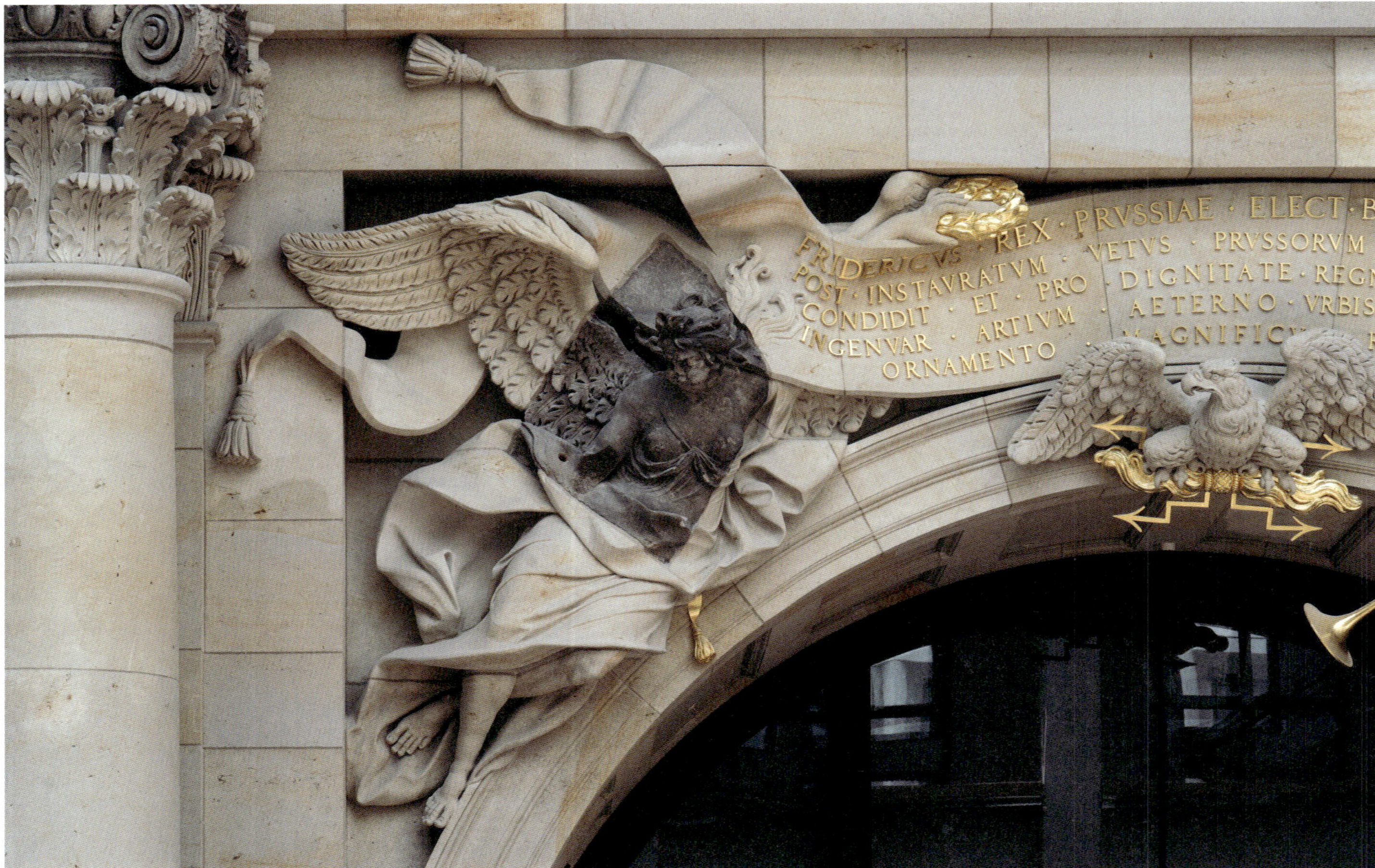

Crowning element of courtyard
Portal 2, left genius, pre-assembly
in the Palace Workshop

Fragment of a genius seen from
the interior courtyard side of the
Eosander Portal, reintegrated in the
reconstruction

**The Reconstruction of the Historical Facade, Modern and
Historical Windows**

In the design of the architect Franco Stella, the historical facades were
accurately reconstituted along a length of altogether 750 metres. The east
side (called the Belvedere) is, by contrast, agreeably restrained and makes
a positive impression by virtue of its lucid composition in prefabricated
exposed concrete elements of high-quality white cement with an
admixture of ground sandstone. With their columnated order, the new
facades in the public passage traversing the building, also in white cement,
represent a modern reminiscence of the Uffizi in Florence.

The facade reconstruction relies in particular on survey photographs
dating from the late nineteenth century, photographs of details as well as
salvaged fragments that survive today. The reconstruction of the historical
facade, with its 2828 figural sculptures and more than 22 000 sandstone
parts, represents a tour de force in structural engineering, cultural
conservation and craftsmanship. The facades in front of the concrete
supporting structure consist for the most part of a masonry structure
composed of 3.5 million bricks, which forms a massive outer wall of sixty
centimetres in thickness, as well as various sandstone elements. The total
depth of the facade, including the concrete supporting structure, measures
up to 1.3 metres.

The restoration of the figural sculptures required more than only
artistic and technical skill. Above all, it called for scientific analysis and
for transfer of know-how among all of the specialists involved. For this
federally funded building endeavour, the client had recourse to a singular
institution: the *Schlossbauhütte* or Palace Workshop. It was here that the
surviving fragments were restored, and at the same time the models for
the reconstructions were created; here the extensive work was carried out
carving the sculptural stone elements. As a rule, a clay model was created
in order to produce a silicone mould, which was then used to fashion a
one-to-one plaster model. This model could then be realized in sandstone
by a stone-working firm. The entire process was continuously supervised
by Bertold Just, head of the Palace Workshop, and by a commission of
experts.

A very small number of surviving historical fragments have been
returned to their original locations. The visible damage that still mars them
is eloquent testimony to the fragility of great art.

The windows represented special technical challenge. There are
513 historical windows in the reconstructed facades and 500 modern
windows in the contemporary facades. Outwardly, the historical windows
must maintain the appearance of the historical facades, while fulfilling on
the inside all of the modern requirements of indoor climate technology,
burglary resistance, use of daylight and so forth. White-coated wood
was used for a one-to-one reconstruction. The choice of materials was a
response in particular to sustainability concerns. Investigations showed
that by virtue of their limited resilience, gross density, hardness and
flexural rigidity, both pine and larch were only to a lesser degree suitable
for the planned construction and utilization. Also considered due to their
greater gross density were woods such as robinia, oak and teak. Chosen in
the end was the highly durable European white oak.

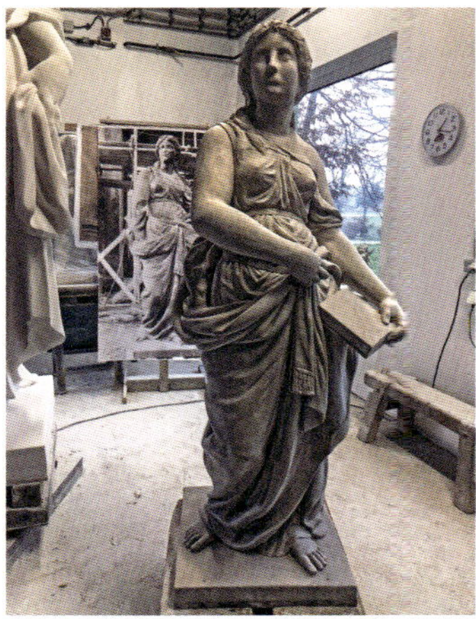

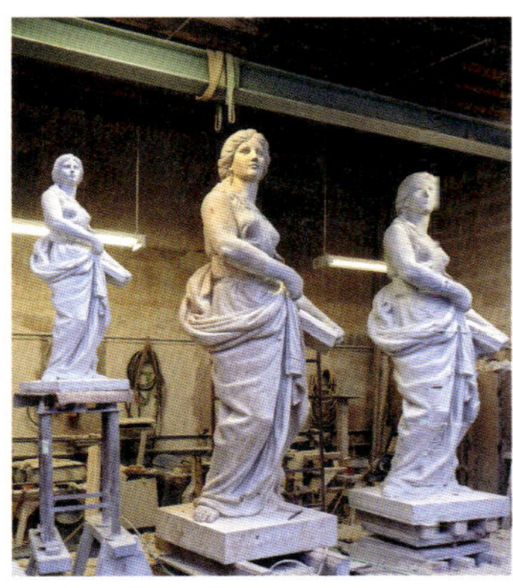

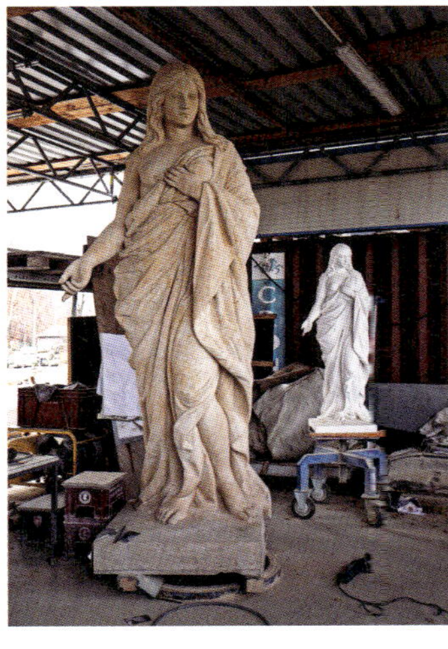

Bozzetto of the colossal figure of
Love for Portal 3

1:1 model of the colossal figure of Love

Plaster model and colossal figure
of Faith for Portal 3

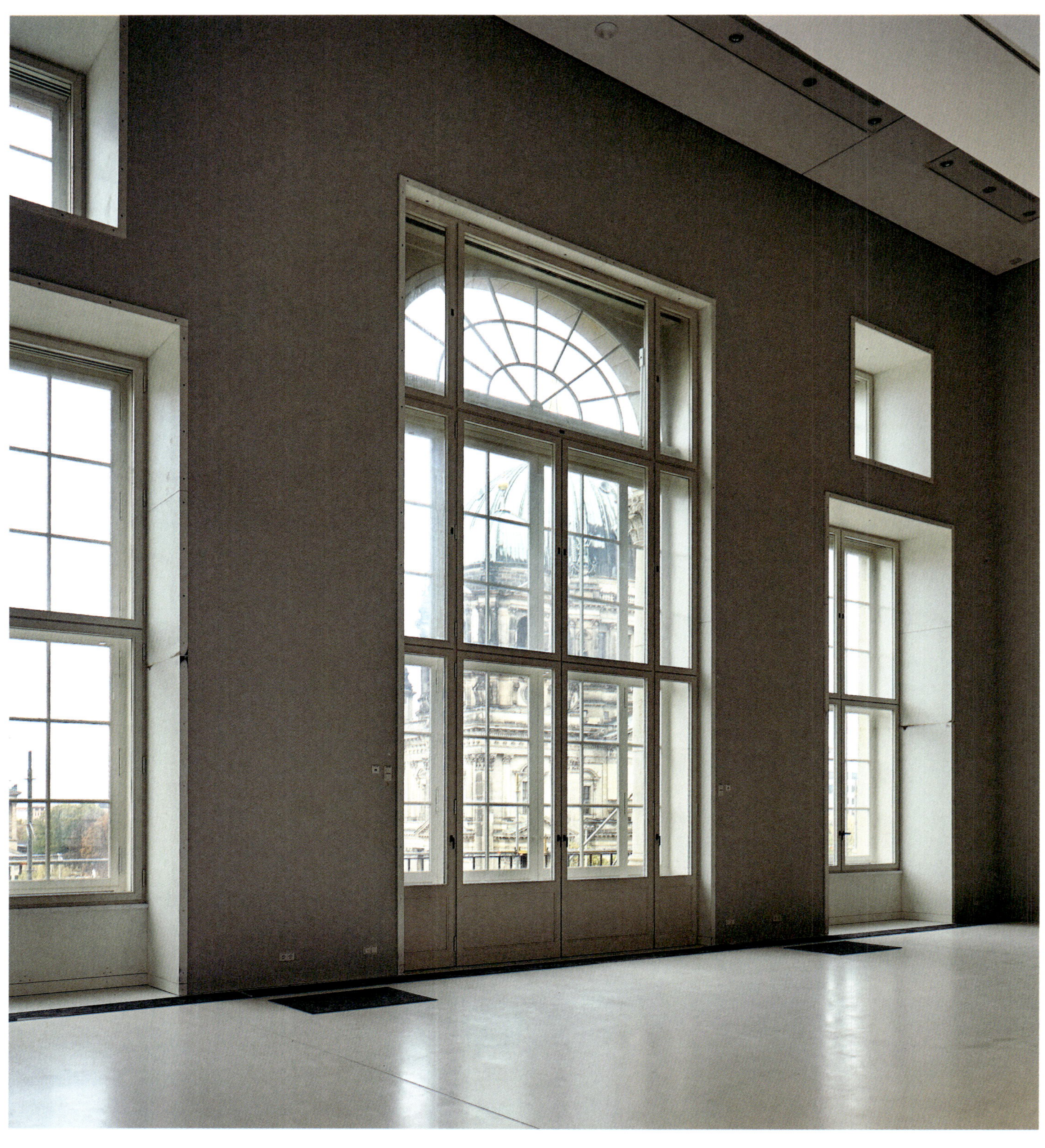

2nd upper floor, room above Portal 4,
view towards the Cathedral through
the large portal window

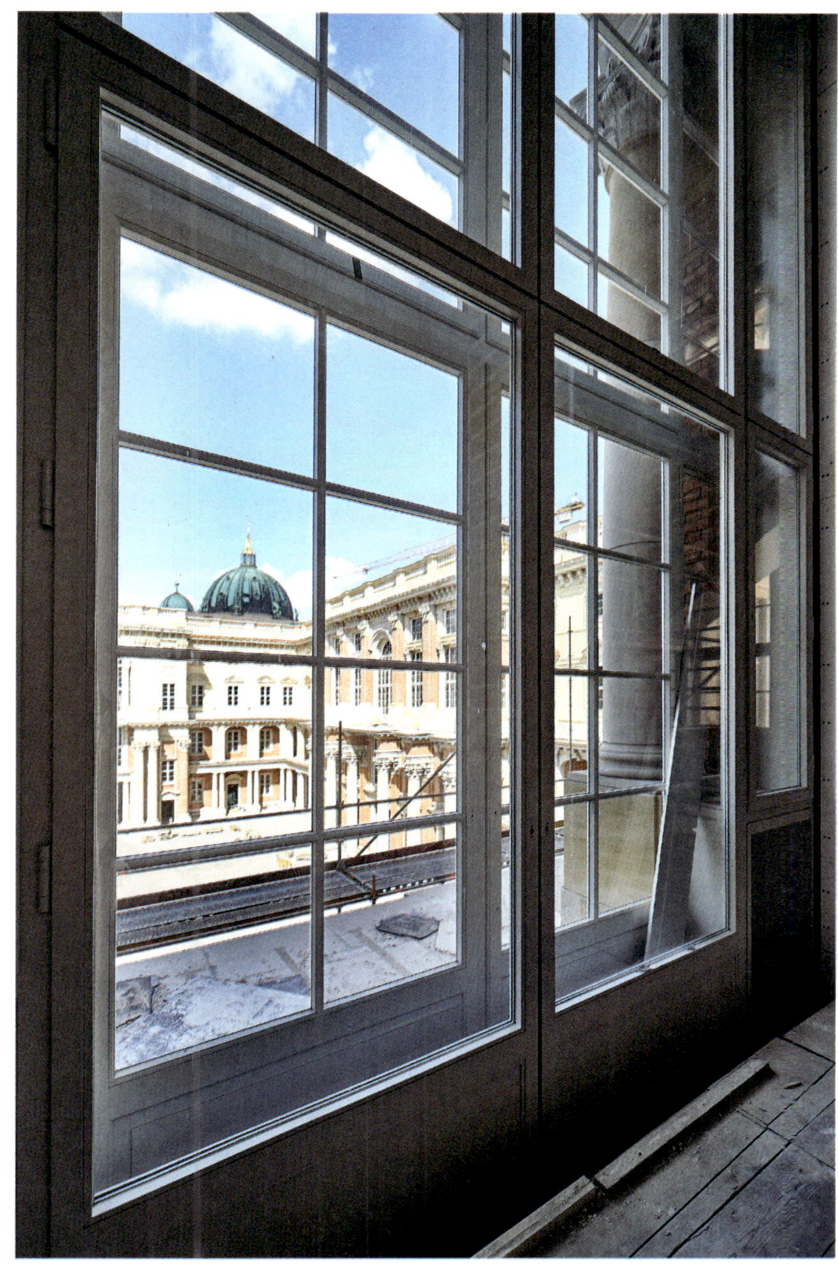

Casement window construction,
2nd upper floor, the room above
Portal 1

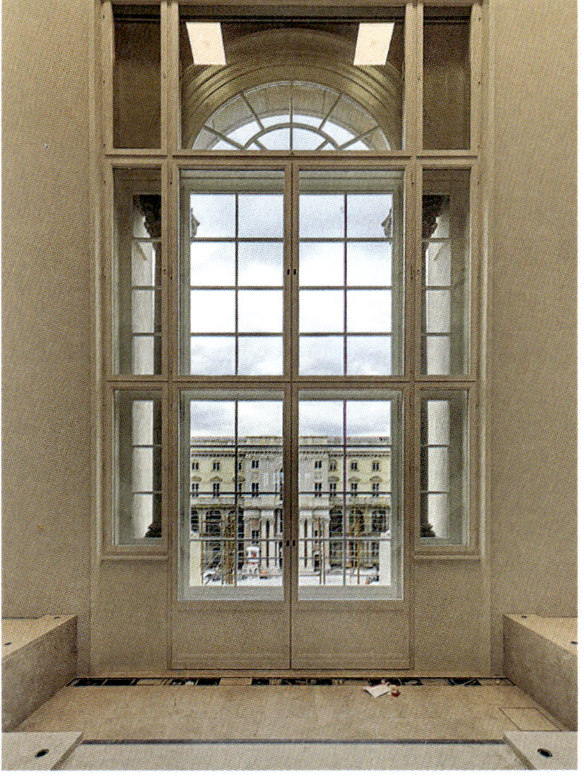

Casement window construction,
2nd upper floor, the room above
Portal 5

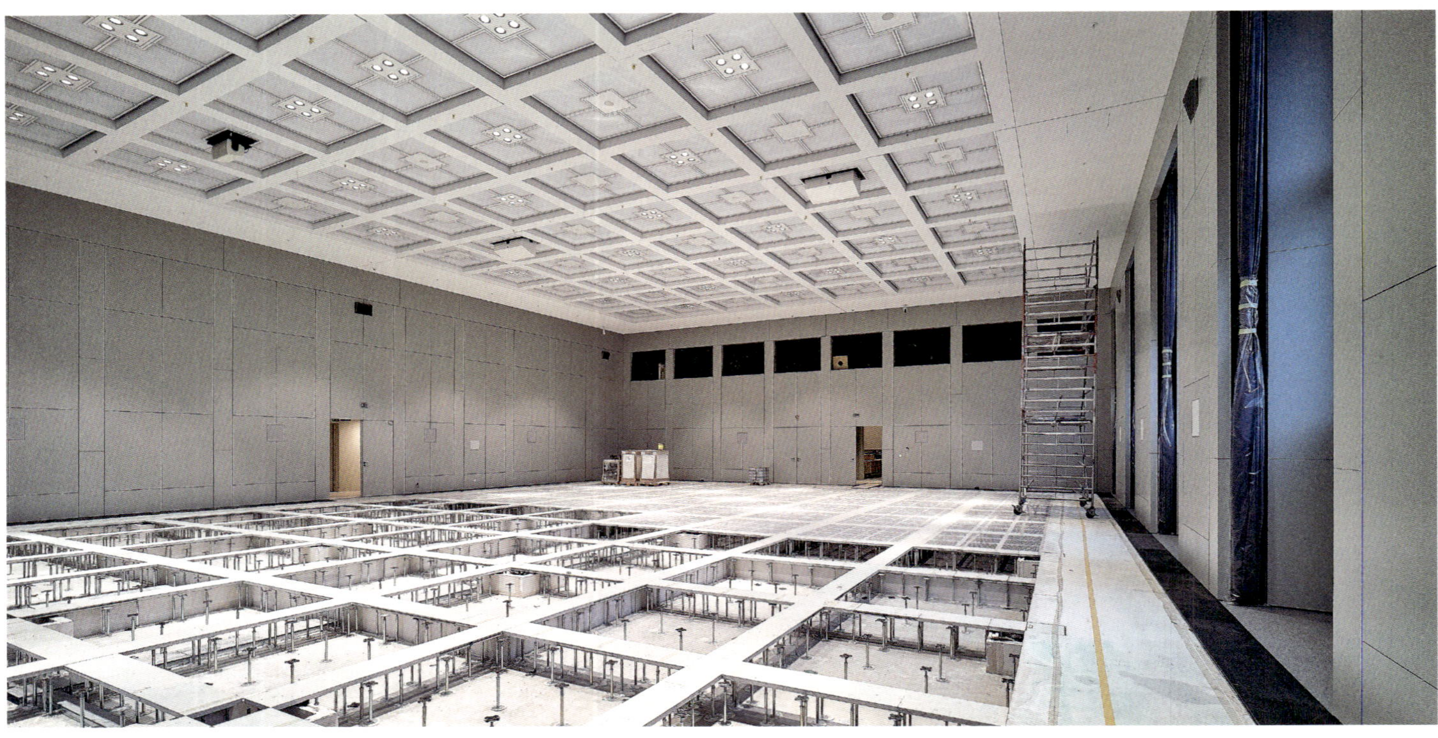

Cavity floor, ground floor, view into
Hall 1. Located above the entrance
are the control rooms and the
interpreters' cabins

The dimensions of the windows resulted from the architectural reconstruction of the facade. The large portal windows have dimensions of up to 5.5 by 9.5 metres. In order to improve dimensional stability and prevent distortion or warping of the window profiles, five-fold laminated oak scantlings, among other things, were manufactured. Some of the windows are also stabilized by steel braces.

The box window constructions have four millimetre restoration glass (low iron) on the outside and 24 millimetres of mulitpane insulating glass on the inside, which results in an particularly low heat transfer coefficient (U_W = 1.2 W/m²K); in the ventilated space between the interior and exterior casement they have curtains for sun protection and dimming. Moreover, dimming options were designed variably for individual zones of use. Depending upon the size of the window, the heavy interior casements weigh between less than 90 kilograms and up to a quarter ton. For this reason, the necessary fittings were tested under real boundary conditions for up to 20 000 cycles.

In order to ensure sufficient airtightness for the air conditioning system within, steel frames were installed air-tight in the primary structure. They incorporate the actual windows, which must also fulfil high sound insulation requirements.

All window elements were constructed to provide maximum protection against burglary. Their performance in this regard was validated by a test report from the renowned Institut für Fenstertechnik (Institute for Window Technology) in Rosenheim.

In the modern parts of the facade metal windows are installed which were also designed as box windows. The external casements have single glazing and as a rule steel frames. The air space between the exterior and interior casement is back-ventilated towards the outside. Incorporated at a height of 180 millimetres are gaps for intake and exhaust. Here, the inner casement also provides thermal insulation and has a triple-pane thermal insulation glazing with infrared reflective coating and a gas filling. The windows have a low U_W-value of 1.1 W/m²K.

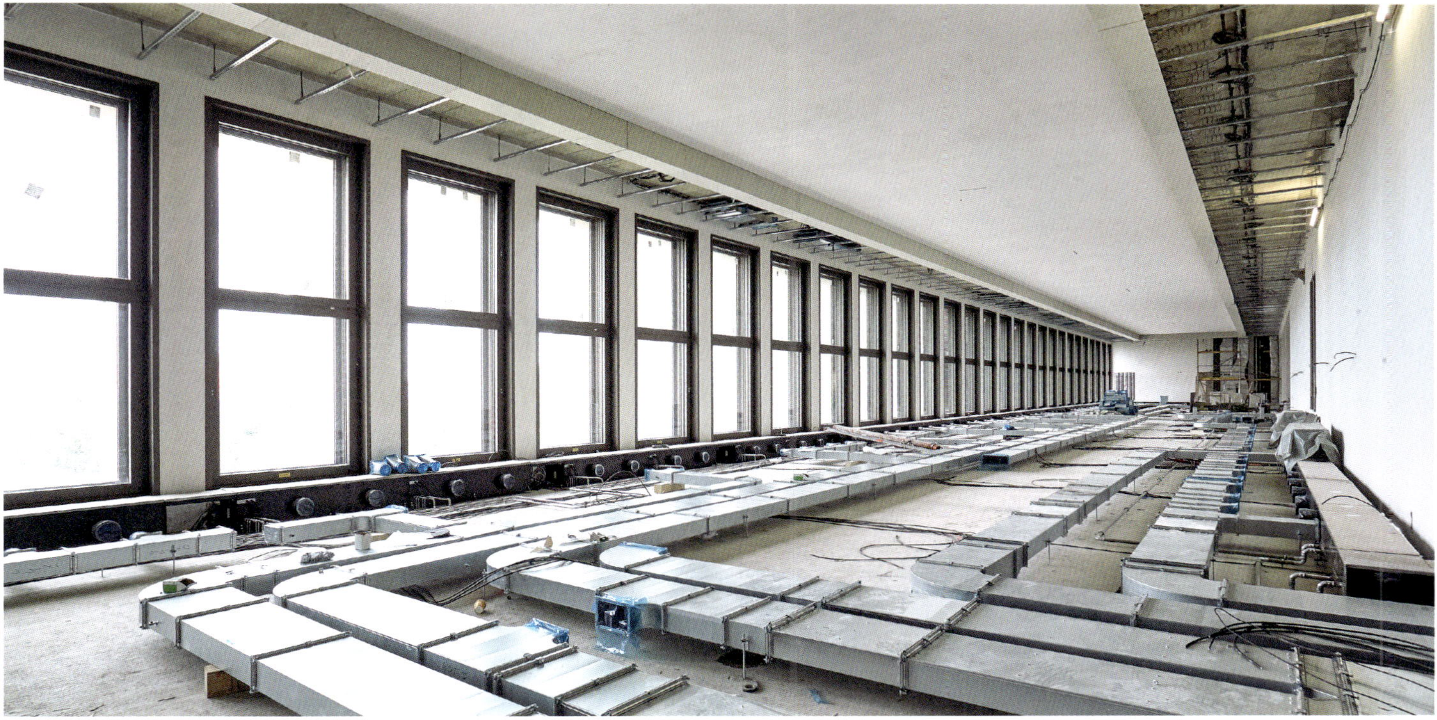

Sustainability, Energy Concept

In building the Humboldt Forum, it was not solely a question of reinserting the Berlin Palace into the urban environment, but also of constructing a building that amply satisfies the demand for sustainability. Here, sustainability is grounded in particular in ecological factors, cost-effectiveness and sociocultural aspects. Regarding cost-effectiveness, it is worth noting that the planned building costs were adhered to – taking inflation into consideration. For the most part, good construction management succeeded in compensating for the rising building costs that emerged during the seven-year construction period. Requests for bids for individual technologies took maintenance costs into consideration as well as investment costs. This made economical operating costs possible as well.

In a building with high demands for climate control, the energy budget plays a substantial role alongside cleaning costs. For this reason, the energy concept was the centrepiece of sustainable building planning. The entire building was calculated according to the German Energieeinsparverordnung (Energy-Saving Ordinance, EnEV) of 2009. Primary energy costs are at least thirty percent below the maximum permissible level. This was achieved first of all through structural insulation that is substantially superior to the value of the reference building of the EnEV 2009. Secondly, heating is supplied for the most part by district heating. The source is the Heizkraftwerk Mitte in the immediate vicinity, whose high efficiency makes it one of the most modern gas and steam turbine power stations in Europe.

In addition to the use of district heating, geothermal energy found near the earth's surface is used for heating purposes as well. In the middle of Spree Island, the hydrogeological conditions of the subsurface are opportune for the use of geothermal energy. The system concept incorporates the use of the subsoil as alternating charged thermal storage. This means that thermal loading in summertime and heat withdrawal in wintertime are equalized in the annual balance. This allows the expense

Rooms in the 3rd upper storey, east facade, installation of the technical equipment (including air supply ducts, electrical and media cables, which are accommodated in the cavity floor)

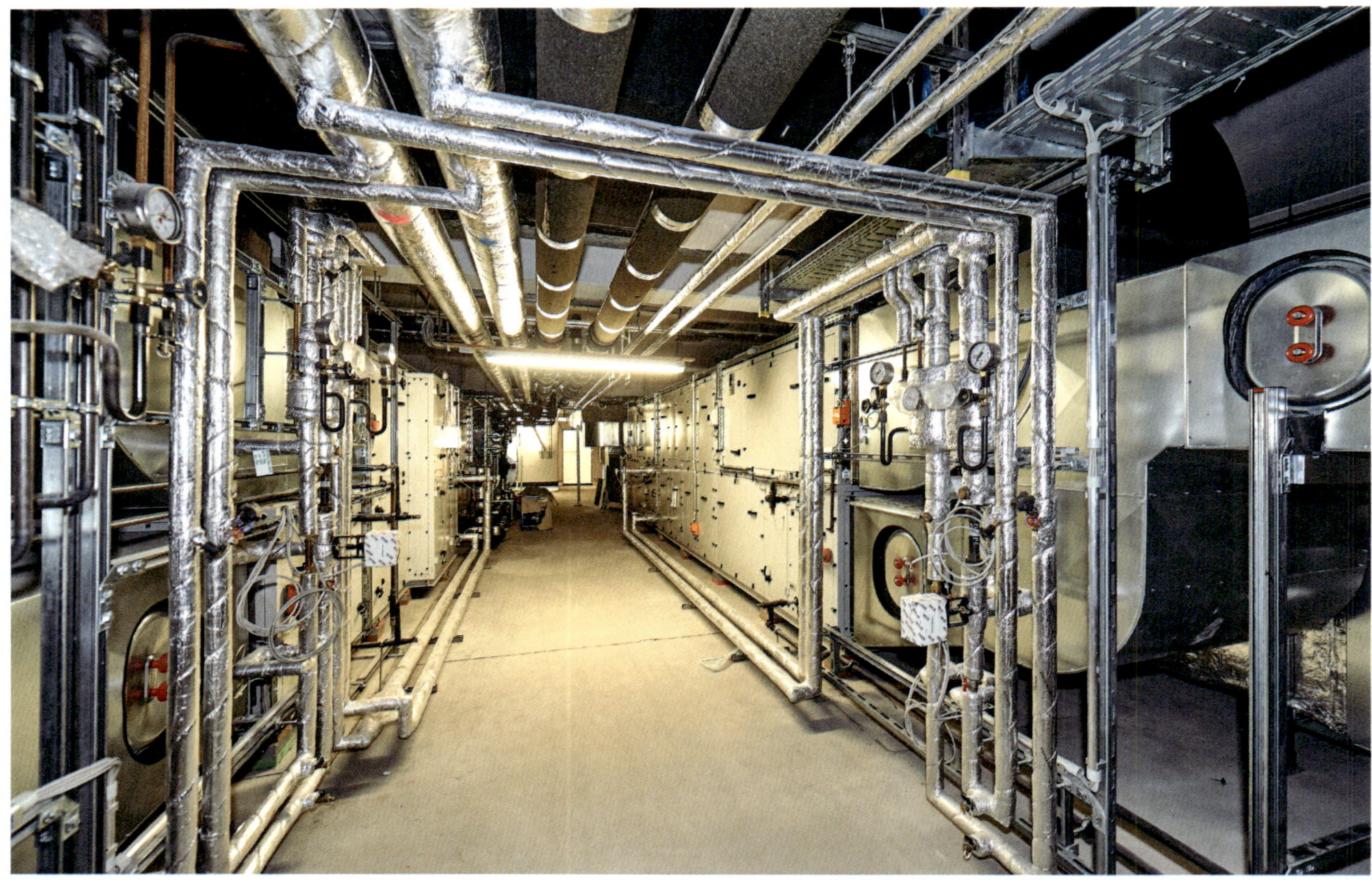

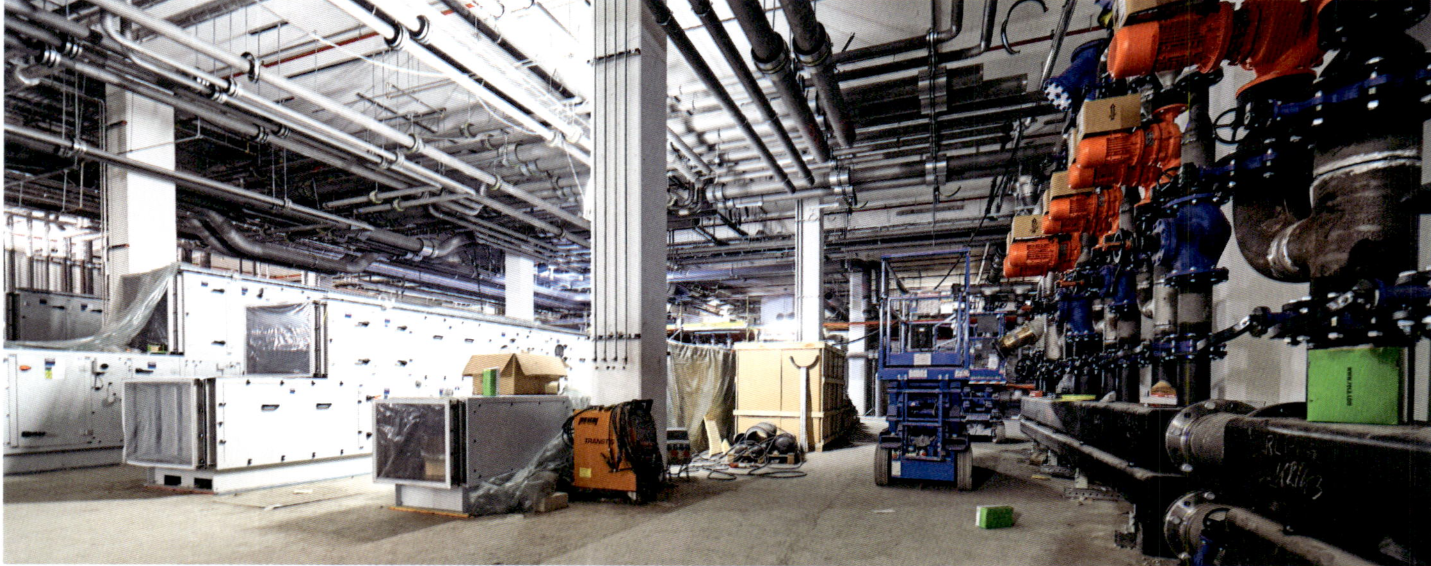

Climate technology for the
museums in the attic storey

Technical centre in the basement

of compression refrigeration for the permanent load to be reduced. Two earth probe fields (115 geothermal heat probes with a depth of about 100 metres in the southern part of the Lustgarten) have been opened up to the north of the building and 54 foundation piles (about forty metres in depth) activated.

Our museum conservators insist upon strict standards for ventilation and air-conditioning technology in the exhibition galleries, which are designed to ensure that the highly sensitive exhibits of both main users, the Ethnologisches Museum and the Museum für Asiatische Kunst, are preserved for posterity. Temperatures in the galleries cannot be allowed to rise above 25° C, with a maximum relative air humidity of 52 percent, with a maximum tolerance of +/- 3 percent and a tolerance for internal temperature of only +/- 1 Kelvin. Due to the reduced transmission heat loss achieved by the energetically efficient outer wall and the windows, it is almost exclusively internal heat loads that are decisive. Hence, during exhibition opening hours, a 'cooling problem' exists year-round. Installed as a sustainable solution to this problem was what is called a building component activation. This means that the ceiling is cooled via small water mains in the concrete ceiling, which in turn cool the ambient air. Additional cooling is provided by incoming air from floor intakes.

Deployed for the additional optimization of cooling processes are heat exchangers (on the roof) using adiabatic evaporation-based cooling. The hybrid construction is necessary so that the refrigerating machines can operate at peak summer temperatures without output losses. Installed for the additional safeguarding of cooling for museum areas and to reduce peak electricity demand in the Humboldt Forum was an ice storage unit.

Sustainable building also means satisfying socio-cultural requirements. One of these aspects is handicapped accessibility. In accordance with current regulations, all parts of the building open to the public are completely barrier free. At the same time, special concepts have been developed for the exhibitions. A tactile guidance system leads to all highlights. Touch-based displays allow visually impaired visitors to experience the exhibitions and the building itself. The visitor guide is also available in simple language and in sign language. Altogether 75 percent of the areas designated as workstations are also handicapped accessible.

The safety and security of both visitors as well as the cultural treasures stored here are of the utmost concern to the Humboldt Forum Foundation in the Berlin Palace. Comprehensive safety, fire protection, evacuation and emergency concepts have been developed and fully implemented. The security control centre of the building is staffed around the clock. In constructing the building, the use of fire-safe materials was given the highest priority.

Modern building technologies and a convincing architectural and technical concept will contribute to making a visit to the Humboldt Forum a memorable experience.

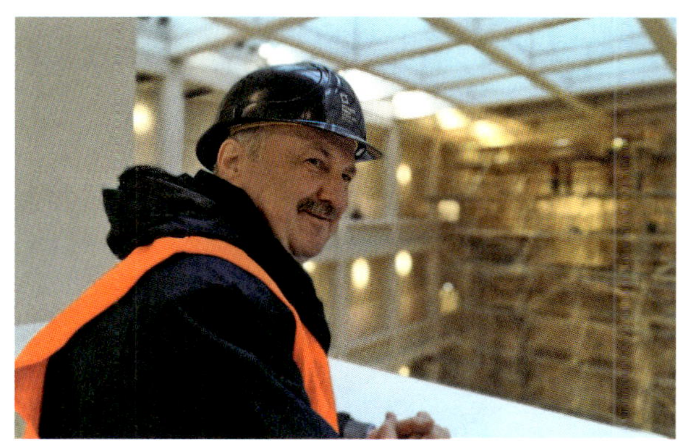

Hans-Dieter Hegner

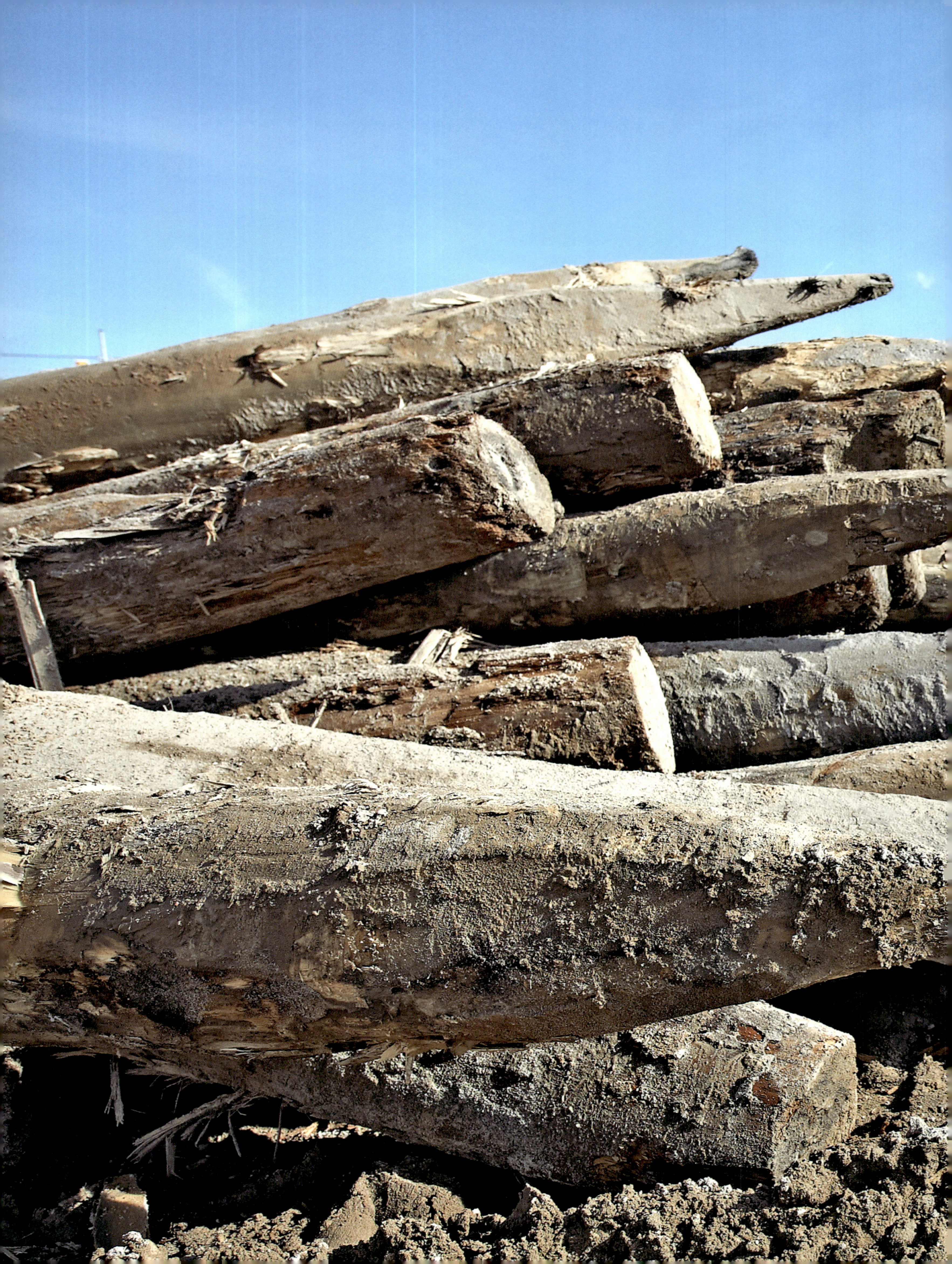

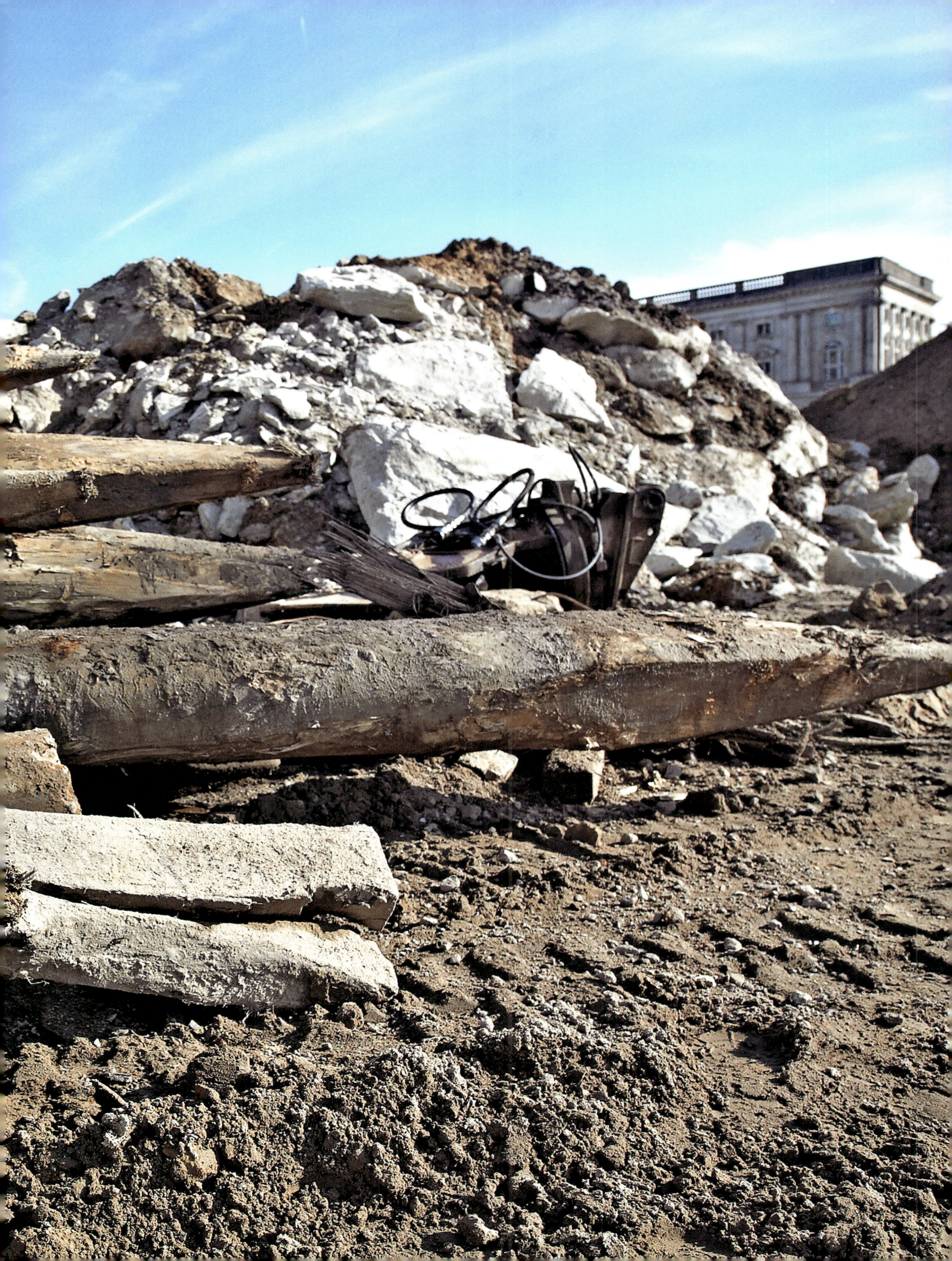

Fig. pp. 142–143:
The sight of these oak posts is
almost reminiscent of Caspar David
Friedrich's *Das Eismeer* (*The Sea of
Ice*): they are the 300-year-old tree
trunks Schlüter had rammed into
the earth by the hundreds for the
foundation of the Mint Tower.

The posts were pulled one by
one from the muddy ground of
the building site like teeth. They
would have been too close to the
underground tunnel for the new U5
Line which runs diagonally beneath
the Palace. Visible at the centre
of the image is the Humboldt Box,
a privately financed marketing
initiative whose roof featured a large
panoramic terrace.

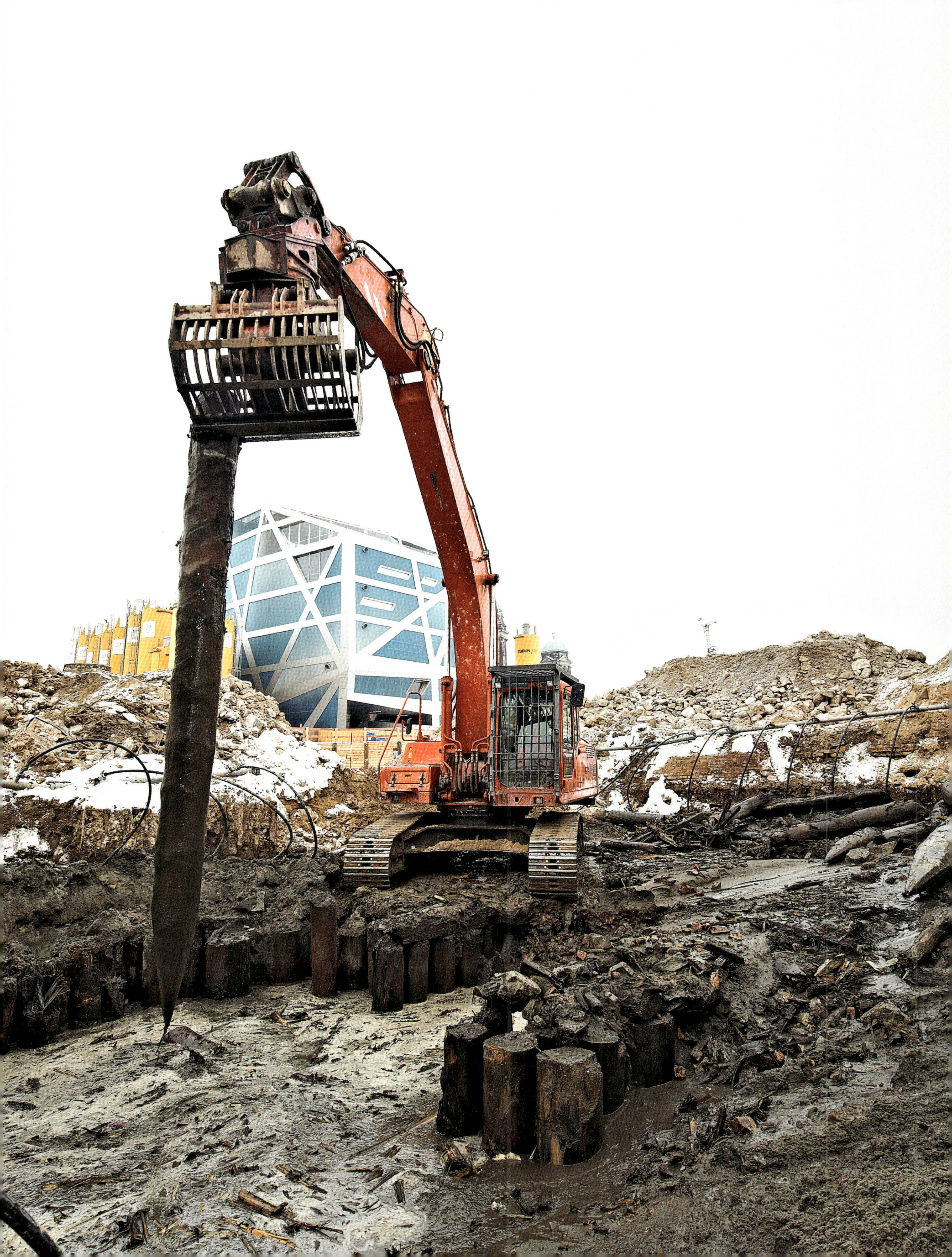

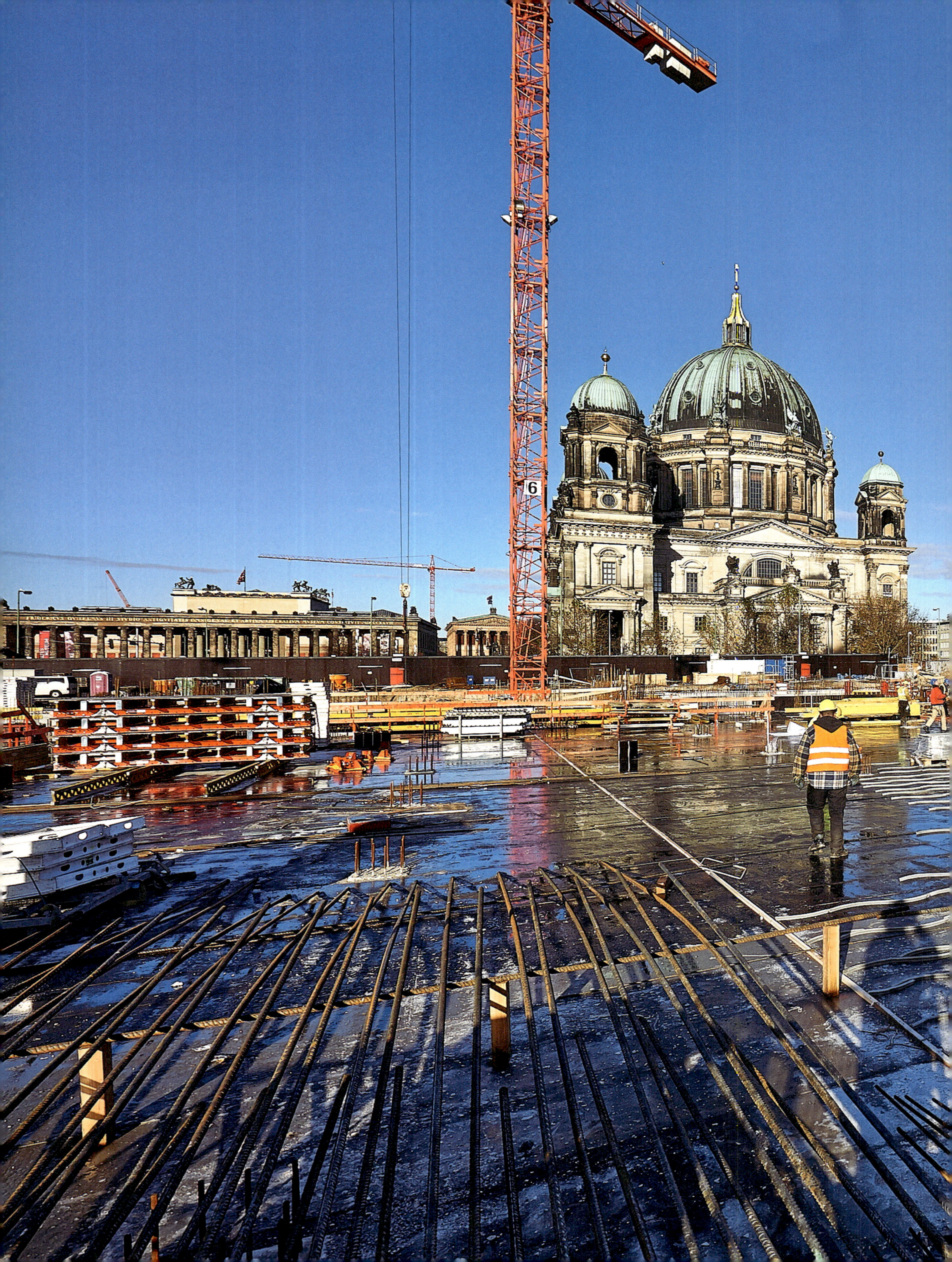
6

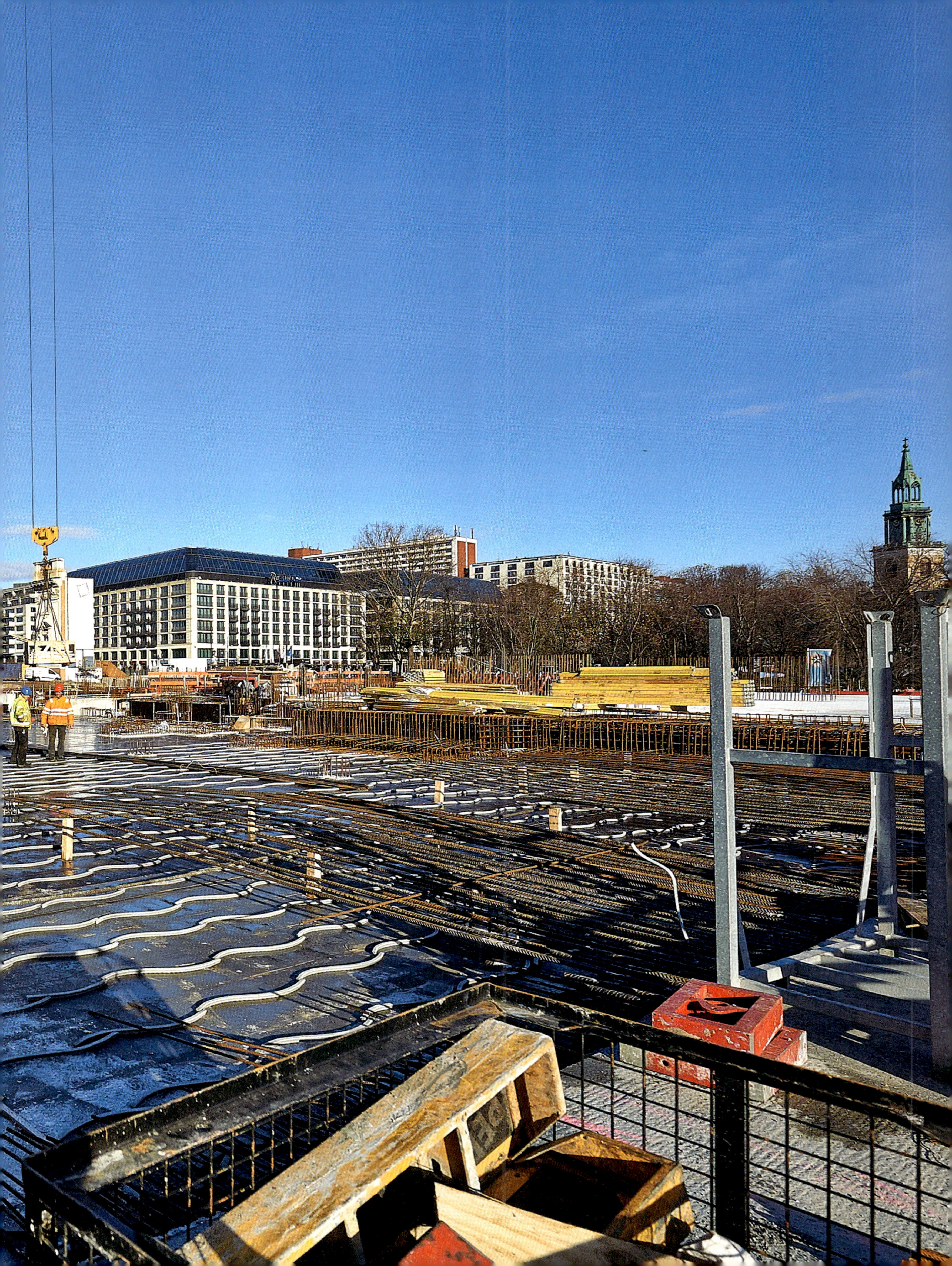

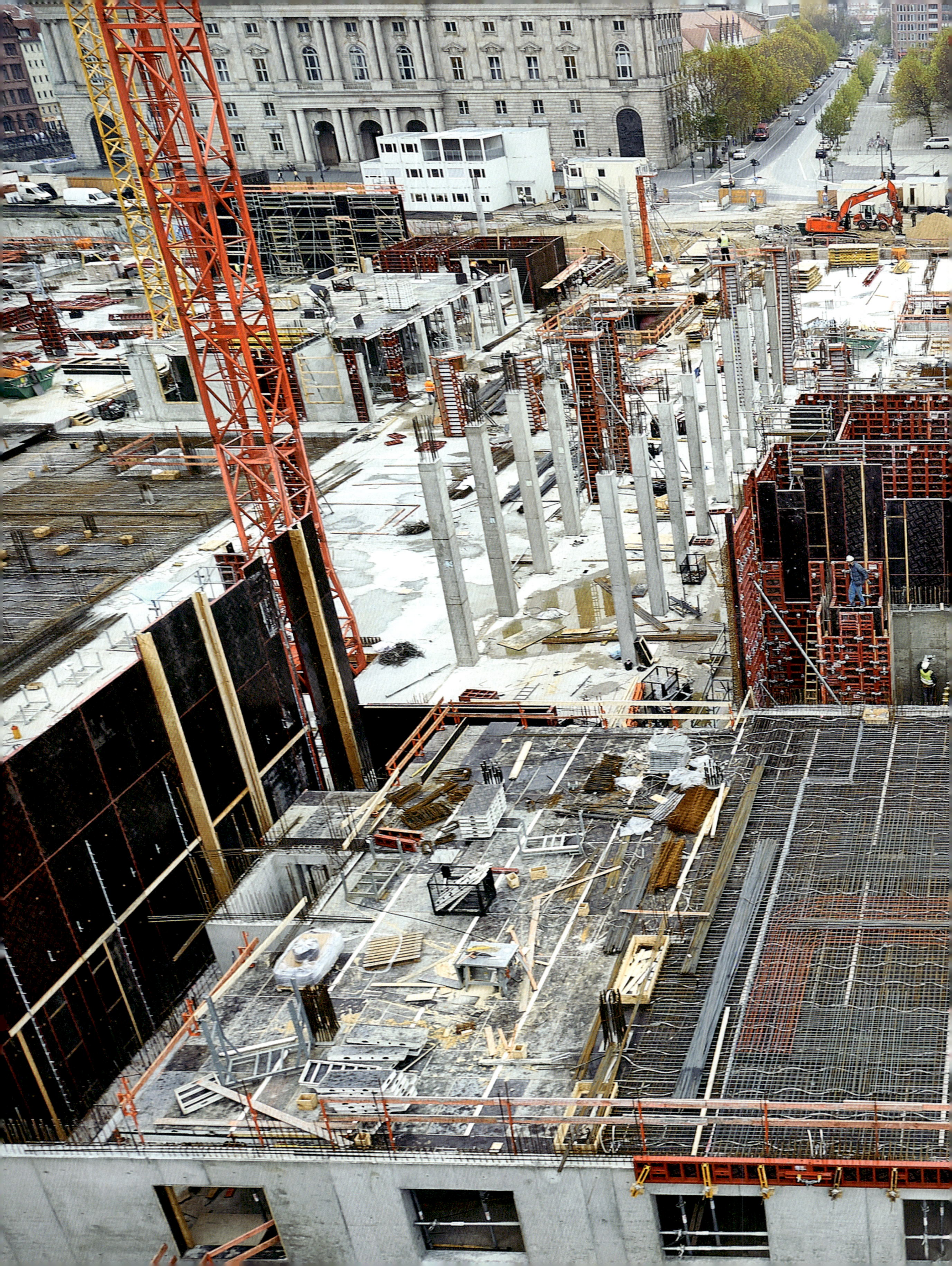

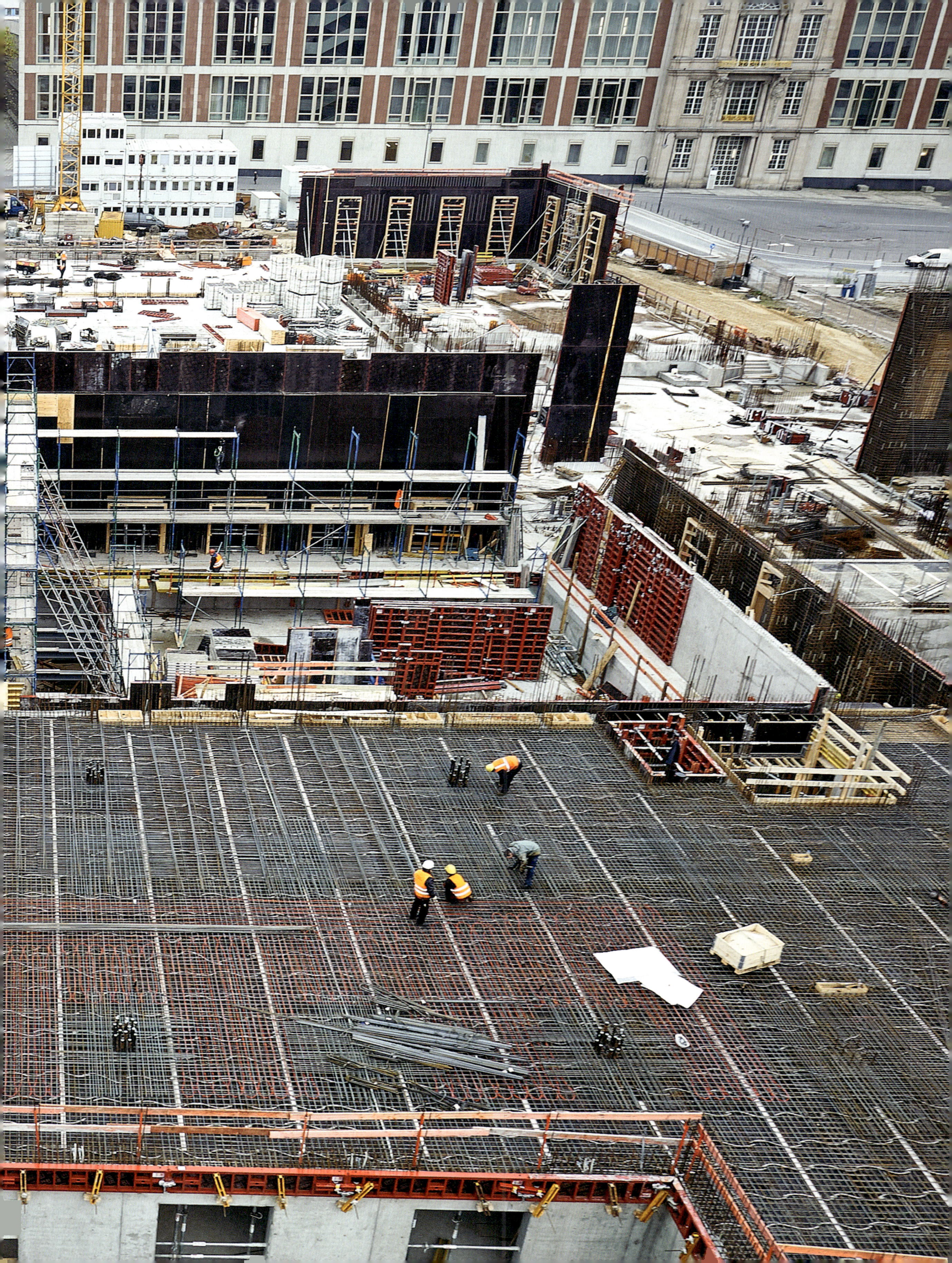

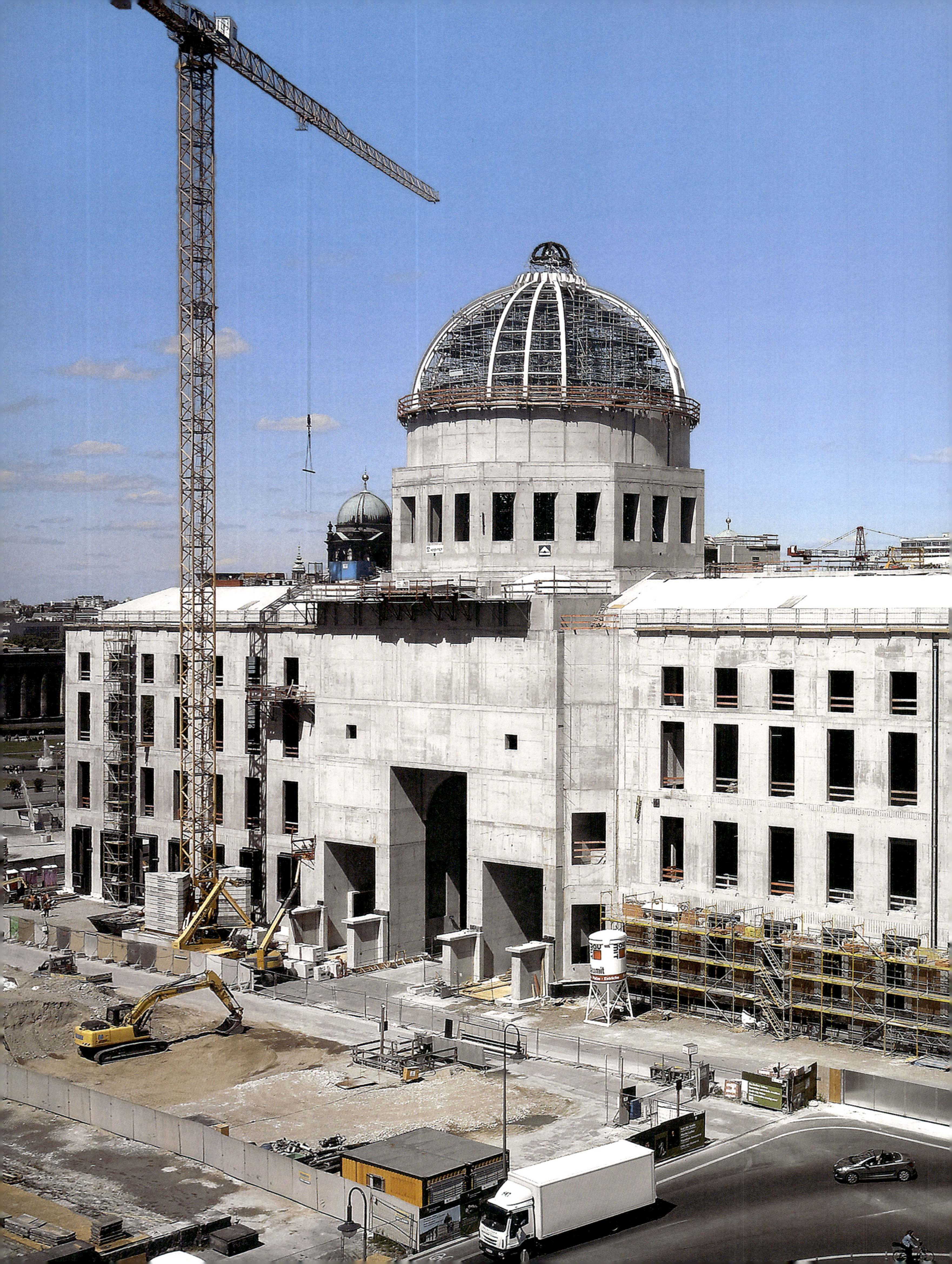

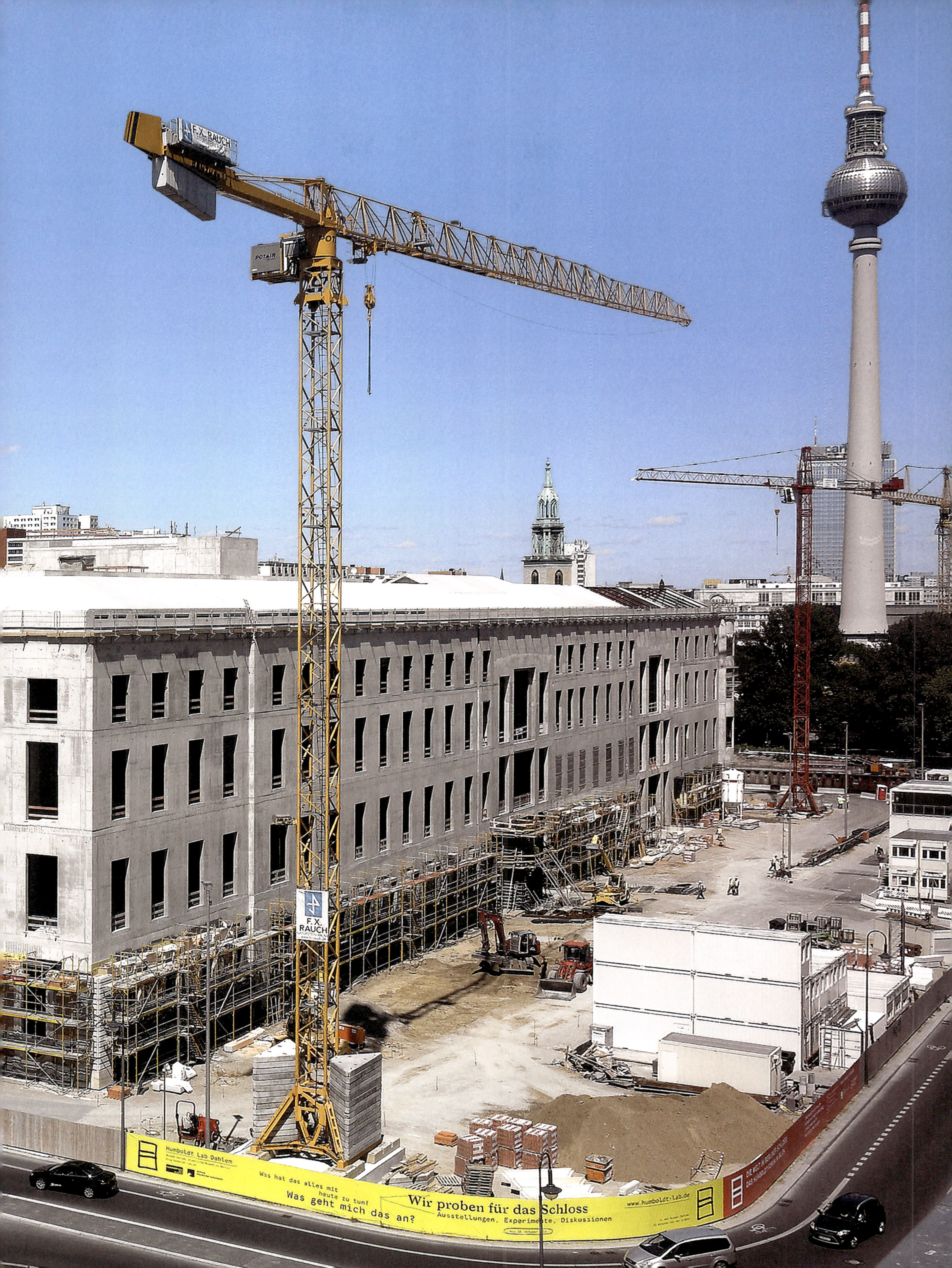
F.X. RAUCH
POTAIN
F.X. RAUCH
Humboldt Lab Dahlem
Was hat das alles mit
heute zu tun?
Was geht mich das an?
Wir proben für das Schloss
Ausstellungen. Experimente. Diskussionen
www.humboldt-lab.de

Fig. pp. 146–147:
In November, just half a year after
the laying of the foundation stone,
the basement ceiling was concreted.
Visible in the image is the Schlüter
Courtyard, with its full basement
level, which accommodates delivery
and warehouse facilities, as well as, in
the basement as a whole, the building
services for the ground floor and the
1st upper level.

Fig. 148–149:
In late 2013, the construction site
resembles a large puzzle – one that
excites admiration for the planning
and coordination brilliance of the
architects and engineers. Visible in
the background of this view of the
western part of the building are the
former Marstall (Stables) and the
Staatsratsgebäude (State Council
Building).

Fig. pp. 150–151:
June 2015: an impressive site: the
shell construction with the topping-
out wreath above the partially
assembled steel structure of the
cupola. On the ground floor level,
work has already begun on the
60-cm-thick masonry wall, which
rose freestanding independently of
the reinforced concrete structure.

The interior of the Palace cupola was
once occupied by Stüler's Palace
Chapel. In the reconstruction, a
prominent exhibition space, the 'Cave
of the Sword Bearers', belonging to
the Museum für Asiatische Kunst
(Museum of Asian Art), was installed
there beneath the 14-meter-tall
vaulted false ceiling.

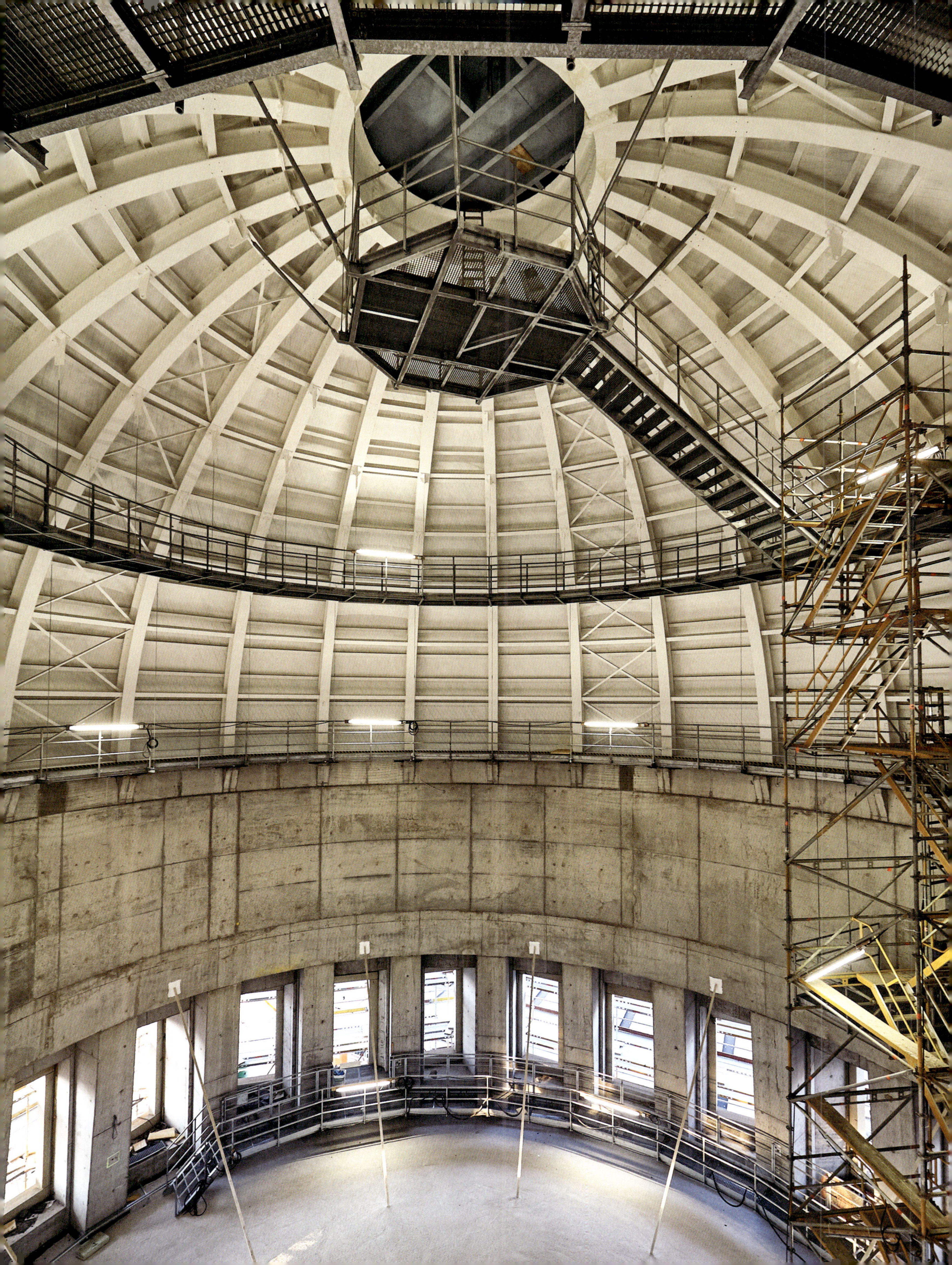

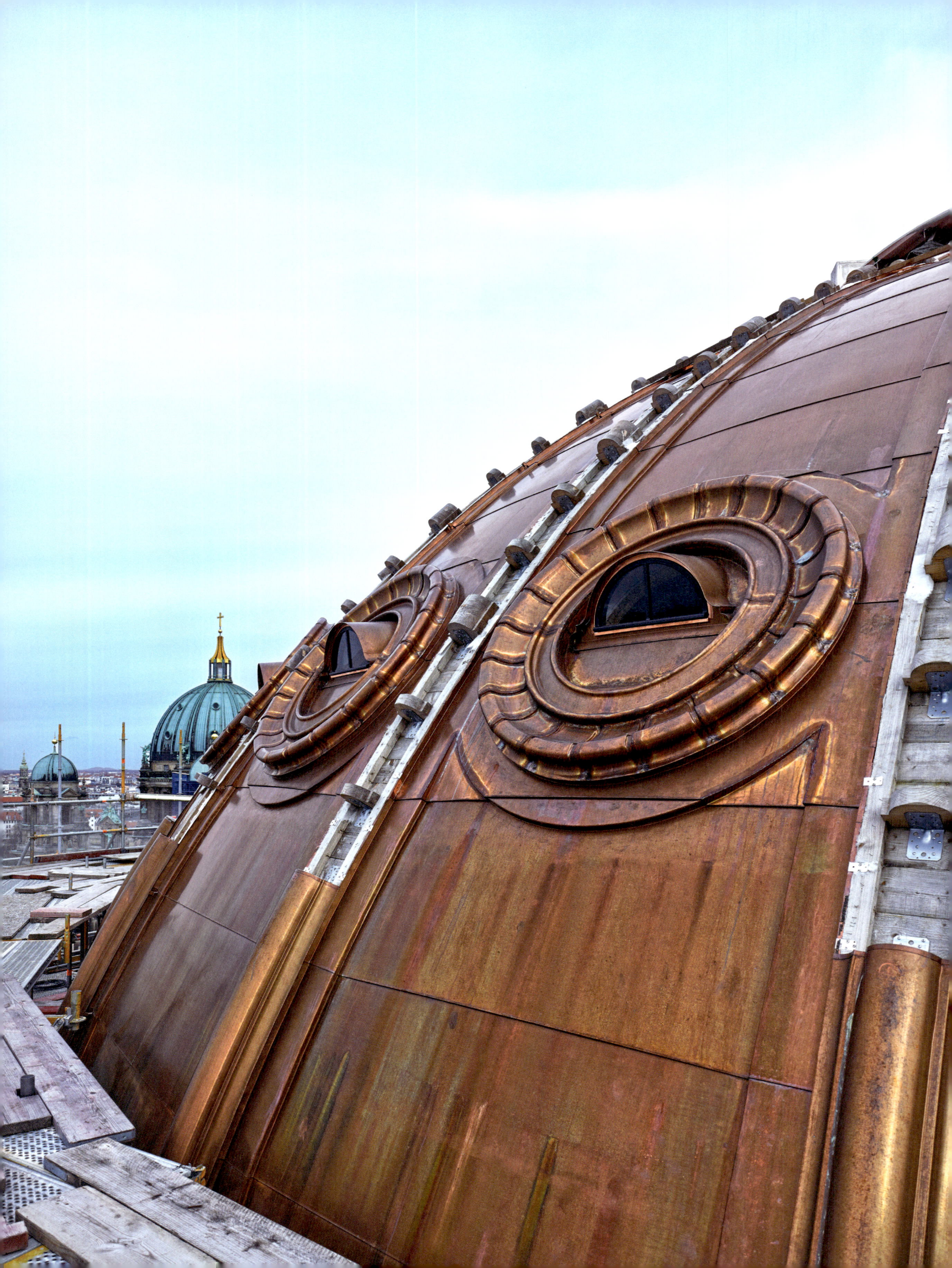

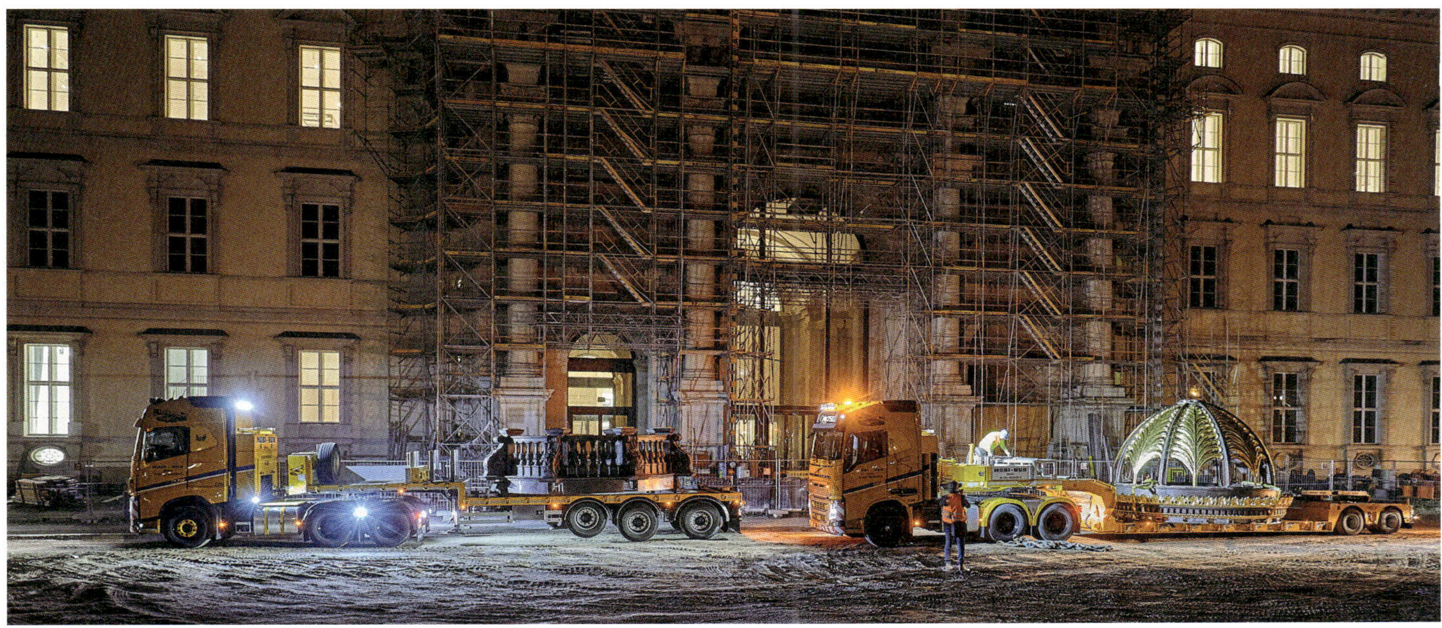

During months of manual labour,
the tinsmiths of a small Thuringian
workshop artfully clad the cupola
with the copper elements
prefabricated in the workshop. It
will take another generation before
it acquires a dark green patina.

Fig. above and figs. pp. 156–157
After two years of building activity,
the assembly of the lantern and
cross on the cupola required a full
day's work. Only during the evening
hours of 29 May 2020 did a gigantic
truck crane position the jewel-like
ornament atop the 60-meter-tall
Palace cupola.

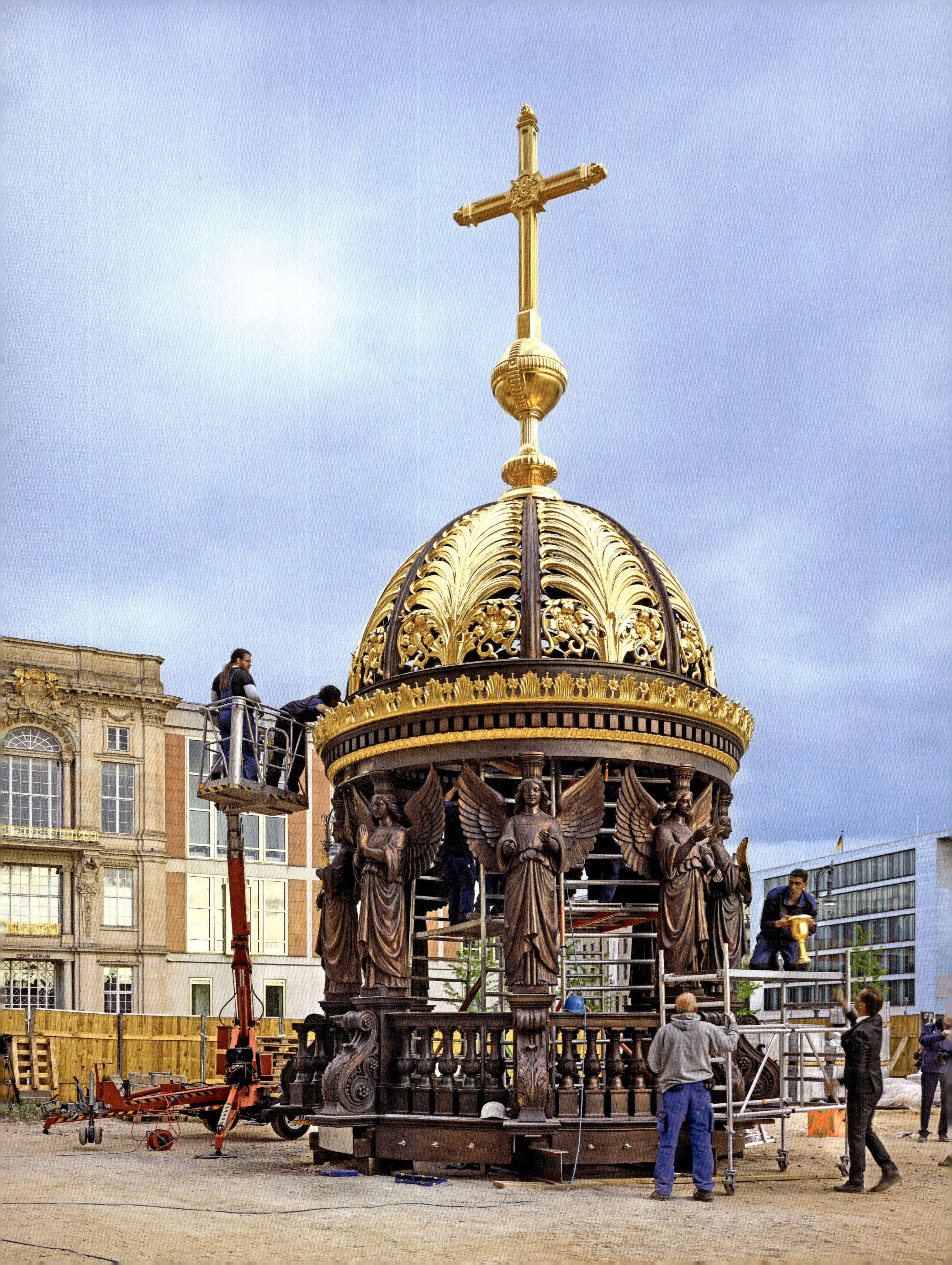

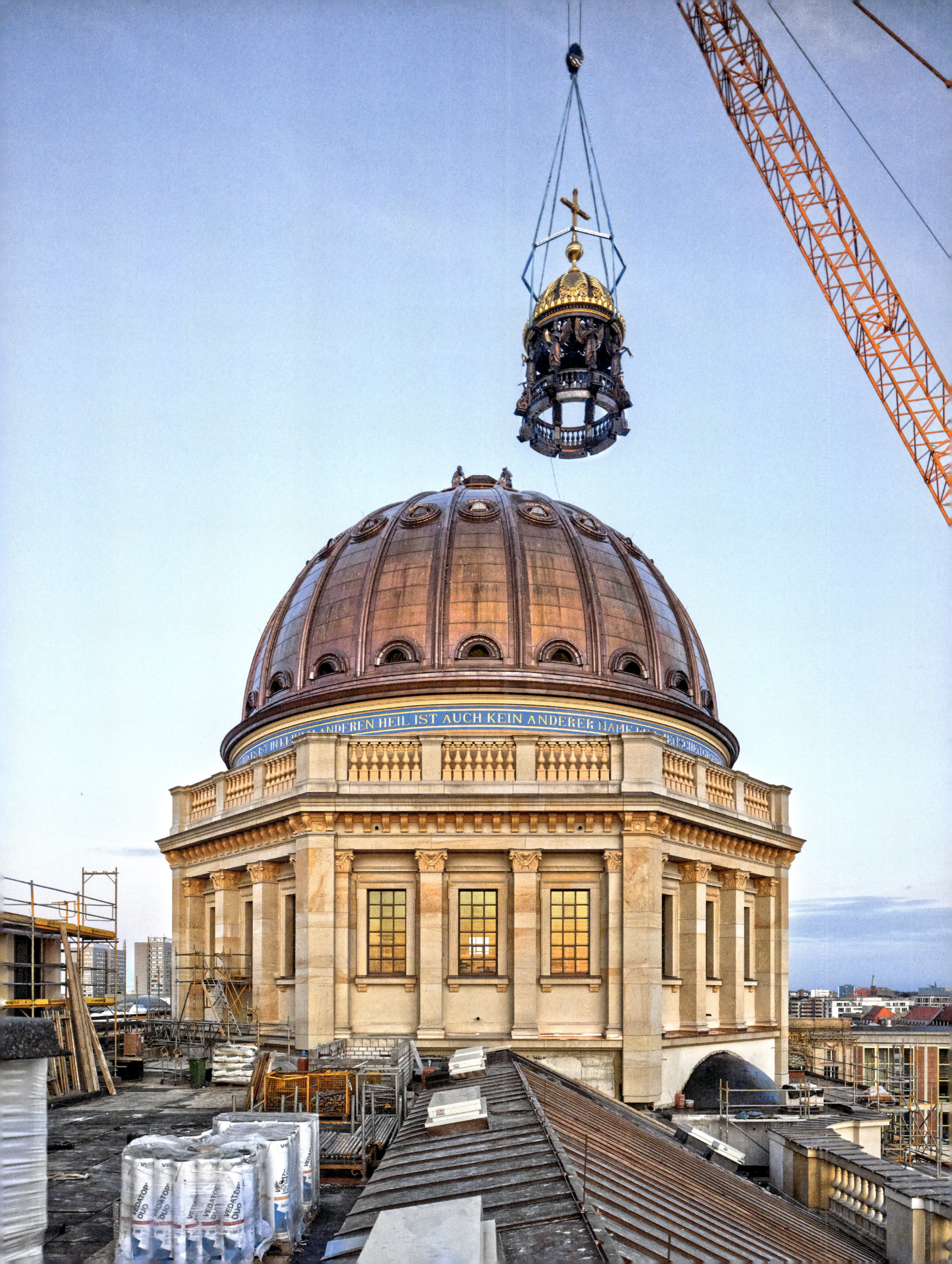
ANDEREN HEIL IST AUCH KEIN ANDERER NAME

During construction of the shell,
traditional masonry work displayed
its full artistry in the fashioning of
the conches here in the passageway
of Portal 5 – with a view towards the
Schlüter Courtyard.

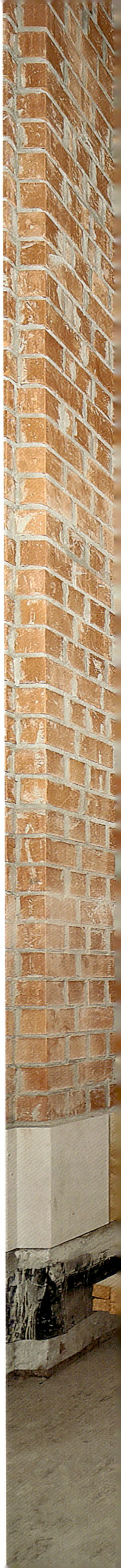

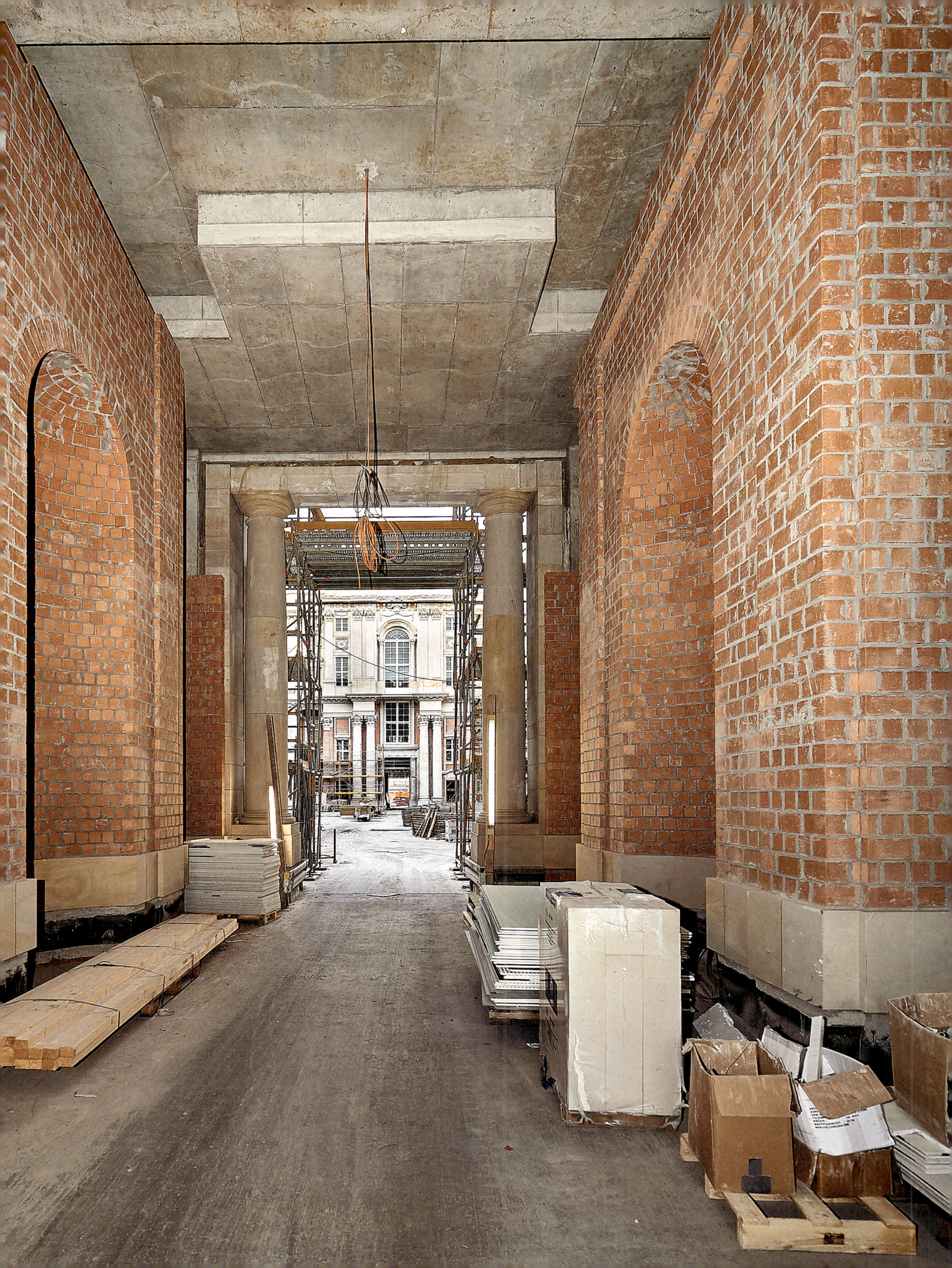

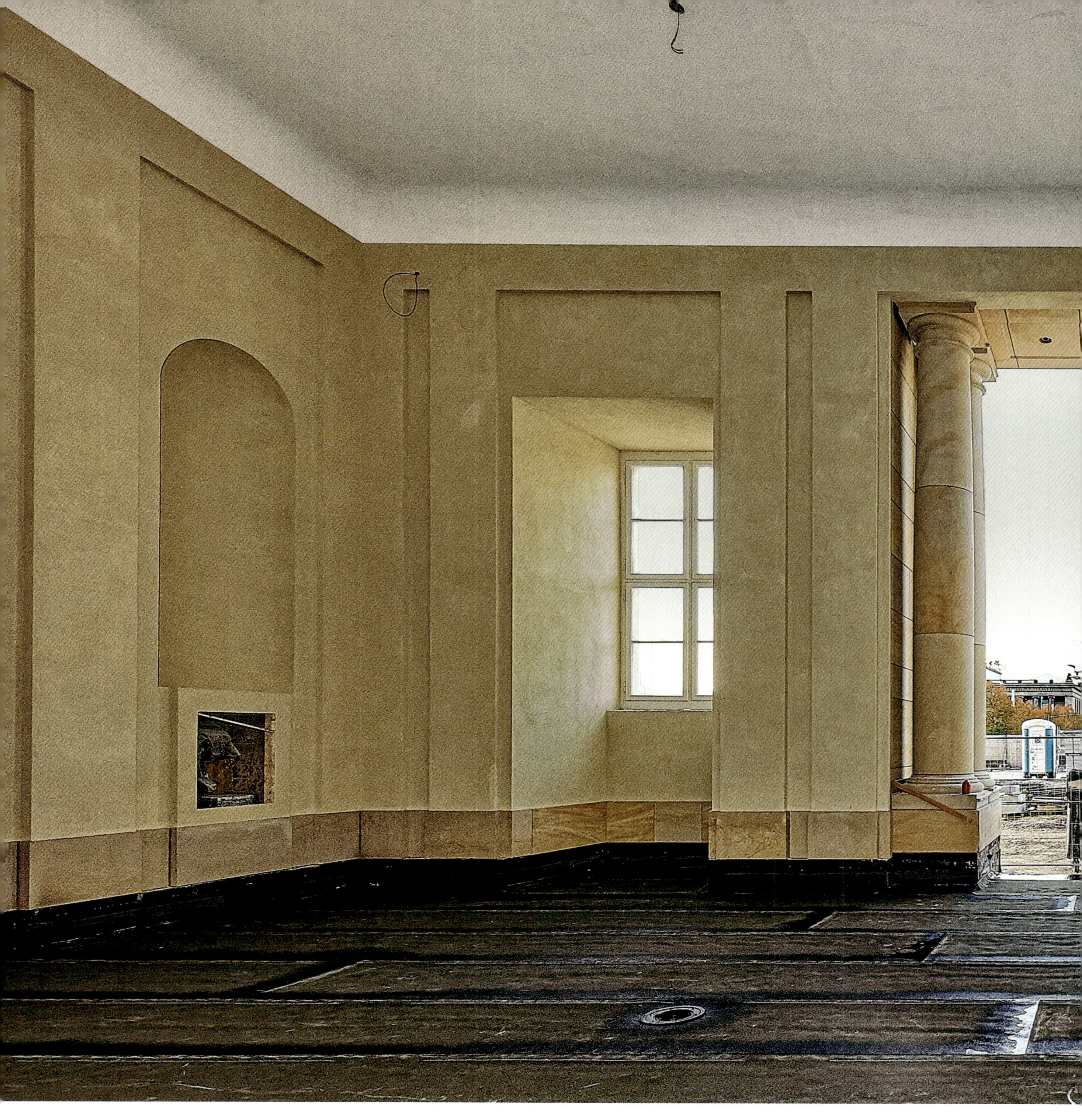

After the application of plaster, but prior to surfacing, the outer area of the passageway of Portal 5 already suggests the future elegance of this entryway to the Schlüter Courtyard.

Fig. pp. 162–163:
The high requirements of the curators for constant air temperature and humidity in the museum areas demand a climate technology and building services that occupy the entire attic storey as well as large areas of the basement level. Seen here are two central air conditioners in the basement level.

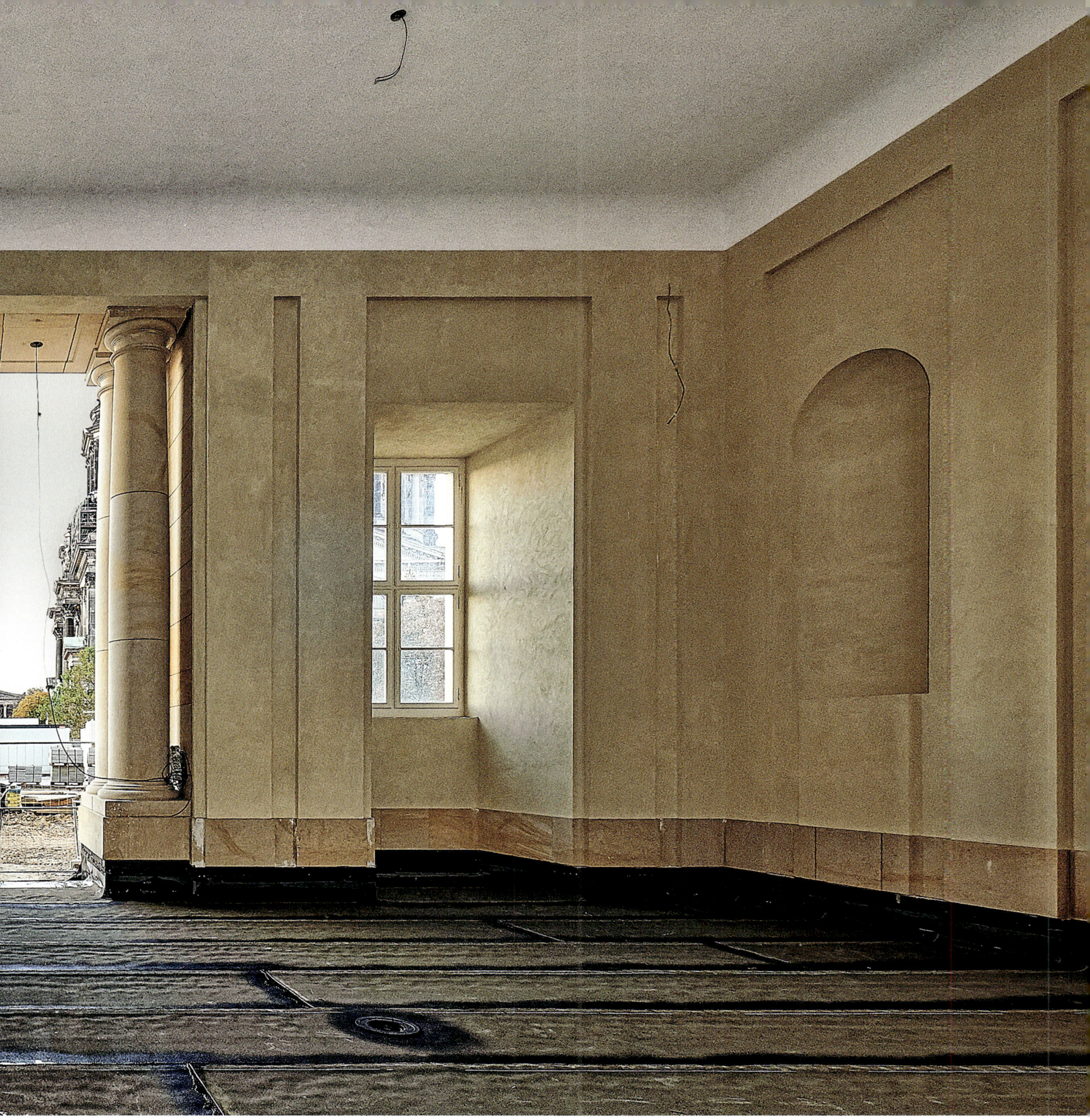

This blue monster is an emergency power diesel engine that ensures that 'the lights in the Humboldt Forum will not go out' during a power outage. Electricity for the Humboldt Forum comes from certified green energy, about 22.5 million kilowatt hours annually; this corresponds to the usage of approximately 7500 four-person households. The building therefore exceeds targets for the energy savings regulations adopted by the Federal State of Berlin by 30 percent.

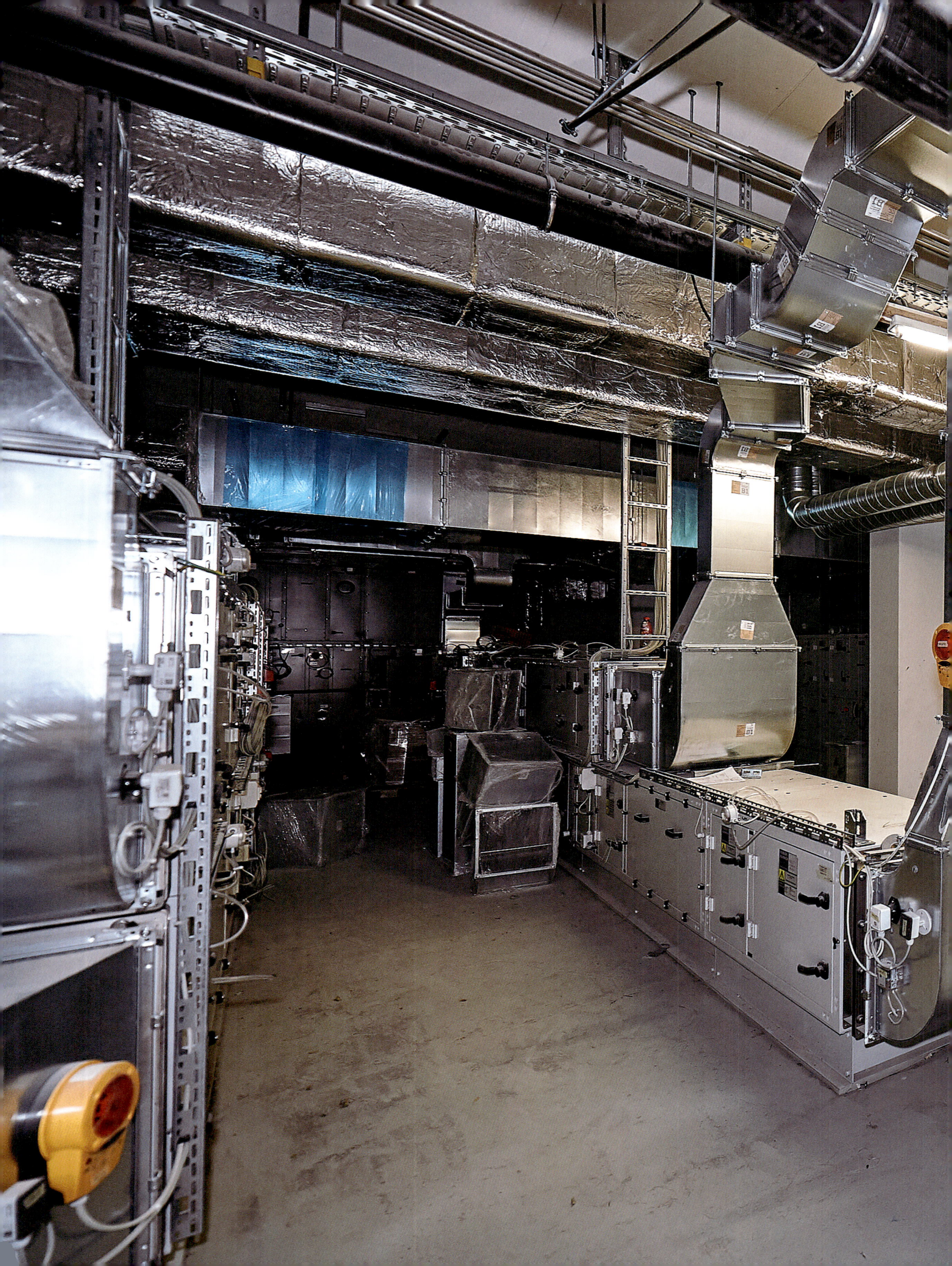

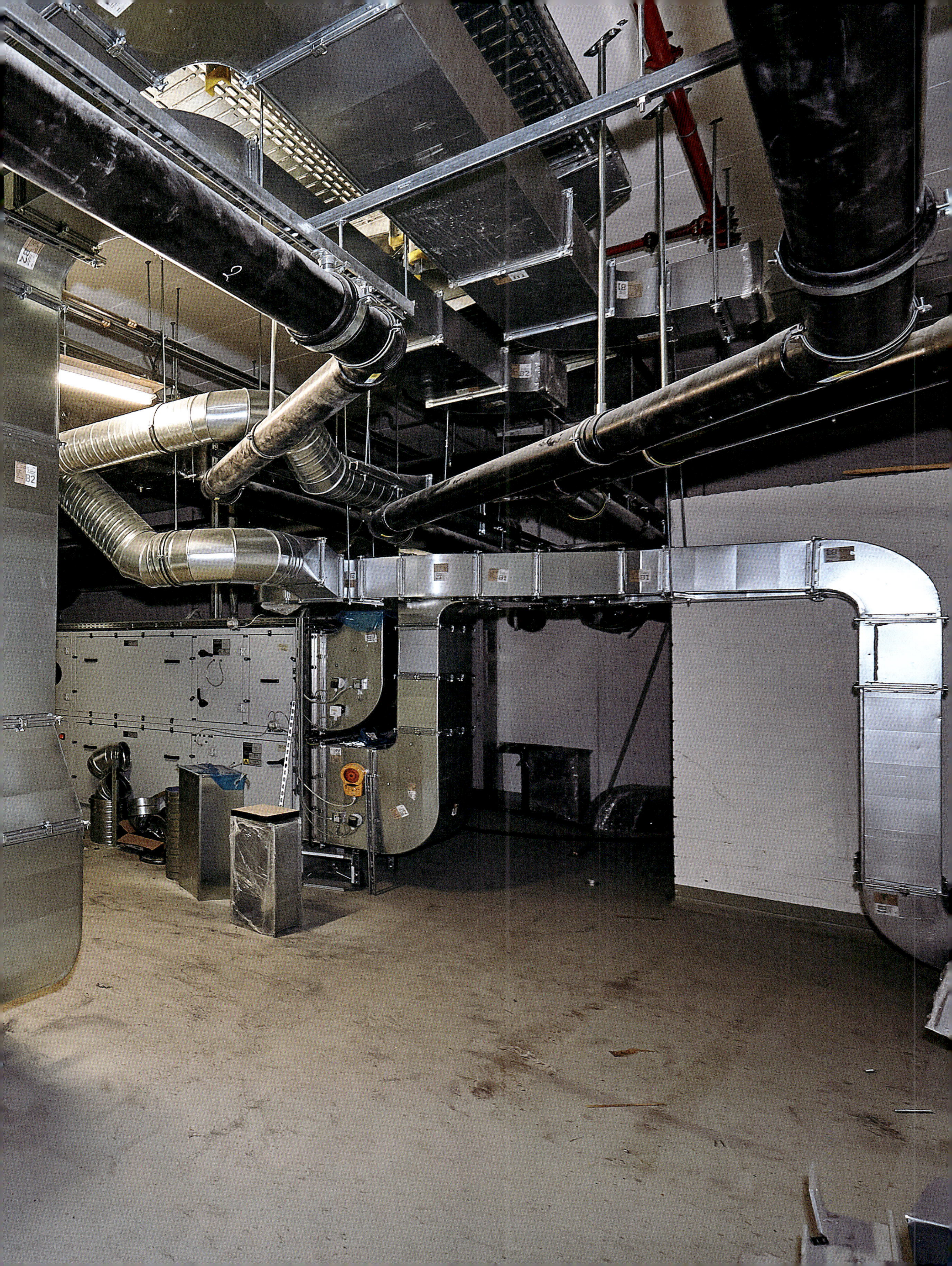

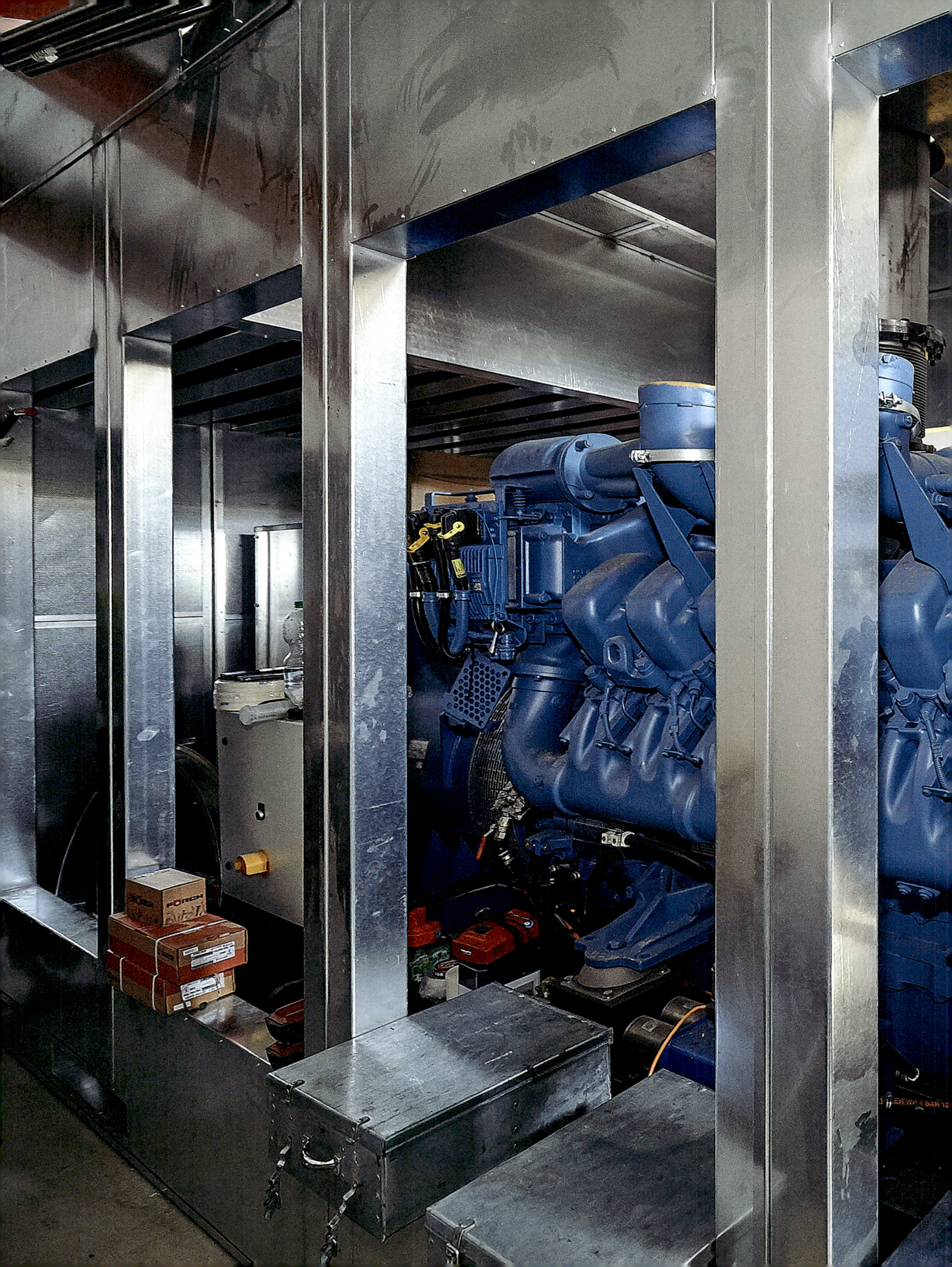

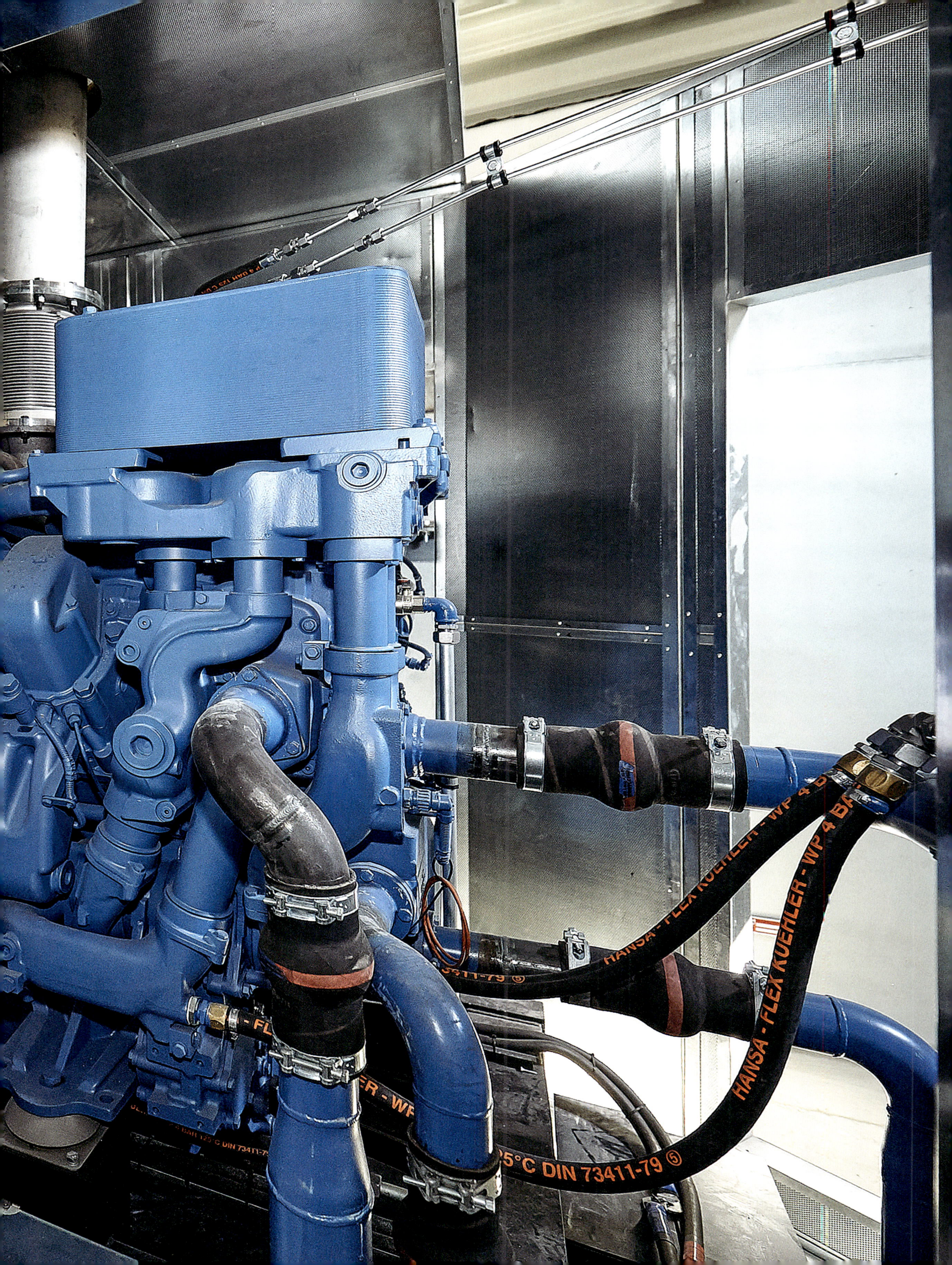

HANSA · FLEX KUEHLER · WP 4 BAR
°C DIN 73411-79
DIN 73411-79

Cultural Management through Collaboration between Institutions

*An Excursus by
Johannes Wien*

Considerably more than 1000 people will work in and for the Humboldt Forum. Whether in services, at information desks, as exhibition security, leading guided tours or seminars, or in housing technology or gastronomy: a large team is required to ensure that everything functions, that visitors feel comfortable. Responsible for cultural and technical operations is the Stiftung Humboldt Forum im Berliner Schloss (Humboldt Forum Foundation in the Berlin Palace), which receives support from its subsidiary, the Humboldt Forum Service GmbH, and other actors. All of the things that visitors are meant to experience as self-evident and unobtrusive require the background presence of a highly professional and discriminating management team. Over the past few years, this infrastructure, too, needed to be constructed.

On 4 July 2002, when the members of the German Bundestag voted across party lines in favour of the partial reconstruction of the Berlin Palace and for its utilization as the 'Humboldt Forum', they ended years of controversy about the development of the historical centre of the German capital. For most of the decision-makers, urbanistic and architectural topics stood in the foreground. Far less was said about the building's envisioned use, although early on it was clear that several cultural and educational institutions would work closely together here. The relocation of the Ethnologisches Museum (Ethnological Museum) and the Musum für Asiatische Kunst (Museum of Asian Art), formerly located in Dahlem, emerged as winning ideas. And the spacious event area, initially called the 'Agora', which Franco Stella had conceptualized in concrete terms in his successful competition entry of 2008, was initially more an idea then a fully fleshed out event organization.

In 2009, a new player joined the Staatliche Museen (State Museums of Berlin) of the Stiftung Preussischer Kulturbesitz (Prussian Cultural Heritage Foundation), the Humboldt Universität zu Berlin and the Zentral- und Landesbibliothek Berlin (Central State Library). Functioning ever since as the owner and future operator has been the Stiftung Berliner Schloss – Humboldt Forum (Berlin Palace Foundation – Humboldt Forum), established by the Federal Government as a non-profit foundation under public law, with one half of the land donated by Berlin. It was created in particular

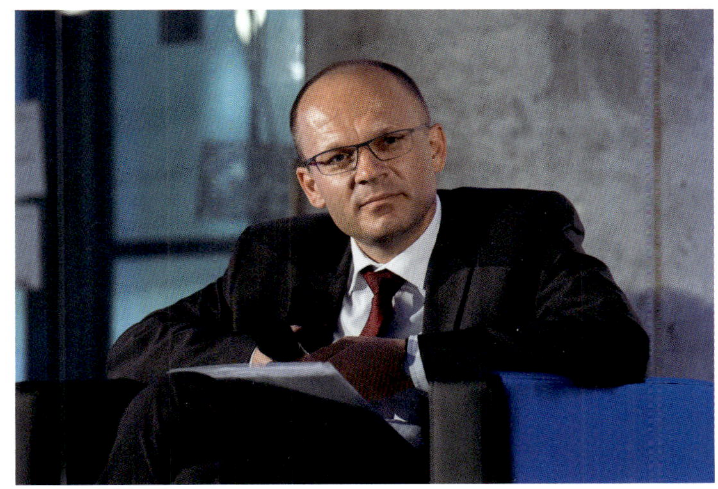

to function as the construction client, and was responsible for compliance with the building budget plan and timetable. Moreover, working together with the association of friends Förderverein Berliner Schloss e.V. (Association Berliner Schloss e.V.), it raised the more than 100 million euros in private donations that were needed for the project. For a long time, many people failed to realize that the Foundation was created as a new cultural facility, and was not simply a 'construction foundation' dedicated to the realization of the building itself. For with respect to tax law, all donations for the historical facade were classified as contributions to provide the current cultural utilization with a suitable and worthy architectural frame. The Foundation therefore plays an important and active role when it comes to the cultural utilization of the Berlin Palace, in particular with regard to the history of the site.

In the year 2016, a number of events set the stage for the forms of cooperation found today at the Humboldt Forum. Berlin once again reconsidered its plans and resolved to present itself, alongside the Humboldt Universität, through the Berlin Exhibition of the Stadtmuseum Berlin (City Museum of Berlin). Meanwhile, a different solution was found for the Zentral- und Landesbibliothek (Central State Library). This resulted in considerable changes to the utilization concept. Through the appointment of the renowned founding directorate, overall curatorial responsibility was placed in the hands of Neil MacGregor, Hermann Parzinger and Horst Bredekamp. They went to great lengths to develop a cultural programme that would harmonize the interests of all participants. They were supported in their efforts by the Humboldt Forum Kultur GmbH as the subsidiary of the construction client, which was renamed Stiftung Humboldt Forum im Berliner Schloss (Humboldt Forum Foundation in the Berlin Palace). In the further course of the extensive and highly complex technical planning, it became increasingly evident that an independent operational organization would be necessary for the Humboldt Forum. Subsequently, the Foundation assumed overall responsibility for the cultural and technical operations of the Humboldt Forum.

Since then, the interaction between the various cultural facilities has been organized productively and on a cooperative basis. Through a long-term license agreement between the Humboldt Forum Foundation in the Berlin Palace and the Federal State of Berlin, the Humboldt Universität and the Stadtmuseum Berlin have practically become long-term tenants, and several cooperative agreements now exist between the Stiftung Preussischer Kulturbesitz (Prussian Cultural Heritage Foundation) and the Humboldt Forum Foundation. The thematic programme, along with educational and outreach offerings, and even some ideas for the books, games and fan merchandise available in the shop, emerge only when all of the participating institutions work together in concert. Here the jointly prepared mission statement for all staff members has proved extremely helpful. A central aspect for us is the prioritization of services. Our own service company, the Humboldt Forum Service GmbH, forms the linchpin of the entire operation.

Developed under the umbrella brand the 'Humboldt Forum', and with support from the German Federal Government and the Federal State of Berlin, a cultural management organization is emerging that facilitates the realization of the ideas of the various protagonists, thereby ensuring that a visit to the Forum is a very special experience for guests from both near and far. As was already the case in the old Berlin Palace as well as in the Palace of the Republic, today this still requires well-coordinated and committed teamwork between many different actors.

How are the Stiftung Humboldt Forum, the Staatliche Museen zu Berlin, the Humboldt-Universität zu Berlin and the Stadtmuseum Berlin joining forces here?

Three Questions to Four Protagonists: Hartmut Dorgerloh, Lars-Christian Koch, Gorch Pieken and Paul Spies

Lars-Christian Koch, Hartmut Dorgerloh, Gorch Pieken, Paul Spies (from the left)

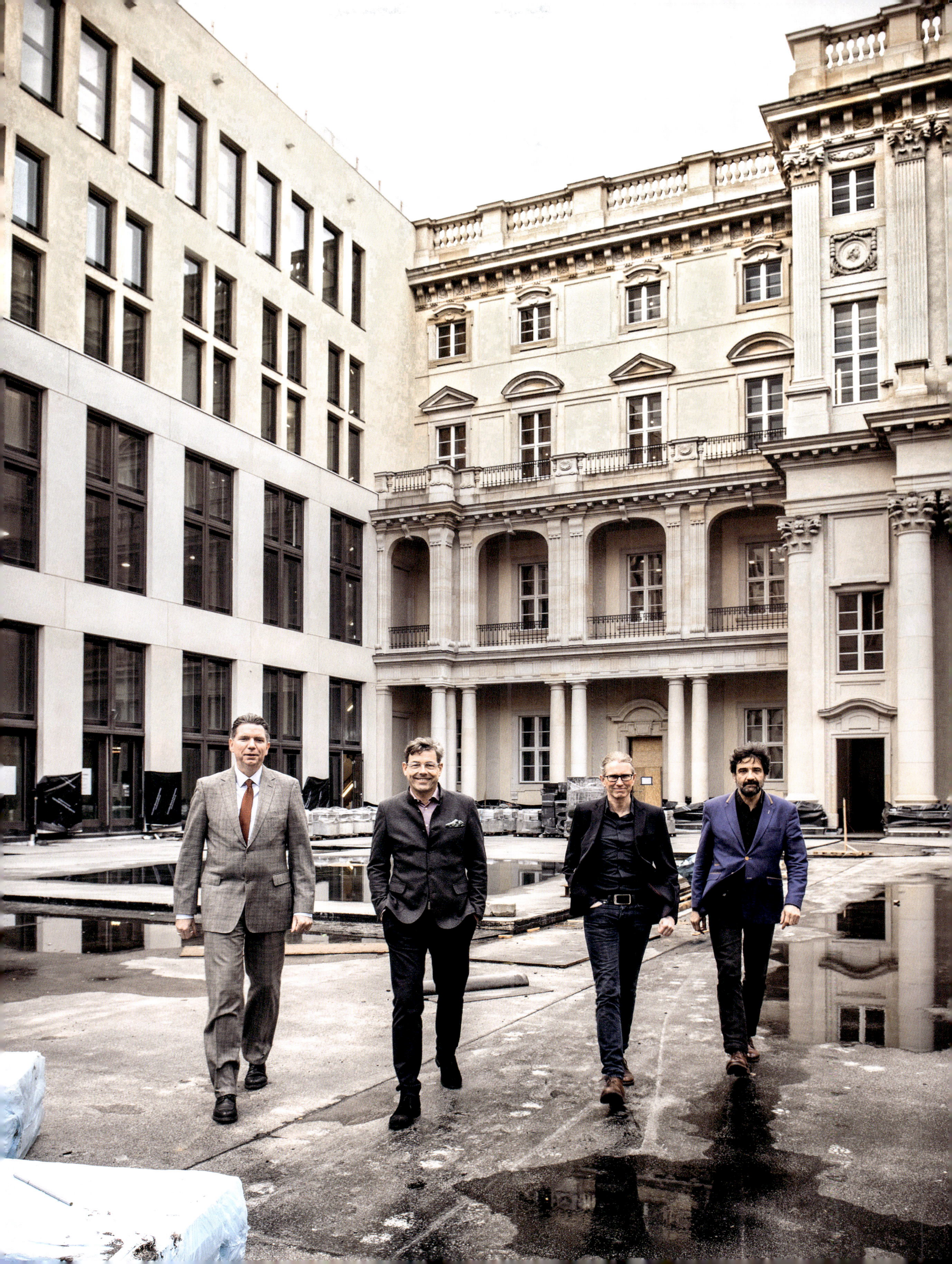

For you personally, what is the greatest attraction of participating in the Humboldt Forum?

Hartmut Dorgerloh: Both personally and professionally, my biography is closely bound up with Berlin and Brandenburg, from pivotal life experiences related to the Berlin Wall and its fall, all the way to my intense preoccupation with the monuments and the cultural landscape that is found between the rivers Oder and Elbe, in particular the palaces and gardens of the Hohenzollerns. In this context, I have been consistently interested in how history is dealt with in various social systems, how it is interpreted, forgotten or made serviceable for other, new aims and purposes. Playing a central role here is our handling of the cultural heritage when it comes to the preservation of monuments, to urban planning, to museums and exhibitions, but also to gardens, which are not simply green spaces, but are also saturated with historical citations and messages.

And as we have learned from the debate about the reconstruction of the Berlin Palace, which has extended now across a quarter century, this process rarely proceeds without controversy and vigorous debate. Again and again, we realize that we are never free from history, that we cannot escape it.

In a place like Berlin in particular, it becomes strikingly evident just how multifarious the forms of appropriation, memory and confrontation with history are, and how many metamorphoses locales and buildings experience over time. The Berlin Wall, the Reichstag (parliament building) and the permanent exhibition 'Topography of Terror' are key examples of such places of memory, as Pierre Nora has called them.

Coming together, then, in the Humboldt Forum in the Berlin Palace are a number of these various elements: Berlin's history all the way from the medieval remains in the Archaeological Cellar to the new underground metro, which was drilled and constructed underneath and at the same time as our new building; Prussian history from the electors all the way to the last German emperor; revolutions and wars; celebrations and parades; debates about the reconstruction of the Palace; decisions about the former Palast der Republik (Palace of the Republic); and finally the question of the potential impact of this new urban quarter on the future development of the adjacent areas, for example on the Marx-Engels-Forum across the Spree.

The Berlin Palace was important as well for the history of science and culture. The history of museums and collecting in Berlin begins with the Kunst- und Wunderkammer (Chamber of Art and Curiosities) in the third upper storey, and after the demise of the monarchy, not just the Schlossmuseum (Palace Museum) and the Kunstgewerbemuseum (Museum of Decorative Arts) were accommodated here, but also pioneering scientific facilities, among them the university's Institute for Gestalt Psychology.

But I am fascinated not just by the question of how the Humboldt Forum can grapple with history, but also by the question of what new layer of meaning the Forum can add to this central location at the heart of the German capital. How can we ensure that the tension between the reconstructed

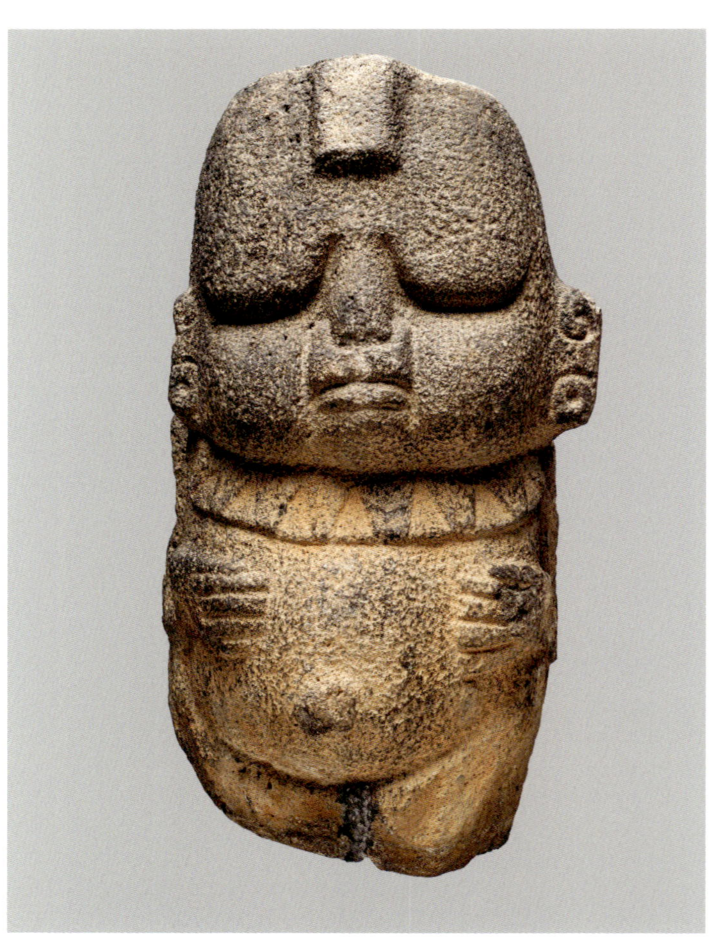

The Barrigón deity, Guatemala,
500–300 BC, Ethnologisches Museum
(Ethnological Museum)

facades and courtyards and the radical contemporaneity of the interior architecture and its functions becomes productive, both today and in the future, for as many people as possible, for the city, for the federal state? What is the potential for something new to emerge here, for example through a multiplicity of actors and their proposals? And what does it mean to be a forum in the twenty-first century? For me, this is a very exciting challenge.

Lars-Christian Koch: The historical and contemporary collections of the Ethnologisches Museum (Ethnological Museum) and the Museum für Asiatische Kunst (Museum of Asian Art) are moving to the very centre of Berlin, where they will be accessible to a broader public. In direct correspondence with the museums and collections on Museum Island, this results in a global perspective on the activities of the Staatliche Museen zu Berlin and of the Stiftung Preussischer Kulturbesitz (the Berlin State Museums and the Prussian Cultural Heritage Foundation).

At the same time, the 'historical' placement of the Humboldt Forum as a building, as a reconstruction of the Berlin Palace, makes the history of the collections of the Ethnologisches Museum and the Museum für Asiatische Kunst – assembled in part in colonial contexts – central to an important contemporary discussion. In a number of respects, these ongoing and emerging debates compel us to invent new ways of working with the collections, to make our own contribution to the reappraisal of European colonial history and to reflection on current postcolonial relations.

The singular constellation embodied by the Humboldt Forum as a consortium of a number of different museums, the Ethnologisches Museum, the Museum für Asiatische Kunst, the Stadtmuseum Berlin (City Museum of Berlin), as well as the Humboldt-Universität, is exciting in a number of respects. It is interesting in part because in some areas collections correspond to each other, for example in the field of audio-visual media. Here there are overlaps between the sound recordings owned by the Humboldt-Universität (Laut Archiv/Sound Archive) and those of the Berliner Phonogramm-Archiv (Berlin Phonograph Archive) in the Ethnologisches Museum. Between them, these collections and archives share the inventory of the Phonographic Commission, recordings that were made in German prisoner of war camps during World War I. The collection was already subdivided during the 1920s: the speech recordings are found today in the Humboldt-Universität, the music recordings in the Ethnologisches Museum. These collections have been digitalized and will be housed together, along with their accompanying documents, in the Humboldt Forum, where they can be appraised jointly by scholars from a number of different fields, becoming the subject of refocused research activity.

Things are similar with the holdings of the International Institute for Traditional Music (IITM), established in 1963 and in operation until 1996. Subsequently, the sound recordings,

photographs and other documents were relocated to Bamberg University, and were transferred back to Berlin in 2008. They are now housed in the media department of the Ethnologisches Museum. Captured by the sound recordings and photographic documents are important aspects of cultural life in Berlin during the Cold War. These collections will also be transferred to the Humboldt Forum, where they can be researched jointly and made accessible to the public.

Gorch Pieken: In December of 2017, when Sabine Kunst, President of the Humboldt-Universität zu Berlin, asked me whether I would curate the exhibition of the Humboldt-Universität in the Humboldt Forum, I agreed without hesitation. The possibilities and potentials of the Humboldt Forum are simply too tempting to resist – even for a fan of the old Palace of the Republic, which I am.

The Humboldt Forum offers an ideal frame for creating an exhibition 'for all' – something regarded in museum circles as extremely difficult, if not simply unattainable. As a rule, museums appeal to delimited target groups, not to everyone, although that is actually their goal. Only around fifty percent of the German population, and not all of our guests from abroad, visit museums.

But the Humboldt Forum is not a museum. And although museums will occupy parts of the Humboldt Forum, it is actually a conference centre, art gallery, university campus, laboratory, salon, speaker's corner, gazebo, dance stage and palace of culture, all in one. The Humboldt Forum is to become an integrated culture machine in the spirit of the great exhibition magician Pontus Hultén, the founding director of the Centre Pompidou in Paris, and will offer an overarching perspective that spans the continents, from art to politics, and all the way to ethnology. With highly diverse categories of visitors and a common core set of visitors, a group that takes an interest in the new architecture of the palace facades and the wide-ranging events programme.

During the daytime, and on some nights as well, the Humboldt Forum will be transformed into a social sculpture made up of people who stroll and muse, dream and reflect, dispute, demonstrate, eat and drink. This makes the Humboldt Forum an outstanding setting for the 'third mission' of science, namely – on the foundation of research and teaching (the 'first and second missions') – to have a profound impact on society by stimulating interest in – and even excitement about – science and scholarship among people with highly divergent origins and educational backgrounds.

That is the task of the Humboldt-Universität in the Humboldt Forum. It is not an end in itself. Access to science and scholarship must be opened up 'to all', hence also making a contribution to democratization and to the potentiation of scientific knowledge and scientific debate.

This is not just an exciting project, but a vital one as well, and one I have passionately enjoyed accompanying and helping to shape right up to the opening.

Paul Spies: It is a marvellous opportunity to display the networking of an urban community with the wider world in an exhibition – it is entitled BERLIN GLOBAL and was developed in cooperation with Kulturprojekte Berlin. Normally, a city museum focuses on local history and local events. But of course we realize that the history of a metropolis like Berlin has always been and remains strongly interconnected with world history. We are finally in a position to illustrate the ways in which a city, and in particular a capital city, can influence the world. Since the Humboldt Forum will be a venue for exhibiting world cultures, the obvious thing to do was to reflect in a concentrated way on such interconnections. In Berlin, people come together from all over the world. They come here to live, to work, to visit or to cultivate economic relationships. At the Humboldt Forum, we have an exhibition surface measuring 4000 square metres to address these multifarious connections. This represents a unique opportunity. Not to mention our prominent location at the centre of Berlin: for the director of a city museum, that is an opportunity that simply cannot be missed.

What exactly can visitors to the Forum expect?

Hartmut Dorgerloh: As the proprietor, the Humboldt Forum Foundation in the Berlin Palace is responsible for the operations of the Humboldt Forum, and one central aspect of this is the provision of excellent services to all visitors. Our guests are the core concern, and it is vital that they feel at home here, that they feel welcome, that they want to visit again. Solely by virtue of its size, the Humboldt Forum represents a gigantic adventure space with an equally variegated, wide-ranging programme. There are permanent exhibitions that can be visited regularly, but also continually changing temporary exhibitions and programme events, from children's workshops all the way to film screenings, from performances to hackathons. Attracting visitors as well are culinary offerings, all the way from the Schlüterhof to the roof terrace, with its spectacular views. Visitors may attend specific events, or take advantage of the educational offerings of the Academy, or instead simply browse the museum shops. The Humboldt Forum is designed to be an inviting place. But it is also intended to be a place that has an impact, that leaves a lasting impression when it comes to the way we see, think, understand and act. It strives to generate multiple trajectories between cultures, traditions and forms of knowledge, always in exchange with the wider world. That is the central idea of a twenty-first-century forum that functions as a common space for a highly heterogeneous visiting public, one that arrives here from every part of the world, and which ranges from children

from a local kindergartens all the way to specialists from overseas. For me, one of the most challenging, but at the same time most rewarding aspects is the task of bringing all of these elements together to form a whole that is composed of many different voices.

Lars-Christian Koch: On the one hand, there are the 'classical' exhibition areas and display collections, on the other hand, the possibility of a deepened interaction with contemporary questions about the collections, facilitated by comprehensive educational programmes and the presentation of the latest research results. At the same time, important parts of the collection are confronted with questions of current social relevance in the framework of temporary exhibitions, which are conceived in close cooperation with the Humboldt Forum Foundation. These activities, moreover, have an impact on the adjacent permanent exhibitions of the museums, which are thus continually kept up to date.

The presentation of intangible cultural heritage – in particular through the important collections of sound recordings, films and photos owned by the Ethnologisches Museum and Museum für Asiatische Kunst – is accorded a prominent status. The audio archive, for example, is presented in a special area and offers an exceptional auditory experience. The high density of media offerings leads to new structures of knowledge transfer, and offers the public deeper access to the collections. All of which is, of course, coordinated with an overarching events programme and with the public and scholarly exchanges taking place in the Academy.

Gorch Pieken: They can expect a world of shifting perspectives, where natural and social scientists from Europe and beyond as well as people with invaluable practical knowledge seek to come to terms with the theme of the exhibition: 'After Nature'.

The contributions of the researchers will be updated continually. The Humboldt Lab is not a museum, of course, we will not be installing a permanent exhibition in the Humboldt Forum. It is precisely this changeability that characterizes the Humboldt Lab – and science as well.

In the inaugural exhibition of the Humboldt Lab, we categorize all of the research we are presenting in relation to the history of science and to general history, and we interrogate every object with regard to its provenance and levels of meaning. Individual objects from the university collections hence become tokens for larger contexts. Objects do not simply exist; instead, we ascribe meanings to them. At the same time, they are always endowed with political significance as well – through material or intellectual appropriation, through the interpretation and seizure of reality.

Paul Spies: In our exhibition, visitors will experience Berlin in very different ways in each room – in particular, thanks to the spectacular interior design. Each room is devoted to a different theme: Thinking the World, Berlin Images, Revolution, Free Space, Boundaries, Entertainment, War, Fashion and Interconnection. As visitors encounter these different aspects

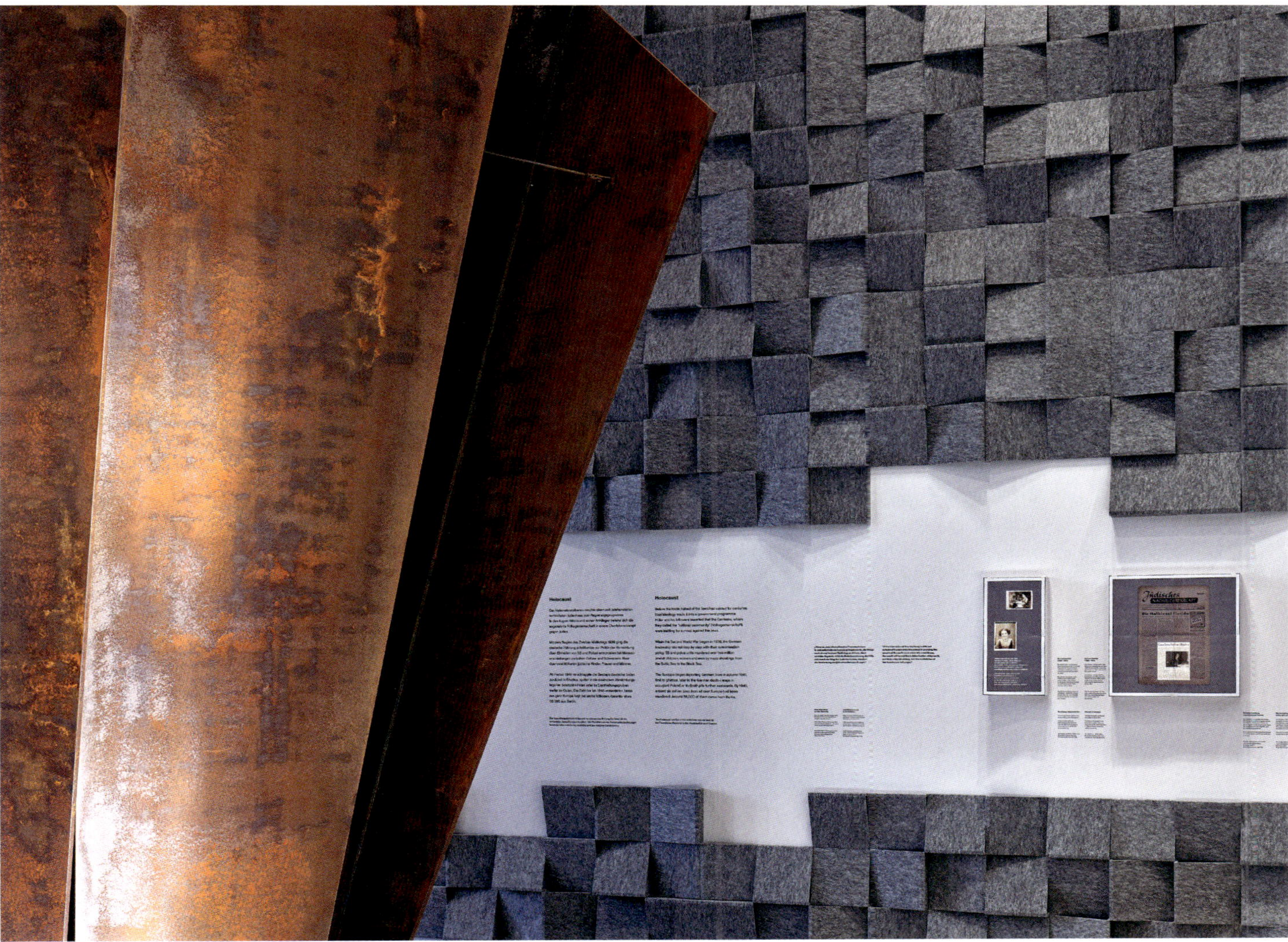

of Berlin, they are also encouraged to critically examine various Berlin clichés. We consider each theme in terms of its familiarity, but also its complexity – which is to say from highly divergent points of view. Moreover, the public becomes active in the exhibition: while touring the presentation, visitors are continually interviewed about the individual themes, about their opinions. Upon entering, each visitor is given a chip wristband, which makes it possible not just to activate objects in the exhibition or to set them into motion, but also to construct a visitor profile interactively in relation to specific questions and answers while touring the exhibition. This means that upon concluding the tour each visitor then has an opportunity to engage in networking; people will get to know one another by discussing the themes of the exhibition. We incorporated this feature right from the start – it is the basis of our concept. In remembrance of the Humboldt brothers: everything is interconnected, we connect with our visitors, they become connected with one another and with the world.

There are also a number of astonishing objects that have come to our attention, and which we have re-categorized, for example the famous vault door from the former nightclub Tresor (vault). We have positioned it as a historic object, as part of a historical narrative within the museum exhibition. We also

Berlin Exhibition: the walls in the War room are covered with grey felt squares that restlessly protrude and recede and are surrounded by light boxes and showcases.

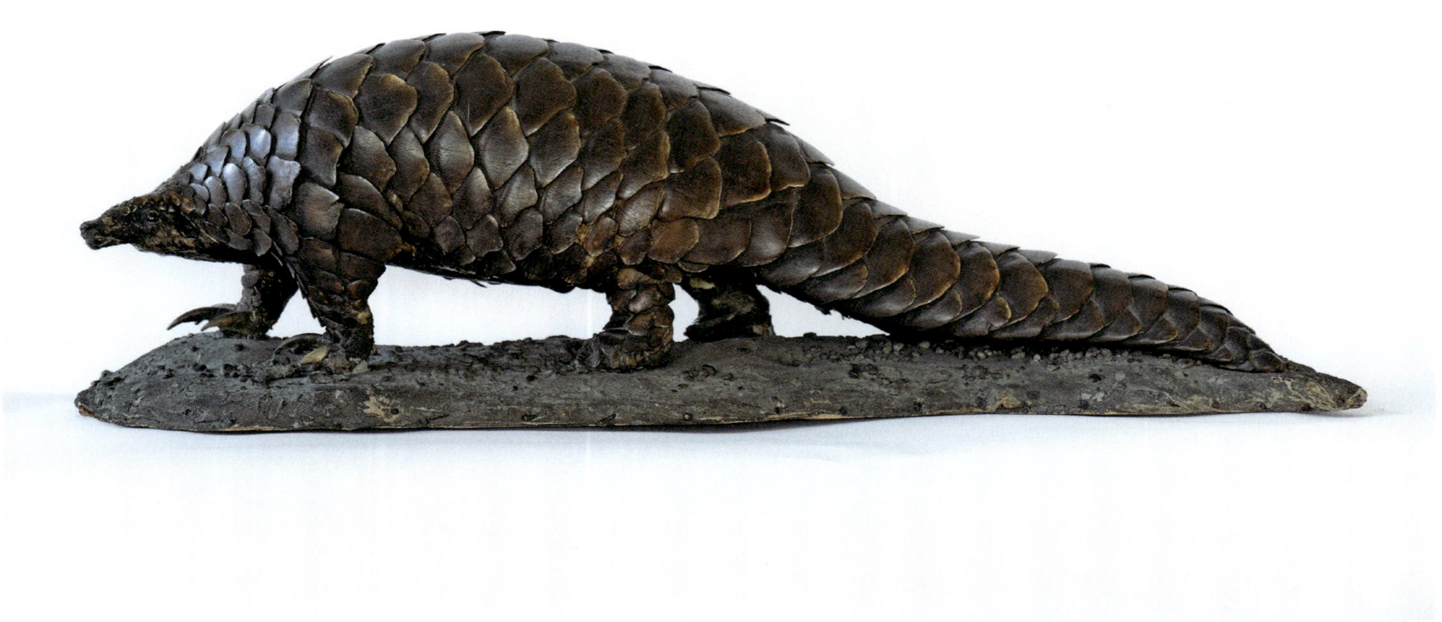

show numerous new works of art, in particular by artists from the urban art scene – a typical Berlin phenomenon, but with an international character. These works have never been exhibited before. And it is this kind of diversified mixture, I believe, that should be offered by the Berlin Exhibition.

Which new aspects and ideas are you contributing?

Hartmut Dorgerloh: Again and again, I find it exciting to realize that many of the ideas and insights of our two namesakes, Wilhelm and Alexander von Humboldt, remain as relevant as ever. In a globalized world, the idea that knowledge is power, but that it needs to be popularized and shared, is just as relevant as the necessary diversity of perspectives or the question of my individual connections with the world. Absolutely central for us, without any doubt, is the 'basic Humboldtian principle' according to which everything is interdependent. And it is not only acute pandemics or climate change that demonstrates this with the utmost clarity. What does it mean for our programmatic work that we are striving to orient ourselves towards 'Humboldtian principles'?

Dried specimen of a ground pangolin (Manis temminckii), Humboldt-Universität zu Berlin, zoological teaching collection

It already begins with the building's architecture. To expose, to render visible the contradictions, breaks and continuities between its outer form and its new contents, to link things with one another which do not necessarily belong together, to organize diversity, to develop the idea of a common future – these are the most exciting, challenging and enticing tasks. And we can only address them when we continually track down contemporary references, when we work in an interdisciplinary way, seeking out dialogue, listening, developing complex programme offerings for a complex world through collaboration with partners from around the world.

Only in this way can the Humboldt Forum become a space of encounter and negotiation, a place where a multiplicity of perspectives come together and achieve expression. In thematic terms, the Humboldt brothers set no limits for us. Actually, they were interested in everything of importance to the country and to society, and often adopted progressive, nonconformist attitudes. Much of this is still cutting edge: education and human rights, slavery and the heritage of colonialism, religion and science, languages and cultures, minorities and their rights and, at a quite elementary level, the exploitation of nature by human beings. All of these will become central topics in the new Humboldt Forum behind these Baroque palace facades. This phenomenal building has been completed, and now the history of the Humboldt Forum can begin!

Lars-Christian Koch: Our collaboration with the Humboldt Forum Foundation, in particular with regard to the areas devoted to temporary exhibitions, harbours great potential for our future work. Here, interdisciplinary curatorial teams will work together, with representatives from the originating cultures playing a central role.

This leads towards joint provenance research, through which knowledge about the collections will be cooperatively compiled and evaluated. The results are to be presented in the Humboldt Forum, which will also endow the collections with an enhanced contemporary relevance. Discussed in this context will be topics such as ownership, possession, legality and cultural meaning, along with many other aspects of significance to contemporary cultures in a globally networked world. This includes not least of all the issue of the restitution of cultural assets, along with strategies for joint attempts to come to terms with the history of various forms of cultural interaction, ranging from inhumane practices to productive processes of cultural exchange.

The Humboldt Forum is not just a museum. Beyond the museums that are housed there, the Forum functions as a platform for global discussion, and this involves, centrally, the task of initiating, facilitating and supporting processes of cultural negotiation. In the coming years, the prestige of the collections in Berlin-Dahlem (at the Humboldt Forum, only about three percent of the total inventory of the Ethnologisches Museum and the Museum für Asiatische Kunst will be on view) will be noticeably enhanced by the activities of the ResearchCampusDahlem, still in the planning stages, in cooperation with the Humboldt Forum. In close collaboration with Berlin's universities and research institutes, a major cooperation partner is the Freie Universität (Free University), which will be intensifying research in the area of material culture studies. Also vital is our collaboration with the Humboldt-Universität with its research focus in the area of immaterial culture studies.

These efforts will be combined with reoriented provenance research, undertaken jointly with representatives from the cultures of origin, which will go beyond simply clarifying the identities of former owners and the legal status of individual objects, and examine the contemporary significance of research results for the cultures of origin and for the relevant nation states. In this way, we hope that our activities at the Humboldt Forum will give rise to new forms of global collaboration in the areas of anthropology, cultural studies and art history, as well as to innovative efforts to convey the results to a wider public.

Gorch Pieken: We intend to revive the old idea of the 'Wunderkammer' (cabinet of curiosities), which goes beyond a mere overview of facts and the dissemination of knowledge. In the early modern era, cabinets of curiosities were places of sensuous experience, and addressed not just rationality, but the emotions as well. In our contemporary adaptation of the cabinet of curiosities, we hope to use playful and aesthetic elements to captivate visitors in a science exhibition, in particular by delighting the eye through the kind of astonishing imagery so typical of such collections. We encounter something similar in the work of Alexander von Humboldt, who possessed – to cite Hans Magnus Enzensberger – the 'the gift of wonder, of astonishment', which is why his 'scientific work' is also characterized by a 'poetic dimension'. And this makes Humboldt a pioneer of the popularization of science.

And it is in this spirit that the exhibition of the Humboldt-Universität in the entry area becomes a floating network of virtual fishes, and the main hall a marvellous knowledge factory for research and teaching, with motorized walls and mobile object machines that are suspended from the ceiling.

Many of the exhibits come from the collections of the Humboldt-Universität, which were founded in 1810 with objects from the cabinet of curiosities from the Berlin Palace. The arrival of the Humboldt-Universität in the Humboldt Forum is hence in a sense also a homecoming story, a return to its historical point of departure.

Unfortunately, very few original objects from the historical cabinet of curiosities still exist; nor does the interior of the newly constructed Palace recall it to memory. Attentive visitors to the exhibition of the Humboldt-Universität, however, may still discover allusions to the historical cabinet of curiosities, for example in the large windows of the Palace. Displayed in these windows, to their full height, were conch shells. 'Shells and various sea snails fill the window boxes', reported a Venetian visitor as early as 1708, when he visited the then brand-new rooms of the Palace, and entered the third room of the cabinet of curiosities.

Paul Spies: All I can say is: they are countless (laughs).
To begin with, the exhibition will have an atmosphere that is
unusual for a classical historical exhibition. We are creating
an exhibition that strives to include and to address the entire
spectrum of citizens of the city, but also visitors to Berlin.
The presentation offers low-threshold forms of access to critical
topics. The public is encouraged to actively participate. It is a
popular exhibition, and also a critical one. This combination is
something I have never seen before. It is, so to speak, a popular
exhibition against populism.

We assembled the exhibition together with people from
the various communities. Which is to say with people who
are directly involved, in their own lives, with the themes of
the exhibition. In particular, we had them tell their stories
to us. That is something new: as historians, we work in this
instance as intermediaries, rather than claiming scientific
authority for our investigations and research. Here the curators
take up a role that does not involve dominating the narrative.
Of course, we have elaborated an overarching concept and
we are attentive to questions of balance, but we have given a
voice to many of the citizens of the city with their contrasting
experiences.

This becomes visible as well in the presentation: repeatedly,
visitors encounter elements that display personal objects
or make voices audible – in recordings of people who have
experienced something that is worth relating to others.

Our aim is to integrate variety, unknown things that it is
important to make known: for nothing is as simple or self-
evidently true as we initially believe. For a history exhibition,
that is essential. Every individual has their own history.
We keep in mind how many different perspectives are inherent
to any given historical topic. And we must never forget just how
many people are affected by what happens. Then it becomes
possible to reflect upon and deal with situations, people and
minorities in society in an equitable way. In this sense, the
exhibition is a plea for diversity – which is ever-present in the
city, and is also the grand theme for the Humboldt Forum.
We seek to explain this diversity, but we also pose the question:
Do we already know everything there is to know, or is there still
much more? Are we genuinely accessible to all? The exhibition
seeks to convey this, but also to embody it.

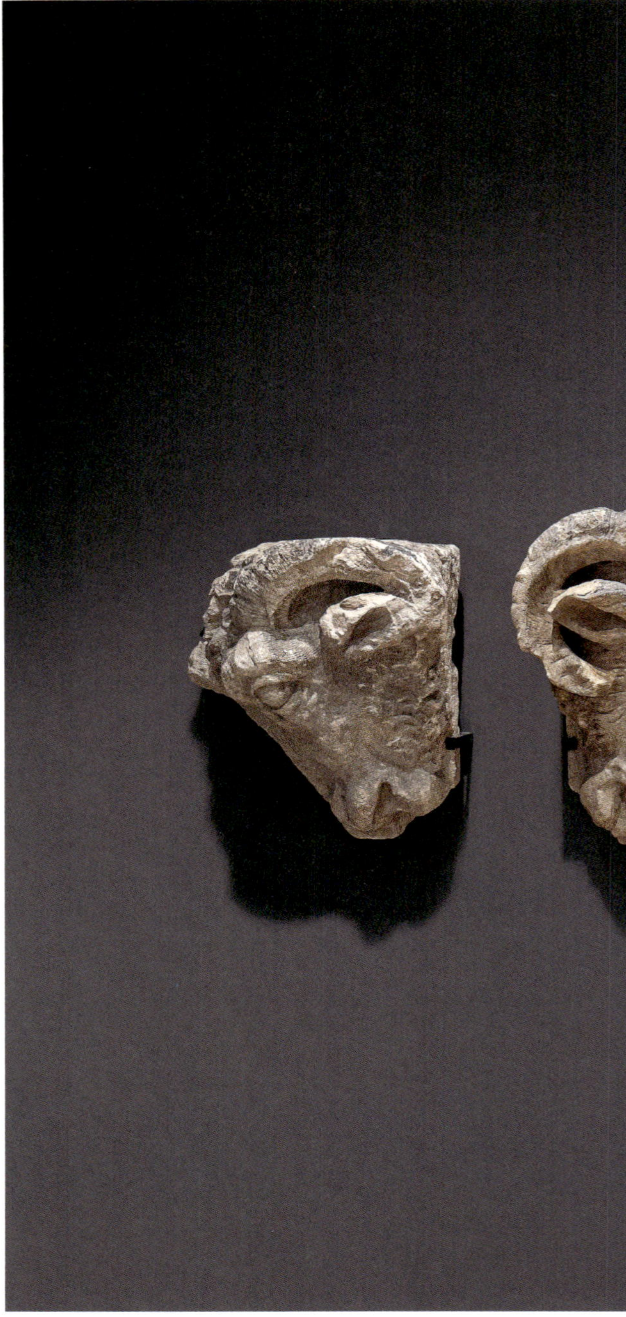

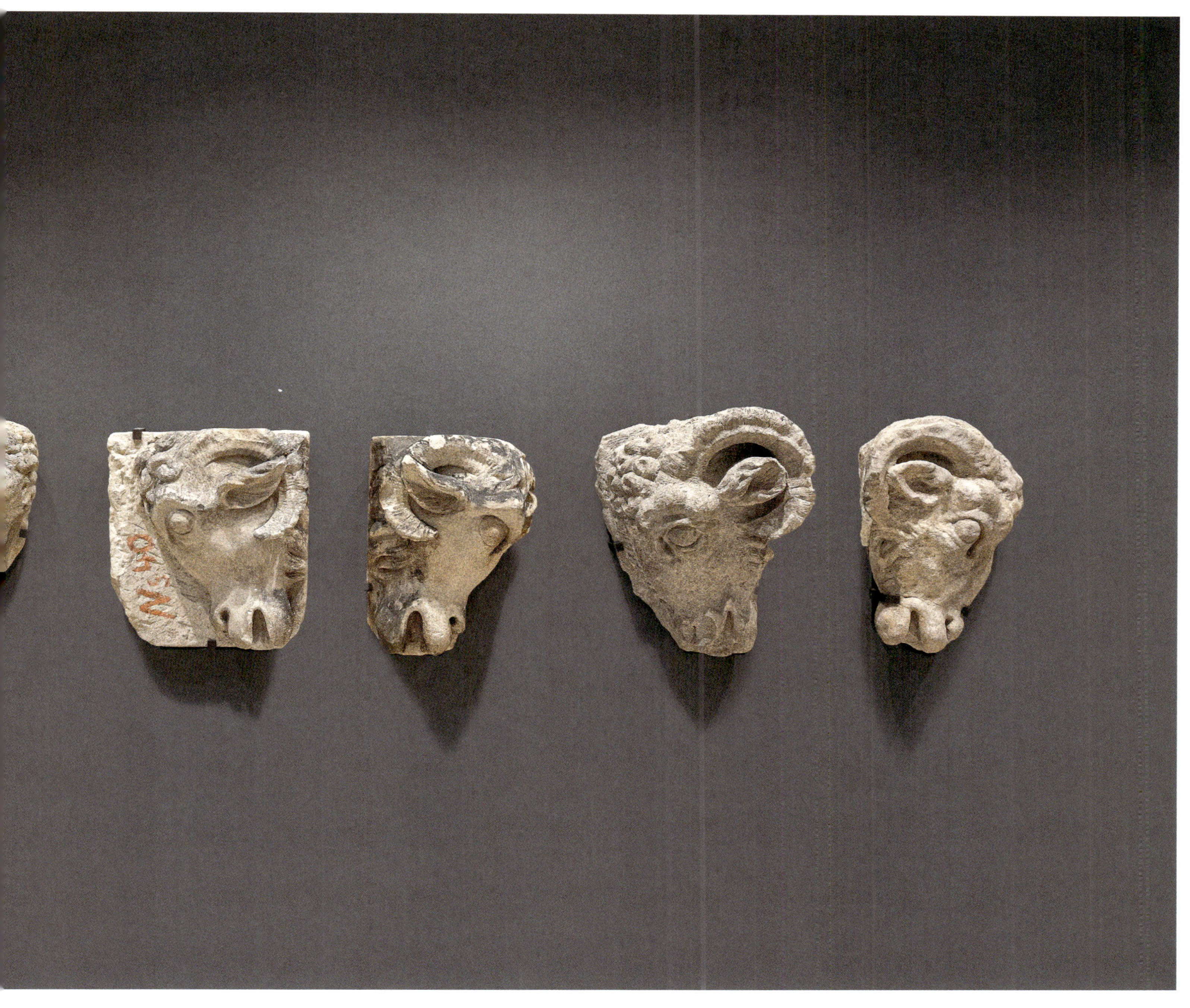

History of the site: mounting of the
original surviving fragments of the
facade ornamentation in the gallery
of the sculpture hall

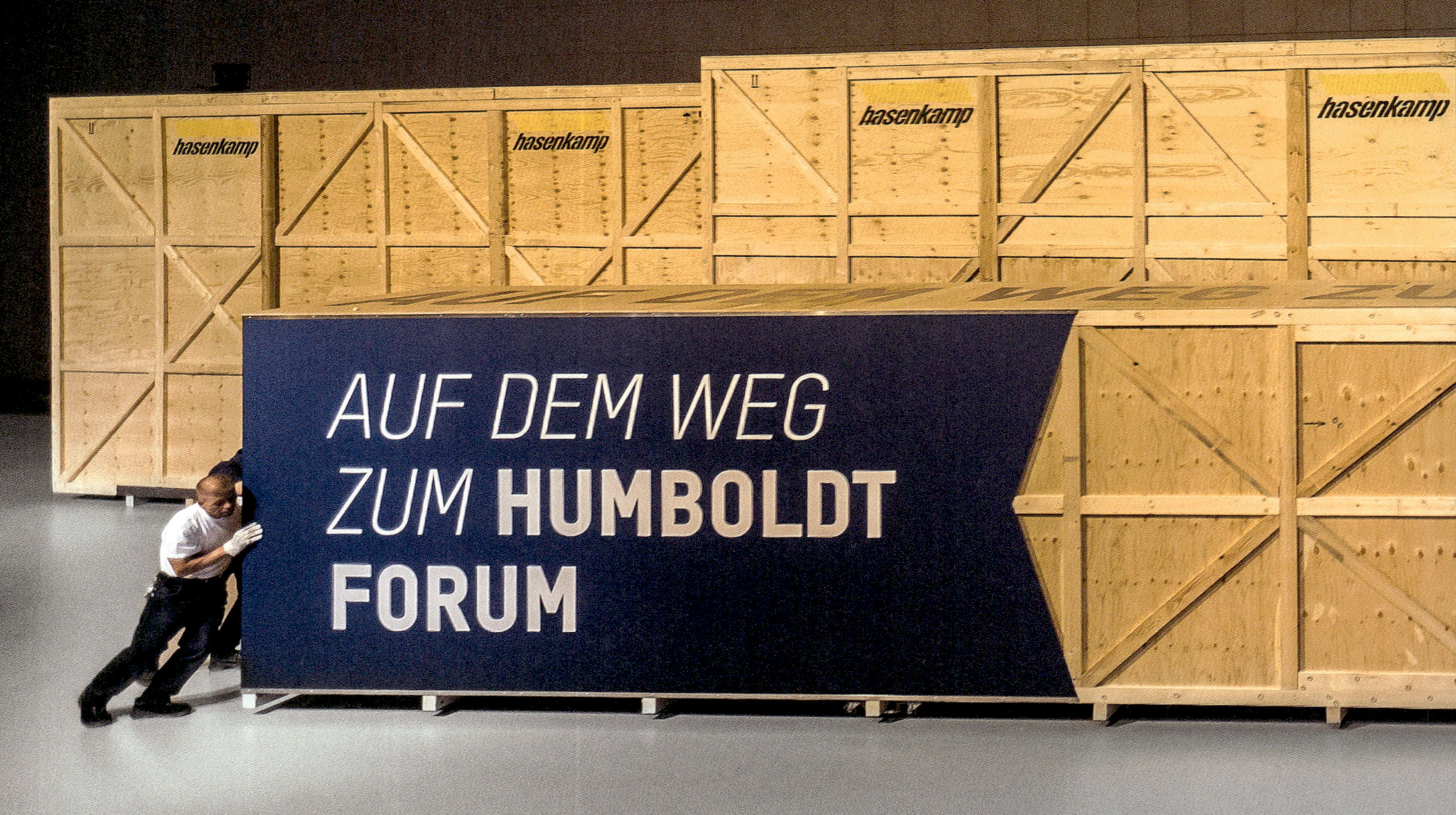

hasenkamp
hasenkamp
hasenkamp
AUF DEM WEG
ZUM HUMBOLDT
FORUM

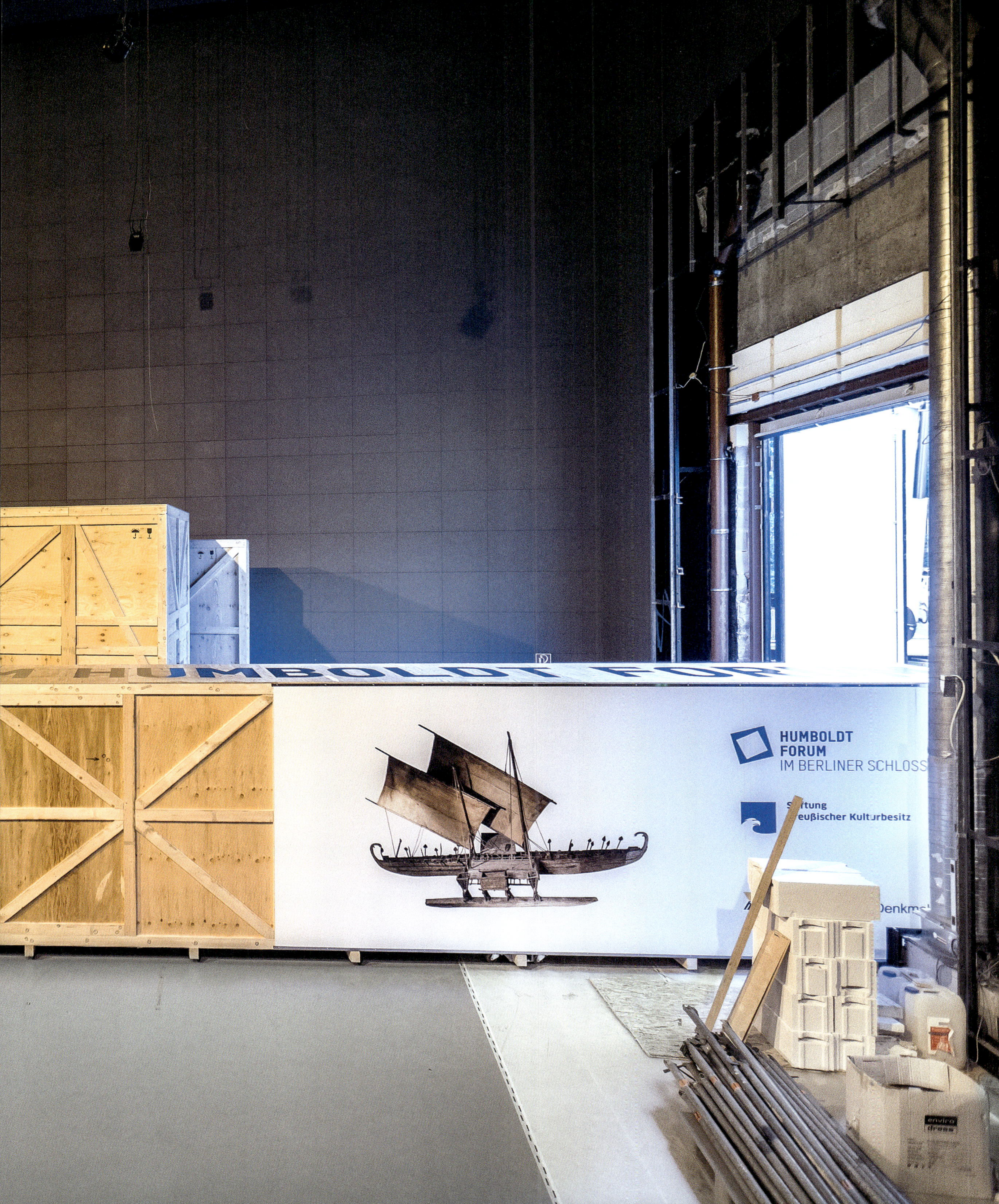
HUMBOLDT FOR
HUMBOLDT
FORUM
IM BERLINER SCHLOSS
Stiftung
Preußischer Kulturbesitz

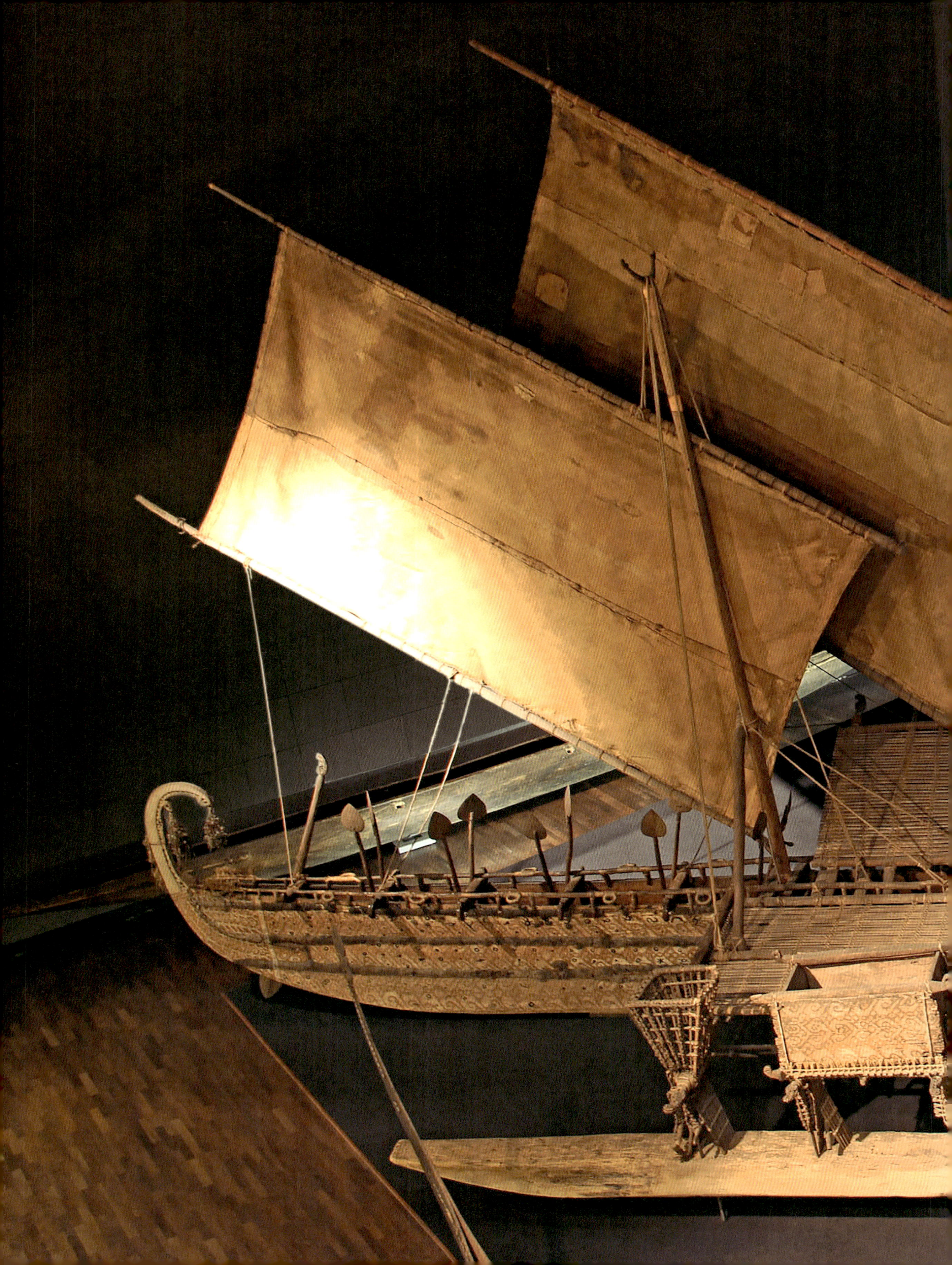

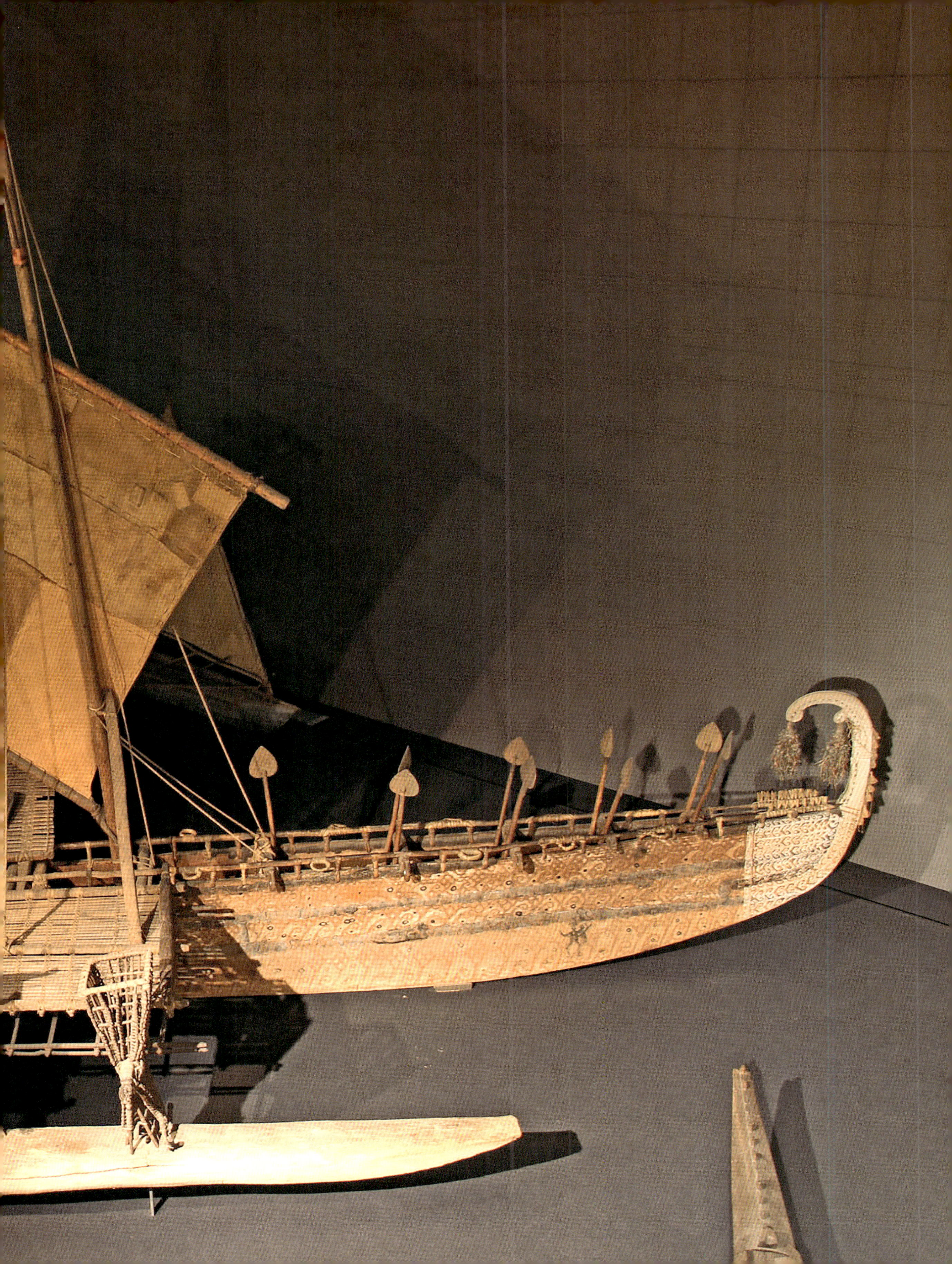

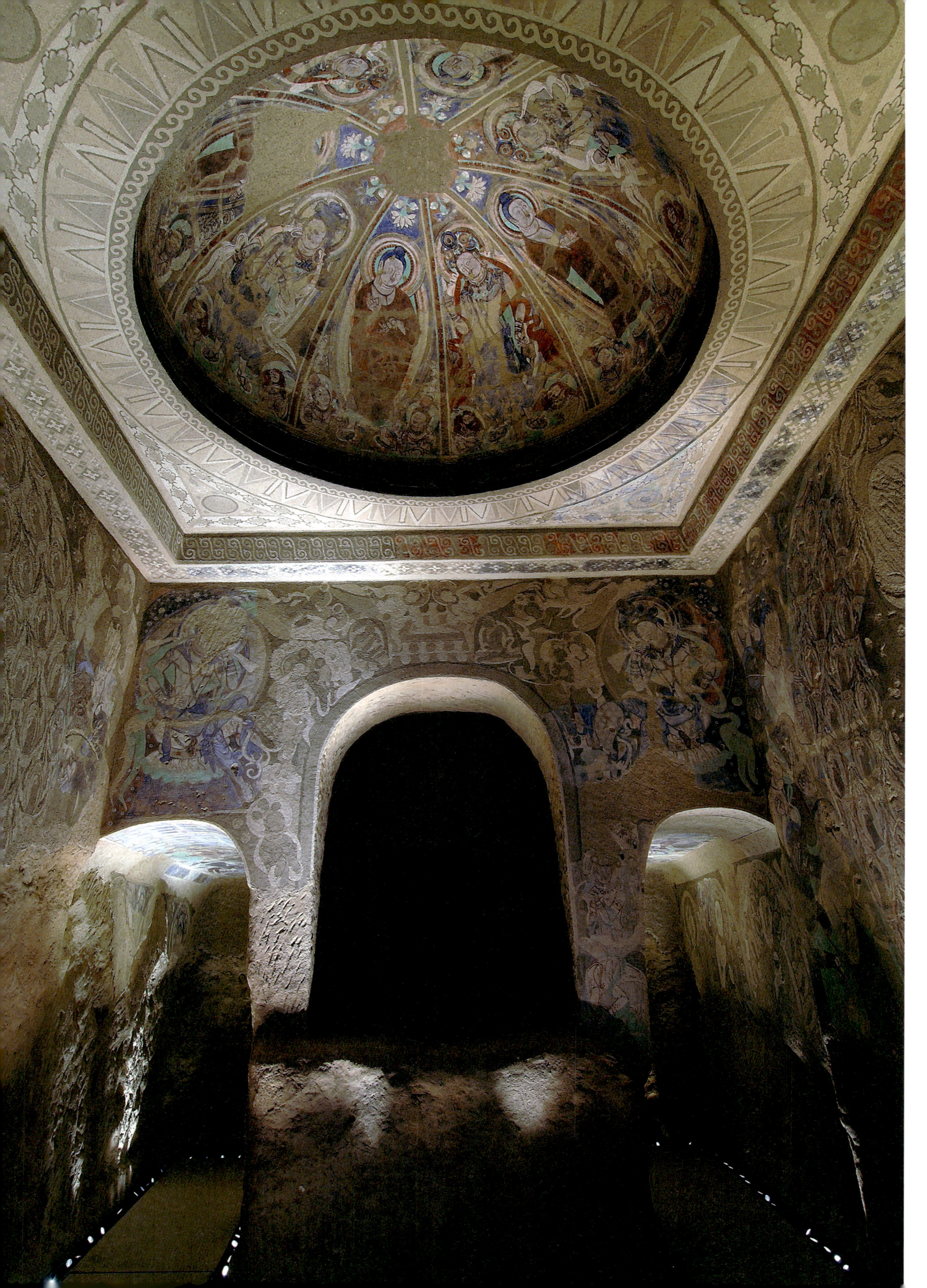

Fig. pp. 178–179:
In May of 2018, two-and-a-half years
before the inauguration in December
of 2020, the first exhibits entered
the Humboldt Forum. Among them
is the famous, well-packed Luf boat
from the South Seas Collection
of the Ethnologisches Museum
(Ethnological Museum). Because
of their size, these objects had to
be heaved through an unobstructed
opening in the 'cubes' of the two-
storey exhibition halls on both sides
of the Grand Foyer, which was then
walled up.

Fig. pp. 180–181:
The two-mast outrigger boat owned
by the Ethnologisches Museum
(Ethnological Museum) comes
from the island of Luf in the north of
what is today Papua New Guinea.
Using such vessels, the men of Luf
travelled on the open sea, trading
or engaging in warfare. Such boats
accommodated up to 50 people. Max
Thiel, a partner in the German trading
company Hernsheim & Co, acquired
the boat in 1903, when the island
belonged to the colony of German
New Guinea.

The Cave of the Ring-Bearing Doves,
dating from the fifth–sixth century,
is the only accessible museum
reconstruction worldwide of a cave
featuring original paintings. In 1914,
it was transported to Berlin from
Kizil at the edge of the Taklamakan
Desert (today in China) by the fourth
Turfan expedition. The researchers
had discovered it in a singular system
consisting of hundreds of Buddhist
cave temples, some decorated with
elaborate paintings.

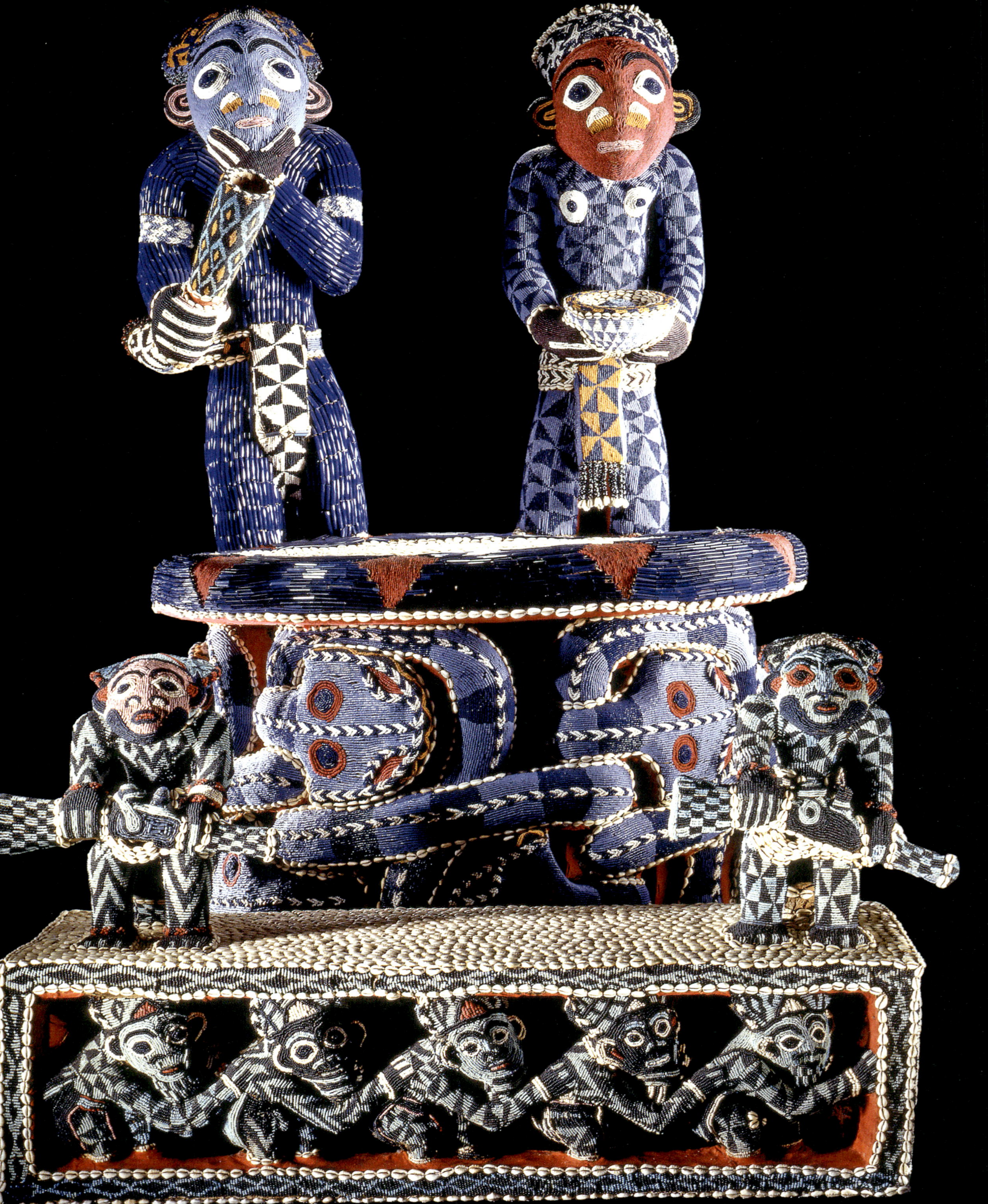

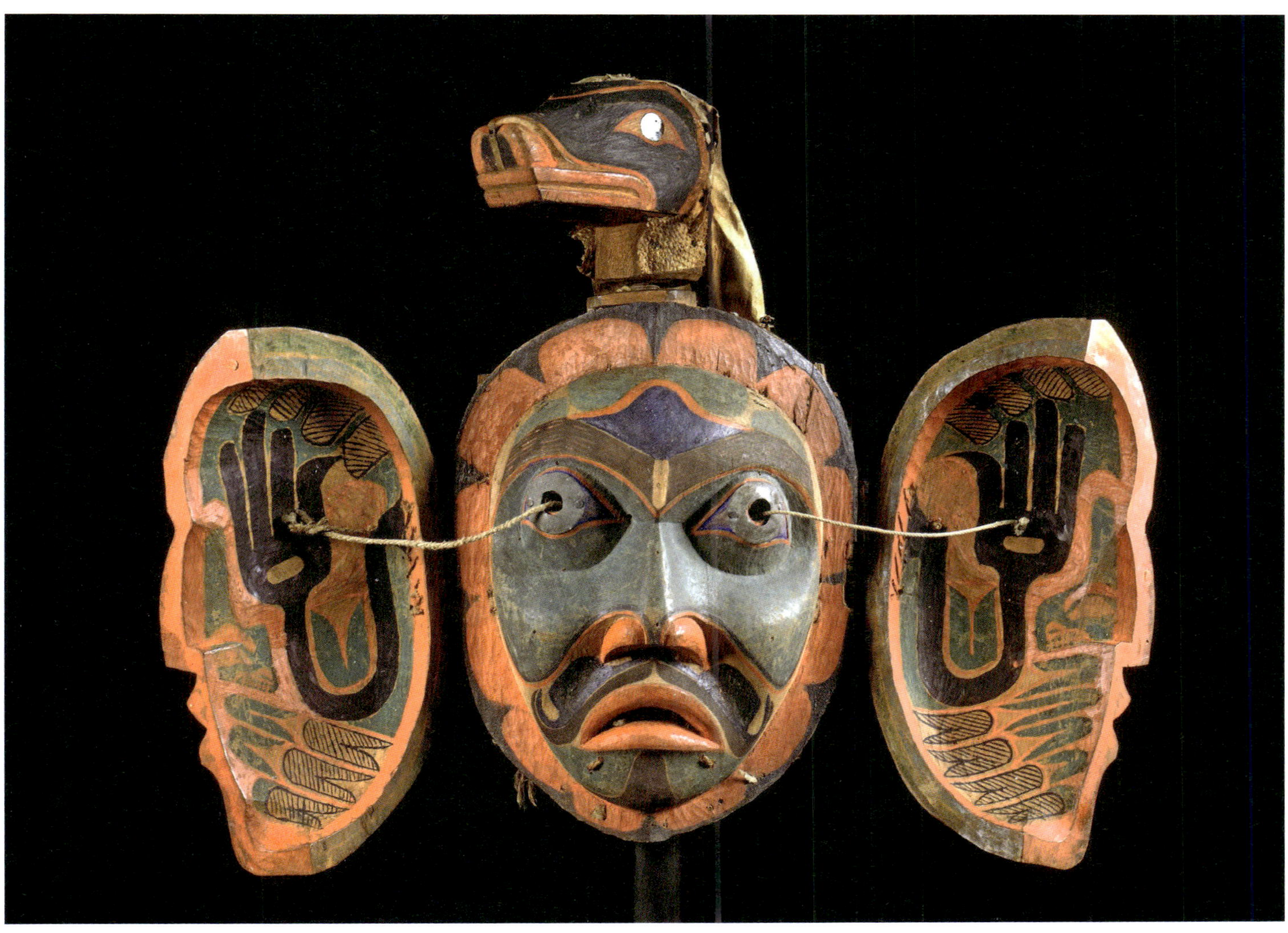

An imposing object in the Humboldt Forum is the 'Mandu Yenu' throne from the kingdom of Bamum in Cameroon. Sultan Njoya of Bamum presented the throne to the German governor of the colony of Cameroon as a gift for the German Emperor Wilhelm II. The gesture raises many questions, and by the same token it is indicative of the relationship between local elites and the colonial power.

The Norwegian captain Adrian Jacobsen collected this transformation mask, created by a Kwakwaka' wakw artist from the Pacific Northwest coast of North America, and brought it to Berlin in 1883. It was worn during potlatches, and symbolizes rivalry between chiefs. When closed, the mask displays anger towards the rival. When open, it expresses the generosity with which gifts were distributed to guests at the potlatch.

The Ethnologisches Museum
(Ethnological Museum) owns one
of the most important collections
of historical and contemporary
sound recordings worldwide. At the
time, the use of such wax cylinders,
assembled beginning in 1902, was
the only option for making recordings
on site. These fragile sound recording
media, numbering nearly 30 000,
have been gradually digitalized, and
are accessible today to interested
specialists worldwide for research
purposes.

Alexander von Humboldt brought this
mosaic, originating from Pátzcuaro,
back from Mexico after his journey to
the Americas in 1803–04. It testifies
to reciprocal cultural appropriation:
here the pre-Hispanic tradition of
featherwork was placed at the service
of a Christian motif. The Madonna

and her splendid background
consist of feathers from at least
thirteen different bird species. When
viewed from a certain angle, the
hummingbird feathers that make
up the Madonna's cloak begin to
shimmer in metallic blue.

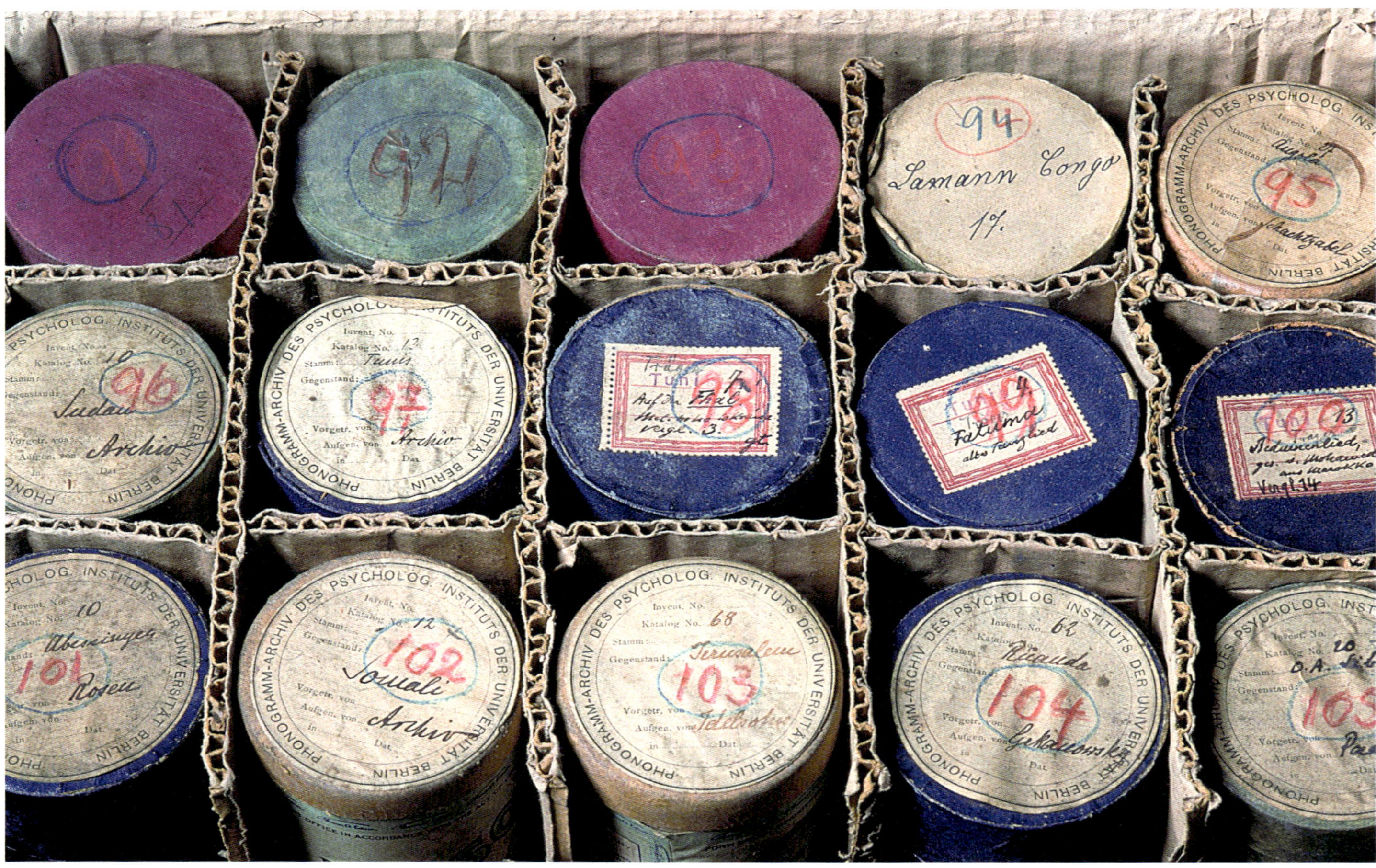

Fig. pp. 188–189:
The life-sized wooden effigy of the
bull Nandi once served the god
Shiva as a mount during ceremonial
processions in a Hindu temple in
South India. It is among the special
attractions of the Museum für
Asiatische Kunst (Museum of Asian
Art) in the Humboldt Forum, and will
be on view on the 3rd upper floor.

Fig. pp. 190–191:
This life-sized wooden figure (tino
aitu) of the divinity Sope comes
from the main temple of Nukuoro,
a Polynesian exclave in Micronesia.
Johann Stanislaus Kubary collected it
in 1877 as an employee of the private
Godeffroy Museum in Hamburg,
founded by a merchant. It will be on
view on the 2nd upper floor of the
Humboldt Forum.

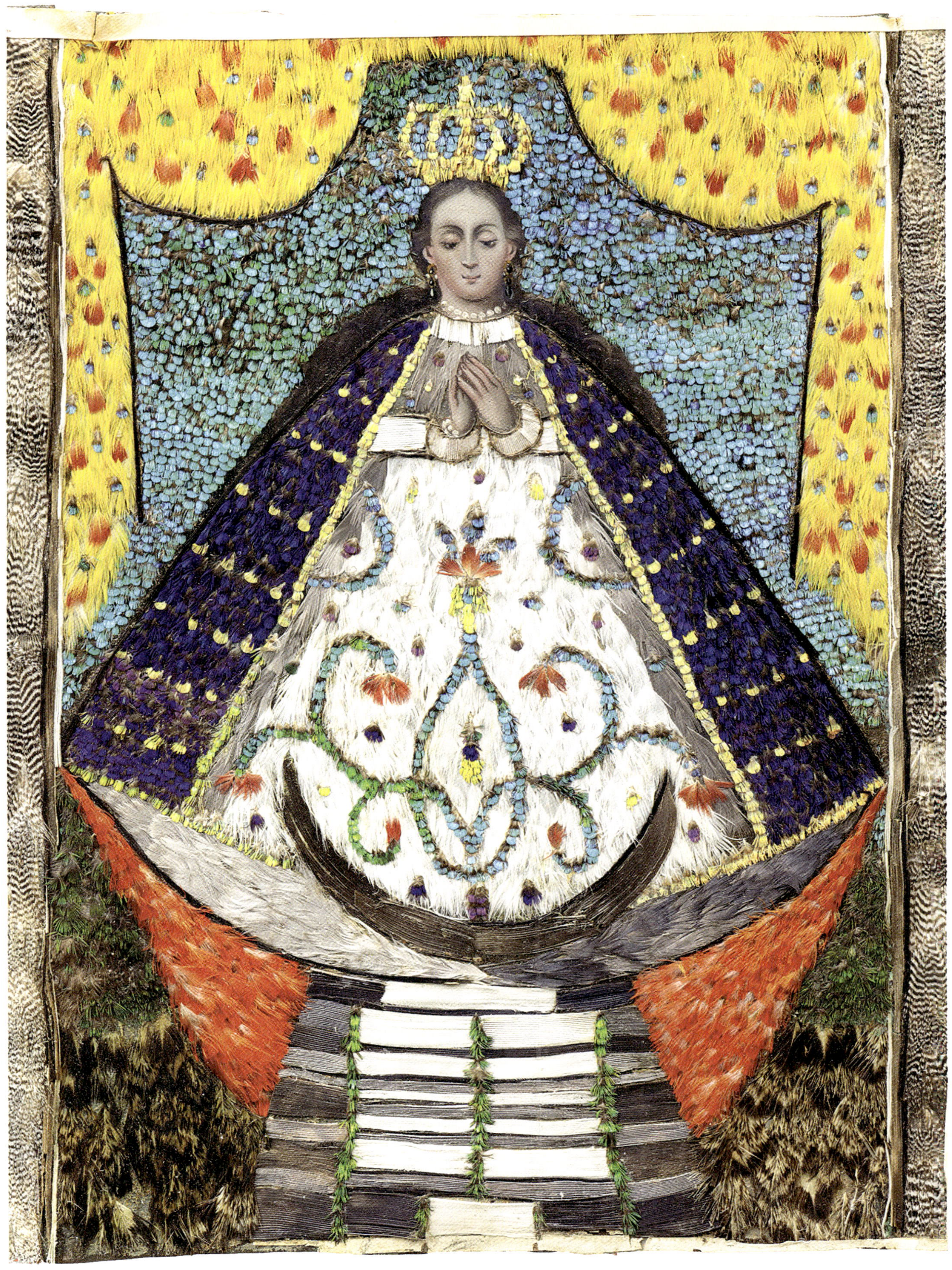

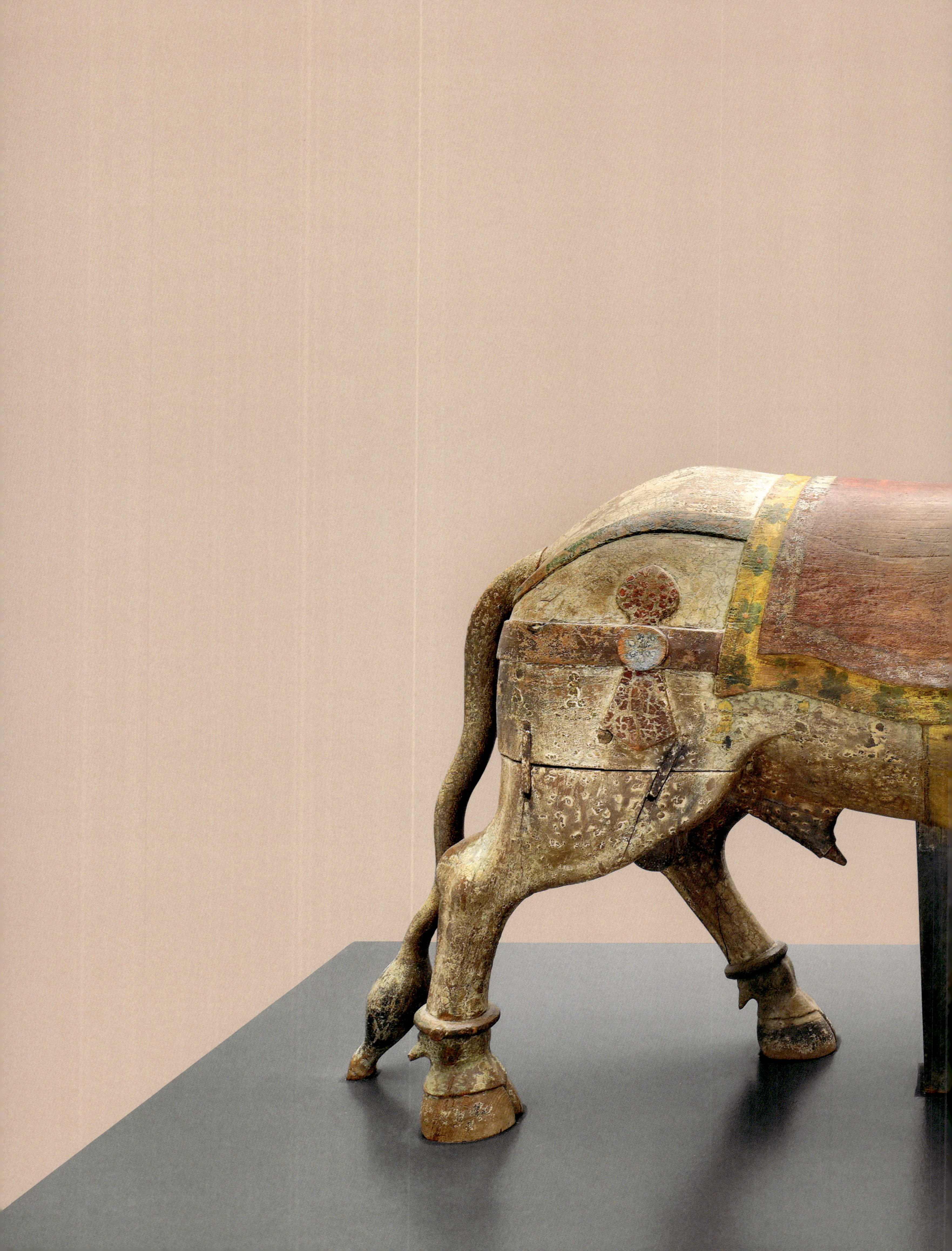

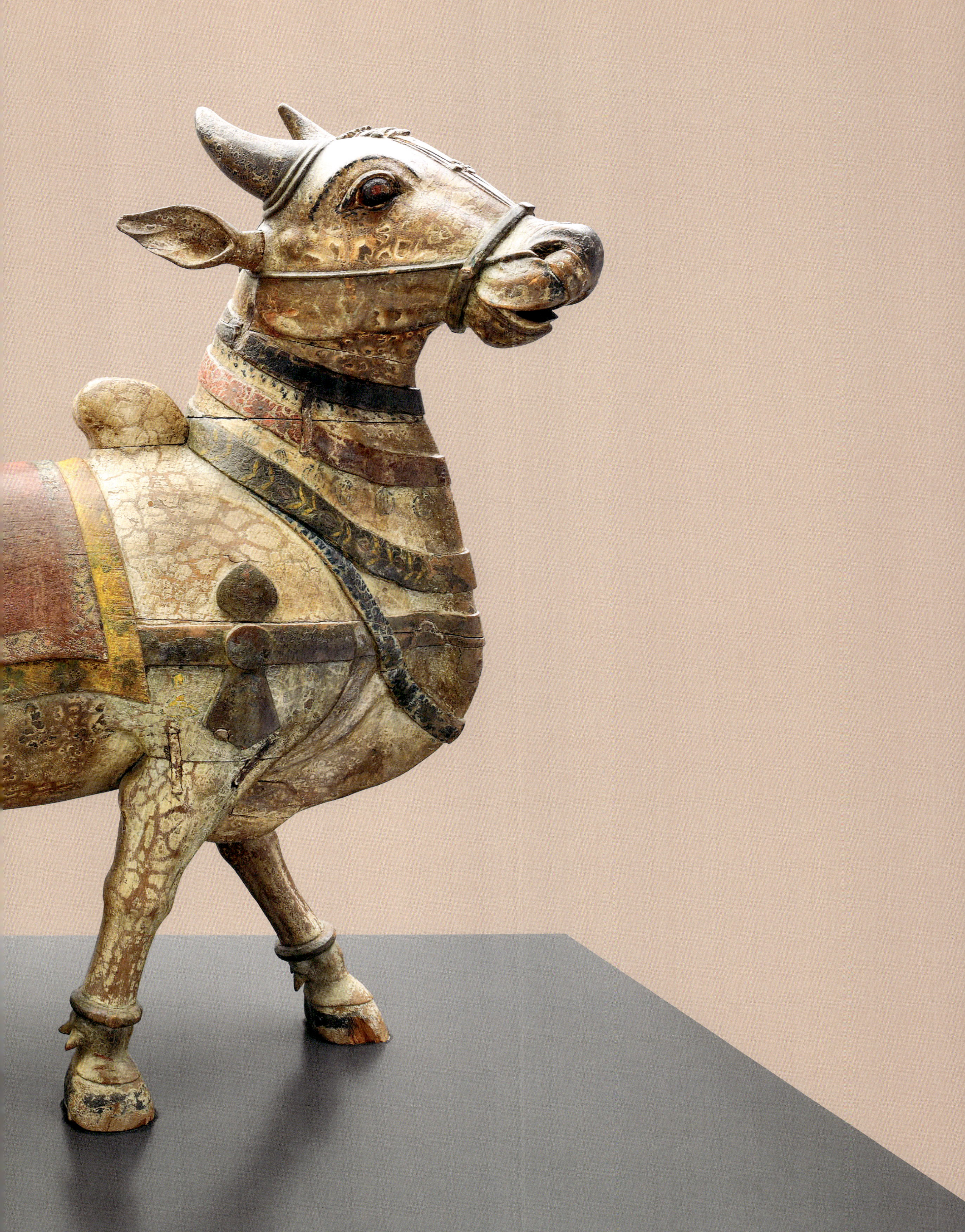

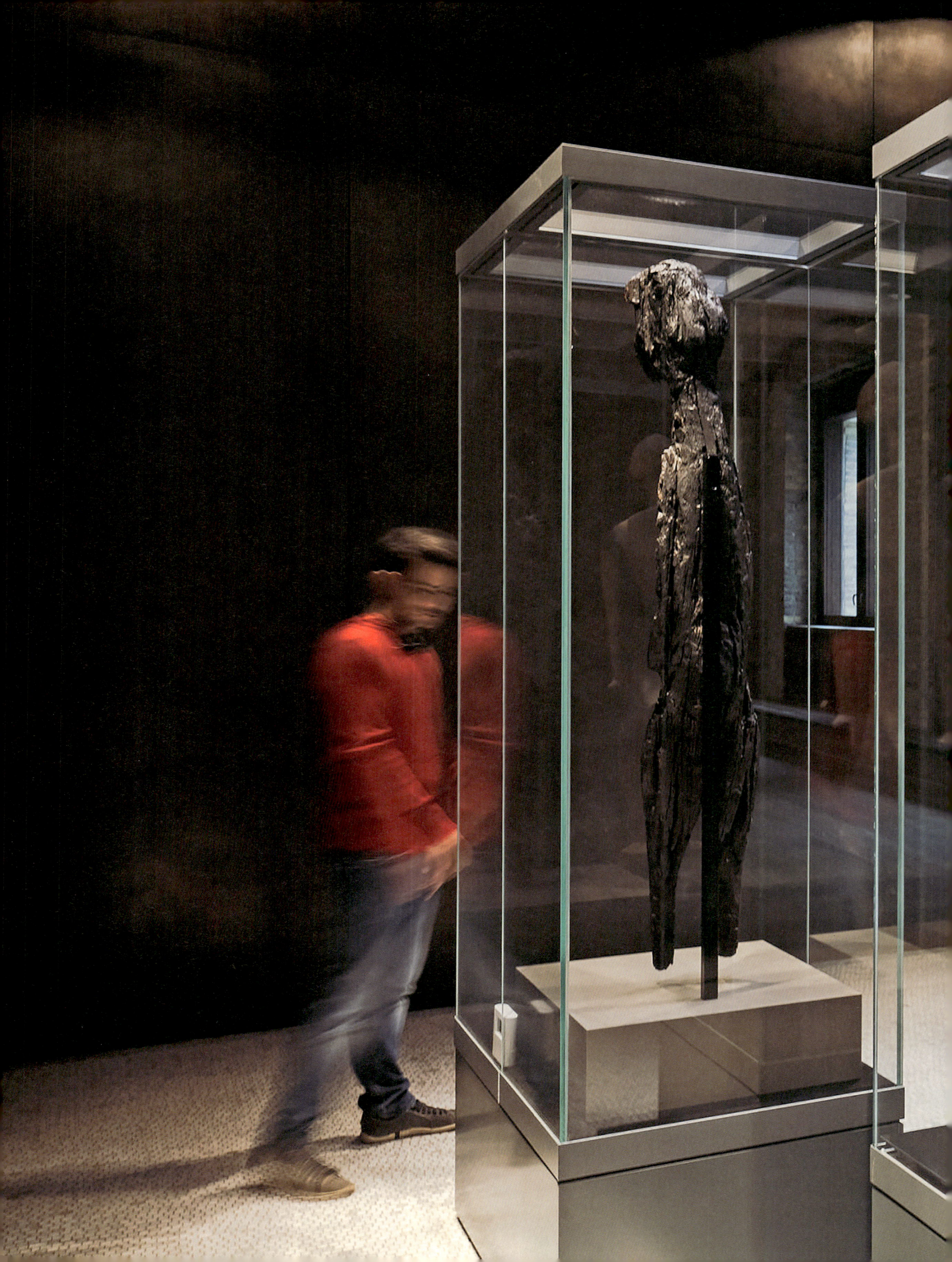

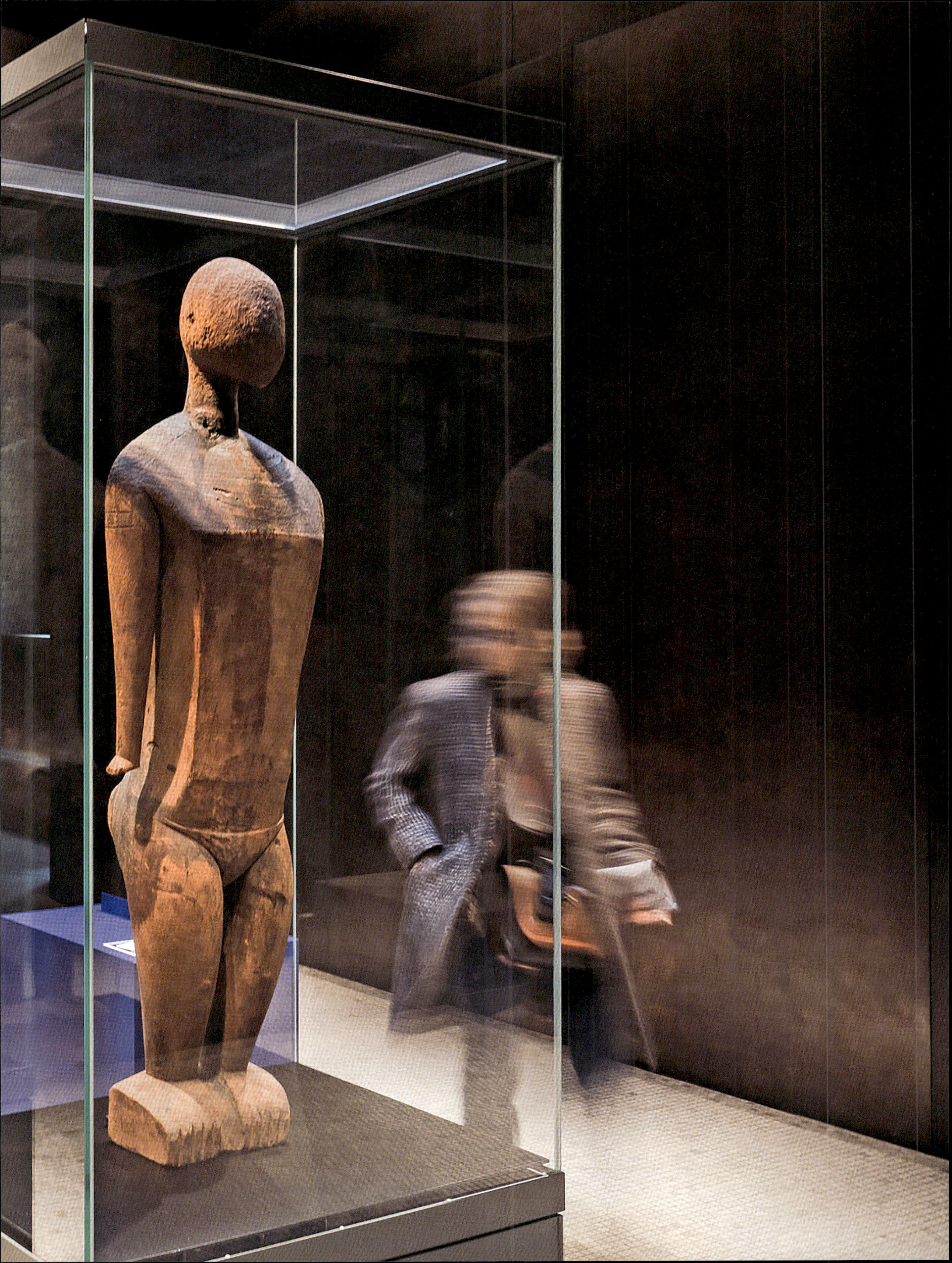

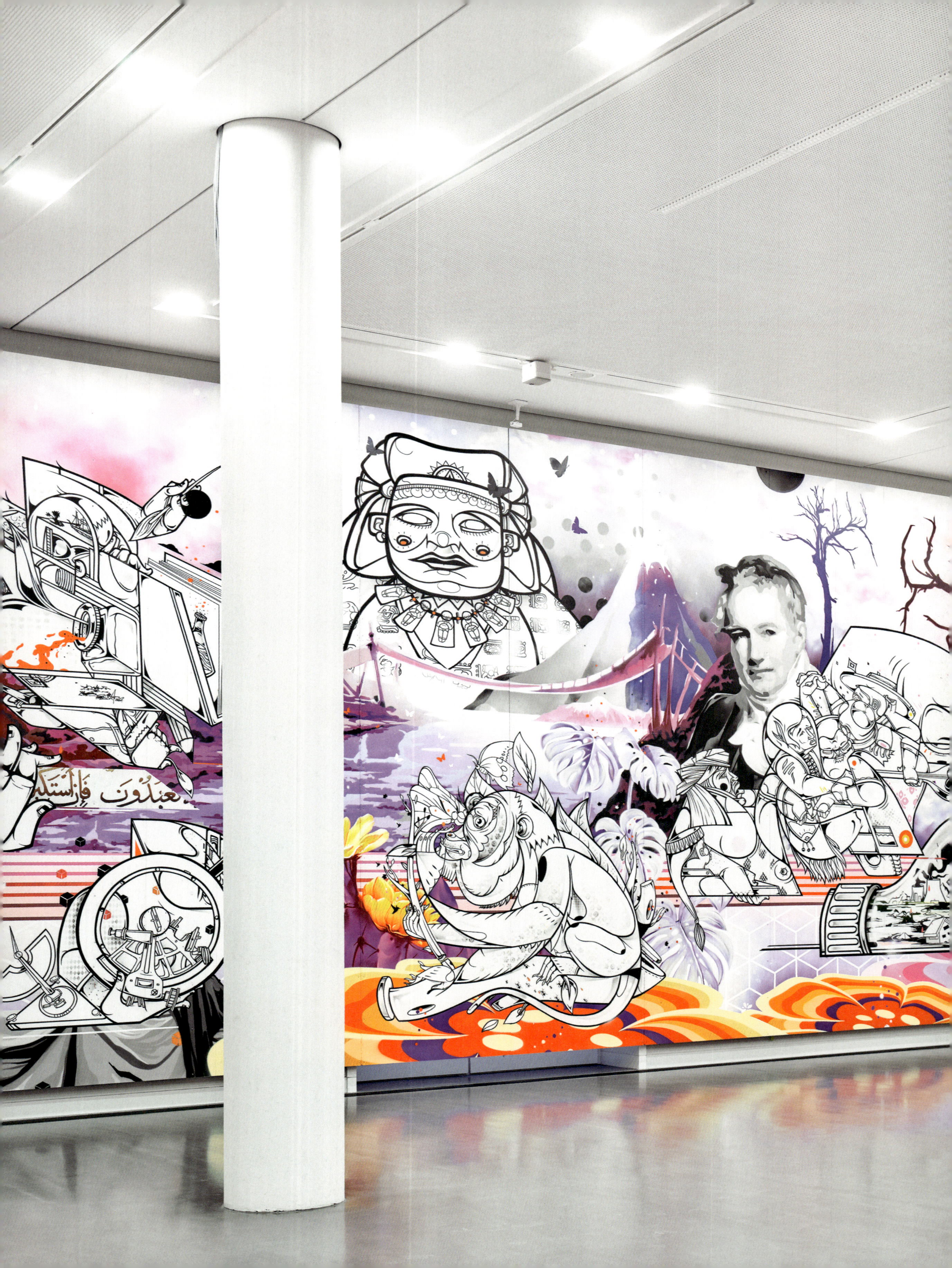

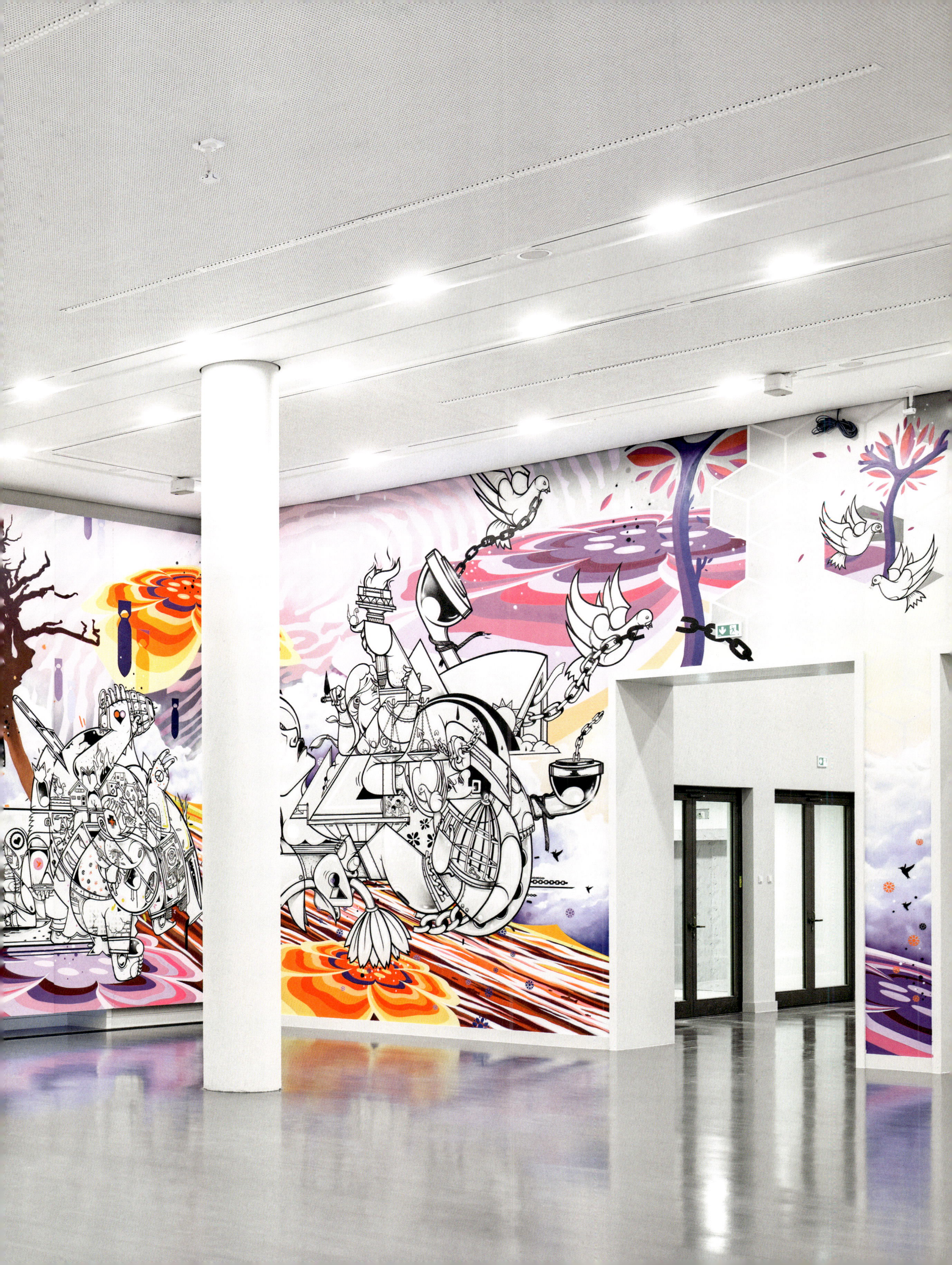

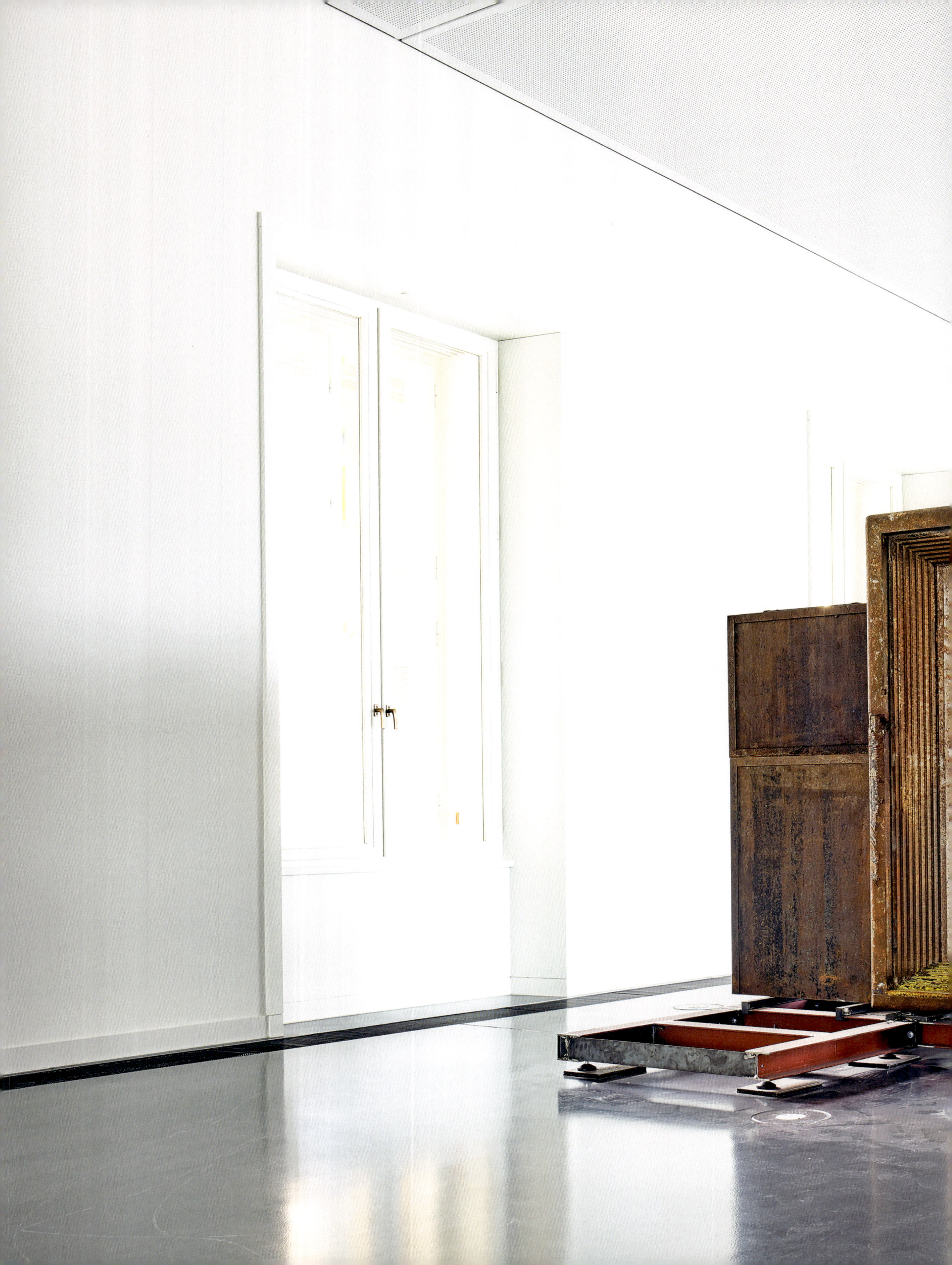

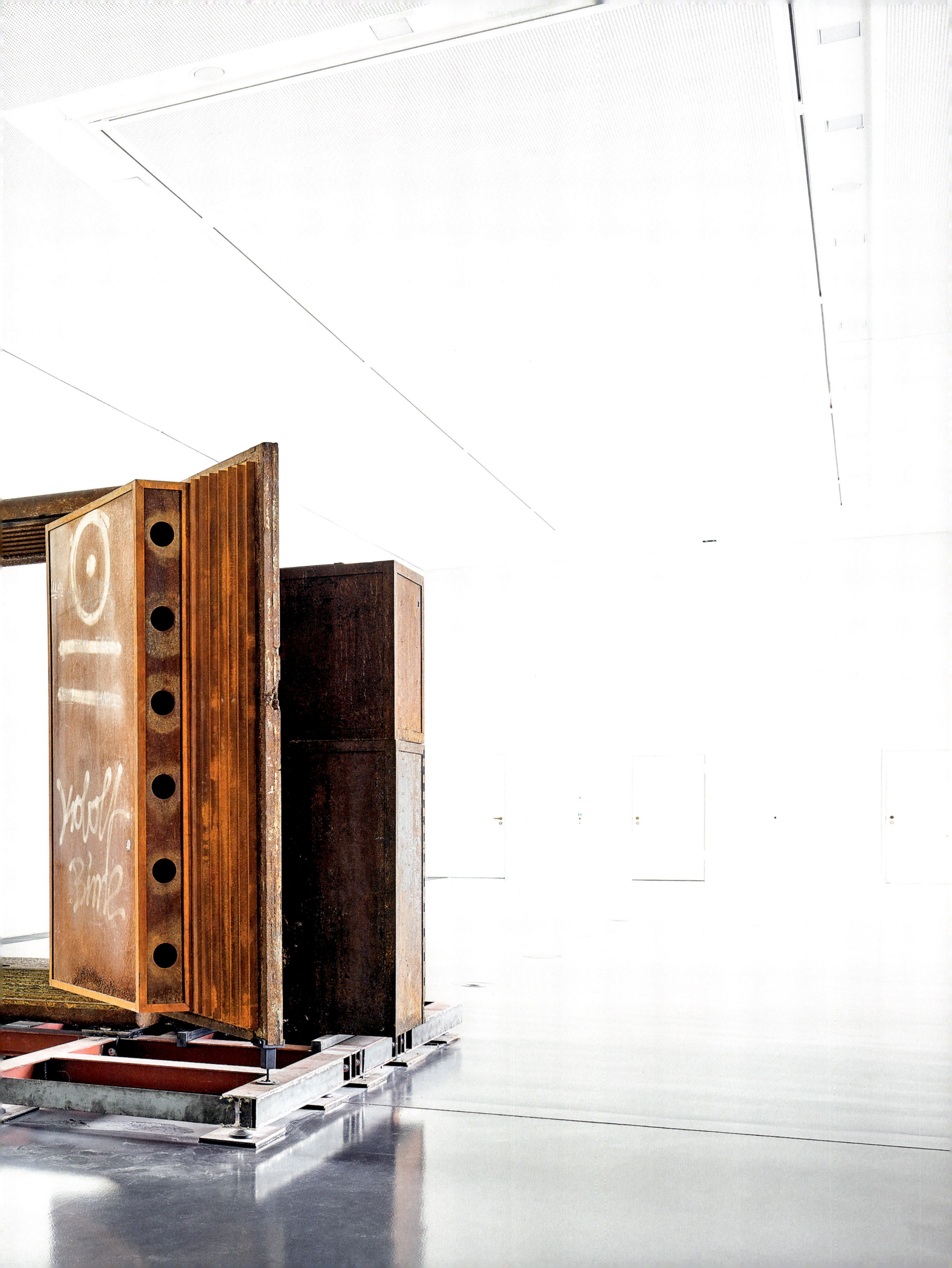

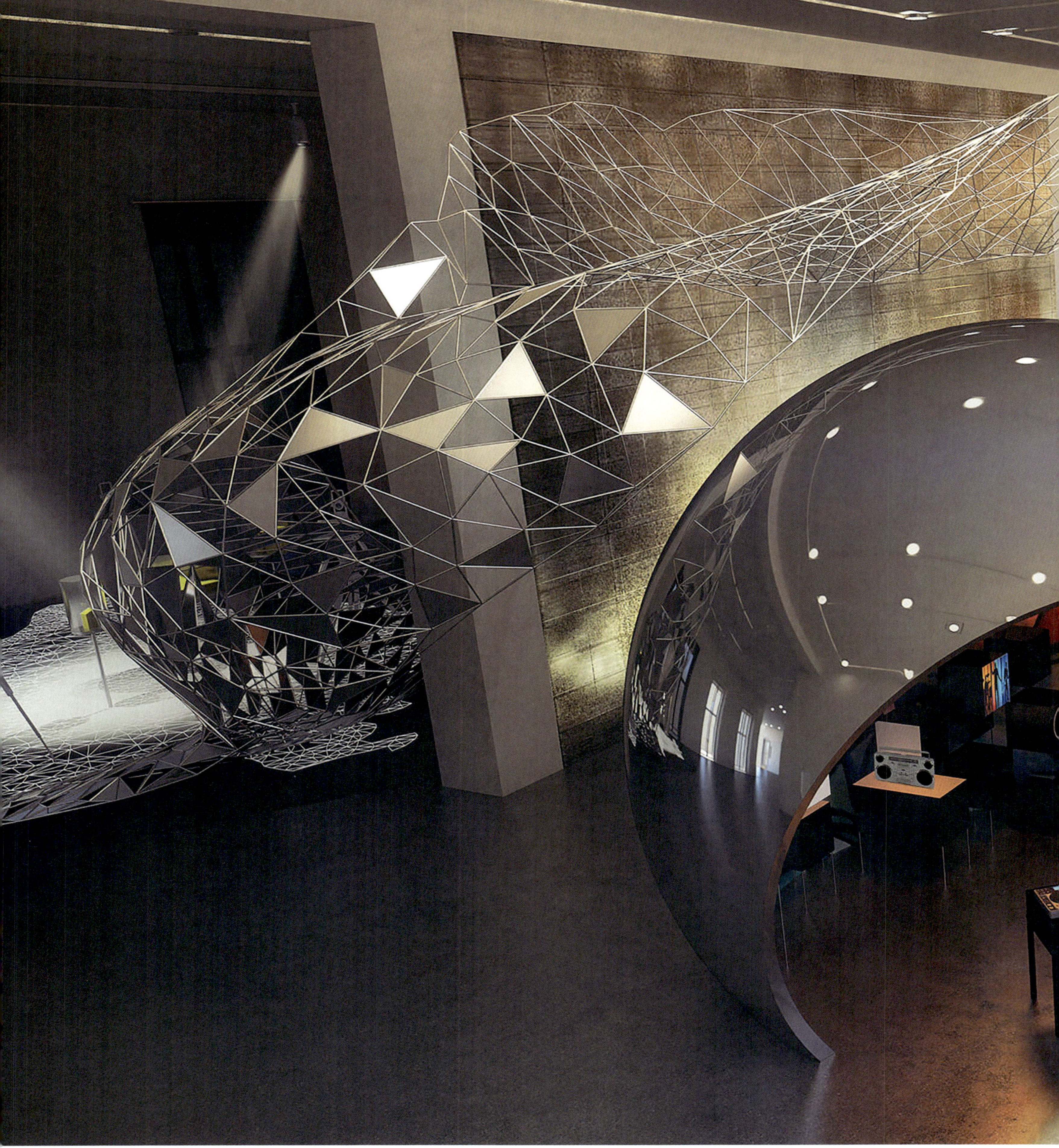

Fig. pp. 192–193:
The gigantic mural *Thinking the World* by the artist duo How and Nosm takes up events from the story of the conquest and exploitation of the world. It welcomes visitors to the exhibition BERLIN GLOBAL.

Fig. pp. 194–195:
This safe door was the first object to occupy the still empty exhibition area. At one time, it secured the safe room of the former Wertheim department store. After the fall of the Berlin Wall, Tresor (safe) became a world-famous techno-club.

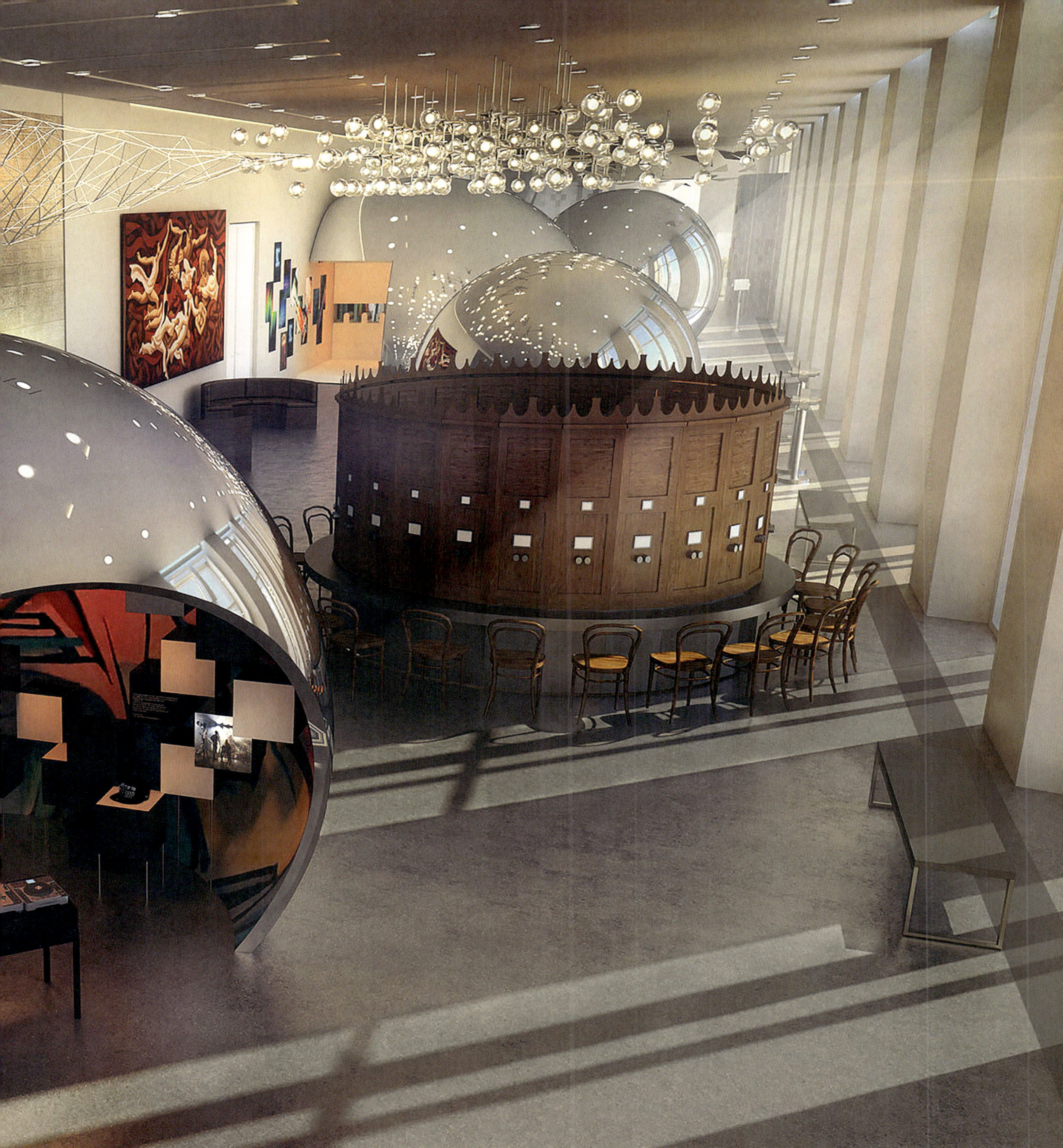

In the thematic room Entertainment, visitors can wander through oversized, accessible spheres, dance to the sounds of Berlin, or travel through time back to the Palace of the Republic.

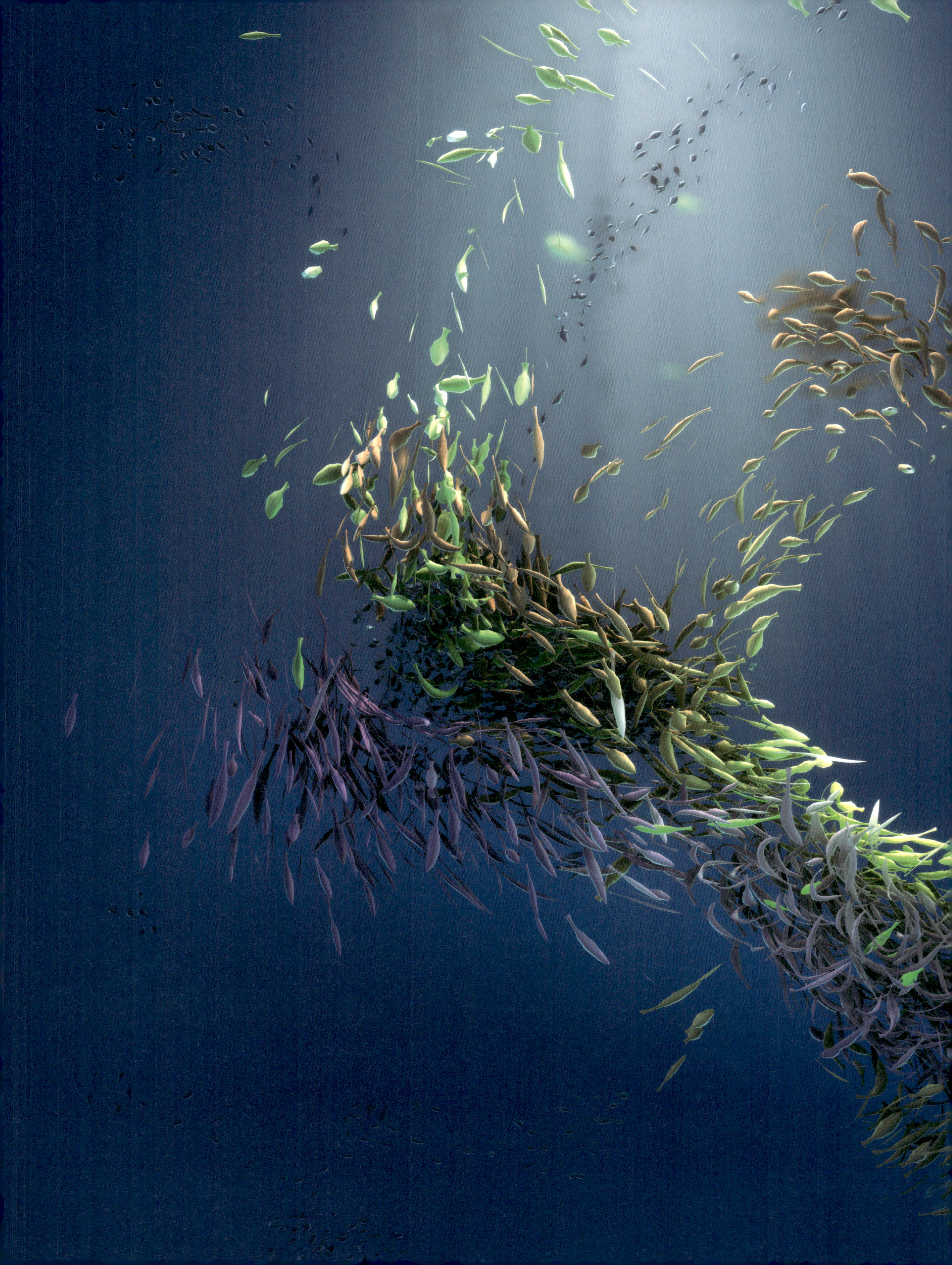

The interactive school of fish
in the foyer of the Humboldt
laboratory reacts to the behaviour
of visitors through changes of
movement or configuration. The
10 000 fish form five subgroups,
which are distinguished from one
another through appearance and
temperament.

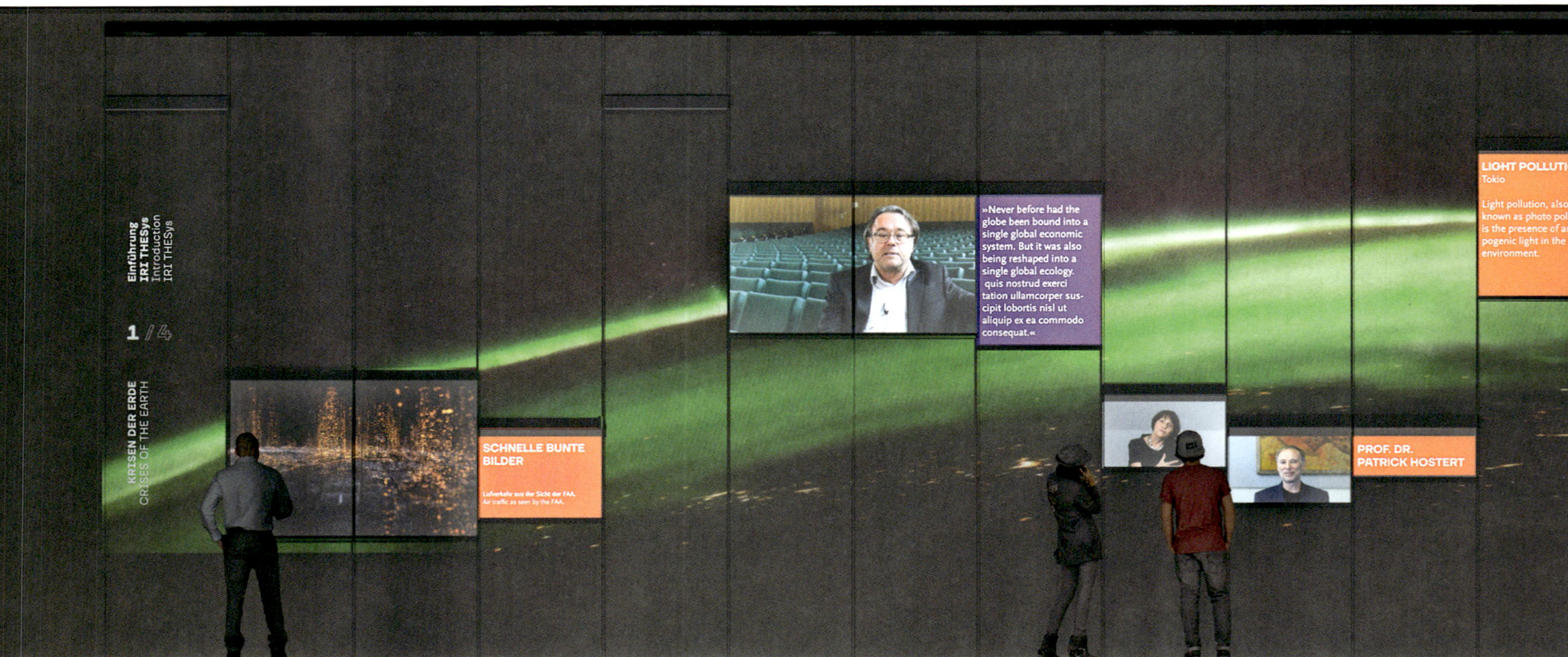

On a surface measuring 125 square
metres, and via 24 mobile and
extendable textile elements, the
kinetic research wall in the main hall
of the Humboldt Laboratory unfurls a
panorama of current research issues.
It thereby becomes a cybernetic
apparatus that responds to the
visitors.

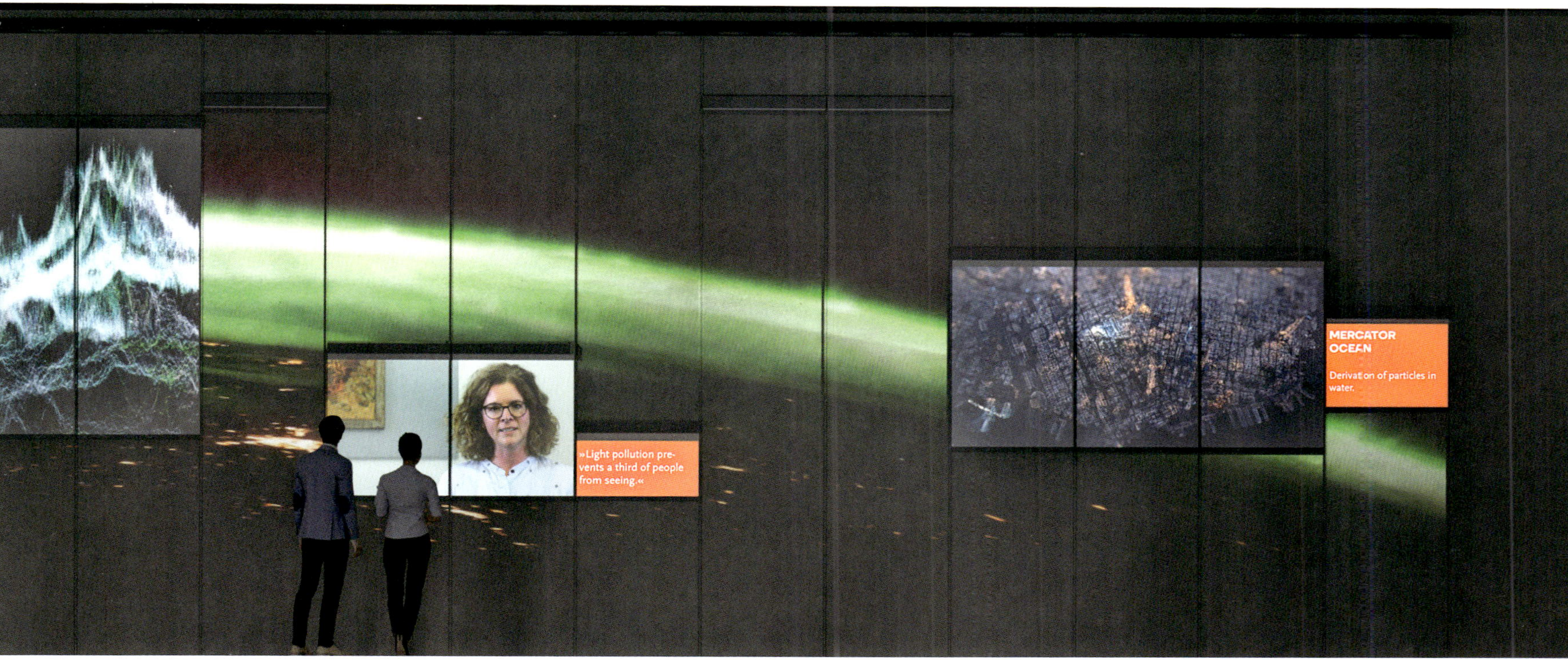

Fig. pp. 202–203:
The lecture notebook 'Prof. Friedrich Paulsen's Lectures on Psychology and Anthropology' was written by Friedrich Blanck (1855–1939) in Berlin. Science and scholarship are nurtured by scepticism as the pathway toward knowledge. In these university lecture notes, which date from summer semester 1885, the student contradicts the professor in capital letters: 'I DOUBT THAT!'

[illegible] gleiche

[illegible] erhoben w[illegible]

[illegible] als die glei[illegible]

[illegible] =DIES[illegible]

Rahm[illegible]

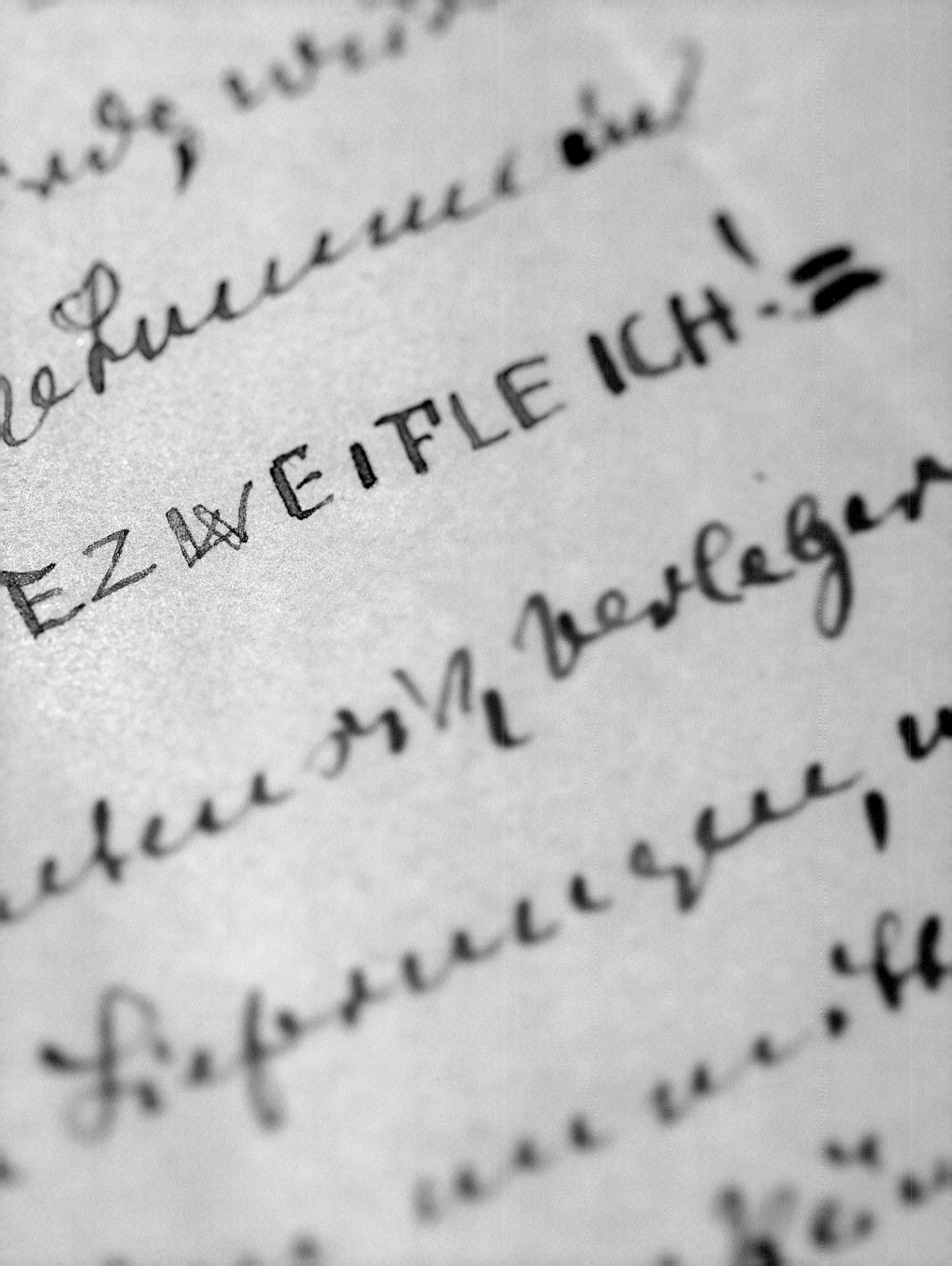
EZWEIFLE ICH!

Via the staircase to the palace basement at Portal Passageway 3, visitors enter an installation that deals with the history of the site and offers insights into the foundation of the historical Palace, consisting of oak piles, which were stabilized by a massive wooden grid.

Fig. pp. 206–207:
As a 'flashback' of history, a large piece of plastic tarpaulin from the facade simulation of 1993 decorates Hall 3 on the ground floor of the eastern wing along the river Spree. With her perfect one-to-one simulation, commissioned by the association of friends Förderverein Berliner Schloss e. V., the Parisian artist Catherine Feff succeeded in persuading the citizenry of Berlin of the beauty of the former Baroque palace.

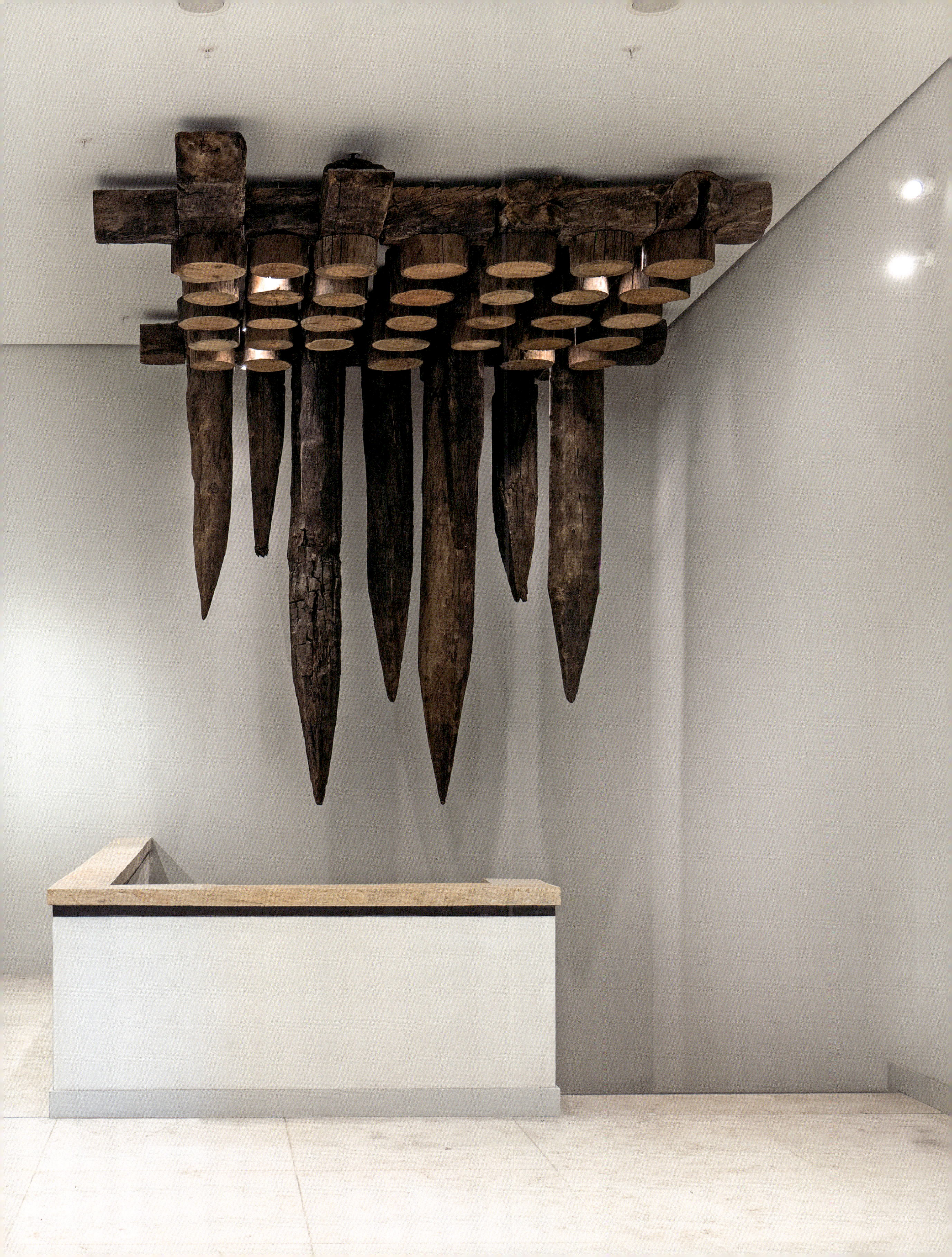

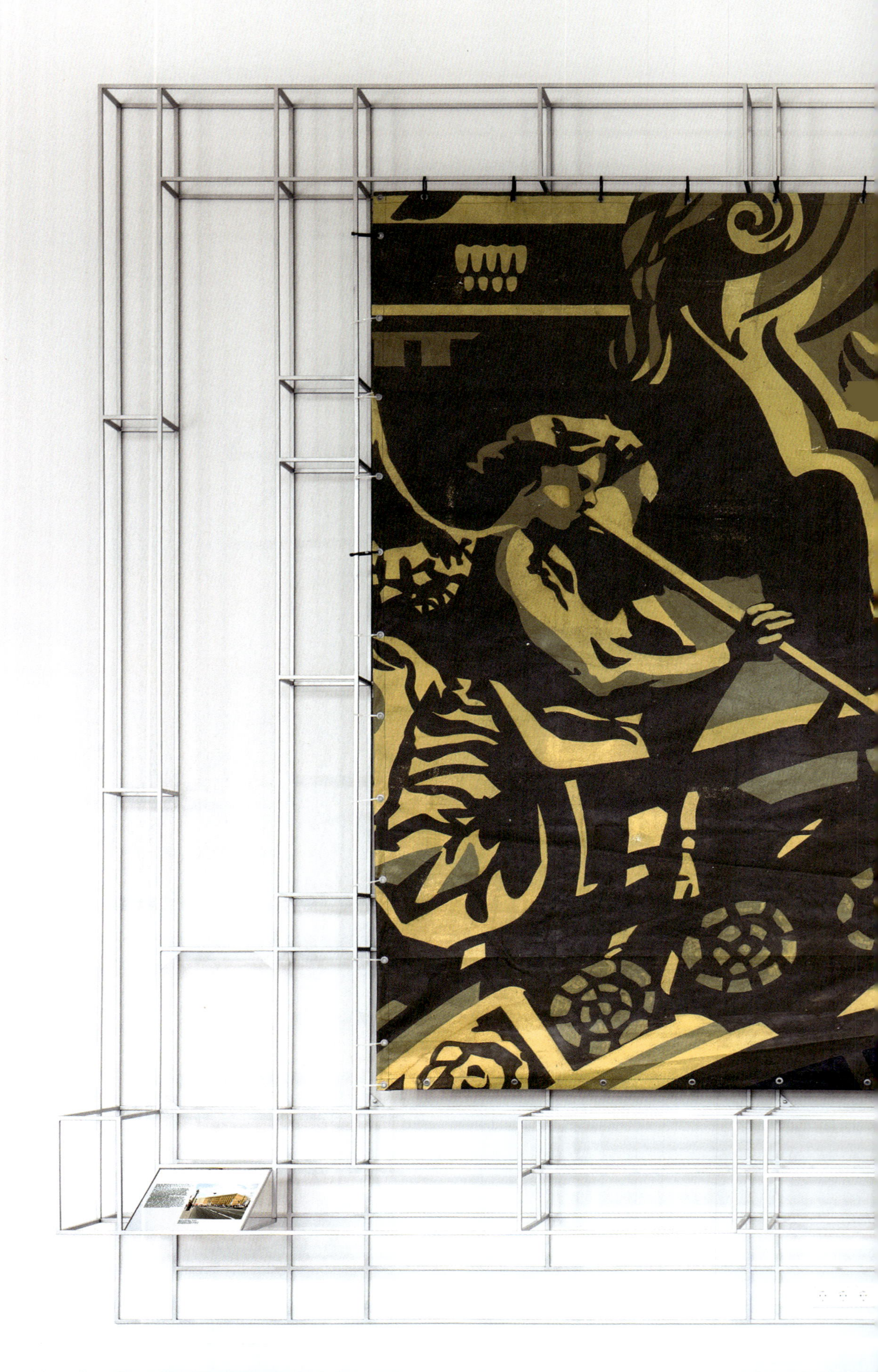

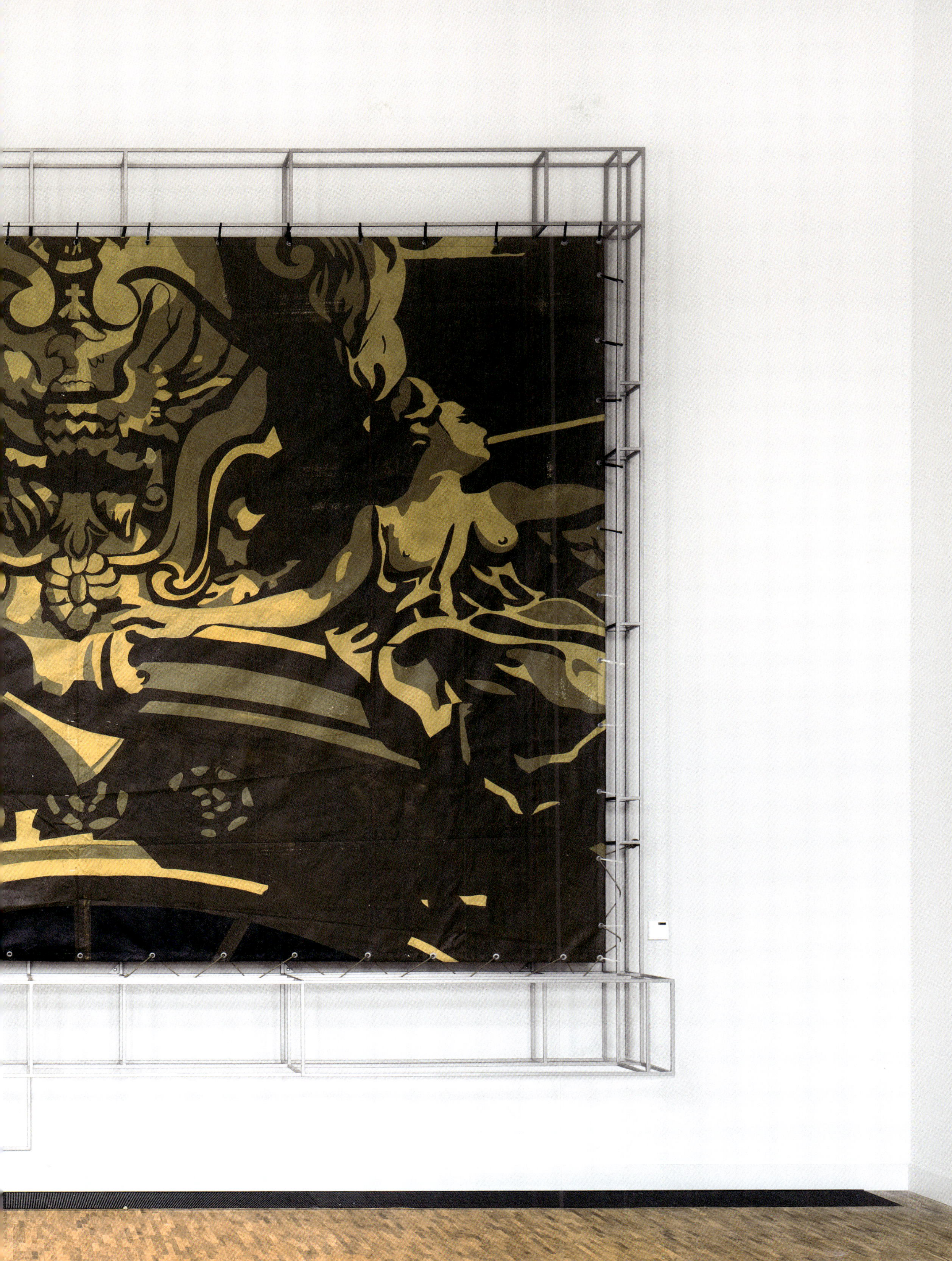

Lectures, Concerts, Performances –
Synergy between Events and Collections
at the Humboldt Forum

*An Excursus by
Lavinia Frey*

Dakar, winter of 2019. On this Saturday morning, the auditorium of the new Musée des Civilisations noires (Museum of Black Civilizations) is full almost to capacity. Important West African specialists from the realms of scholarship and art, representatives of cultural institutions, along with a number of guests from Europe and the United States, have come together for a two-day symposium on the invitation of the Senegalese economist and author Felwine Sarr. Under discussion are the questions of material and non-material cultural heritage and of alterity. The question is raised as to how cultural heritage, in particular the West African cultural heritage can be narrated today, in the wake of colonialism and under the impact of post-colonialism. Are museums nothing more than refrigerators and mausoleums? Are the exhibited objects shown aseptically in display cases for all eternity, robbed of their original contexts? Is it not instead only the practices that are associated with the objects, whether music or dance, ritual or handicraft production, that generate a fascination and a deeper appreciation for culture? Can these be brought into relationship with a museum, which then becomes a living place? Or would it then still be a museum at all? And what happens when these traditions are mixed with contemporary southern, western, eastern traditions, when art producers appropriate these practices and create something new?

These are central questions for both Dakar and Berlin. The task of museums and cultural institutions is to narrate the history of objects, cultural entanglements, interdependencies, ruptures and questions in a multi-perspectival way so that they enthral, fascinate, make a deepened understanding possible and stimulate curiosity.

When an Indonesian gamelan ensemble that has been admired as an object by generations of Berliners in the Ethnologisches Museum (Ethnological Museum) in Dahlem is now combined with other art forms and narratives, it expands into new dimensions of experience. Precisely this occurred in the presentation of *Setan Jawa*: a black-and-white silent film with Indonesian shadow theatre and modern dance in a synthesis with a European orchestra and a traditional gamelan orchestra – not the historical one, however, that is also on

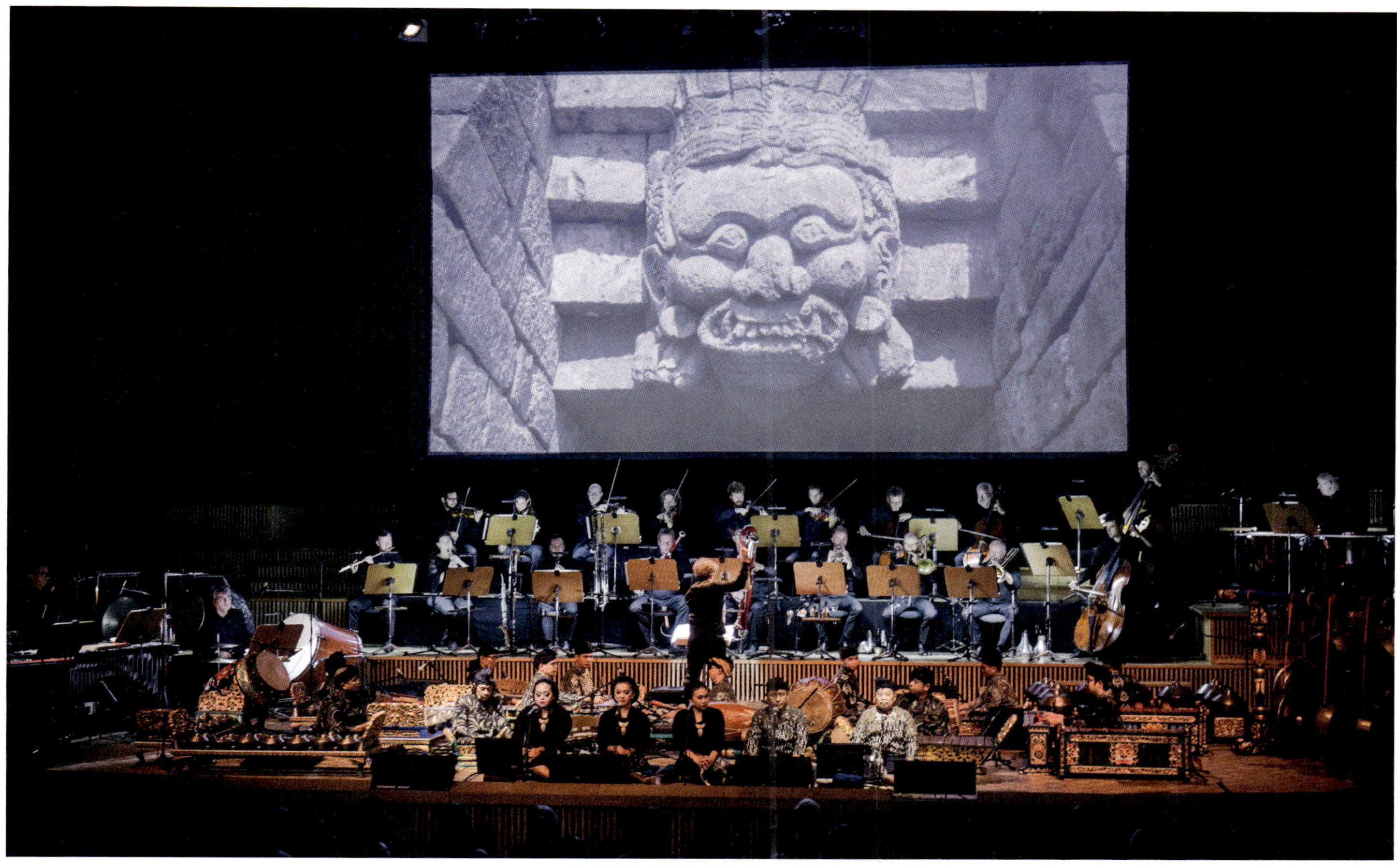

view in the exhibition – formed a fascinating work of art that was given its German premiere in 2018 in the context of the Humboldt-Box exhibition *[laut] Die Welt hören / [Sound] Listening to the World* in cooperation with the Rundfunk-Sinfonieorchester (Radio Symphony Orchestra) Berlin. While the performance, a collaboration between the director Garin Nugroho, the composer Rahayu Supanggah and the conductor Iain Grandage together with the Javanese gamelan ensemble Garasi Seni Benawa, had already enjoyed considerable success in Melbourne and London, it had an even broader impact in Berlin in connection with the Humboldt Forum. Why? Not only the performance itself contributed to the impact, but also the gamelan orchestra as an object. Before and after the performances, the musicians offered audience members an opportunity to examine the individual instruments close-up, explaining their functions, their special features, their traditions, the techniques used to play them. This collaborative project, involving a nineteen-piece Javanese gamelan ensemble and twenty musicians from Berlin, was exemplary of the aims and objectives of the Humboldt Forum, which brings together the exhibited objects with artistic production, allowing them to serve as points of departure and inspirations for continually new event formats.

With two large spaces on the ground floor and numerous smaller halls and spaces in the exhibition galleries, the Humboldt Forum is in an ideal position to generate such connections in intimate ways and to render them accessible to experience.

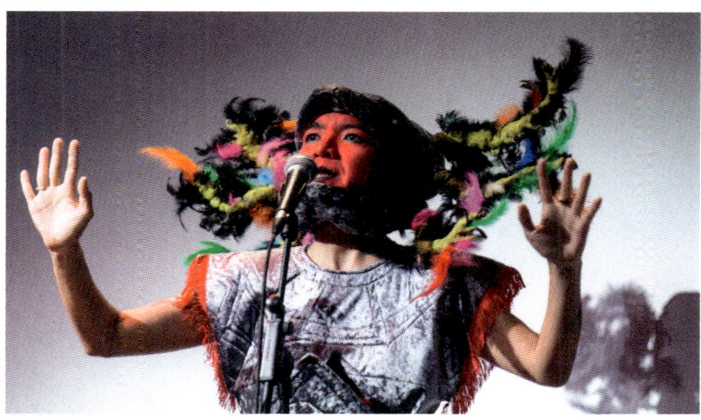

Setan Jawa – Der javanische Teufel (The Javanese Devil), silent film with live orchestral music by the Javanese gamelan ensemble Garasi Seni Benawa and the Rundfunk Sinfonieorchester Berlin (Radio Symphony Orchestra) in the Haus des Rundfunks Berlin, 2018

Performance of El viaje de formol (Formaldehyde Trip) by Naomi Rincón Gallardo in the programme on the occasion of Alexander von Humboldt's 250th birthday at the Humboldt Forum, 2019

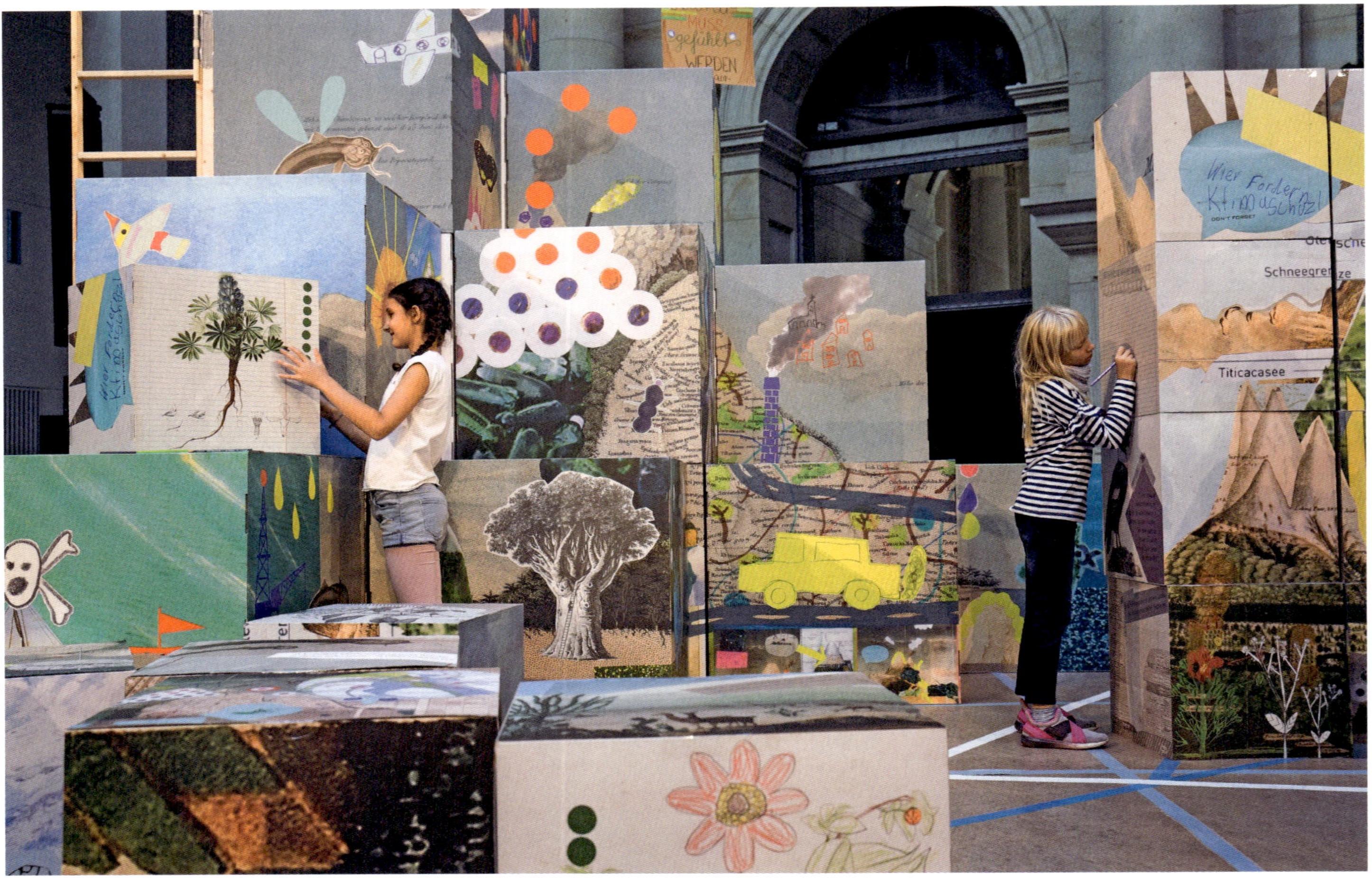

Participatory installation Narrated
Histories on the occasion of
Alexander von Humboldt's
250th birthday at the Humboldt
Forum, 2019

But the Humboldt Forum would not be called a forum if it
did not provide a space for other forms of expression as well.
Film and literature in particular provide very different forms
of access to the themes addressed in the collections. Not just
the performance of a cultural practice itself, but also a poetic
approach to it, whether in language or imagery, can open up
perpetually new and unexpected perspectives, engendering
emotional connections or eliciting a sense of wonder. Here, film
screenings and lectures play central roles. In coordination with
the exhibitions, these media produce a more complex picture
of the theme under investigation, complementing the image,
enriching experience. For us, the great opportunity – and the
biggest task – is to clarify the link to the present moment.
Contemporary film and literature catapult very different
African and Asian images and voices into our minds than the
ones many of us grew up with. They demonstrate in particular
how intertwined divergent cultural forms can be, highlighting
the questions that are central elsewhere, which in turn pose
new questions for us or situate local themes in new contexts:
identity, homeland, faith and migration, to mention only a few
catchphrases.

Central here is participation, direct involvement. 'If you do
it for me but without me, it's against me.' This sentence was
conveyed to us as a challenge by George Abungu, a member
of our team of international experts since 2015. In concrete
terms, this means collaborating and cooperating with various
institutions, groups and individuals worldwide and in Berlin.
Essential to the mission of the Humboldt Forum are the insights

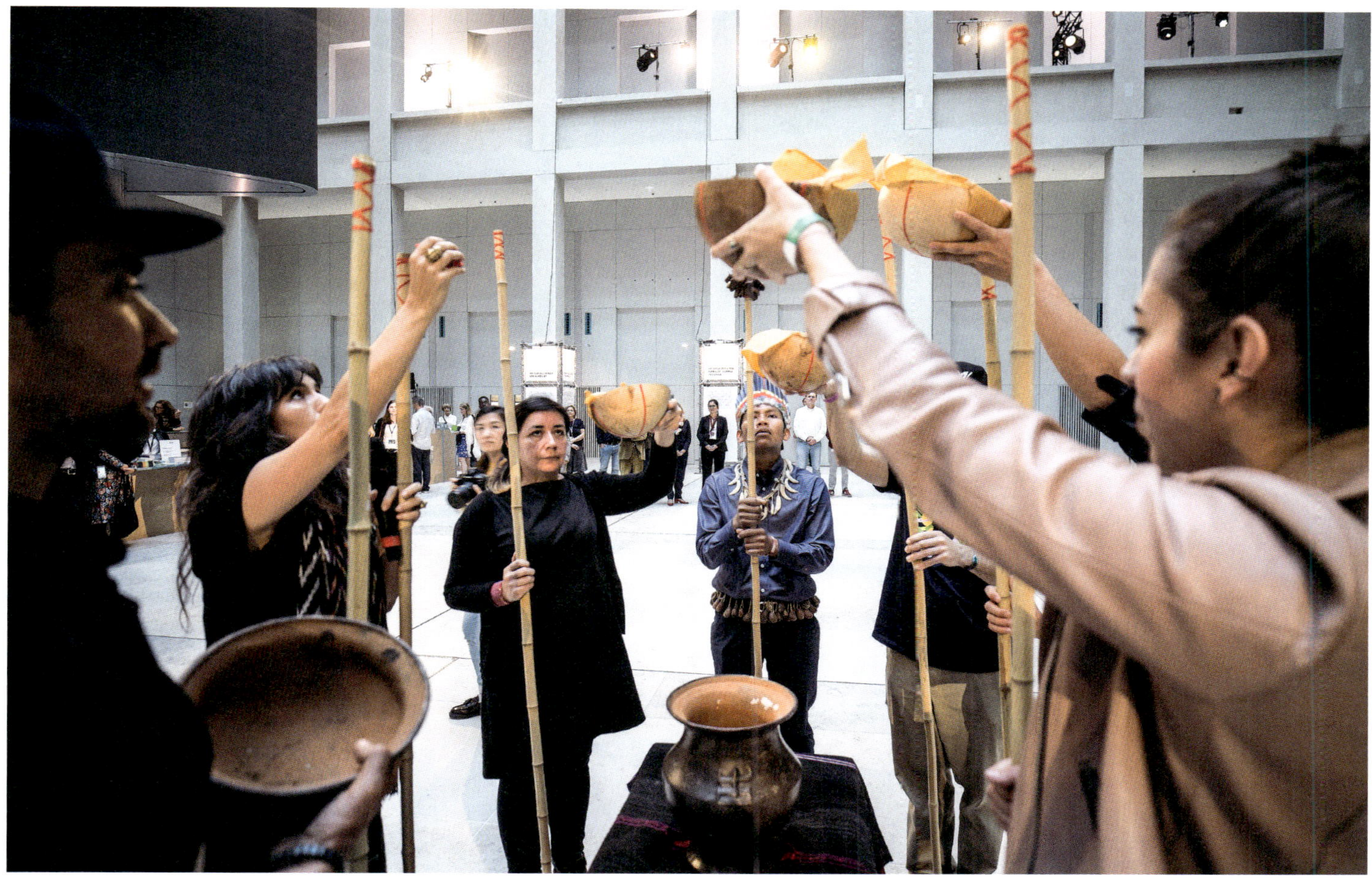

that emerge here through new contents and new forms.
For our performative and artistic formats, the proximity to the
collections makes possible approaches to a range of themes
that transcend boundaries and borders.

With Wilhelm and Alexander von Humboldt as fitting
namesakes, the awareness that everything is interconnected
is positioned at the centre of our concerns: the connection to
Museum Island with its collections, which in turn highlight
these interdependencies from a European perspective; the
connection to Humboldt-Universität and issues related to
current research, in particular ecology and diversity; the
connection to urban society, with its diverse communities,
connected via the Berlin Exhibition, as well as the fascinating
and challenging history of the location itself, as the former site
of the Berlin Palace and the Palast der Republik (Palace of the
Republic).

In this way, the Humboldt Forum becomes a place of
negotiation and contestation: after all, a forum thrives on open
discussion, on a multiplicity of narratives and perspectives.

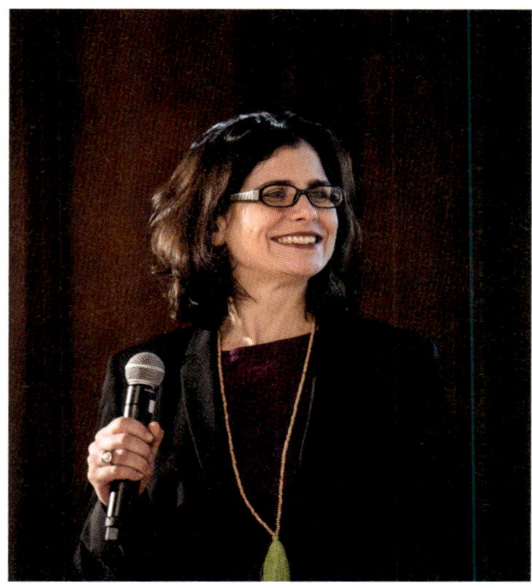

Lavinia Frey

Performance in the Grand Foyer
during the ceremony on the
occasion of Alexander von
Humboldt's 250th birthday, 2019

Fig. pp. 212–213
O Ciclo Anual no Rio Tiquié (Annual
Cycle on the Tiquié): night-time light
projection on the east facade of the
Humboldt Forum on the occasion of
Alexander von Humboldt's 250th
birthday, 2019

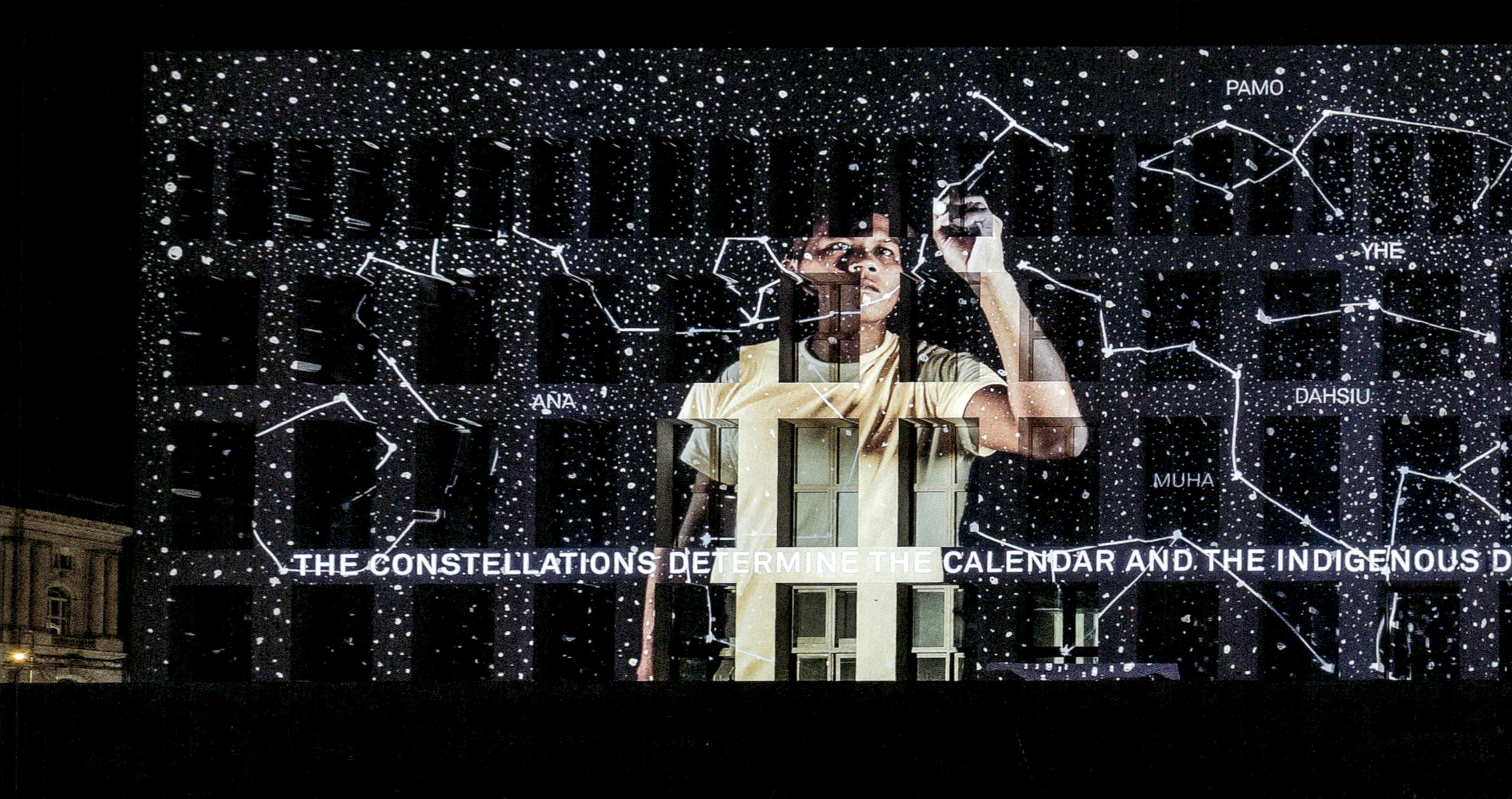
PAMO
YHE
ANA
DAHSIU
MUHA
THE CONSTELLATIONS DETERMINE THE CALENDAR AND THE INDIGENOUS D

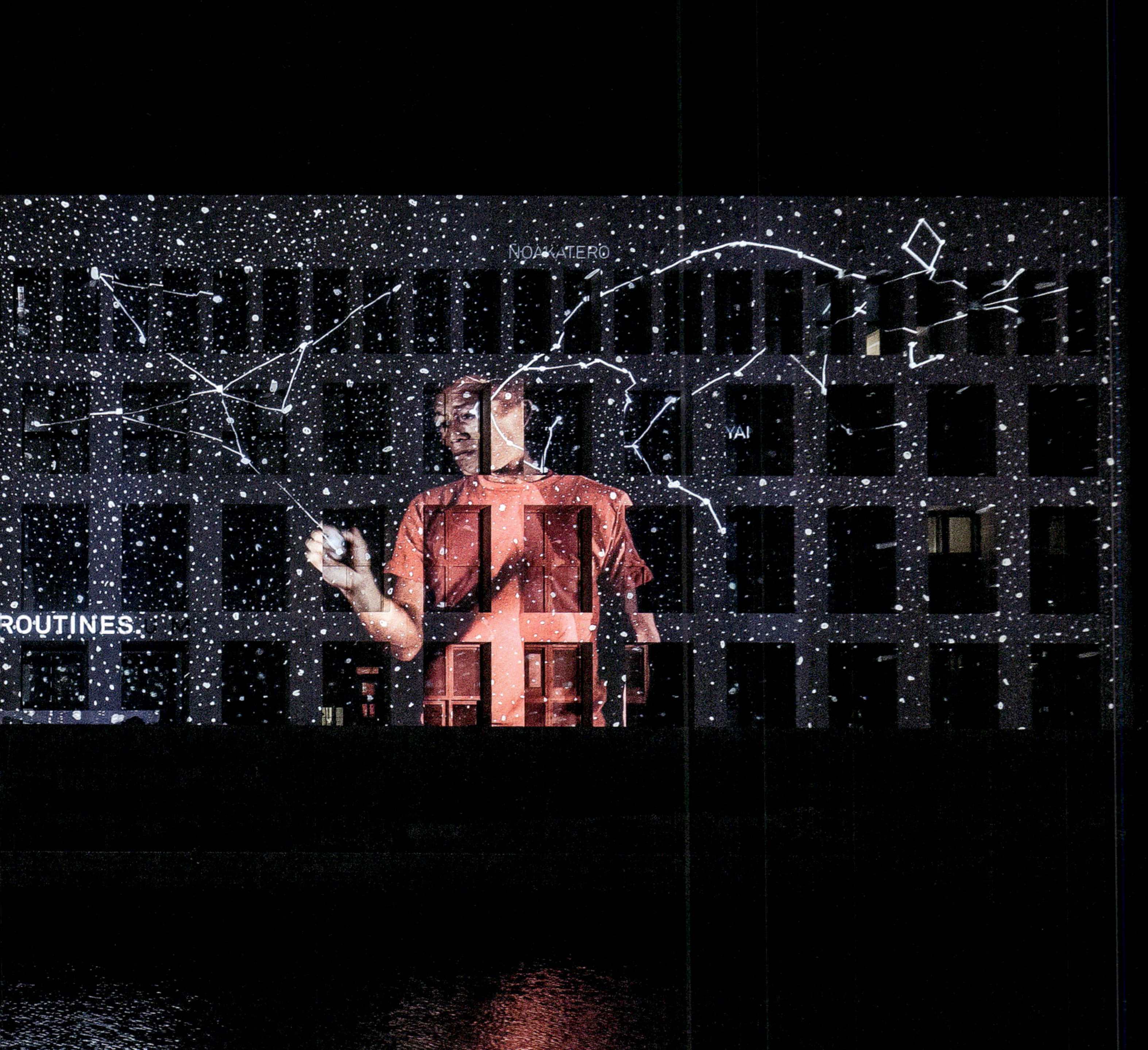

NOAKATERO
YAI
ROUTINES.

'A New Sphere of Action for the Universal Gaze'

A Conversation with Horst Bredekamp, Neil MacGregor and Hermann Parzinger

Horst Bredekamp, Neil MacGregor,
Hermann Parzinger (from the left)

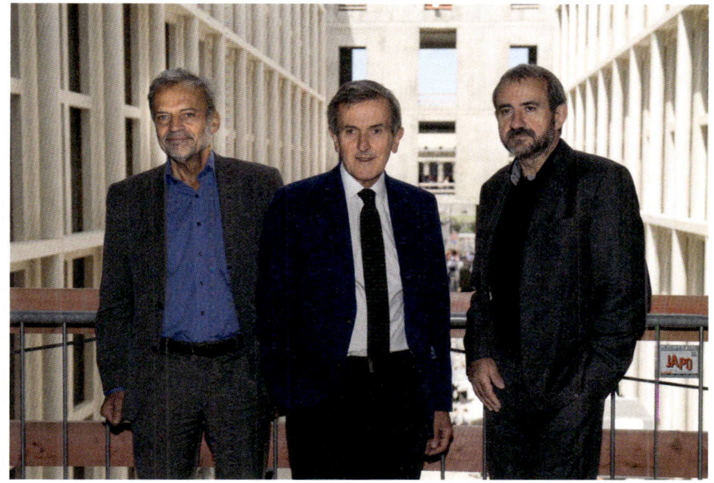

*Herr Parzinger, reviewing the past decade, beginning with
the conclusion of the design competition and ending with the
completion of the Humboldt Forum – are you satisfied with what has
been achieved?*

Hermann Parzinger: It was a process that had to overcome
many obstacles and adapt again and again to altered
framework conditions. When I became president of the
Stiftung Preussischer Kulturbesitz (Prussian Cultural Heritage
Foundation), we organized workshops with experts from around
the world in order to reflect together about the ways in which
non-European collections could be presented in the twenty-
first century. The topic of colonialism was already current at
the time; the topic of restitution had not yet become so central.
An important phase of development was the Humboldt Lab
Dahlem, the rehearsal stage, which Martin Heller organized.
There we were able to try out many things that would later be
integrated into the planning process. In the subsequent phase,
we three founding directors attempted to lay out a number of
major thematic trajectories for the project. Perhaps it would
have been simpler to have simply designated one individual ten
years ago to take responsibility for all aspects of the Humboldt
Forum; but who, back then, would have been willing to take
on such a task when so much still remained uncertain? Under
the circumstances, we can be satisfied with the way things
developed.

*Mr MacGregor, you headed the British Museum before becoming
a founding director of the Humboldt Forum. Do you regard the two
institutions as comparable?*

Neil MacGregor: With regard to the collections as well as to
the larger ambitions of the project, it is certainly possible to
compare the Humboldt Forum with the British Museum. Both
strive to investigate and display cultural objects from around
the world, and both strive to function as places of debate about
society. On the other hand, the organizational preconditions
are divergent. The British Museum is an institution with a very
clear-cut governance structure and a clear-cut approach to
arriving at decisions. In London, I dealt with structures that had

existed for hundreds of years, while in Berlin, by contrast, the
founding directorate was obliged to devise these structures for
the Humboldt Forum project from scratch.

*Herr Bredekamp, one of your central ideas for the Humboldt Forum –
alongside the revitalization of the legacy of the Humboldt brothers –
was to reclaim the idea of the Kunstkammer (Cabinet of Art and
Curiosities) cultivated by the prince-electors of Brandenburg and the
Prussian kings. What remains of these ideas in the Humboldt Forum
in its final form?*

Horst Bredekamp: The idea goes back to Gottfried Wilhelm
Leibniz, whose 'Drôle de pensée' (Strange Thought) of 1675 is
perhaps the boldest, most radical reflection on the museum to
date: the idea of a thinking machine that would be organized
around various collections. Later Leibniz revived his concept
in relation to the *Kunstkammer* in the Berlin Palace when he
founded the Academy. In one of its wings, the Academy
was to house a 'theatre of nature and art'. There is also the
fact that the Humboldt brothers took a strong interest in the
Kunstkammer in the Berlin Palace – which, incidentally, had
been Berlin's first publicly accessible museum beginning
about 1800. Initially, Alexander von Humboldt wanted to use
it to found a world museum that would have been associated
with the Academy of Sciences. In 1809, however, Wilhelm
von Humboldt succeeded in having the natural-scientific and
medical collections of the *Kunstkammer* transferred as an
inaugural gift to the newly founded university. In this sense,
the Berlin University is a daughter of the Berlin Palace. My
proposal to the commission on the historical centre of Berlin in
2001 was to relate this idea of a knowledge laboratory via the
Humboldt brothers back to Leibniz. This concept was realized
in the structure of the Humboldt Forum. It represents a major
success that the Humboldt Forum stands under the motto
'museum as a process'. The most conspicuous expression of
this is perhaps the Academy, to be housed in the first upper
storey. Disappointing on the other hand is the fact that today
there is no place for an object-based reconstruction of the
Kunstkammer; however, the project has not been definitively
abandoned either.

When you were appointed as founding directors, did the three of you expect the colonialism debate to assume such significance for the Humboldt Forum?

Neil MacGregor: No. Through my activity at the British Museum, of course, I was aware that every collection of cultural artefacts from Africa, Asia, the Americas and Oceania raises questions about provenance and the possibility that they were acquired under coercive or inequitable circumstances. The disputes over the Parthenon Frieze or the Benin Bronzes were at the heart of debates about the inventories of today's universal museums. What I did not expect, however, was that the discussion of Germany's colonial history would become so heated. A fundamental difference from the situation in London is that there debates about the origins and optimal places of display of the objects were conducted in the context of long-standing contacts and scholarly collaboration with colleagues and cultural actors from the countries of origin. In Berlin – in particular as a result of the loss of the colonies after World War I – this is not the case. Rather than being international in orientation, the discussion is in large measure internal to Germany. This was true as well for the debate about the role and the function of the objects in the Humboldt Forum that date from the colonial era. In London, to remain with the example of the Benin Bronzes and the Parthenon sculptures, besides the debate about the circumstances of acquisition, a key central question was of the public role that could now be played by these objects in London, Athens, Benin or, very importantly, elsewhere in the world: to explore what they could convey about a historical civilization, and whether it was advantageous to have some of these objects on view at multiple locations. What I found surprising in Berlin was that the question revolved less around the public function of the objects as cultural and historical artefacts, whether in Germany, in their countries of origin or elsewhere, and much more around the circumstances under which they were acquired. I think this relative under-playing of the inherent human significance of historico-cultural collections for the world-wide memory and understanding of a civilisation is concerning.

Hermann Parzinger: I would never have expected the debate to have become so emotional. I was not surprised that we found ourselves obliged to face the topic of colonialism. In our initial considerations regarding the exhibition modules for Cameroon and the Turpan Caves in China, for example, colonialism and acquisition history already played an important role. Meanwhile, this theme has acquired a degree of vehemence that I really never would have expected. For the Humboldt Forum, however, precisely this aspect represents a great opportunity. My approach to the project has always been guided very strongly by the collections. This led to my desire to take as many trips as possible to the countries of origin of these objects, in Asia, Oceania, Africa, and North and South America, in order to establish contacts with experts, cultural actors and representatives of indigenous societies there. This input from outside is necessary in order to develop new perspectives on the objects. I see enormous potential for the future in cooperation with various actors from many different countries, among them Venezuela, Colombia, Brazil, Angola, Tanzania, Rwanda, the United States and China. In a sense, this approach represents a continuation of my earlier work as an archaeologist, since international cooperation is indispensable in that field.

Horst Bredekamp: To my way of thinking, the Humboldt Forum failed to respond adequately to the vehemence of this negativity. At least initially I thought it best not to fuel the debate further. I only reacted publicly during my third year as a founding director. In retrospect I see this as a mistake, since, to invoke Antonio Gramsci, it is a question of cultural hegemony, and the conflict should have been taken on earlier and in a more decisive way. But it is a form of lunacy when, in this context, the programmatically anticolonial and antiracist tradition that culminated in Franz Boas is interpreted as a disguised element of colonial domination. The concept of the Humboldt Forum is one of confidence and grandeur. Together with the university, it is meant to sit in the middle of the capital of a nation that has incurred horrendous guilt during its history, and to serve as a place for non-European cultures and for thinking on a global scale. The post-colonial debate has attempted to discredit

the enterprise as window dressing, with the argument that
every object contained in Berlin's ethnological collections
can only be seen as the product of European colonialism.
In my view, however, this argument represents a reversal of
historical reality. The origins of the Berlin collections are found
in a universalistic point of view: they represent an attempt
to rescue that which modern civilization was destroying
worldwide. Around 1900, the Völkerkundemuseum (Museum
of Ethnology) was officially deemed ineffectual when it came
to serving colonial interests. For this reason, an enormous
museum of colonialism was created in Berlin-Treptow as a
counterweight. I regard it as utterly disastrous to place this
universalizing tradition on the defensive.

*How is the Humboldt Forum responding to debate about the
colonial origins of the collections?*

Neil MacGregor: Concerning this point, I believe that the
governing structure created by the three founding directors is
quite helpful. The circumstance that the Humboldt Forum is not
the owner of the museum collections plays a decisive role here.
This means that the Forum is a place where the significance
and the future of the collections can be discussed freely. Here,
perspectives from around the world can converge, in particular
from the countries – or cultures – where the objects originated.
In this respect, the Humboldt Forum enjoys an institutional
advantage over the British Museum or the Musée du Quai
Branly, where such debates of course already take place, but
always in the context of their own ownership and stewardship
of the collections. It would be helpful in public discussions
if it could be made more explicit that the collections belong
not to the Humboldt Forum, but to the Stiftung Preussischer
Kulturbesitz (Prussian Cultural Heritage Foundation): that
changes the framework of the debate.

Horst Bredekamp: The fundamental ethic of the museum,
namely to ensure the protection of the works displayed in it,
should be perceived as a possibility for cooperation, not as a
means of coercion. Then it will become clear that the Humboldt
Forum has served as a catalyst for an acrimonious and painful

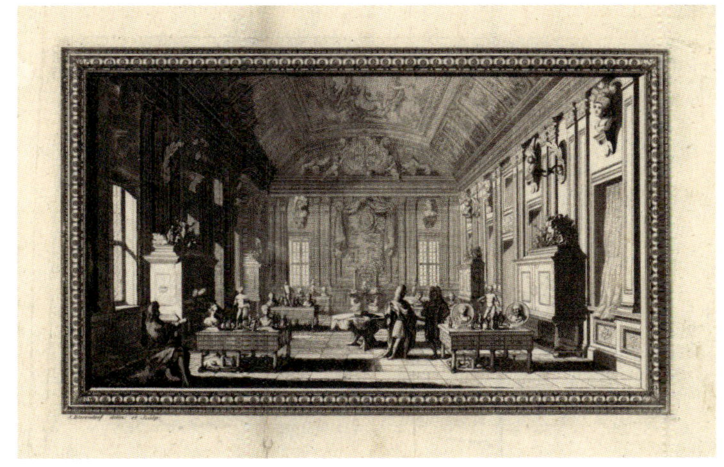

View of the Berlin Cabinet of Art and
Curiosities in the Apothecary Wing
of the Palace, engraving, c. 1695

Following pages:
Design for the exhibition area on
Amazonia in the Ethnologisches
Museum (Ethnological Museum)

Visualization of the cupola hall with
the central Asian Turfan collection
of the Museum für Asiatische Kunst
(Museum of Asian Art)

217

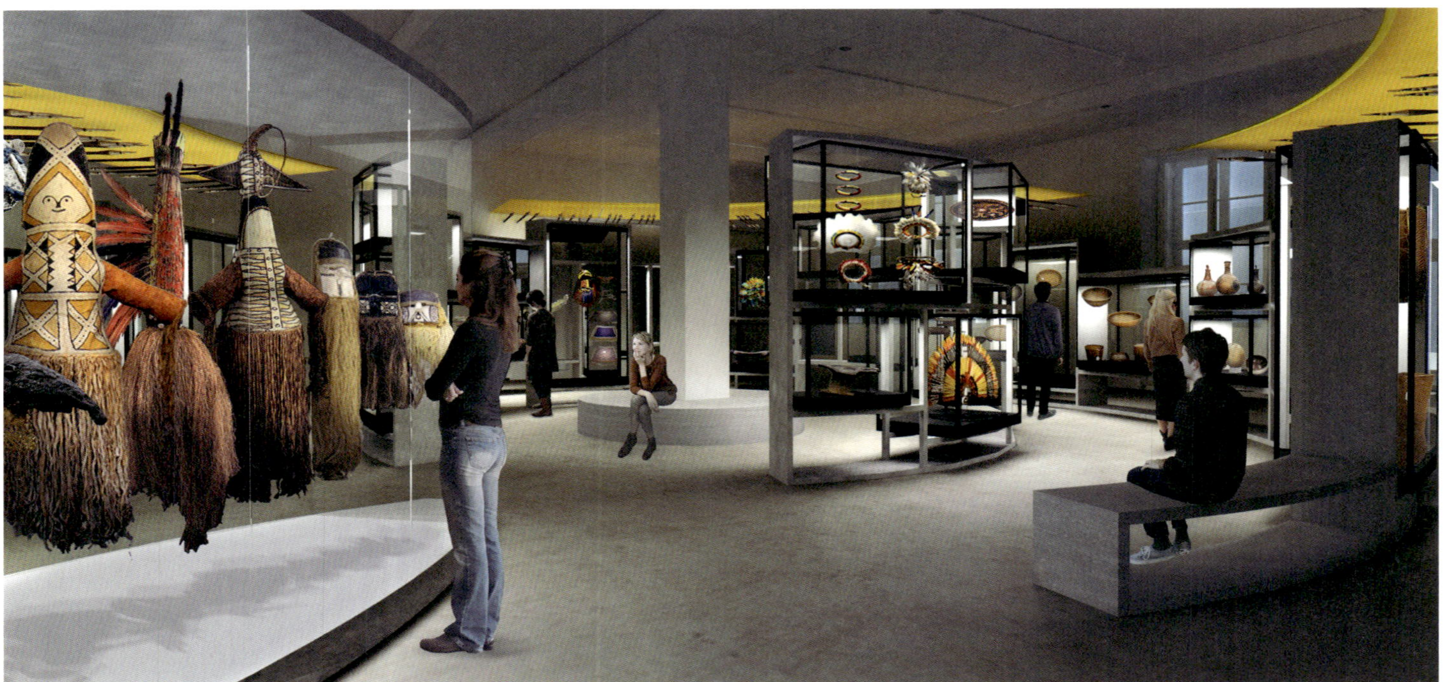

debate, but that in the end a new element has emerged within our picture of German history, one that links up with an Enlightenment that deserves the name.

Is the idea of the universal museum still relevant?

Horst Bredekamp: More than ever. The era of postmodernist fragmentation of knowledge has also meant the discrediting of every attempt to conceive of culture and civilization as wholes. When we consider the global problems that assail us daily, it is an indispensable necessity to expose ourselves to the totality of the world. Exemplifying this alongside Leibniz is Alexander von Humboldt with his idea of the cosmos, which is more timely today than it might have seemed after the appearance of Darwin's *Origin of Species*. The same is true of Wilhelm von Humboldt's proposal to seek access to the languages of the world. Impelled by anticolonial aspirations, both consistently advocated the idea of a world museum where objects could be studied comparatively. If this idea is discredited, we face the danger that the world will revert towards identitiarian spheres – a ghastly prospect.

Hermann Parzinger: Actually, universal museums in the narrow sense exist only in London, Paris, New York, Saint Petersburg and, in the present case, Berlin. In my view, these museums are more important now than ever, with cities like Berlin being strongly shaped by immigration from around the world. Museums need to respond to this, to take account of the expectations and needs of society. They can do much to promote tolerance and respect for foreign cultures. But museums must also face the fact that ownership of their collections involves an obligation to cooperate with the countries of origin, the societies of origin, to research

provenance and to return objects that were acquired unlawfully. The enormous opportunity here is to go in completely new directions when it comes to developing new approaches to dealing with the collections. The 'Universal Museum of Berlin' consists of Museum Island and the Humboldt Forum, which together showcase a singular concentration of world culture. Emerging here at the heart of Berlin is a place where it becomes possible to contemplate the world as a whole in the Humboldtian sense and to seek to understand developments from cultural, economic and climatological perspectives. In the age of globalization, this is enormously important. Decisive here is the search for interconnections and correlations, not the re-regionalization of collections, which leads towards the separation of that which should be considered comparatively.

The contradiction between the Baroque facade and world museum inside has long preoccupied discussions about the Humboldt Forum. Do you regard this as an obstacle or an opportunity for the project?

Neil MacGregor: I see it as a great opportunity. When we view the reconstructed facade of the new museum, we recognize that it stands for a culture that perished, as did many of the cultures displayed in the building itself. All cultures, all civilizations are fragile and impermanent. With the Humboldt Forum, the reconstruction of the palace facades serves as a reminder that cultures must always be reconstructed and reconceived – we use the past while at the same time transforming it, in the process reassessing the significance of its individual elements. I find this extremely helpful in discussions about the Humboldt Forum. Elements of the past are there, but they must be reconsidered and recombined. The building

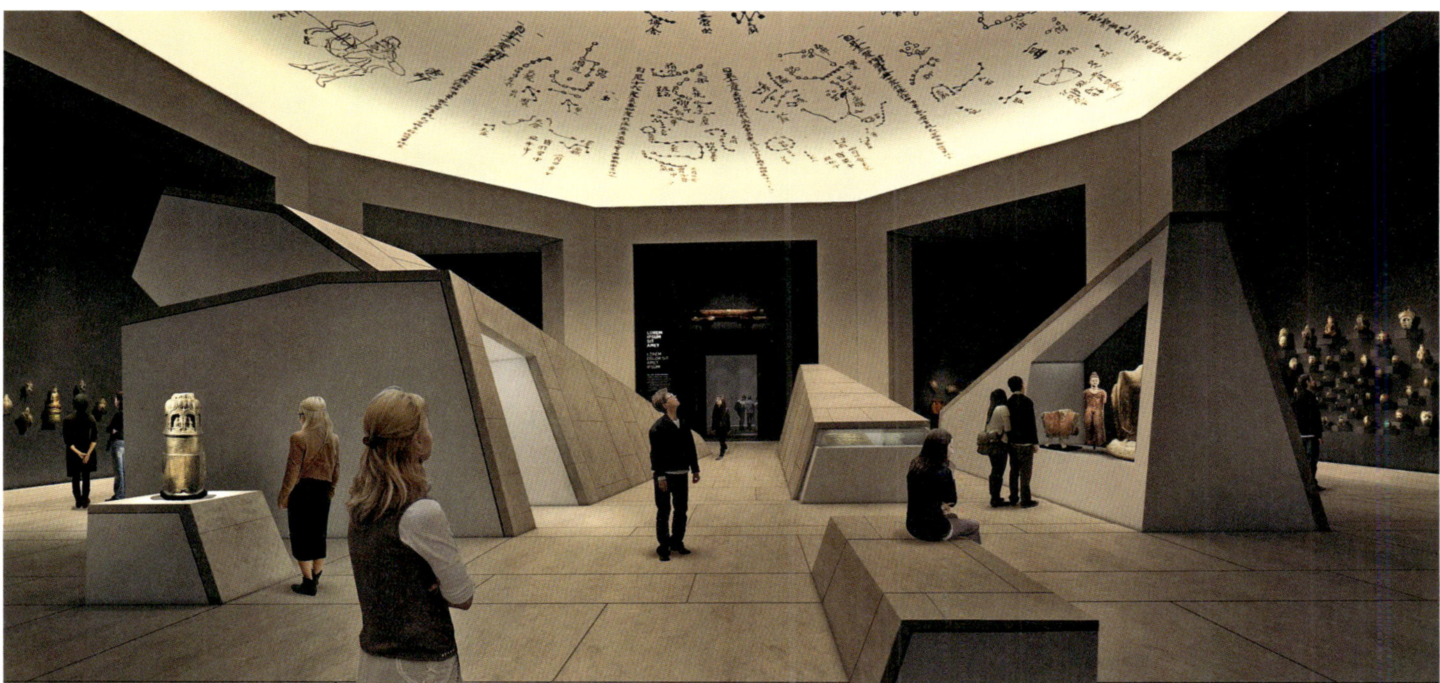

serves as a reminder that we must continually redefine our ideas about any culture, any civilization.

Horst Bredekamp: In the beginning, I wasn't convinced by the architecture of the reconstructed Palace. At that time, a *pasticcio* of the Palast der Republik (Palace of the Republic) and a bold, shrewdly conceived new building seemed to me more plausible. But I've learned that the facade represents a possibility rather than an impediment. Franco Stella is a product of the best tradition of Italian rationalism, and had no intention of producing a kitschy amalgamation of Baroque facade and modern interior. Both as a theoretician and a practitioner, the connection between portals, openings and streets were of elementary importance to him, which is wonderful for the corporeal experience of the building. When it comes to the architecture, I have done a turnaround.

Hermann Parzinger: From the beginning, it was a challenge to bring together form and content. Of course, the fact that the debate about the Humboldt Forum was and remains so emotionally charged has something to do with the building and what it stands for. Had a futuristic building been constructed here, there would have been a discussion, but probably not with this intensity. The reconstruction of the palace facade contributes to shifting the history of the collections even more to the centre of concern. Justifiably so, in my opinion. Berlin is also the city of the Congo conference, and as a colonial power Germany committed serious crimes. For me, an awareness of our own history is a precondition for the further development of society. These things simply cannot be omitted from consideration.

The building is to be characterized by a mixture of permanent and temporary exhibitions. This will demand much concentration as well as time from visitors. What should interested visitors take away from the Humboldt Forum?

Hermann Parzinger: We offer visitors diverse forms of access to the exhibitions. First, there are what we call the highlights, which allow you to experience the most important objects and their histories in a rapid tour. Secondly, visitors can familiarize themselves with the individual collections through repeated visits; here we need to promote a sense of fascination with the Humboldt Forum among visitors. The intention is that they will learn that world art was created in Asia, Africa, the Americas and Oceania, and that we have to know this art. And that cultural developments must always be considered in dependence upon the specific natural environment and climatic conditions. Another important aspect is the interrelatedness of world cultures. Whether the Indian Ocean or the Silk Road, globalized worlds existed very early on. And finally, the history of the collection is a reflection of our own history: among the crucial themes are colonialism, slavery, exploitation, but also the drive to engage in research, curiosity, the scientific impulse to investigate the world.

Neil MacGregor: The large glazed interior courtyard sends a clear message to visitors: although this building resembles a royal palace from the outside, it is in fact a place of encounter for people from all over the world. That the Forum bears the name of both William and Alexander von Humboldt is already an important signal: neither the natural nor the man-made, historical world can be taken for granted. Both are perpetually endangered, and each generation is faced with the task of rediscovering and preserving their value and their dignity.

Today, in an age of globalization and rapid climate change, this message is more important than ever. In this respect, the building's appearance and its contents are thoroughly compatible with each other.

How can scholarship and science profit from the Humboldt Forum? How should it develop after the opening?

Horst Bredekamp: The collections of the Berlin Palace set a task for art history that has yet to be fulfilled. In 1838, Franz Kugler produced a catalogue of sorts of the Berlin collections, which led in 1842 to the first liberal exhibition of world art ever organized: an attempt to conceive of the cultural history of humanity as a process, from the earliest stone artefacts up to the globalized world of the nineteenth century. A new field of action for a universal perspective on artefacts could now emerge from this spirit at the Humboldt Forum. The proximity between seminar rooms and exhibition galleries that will be found there fills me with great expectancy, with joyous anticipation. Here it will become possible, and on a grand scale, to establish a link between aesthetic delight and intellectual discovery – something museums consistently aspire to, but which is regularly compromised by practical necessity. Nothing comparable exists at the moment.

Hermann Parzinger: At the Humboldt Forum, the expectation of further development is particularly intense, but I see this as a great opportunity. More than any other museum, it will be a place for debate, including debate about the collections, and it will be necessary to react. Beyond that, the Humboldt Forum is a platform where museums collaborate, jointly developing exhibitions and other projects: museums of technology and natural history, university collections, botanical gardens and so forth can work together here on a completely new basis with museums of art and cultural history. Available for temporary exhibitions is one quarter of the total surface area of the upper storeys. Collections should not be static, they must remain in movement. That is essential to a vibrant centre devoted to art and culture such as the Humboldt Forum.

What will be the enduring merit of the founding directorate?

Neil MacGregor: That will be for others to decide. But I think we can point to two things. First, we created a structure that enables the different autonomous institutions to work another. That was a particularly German challenge. Every other European museum tradition would have established a clear hierarchy in the organization of the institution. The German model is very different. Our task at the Humboldt Forum was to devise a governance structure that could accommodate and coordinate the various participants, each with their own distinct priorities, roles and histories, and each led by a single individual. Nothing like it really exists anywhere else in the world. A second outcome of the founding directorate is, I think, the fostering of a habit of curators to work outside the boundaries of their disciplines, and to collaborate not only with other museums, but also with specialists from very different fields. In Berlin, this was not a matter of course, and there was, if not resistance, then perhaps some hesitation. But today, this curatorial openness is a defining trait of the Humboldt Forum. Art historical and archaeological questions are discussed in a far broader international context and with different assumptions than was the case just a couple of years ago. The institution that contributed most to bringing this change about was the university: it embodies the tradition of continual renewal and expansion of research fields and objectives. That is the spirit of the Humboldt brothers, and the Humboldt Forum will be a proper home for this spirit. Here museums and university converge in new ways, which will produce new forms of knowledge, of understanding and of cultural awareness. I am proud to have been a part of the process that gave rise to this new institution.

Horst Bredekamp: As its programme, the founding directorate advocated the concept of the 'museum as a process'. Accordingly, in a very challenging procedure it brought dynamism into the plans – already largely finalized – for the second and third upper storeys. This intervention pursued the systematic attempt to make the museum an organ of thought, not unlike a university. As far as I can judge today, this switch can no longer be turned off again, and this is the decisive contribution of the founding directorate to the realization of the Humboldt Forum. I myself belong to a circle of altogether three individuals who pursued and followed the entire project from the very beginning through various committees. In the process, I had to witness how a radical idea, probably unavoidably, must endure compromise before being translated into reality. At times, this disappointed me, but on the whole, I remain convinced that the framework and the foundation of this idea have been implemented.

The Humboldt Forum will open incrementally beginning at the end of 2020 and continuing into 2021. Are you happy with this staggered arrangement?

Hermann Parzinger: Of course, the ideal for all of us would have been having everything ready all at once. But we are talking about a gigantic building with 40 000 square metres of total usable surface area – why delay opening areas that are ready now until the last rooms are finished? To that extent, I'm very pleased with the dramaturgy of an opening in stages. There will be a main opening at which the Humboldt Forum can be experienced by the public. In my view, it's very smart to open up the building successively, making it accessible from the lower level and working upwards. It is and remains a tremendous logistical, curatorial and technical challenge.

Interview: Andreas Kilb, Berlin, April 2019

'*At the Humboldt Forum, the expectation of further development is particularly intense, but I see this as a great opportunity.*'

Hermann Parzinger

Timeline:
What Happened on and around the Building Site …

Bernhard Wolter

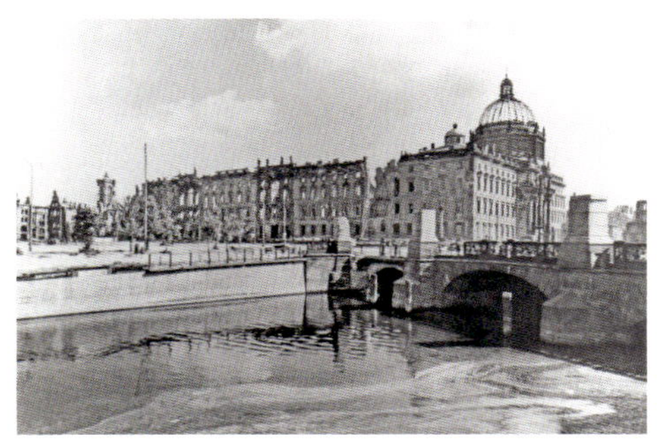

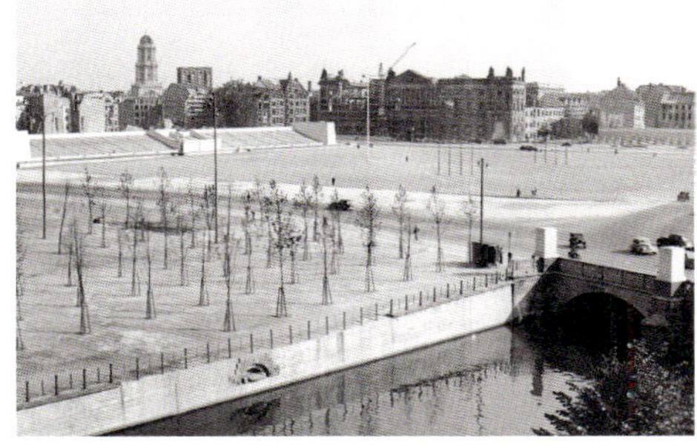

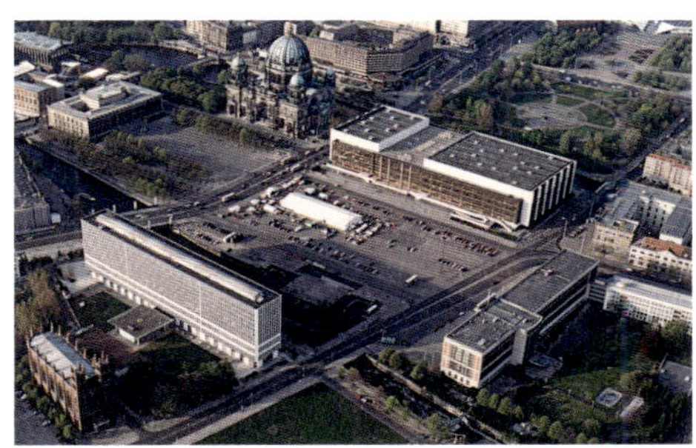

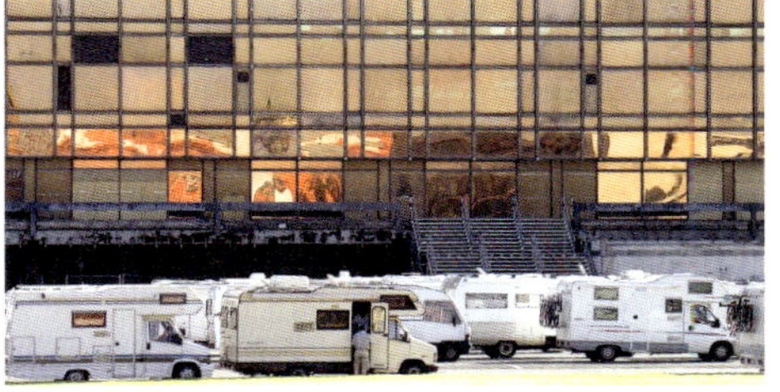

Few people are aware of the enormous cost to the young German Democratic Republic (GDR, more commonly known as East Germany) entailed by the destruction of the Berlin Palace in autumn of 1950: three months of demolition work cost approximately 16 million GDR marks! Immediately before demolition, the precious Baroque sandstone sculptures of Schlüter and Böhme were provisionally documented by students from Humboldt-Universität.

Before the Palast der Republik (Palace of the Republic) opened in 1976, Schlossplatz (Palace Square) remained empty for twenty-five years – only the eastern side was outfitted with a large wooden grandstand. Hundreds of thousands streamed into the square for the annual First of May festivities. To accelerate the procession on the occasionally still cool spring days, Breite Strasse (Broad Street) was widened by demolishing the buildings on its western side.

The Palace of the Republic was the prestige building of the 'capital of the GDR' (East Germany), and it beat the International Congress Centre (ICC) in the western part of the city in a race for rapid construction, yet was soon doomed due to the use of sprayed asbestos. Together with the Staatsratsgebäude (State Council Building) and the Finance Ministry, it formed the new forum of the East German government. For months at a time during the 1990s, the open space in front of the 'Palace' became a much-favoured parking place for mobile homes.

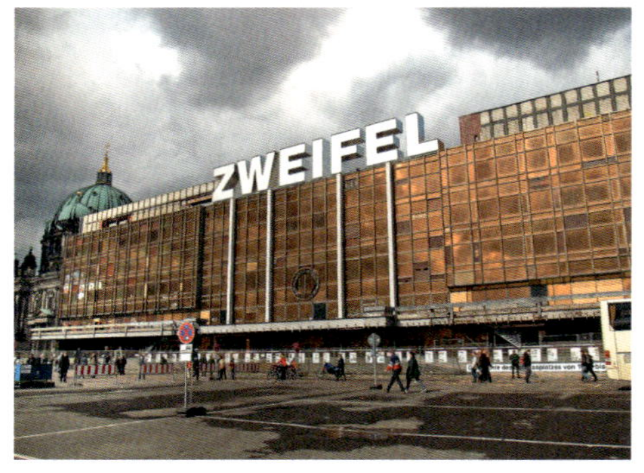

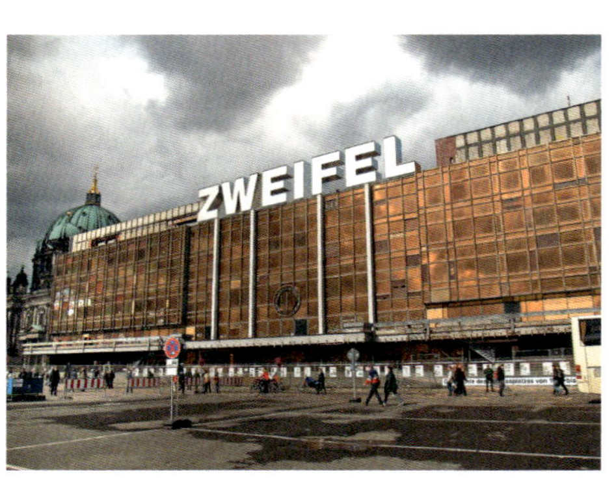

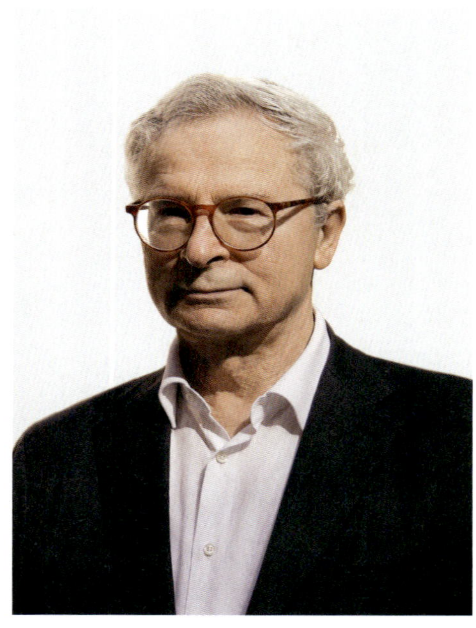

As early as 30 September 1990, the Palace of the Republic was closed in response to pressure from 1700 employees who complained of the danger to their health caused by the asbestos contamination of the interior air. The protracted demolition made possible a multitude of innovative ideas for cultural utilizations before the Schlossplatz (Palace Square) lawn became a further intermediate station prior to the inception of new construction. The Norwegian artist Lars Ø Ramberg attracted great attention with his project PALAST DES ZWEIFELS (PALACE OF DOUBT). The word ZWEIFEL (DOUBT), forty-two by eight metres large, made of aluminium and 900 metres of neon tube, illuminated the night sky of Berlin for six months.

In 2002, based on recommendations from the International Expert Commission on the Historical Centre of Berlin, the German Bundestag (parliament) voted with a large, multiparty majority to rebuild the three Baroque exterior facades and the Baroque Schlüter Courtyard. In 2008, with a design that was remarkable both urbanistically as well as architecturally, the Italian architect Franco Stella received first prize in an international design competition by unanimous decision of the jury.

The German Bundestag charged the federal government with establishing the Stiftung Berliner Schloss – Humboldt Forum (Foundation Berlin Palace – Humboldt Forum, a foundation under private law, which then transpired in summer of 2009. This was the precondition for issuing tax-deductible donation receipts. The reconstruction of the Baroque palace facades, projected to cost about 80 million euros, was to be financed through contributions. Manfred Rettig of the former Bundesbaugesellschaft Berlin mbH (Federal Construction Corporation) was appointed founding chairman. He was later joined on the board by Frank Nägele from the Federal Chancellery as the Foundation's commercial director.

Between 9 July 2009 and 17 January 2010, the partners of the Humboldt Forum in the Berlin Palace presented their ideas in an elaborate exhibition in the Altes Museum (Old Museum), directly opposite the new Schlossplatz (Palace Square) lawn and the future construction site. *Anders zur Welt kommen (A Different Approach to the World)* presented a spectacular conceptual cosmos and showed what the Stiftung Preussischer Kulturbesitz (Prussian Cultural Heritage Foundation) with its non-European collections, Humboldt Universität and the Zentral- und Landesbibliothek (Central State Library) Berlin were planning.

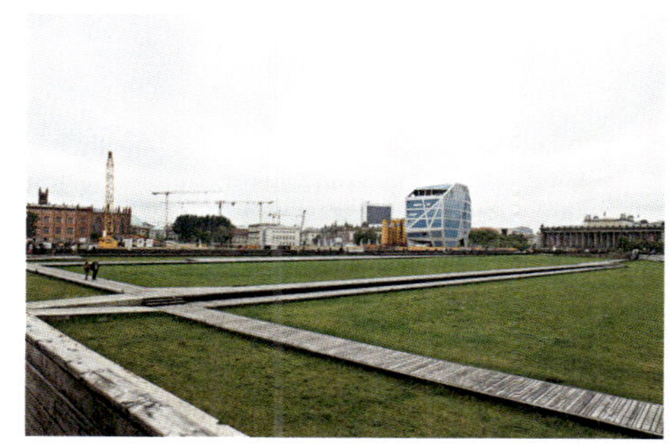

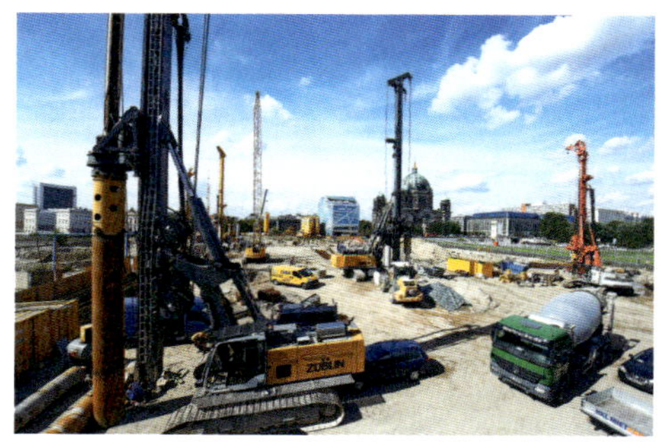

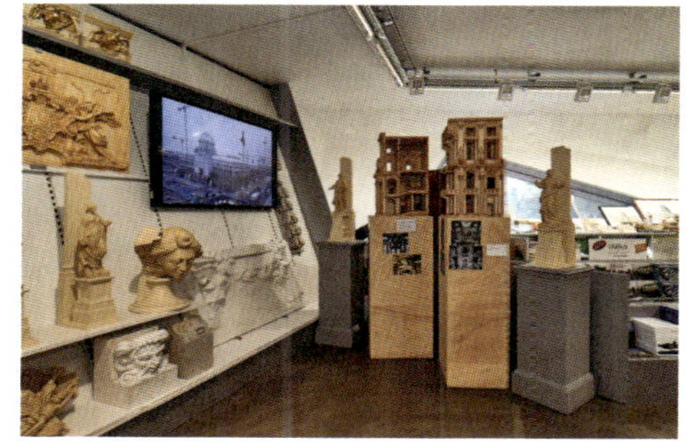

Not long thereafter, in 2010, the European financial crisis threatened to scuttle the project. Manfred Rettig, the founding chairman, saw to it that the inception of construction was delayed for three years, until 2013, during which period, however, the architects could continue their planning work. As a result, it became possible to prepare a set of meticulously elaborated planning documents for the shell construction without time pressure. The *fait accompli* for the inception of construction work was the fact that the excavation of the building pit and the construction of the foundations were brought forward to June 2012. The foundations had to be reinforced in order to allow construction on the tunnel for the Number 5 underground line, which runs between Alexanderplatz and the Brandenburger Gate, to begin on schedule.

The Humboldt Box, designed to serve as a pivotal marketing instrument for the Humboldt Forum in the Berlin Palace, was established in 2011 as a private–public partnership and financed without government funding. Entrance fees to the Box and facade advertisements on the building scaffolding were intended for refinancing of the investors. The applicable contract between the Federal State of Berlin, the Federal Office for Building and Regional Planning and the operators of the Box had been concluded already in 2009, prior to the establishment of the Humboldt Forum Foundation – and very much to its displeasure. The uncompromising modernity of the architecture of the Box stood in stark contrast to its marketing purpose, but succeeded in eliciting considerable public attention.

One section of the basement level, which had only been buried during the demolition of the Palace (and is again accessible today as a part of the 'History of the Site'), was preserved in the course of construction work. Under the north-western corner of the historical building, about 2000 oaken posts – which were still well-preserved after 300 years – were removed from the wet building ground. They had formed the foundation of the legendary Münzturm (Mint Tower), which the palace building master Andreas Schlüter erected here for Friedrich I. However, because the tower, nearly 100 metres in height, leaned to one side, it had to be demolished prior to completion: an unparalleled disaster that cost Schlüter his job. The oaken logs were reutilized and sold for furniture wood and parquet flooring.

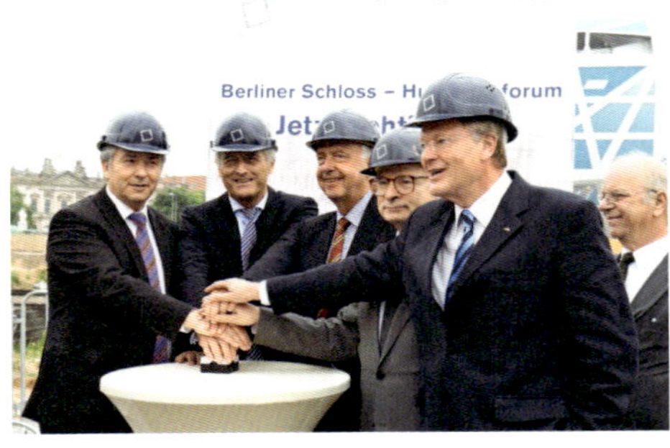

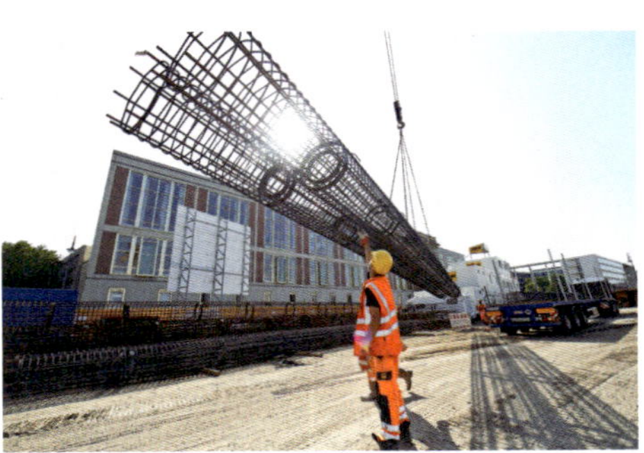

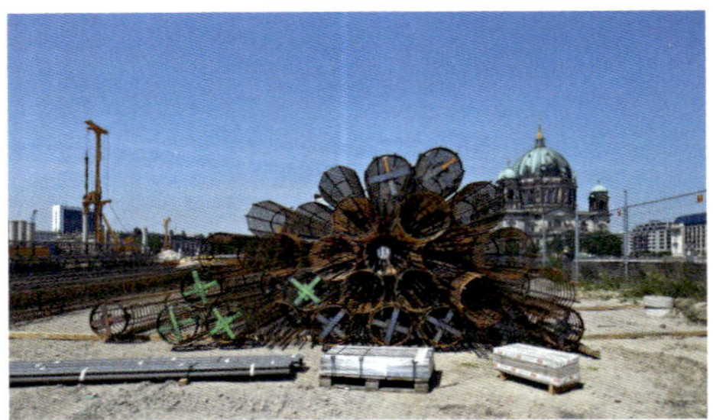

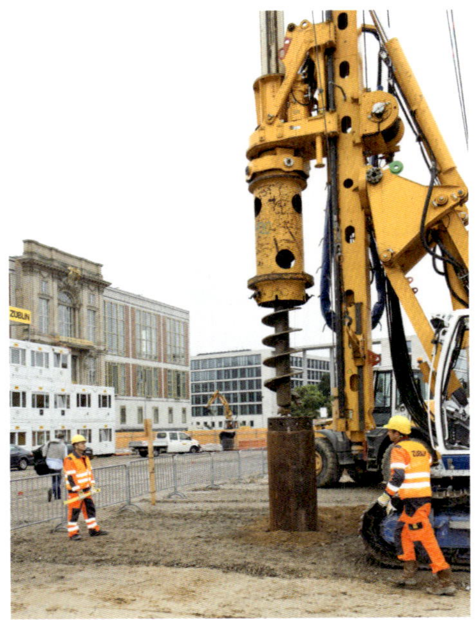

On 12 June 2012, Frank Nägele was sworn in as State Secretary for Economic Affairs of the new government of the Federal State of Schleswig-Holstein. At the twelfth session of the Foundation board, held on 27 June, he therefore resigned his post on the Foundation's board. Only after a number of attempts, and with four abstentions, was the Foundation board able to appoint Johannes Wien as the new commercial director of the Foundation at its fourteenth meeting, which took place on 13 December 2012. The trained palaeontologist had headed the executive management team and minister's office at the Federal Ministry of Transport, Building and Urban Affairs, and had most recently been the ministry's sustainability officer, assuming responsibility for the development of a mobility and fuel strategy.

An inspection of the sealing blanket of the excavation pit revealed a hand-sized lump of coal. Pieces of embedded stone in an otherwise liquid-sandy building ground can result in leakage in the subterranean injected concrete floor; for this reason the Foundation, as the building owner, decided to spend an extra 750 000 euros in order to position the grid of bentonite injection lances much more closely together. This operation proved worthwhile. On completion the construction pit was immediately leakproof, allowing the shell construction to begin without delay.

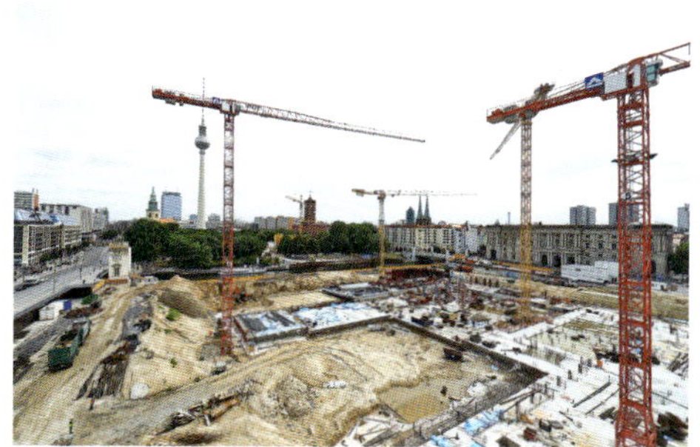

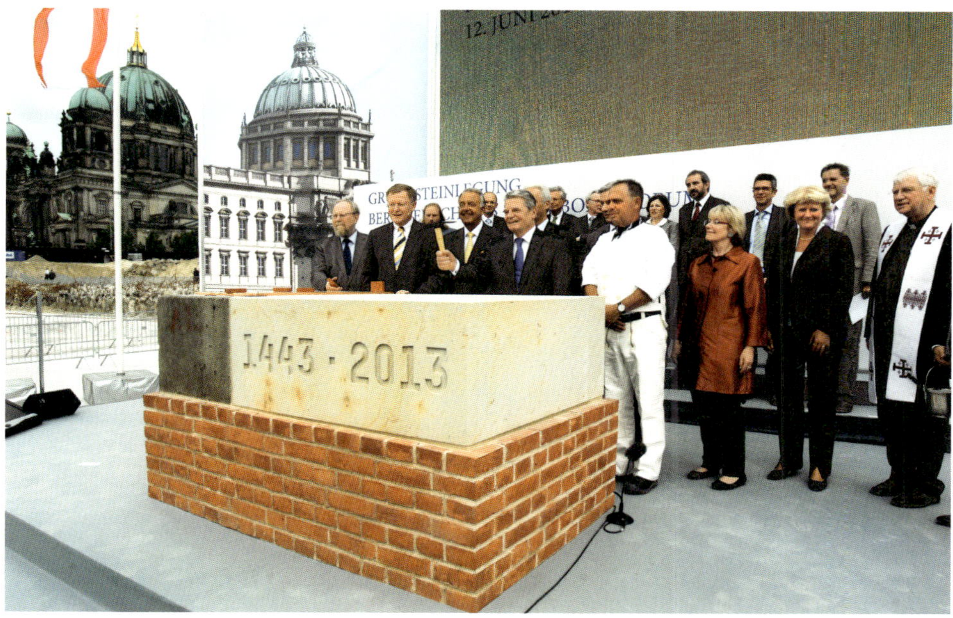

The ceremonial laying of the foundation stone for the Humboldt Forum in the Berlin Palace took place on 12 June 2013 with Federal President Joachim Gauck and many prominent guests from the spheres of politics, business and culture. Taking part in the festive event together with his wife was the head of the House of Hohenzollern, Georg Friedrich, Prince of Prussia. On the ensuing first Tag der offenen Baustelle (Day of the Open Construction Site) 15 000 interested individuals descended into the foundation pit in order to view the foundation stone. Bearing the inscription '1413–2013', the sandstone block was later incorporated laterally into Portal 4.

That same morning, in one of those 'ironies of history', the Foundation received a telephone message from the administration of the District of Berlin-Mitte, which had decided to initiate court proceedings for debt enforcement for road tax for the construction site in the amount of about 80 000 euros. Given its non-profit status, the Foundation was actually exempt and had refused to make the payment; this exemption was later granted by the administration of the Berlin Senate.

URKUNDE

GRUNDSTEINLEGUNG
FÜR DAS BERLINER SCHLOSS – HUMBOLDTFORUM
AM 12. JUNI 2013

Über 500 Jahre stand auf der Spreeinsel in Berlin als Abschluss der Allee Unter den Linden das Schloss der brandenburgischen Kurfürsten, der preußischen Könige und der deutschen Kaiser. 1443 legte der Kurfürst von Brandenburg Friedrich II. den Grundstein für das Renaissanceschloss. Um 1700 erweiterte Andreas Schlüter die kurfürstliche Residenz zum königlichen Schloss für Friedrich I., König in Preußen. Seine Nachfolger vollendeten bis 1716 das Barockschloss. Nach Novemberrevolution und Abdankung des Kaisers 1918 nutzte die Weimarer Republik das Schloss als Museum. Das im Zweiten Weltkrieg schwer beschädigte Gebäude ließ die kommunistische DDR-Führung 1950 sprengen. 25 Jahre später entstand hier der „Palast der Republik". Nach der friedlichen Wiedervereinigung Deutschlands wurde dieser 1990 aufgrund der Asbestbelastung geschlossen und 2006 schließlich abgerissen.

Heute legen wir hier den Grundstein für das Berliner Schloss – Humboldtforum. Damit kehrt das einstige Schloss mit rekonstruierten barocken Fassaden wieder zurück. Hinter den historischen und zeitgenössisch gestalteten Außenwänden schaffen wir auf Beschluss des Deutschen Bundestages mit dem Humboldtforum einen neuen zukunftsorientierten Ort für den Dialog mit den Kulturen der Welt.

Zusammen mit den bedeutenden Museen der europäischen Kunst und Kultur sowie der des Mittelmeerraumes auf der Museumsinsel bilden die großen Sammlungen Afrikas, Amerikas, Asiens und Ozeaniens der Staatlichen Museen zu Berlin – Preußischer Kulturbesitz einen kulturellen Anziehungspunkt in der Mitte Berlins. Mit dem „Humboldt-Labor" der Humboldt-Universität zu Berlin und der „Welt der Sprachen" der Zentral- und Landesbibliothek Berlin, aber auch mit seinem großen Veranstaltungs- und Begegnungsbereich im Erdgeschoss wird das Humboldtforum zu einem neuen kommunikativen Stadtmittelpunkt für die Bürgerinnen und Bürger und die zahlreichen Gäste dieser Stadt aus aller Welt.

Berlin, am 12. Juni 2013

JOACHIM GAUCK
Bundespräsident
Schirmherr der Stiftung Berliner Schloss – Humboldtforum

Der Deutsche Bundestag

PETRA MERKEL
Vorsitzende
Haushaltsausschuss

Dr. ANTON HOFREITER
Vorsitzender
Ausschuss für Verkehr,
Bau und Stadtentwicklung

Prof. Dr. MONIKA GRÜTTERS
Vorsitzende
Ausschuss für Kultur und Medien

Die Bundesregierung

Dr. PETER RAMSAUER
Bundesminister für Verkehr, Bau
und Stadtentwicklung

BERND NEUMANN
Staatsminister für Kultur und Medien

Das Land Berlin

KLAUS WOWEREIT
Der Regierende Bürgermeister von Berlin

Die Bauherrin

RAINER BOMBA
Stiftungsratsvorsitzender
und Staatssekretär im
Bundesministerium für Verkehr,
Bau und Stadtentwicklung

MANFRED RETTIG
Vorstand und Sprecher
Stiftung
Berliner Schloss – Humboldtforum

JOHANNES WIEN
Kaufmännischer Vorstand
Stiftung
Berliner Schloss – Humboldtforum

Die Partner

Prof. Dr. HERMANN PARZINGER
Präsident
Stiftung Preußischer Kulturbesitz

Prof. Dr. JAN-HENDRIK OLBERTZ
Präsident
Humboldt-Universität zu Berlin

VOLKER HELLER
Managementdirektor
Stiftung Zentral- und Landesbibliothek Berlin

Der Förderverein

Prof. Dr. RICHARD SCHRÖDER
Vorstandsvorsitzender
Förderverein Berliner Schloss e. V.

WILHELM VON BODDIEN
Geschäftsführer
Förderverein Berliner Schloss e. V.

Die Bauausführung

RITA RUOFF-BREUER
Präsidentin
Bundesamt für Bauwesen und Raumordnung

Der Architekt

Prof. FRANCO STELLA

In conformity with tradition, the architect's plans, the currently valid coins, a copy of the latest edition of a Berlin daily newspaper, along with a certificate bearing the signatures of the participants were placed inside a copper canister and inserted into the foundation stone. Manfred Rettig, the Foundation's chief construction officer, had two copies of this certificate prepared so that the second original version can be placed on display. Only a few of the signatories – among them the current Minister of State for Culture and the Media Monika Grütters, who signed at that time as the Chair of the Committee on Culture and Media for the German Bundestag, Wilhelm von Boddien, the managing director of the Förderverein Berliner Schloss e.V. (Association Berliner Schloss e.V.), and the architect Franco Stella – experienced the entire construction period, and experienced the joy of inaugurating the new exhibition, encounter and event centre personally and still 'in office'.

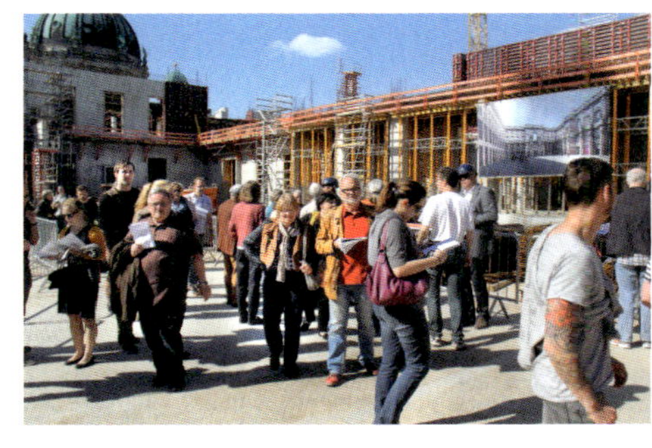

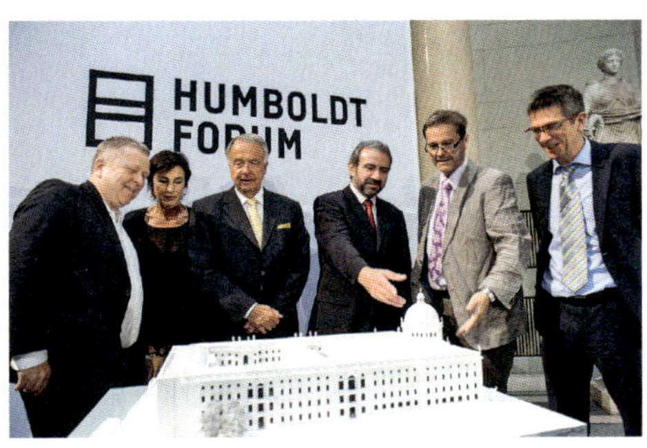

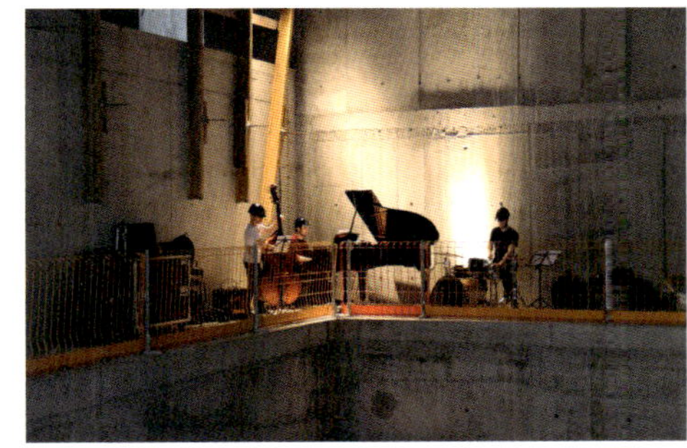

Also launched in 2013 – the year of the laying of the foundation stone – with the appointment of the Swiss cultural entrepreneur Martin Heller by Bernd Neumann, the Federal Minister of State for Culture and the Media at the time, was programme planning for the events sector of the new cultural centre. Among other things, Martin Heller and his team prepared sample event planning for the entire season, with exhibitions, concerts, lectures, film screenings, performances, dance and theatre. At the same time, he installed the Humboldt Lab in the Dahlem museums for a four-year period in collaboration with the Federal Cultural Foundation. Through innovative and challenging exhibition and art events, the Lab explored novel approaches to the handling of ethnological materials and of museum exhibits in general.

In late 2013 and early 2014, when the shell construction was already complete up to the second upper storey, a vehement discussion, mainly in the newspaper *Berliner Zeitung,* agitated the minds of the public. The architect Stephan Braunfels – who had become well-known for his Neue Pinakothek in Munich and his buildings for the Bundestag in Berlin – stridently criticized Franco Stella's design, arguing for another fundamental rethinking of the architectural concept. Drawing on his own competition entry, he proposed rotating the Schlüter Courtyard by 180 degrees so that the palace would form a U-shaped building that would be open towards the river Spree on the east side. In retrospect, this campaign appears to have been an initial and unsuccessful attempt at least to delay, if not to halt altogether, a building project disfavoured by some of the media.

On 1 June 2014, the second Tag der offenen Baustelle (Day of the Open Construction Site) demonstrated the enormous curiosity on the part of the Berlin populace about the new building, now still a shell construction. Lines of visitors stretched along the entrance to the construction site, past the Box, and to the Schlossbrücke (Palace Bridge) across the Spreegraben. Thousands of people explored the building site, where the future Schlüter Courtyard and the Passage were perceptible now only in broad outlines. In the multifunctional hall (today Hall 1), students from the Hochschule für Musik Hanns Eisler Berlin (Hanns Eisler School of Music Berlin) performed musical works from around the world.

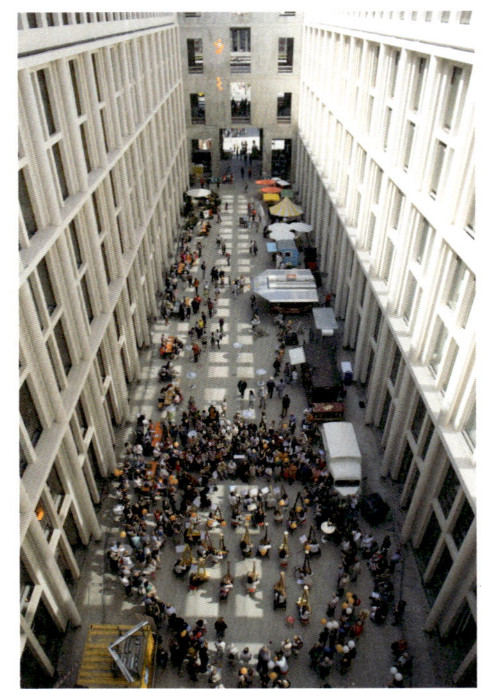

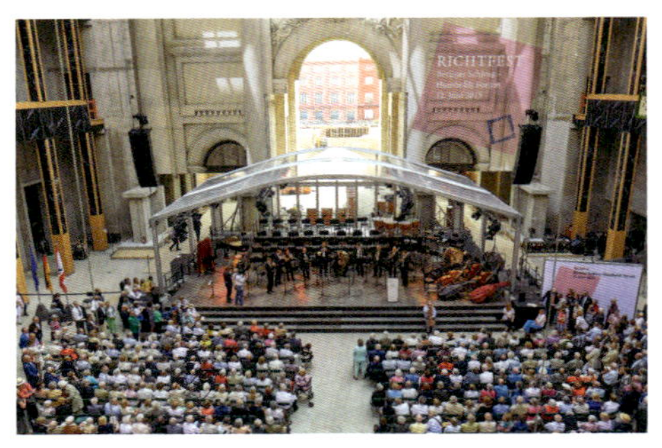

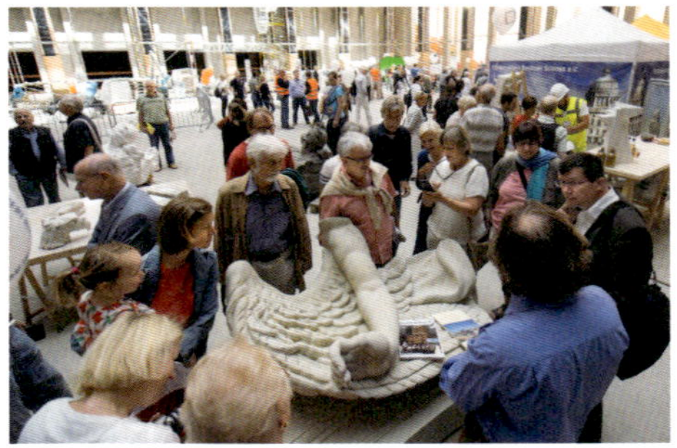

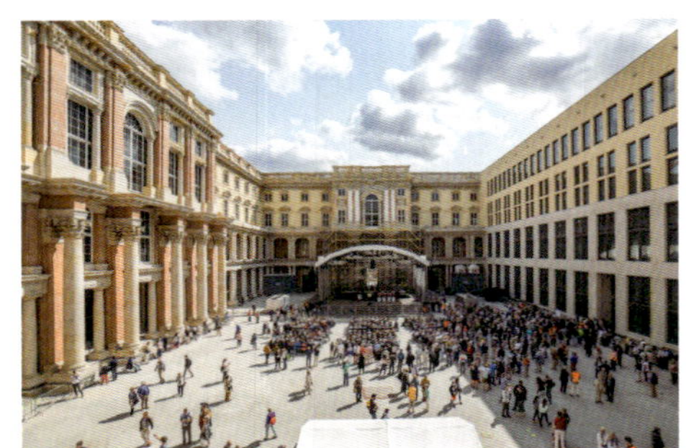

In mid-June of 2015, right on schedule, the Humboldt Forum Foundation held the topping-out ceremony together with construction workers and planners. Under the direction of Daniel Barenboim, the Staatskapelle Berlin – so intimately bound up with the Palace historically – performed Schubert's *Unfinished Symphony in B minor* in the Grand Foyer. Afterwards, and for the entire weekend, the shell structure was accessible to the public during the third Tage der offenen Baustelle (Days of the Open Construction Site). In just three days, about 50 000 people made their way into the unfinished building. With a varied programme, and for the first time with the participation of the Federal Foreign Office and the German Academic Exchange Service, the Humboldt Forum Foundation in the Berlin Palace and the three other actors provided insights into current ideas for future programming.

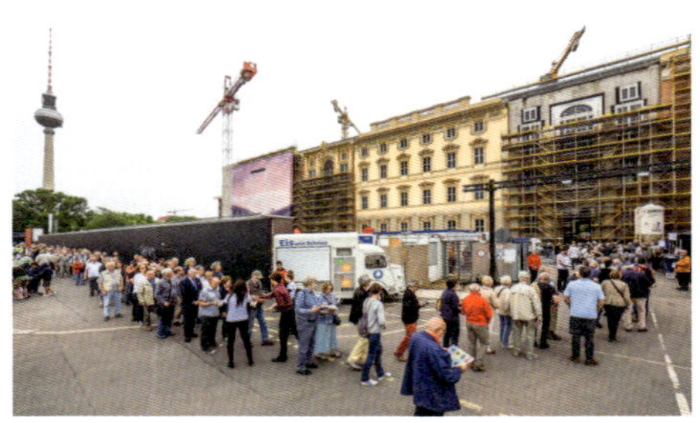

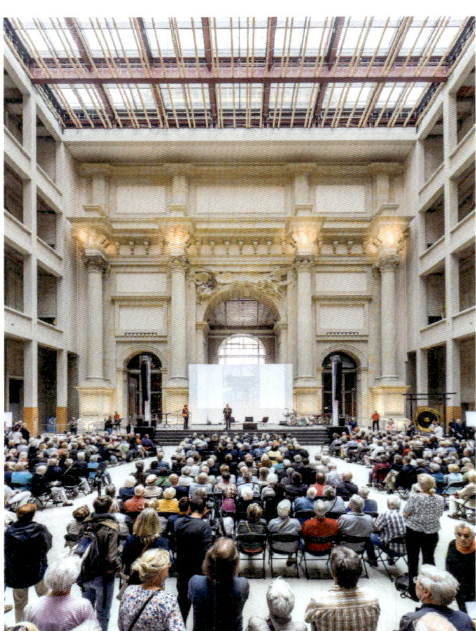

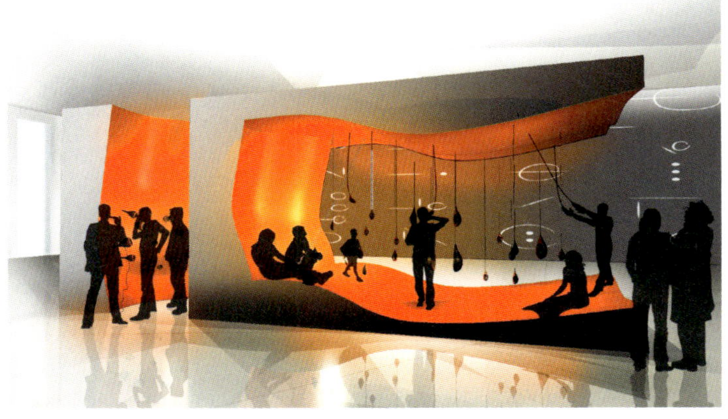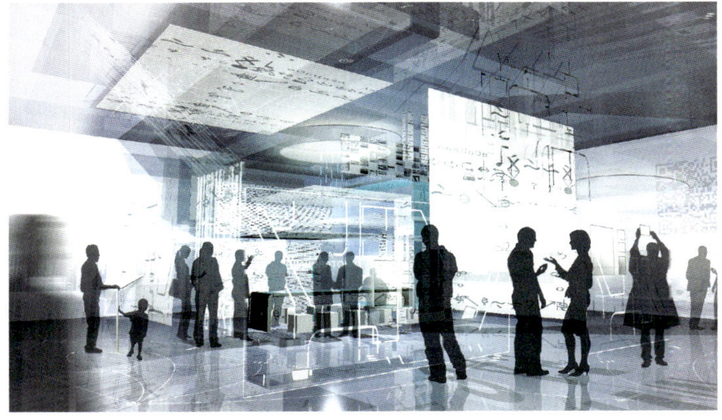

In mid-March, just before the topping-out ceremony, Michael Müller, the governing mayor of Berlin and also the city's senator of culture, indicated that the Zentral- und Landesbibliothek (ZLB) would no longer be moving into a location within the interactive installation *Welt der Sprachen (World of Languages)* in the Humboldt Forum. Instead, the Senate now planned to install the Berlin Exhibition in the former library area, measuring about 4000 square metres of usable surface, in the east wing of the first upper storey, for which the Stadtmuseum (City Museum) Berlin would work out a concept together with Kulturprojekte Berlin GmbH. For the ZLB, this step was a complete surprise. The building owner, namely the Humboldt Forum Foundation in the Berlin Palace, also signalled its disquiet, and warned of the delays and cost increases that could be expected to result from such a belated and fundamental utilization change.

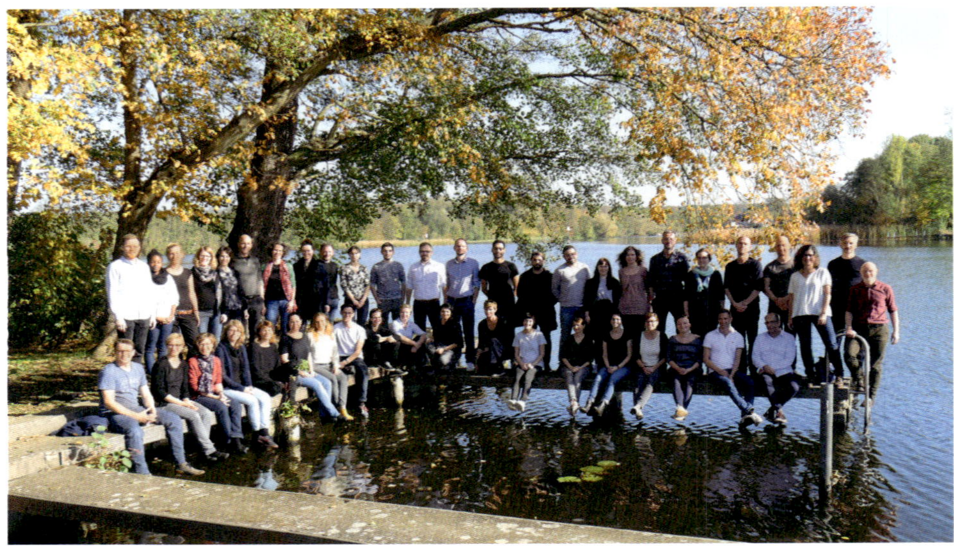

In May of 2015, Monika Grütters, the new Minister of State for Cultural Affairs, who had been in office for about one year, achieved a genuine coup with the appointment of Neil MacGregor as head of the founding directorate of the Humboldt Forum. Neil MacGregor had been director of the British Museum in London since 2002, and had successfully managed the spectacular expansion of the building through the star architect Norman Foster. Optimally networked internationally, he had recently curated the highly acclaimed exhibition *Germany – Memories of a Nation* in London. As the other founding directors, Grütters hired Hermann Parzinger, president of the Stiftung Preussischer Kulturbesitz (Prussian Cultural Heritage Foundation), and the Humboldt-Universität art historian Horst Bredekamp.

Proposals by the new founding directors for updating and restructuring the exhibitions as well as the overall utilization concept led to further decisive planning modifications. MacGregor saw to it that the specialist libraries of both museums, originally to be domiciled in the southwest wing of the first upper storey, yielded to an academy and an office of education and outreach for the Humboldt Forum. Joined by his colleagues, he also proposed rededicating about one third of the areas reserved for the permanent exhibitions of the two museums, which would now be used for temporary exhibition areas, thus allowing presentations to respond more emphatically to topical concerns. Manfred Rettig, the founding chairman of the Foundation, who was responsible for the building process, declined to

endorse these changes, and in early 2016 surprised everyone by handing in his resignation. At that point, the Foundation board appointed Hans-Dieter Hegner from the Ministry of Building as the new chief technology officer, and the cultural manager Lavinia Frey as chief culture officer as well as managing director of Humboldt Forum Kultur GmbH. The task of this newly founded subsidiary of the Foundation was to establish the cultural operations and programming structure of the new centre of culture.

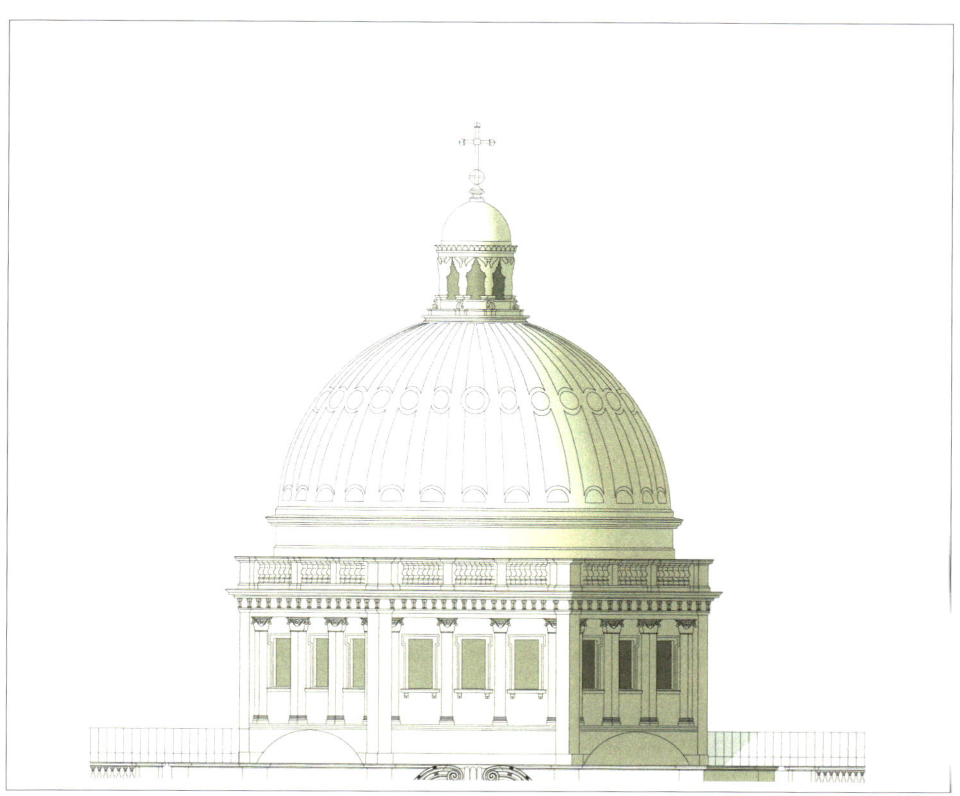

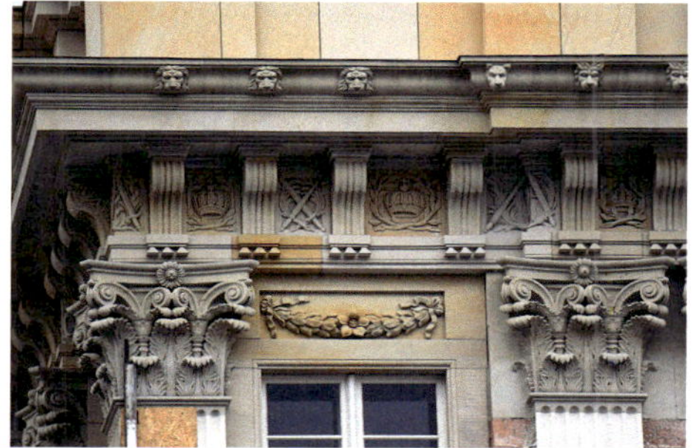

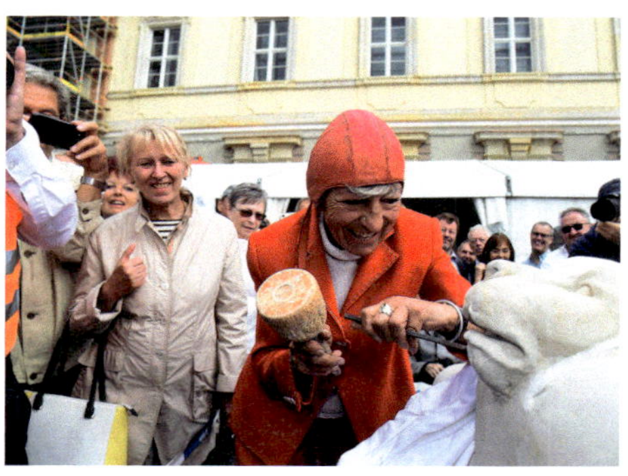

Early in 2017, the Foundation experienced a second negative media campaign, this time focused on the Christian cross on the palace cupola. The trigger was a press release by the Foundation announcing that a donor for this historical detail had been found. In the context of the competition assignment, which stipulated the historically accurate reconstruction of the facades and potentially of the palace cupola as well, the architect had in fact already envisioned the cross on the cupola in his design. Ensuing nonetheless was a discussion about whether the Christian symbol was appropriate to what would after all now be a secular building of culture. Among the most vociferous critics of the cross was Klaus Lederer, the new senator of culture for the Federal State of Berlin. Since, however, no one on the Foundation board proposed a corresponding planning revision, the complete historical reconstruction of the palace cupola, including the cross, was retained as originally intended.

At the Tage der offenen Baustelle (Days of the Open Construction Site) in 2017, the West Berlin icon Heidi Hetzer, who had just turned 80, visited the building site with vintage car fans. During the previous three years she had toured the world in her Hudson Greater Eight, built in 1930. That cay, she donated a sandstone lion's head, but insisted on presenting it as a lioness without mane, so without further ado she personally chiselled off the hair from the already finished lion. The female lion's head is now the fourth from the left on the roof eaves above inner Portal 1, where it is readily recognizable by a practised eye.

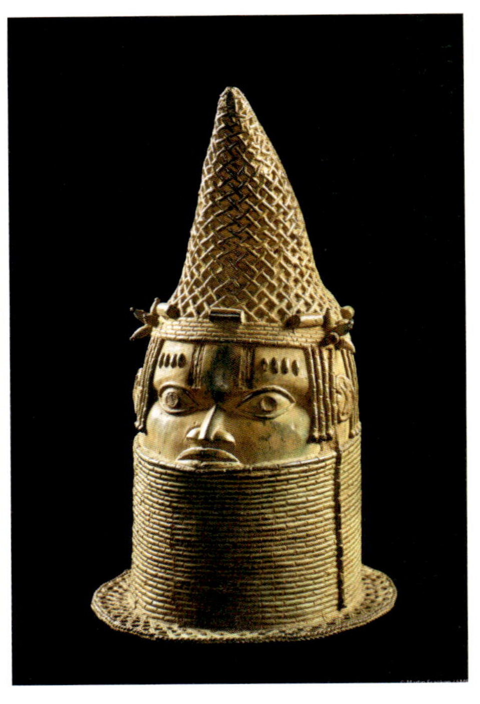

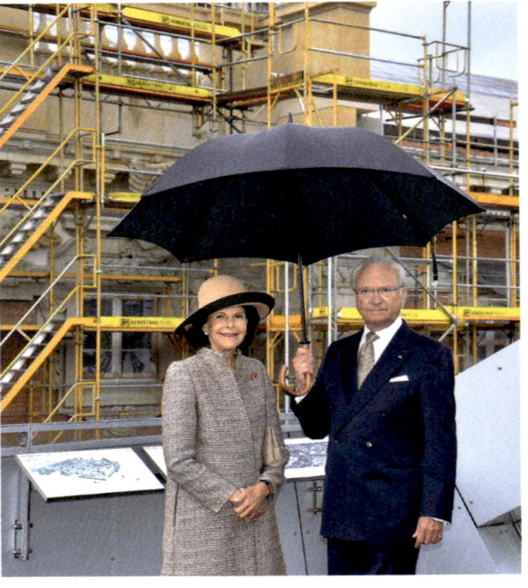

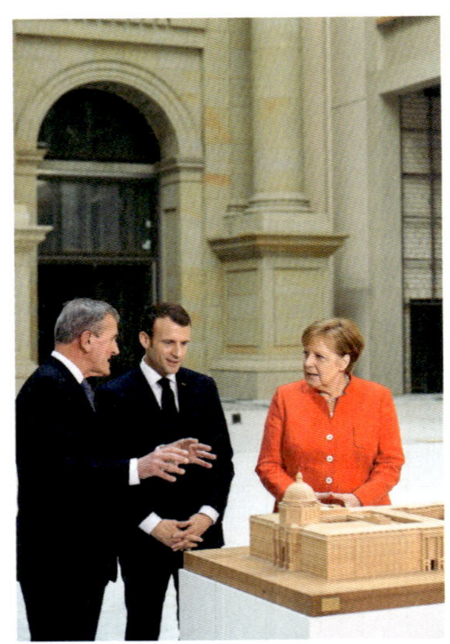

In a much-acclaimed speech delivered to students in Ouagadougou, the capital of Burkina Faso, in November of 2017, French President Emmanuel Macron, who had been in office since May of that year, declared that within a period of five years he wanted to create the preconditions for the restitution of African cultural artefacts from France back to Africa. In the German media as well, this speech led to protracted public discussions about the handling of the colonial legacy found in ethnological collections. The Humboldt Forum quickly became a focus of contention – unsurprisingly since Berlin's Ethnologisches Museum (Ethnological Museum), scheduled to move into the Forum, is the largest in Germany.

As the building's completion approached, the prestigious construction site received attention from prominent figures internationally. The Swedish royal couple paid a visit to the unfinished Palace on 5 October 2016. On 19 April 2018, German Chancellor Angela Merkel, together with founding director Neil MacGregor, insisted on personally greeting French President Emmanuel Macron in the large and now nearly complete entrance foyer.

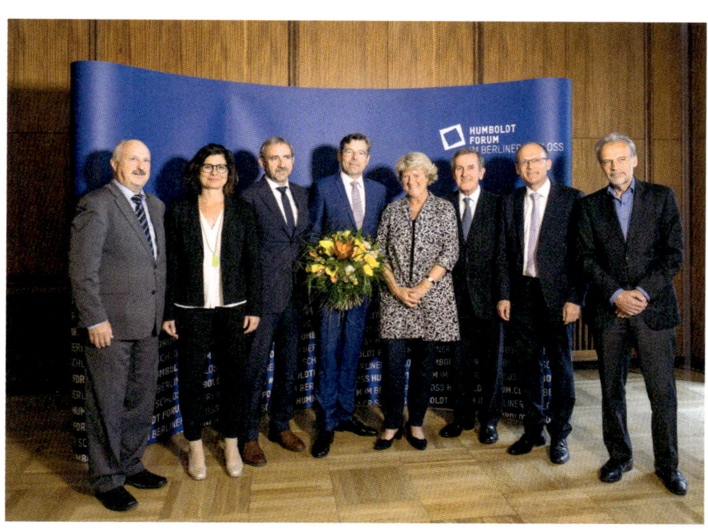

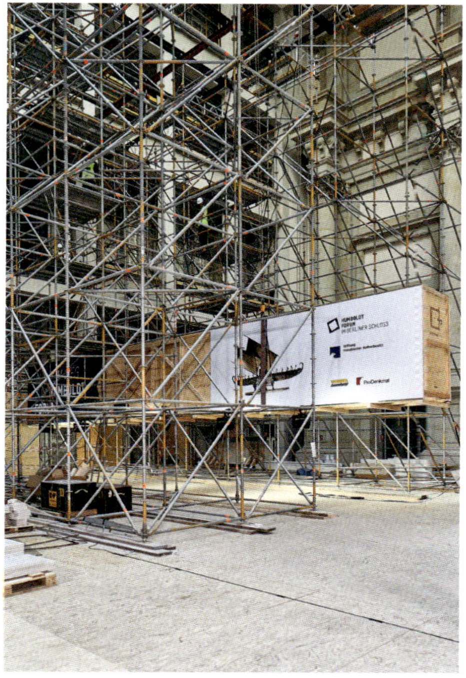

In a session held on 15 May 2018, the Foundation board, acting on a recommendation by Minister of State for Culture Monika Grütters, appointed Hartmut Dorgerloh, then general director of the Stiftung Preussische Schlösser und Gärten (Prussian Palaces and Gardens Foundation), as the new general director of the Humboldt Forum im Berliner Schloss (Humboldt Forum in the Berlin Palace), to take effect on 1 June of that year. With his assumption of office, the previous founding directorship was dissolved.

The new general director was already present in late May of 2018 when the first large objects from the Ethnologisches Museum were brought into the two-storey exhibition halls on either side of the Grand Foyer. Even when disassembled, the celebrated South Sea boat and the houses from the Palau Islands were too large to fit through the doors, and had to be carried through still open wall segments, which were completed only later. In order to store these valuable historical objects properly in their crates until their later installation, both halls were provisionally climate controlled.

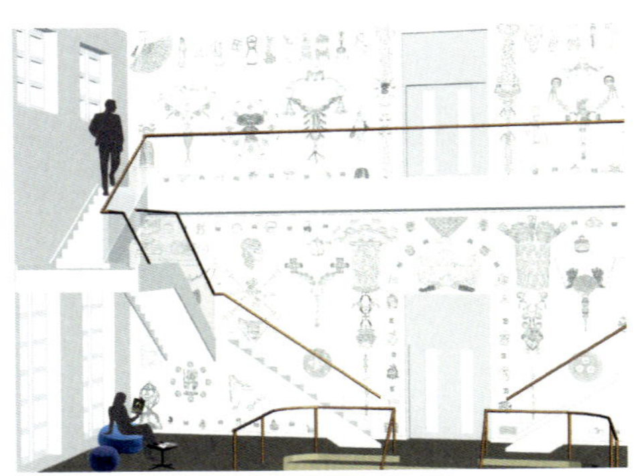

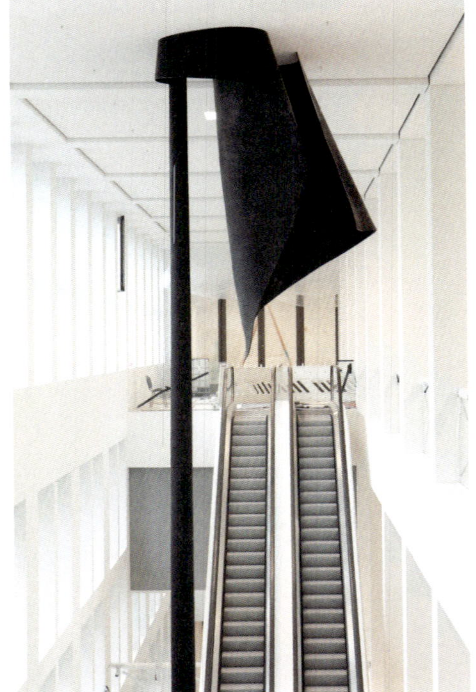

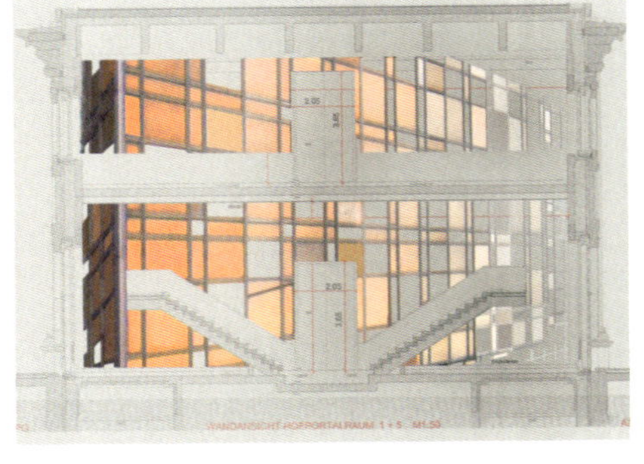

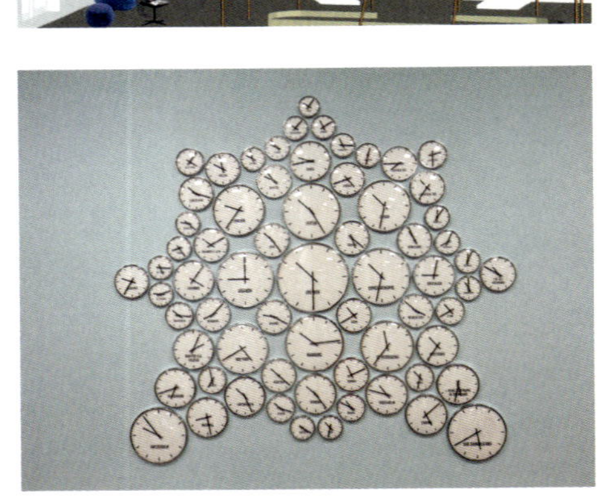

Although the reconstructed baroque palace facades are adorned with manifold masterworks of fine art, and various modern works will be absorbed into the collections as well, the 'Kunst am Bau' (art on public buildings) programme represents yet another discursive level to be integrated into the building. In national competitions, contemporary art projects designed to serve as a stimulus to critical reflection were selected for five locations within the building. Among these is the *Statue of Limitations* by the artist and Ai Weiwei student Kang Sunkoo, two extensive graphic wall pieces in the staircases in Portals 1 (An Seebach and Christiane Stegat) and 5 (Tim Trantenroth), a clock installation by Stefan Sous for the foyer of the Berlin Exhibition and the Academy in the first upper storey as well as *Die Architekten (The Architects)* by Christiane Dellbrügge and Ralf de Moll in the ground floor hall foyer.

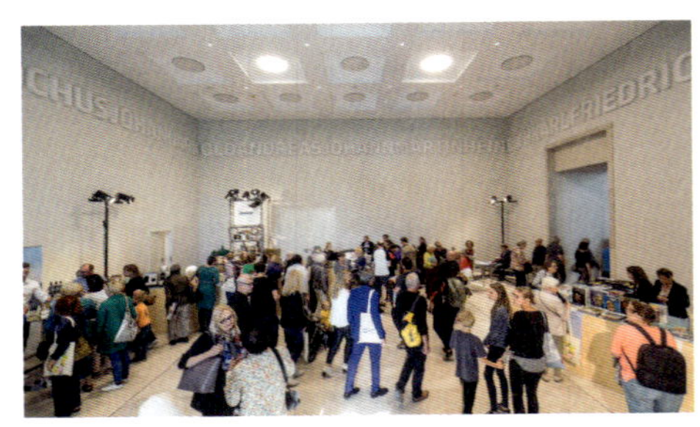

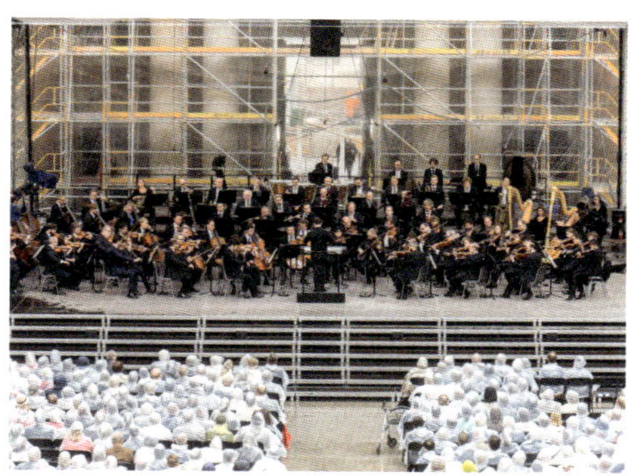

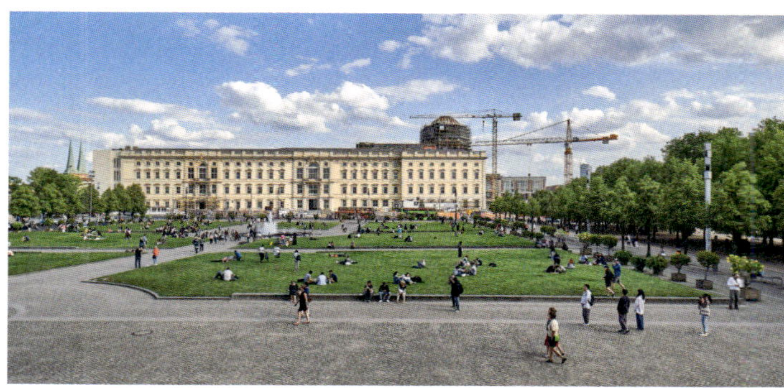

At the Tage der offenen Baustelle (Days of the Open Construction Site), organized by the Foundation as the construction client on 25 and 26 August 2018 for the last time before the building's completion, visitors could take a first look at the reconstructed Schlüter Courtyard, although stucco and sandstone details were still missing in some places. On the initiative of Wilhelm von Boddien, director of the Förderverein (association of friends), the Berliner Philharmoniker under the direction of its new principal conductor Kirill Petrenko were persuaded to perform here under open skies for the first time after an interval of around 80 years – with music by Richard Strauss and Ludwig van Beethoven. Admission fees were linked to a donation, making it possible to gather 500 000 euros on a single afternoon. Even the rain that commenced promptly when the concert began failed to dampen the spirits of the 1500 music lovers.

The first meeting of the newly established Interessengemeinschaft Kultur & Bildung Spreeinsel (Spree Island interest group for culture and education) already took place in June of 2017 on the initiative of the Stiftung (Foundation) Humboldt Forum (SHF). Through this association, the participating institutions located on the Spree Island, which were, in addition to the SHF, the Staatliche Museen zu Berlin – Preussischer Kulturbesitz (Berlin State Museums – Prussian Cultural Heritage), the Hochschule für Musik Hanns Eisler Berlin (Hanns Eisler School of Music Berlin), the Berlin Cathedral, the European School of Management and Technology Berlin and the Stiftung Zentral- und Landesbibliothek Berlin (Central State Library of Berlin Foundation), hoped to receive a better hearing in particular from the Berlin Senate with regard to predictable and increaasing problems involving tour bus traffic, but also unresolved urban issues such as lighting and signage. After a number of press conferences held in 2018 and 2019, the interest group succeeded in persuading the Berlin Senate to close Bodestrasse and the streets adjacent to the Lustgarten entirely to through traffic, so that in the future no tour buses will be able to park in the immediate vicinity of the UNESCO World Heritage Sites on Museum Island.

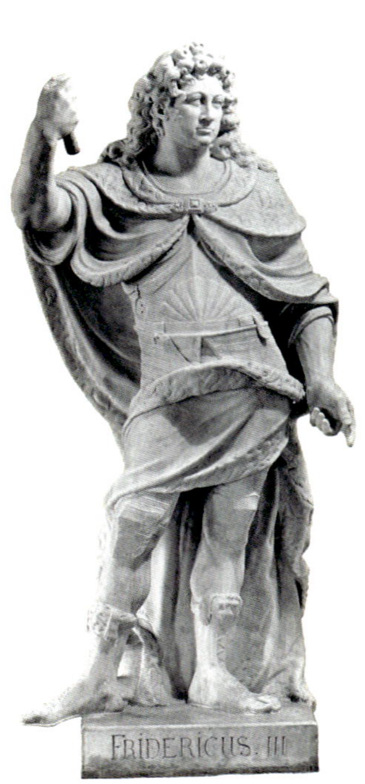

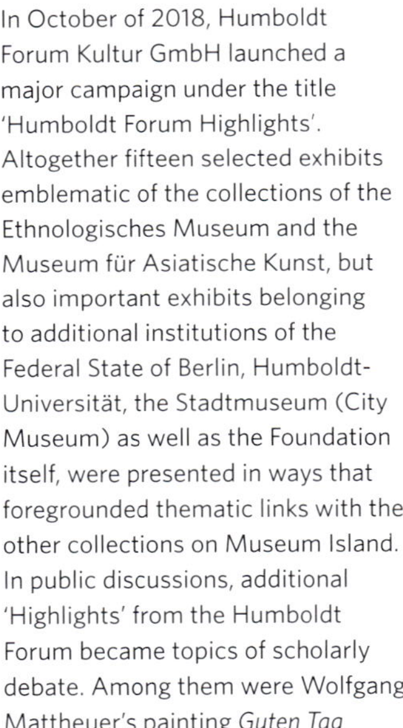

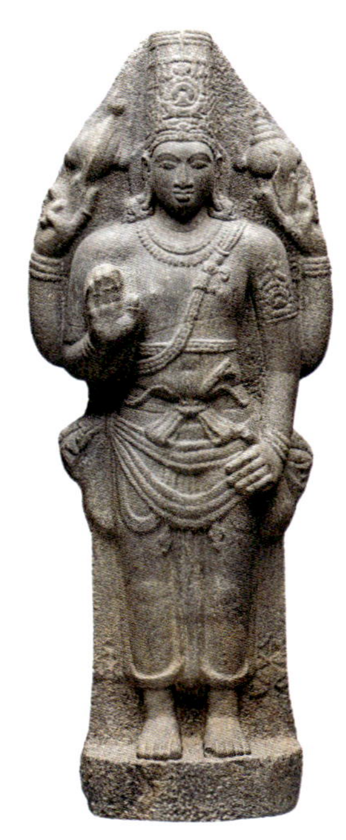

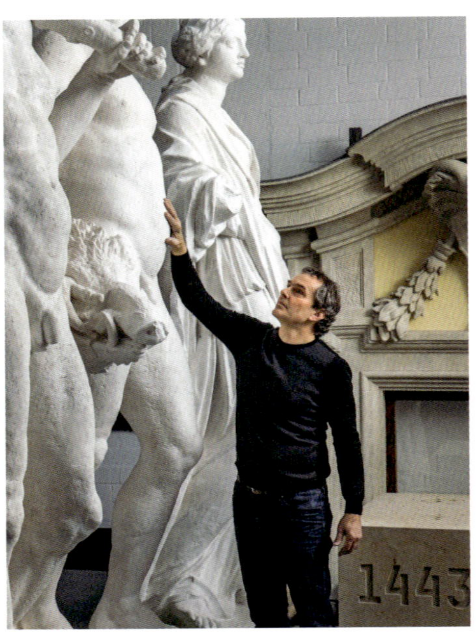

In October of 2018, Humboldt Forum Kultur GmbH launched a major campaign under the title 'Humboldt Forum Highlights'. Altogether fifteen selected exhibits emblematic of the collections of the Ethnologisches Museum and the Museum für Asiatische Kunst, but also important exhibits belonging to additional institutions of the Federal State of Berlin, Humboldt-Universität, the Stadtmuseum (City Museum) as well as the Foundation itself, were presented in ways that foregrounded thematic links with the other collections on Museum Island. In public discussions, additional 'Highlights' from the Humboldt Forum became topics of scholarly debate. Among them were Wolfgang Mattheuer's painting *Guten Tag*

(Good Day), formerly in the painting gallery in the Palace of the Republic, which will henceforth be on display in the Humboldt Forum, a *Feather Madonna* from Mexico and the Hindu god Vishnu from South India.

The colleagues at the Foundation along with the planners and sculptors, were shocked by the unexpected death of Bertold Just, head of the palace workshop, who died of heart failure on 6 November 2018 at the age of only 55 years. For the Foundation, he was and remains irreplaceable. Bertold Just combined a phenomenal expertise in the Baroque sculpture of Andreas Schlüter and his workshop with his own experience as a sculptor, an indefatigable commitment and a passionate dedication to the uncompromising quality of the reconstruction of the sculptural decoration of the palace facade. With his friendly character, he generated the incredibly creative atmosphere found in the palace workshop among the sculptors, stucco artists, conservators and stonemasons. Everyone who had the privilege of knowing and admiring him holds him firmly in memory.

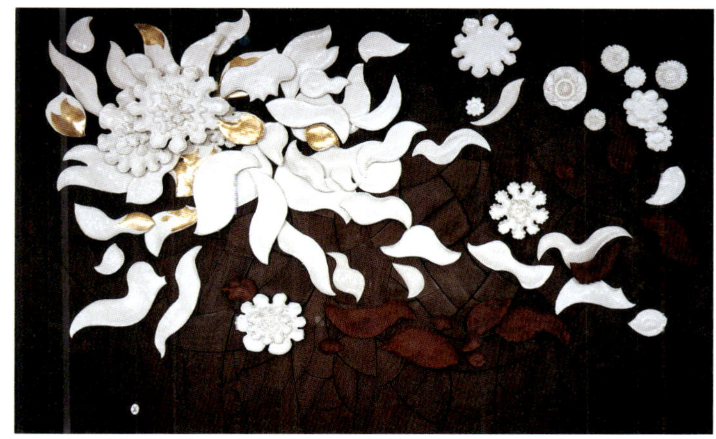

At the end of the year, the Humboldt Box in front of the facade facing Lustgarten (Pleasure Garden) was closed down and was dismantled by early May of 2019. The final exhibition was entitled *Dies ist auch unsere Baustelle! (It's Our Construction Site Too!)*, a project for children and young people that will be integrated in the tailor-made form of a 'family track' into the permanent exhibitions, creative educational offerings and guided tours of the Humboldt Forum. At the end of the year, the operations of the Humboldt Forum Kultur GmbH were amalgamated with those of the Foundation.

Meanwhile, fundraising for the reconstruction of the Baroque palace facades continued successfully, utterly contrary to the gloomy predictions of certain voices in the media. On 1 February 2019 in the Grand Foyer in the presence of Düsseldorf Mayor Thomas Geisel, Ulf Doepner of the Düsseldorf friends of the Förderverein Berliner Schloss e.V. presented the chair of the Foundation with a cheque for 505 000 euros, intended for the 'Düsseldorf window axis', a section of the facade in the full height of the building located in the Schlüter Courtyard to the right of Portal 6. By the end of the year, the Förderverein would fulfil its promise to ensure that the 80 million euros required for the palace facades would come not from tax revenues, but instead from the unparalleled commitment of the citizenry all over Germany.

Through a number of press conferences and other events, the Humboldt Forum retained public attention even after the closing of the Humboldt Box, an example being the press conference held on 15 May on the occasion of the acquisition of original fixtures from the Palace of the Republic. They are called 'Flashbacks' – among them a glass ballot box, porcelain plates and ice cream cups, a floral porcelain wall from Meissen, but also a surveillance monitor used by the state security services – and their presence in the Humboldt Forum will serve as reminders that the Palace of the Republic once stood at this location. Another major press conference held on 4 June presented the collection of objects from the North American Omaha tribe from the Ethnologisches Museum, which had been assembled a century earlier by the Native American ethnologist

Francis La Flesche. A further press conference organized by the Berlin Stadtmuseum (City Museum) together with Kulturprojekte Berlin marked the arrival on 18 June of the famous 'Safe Door' in the completed Berlin Galleries, located in the first upper storey.

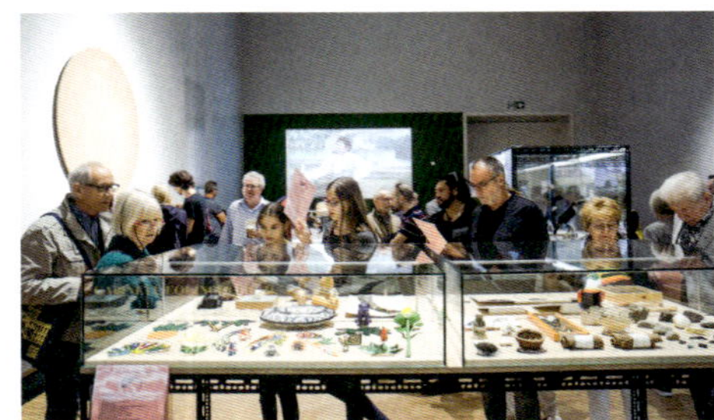

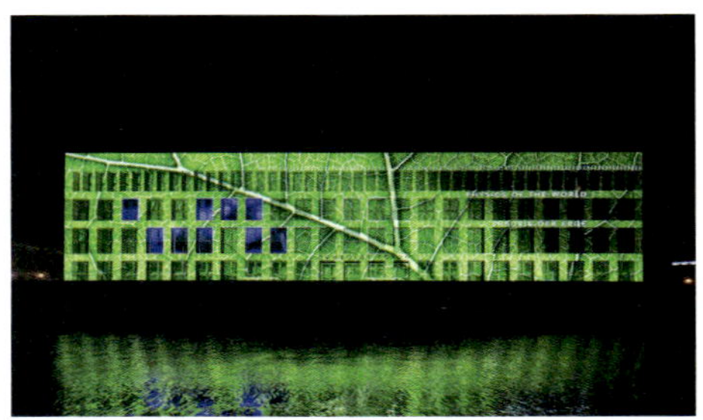

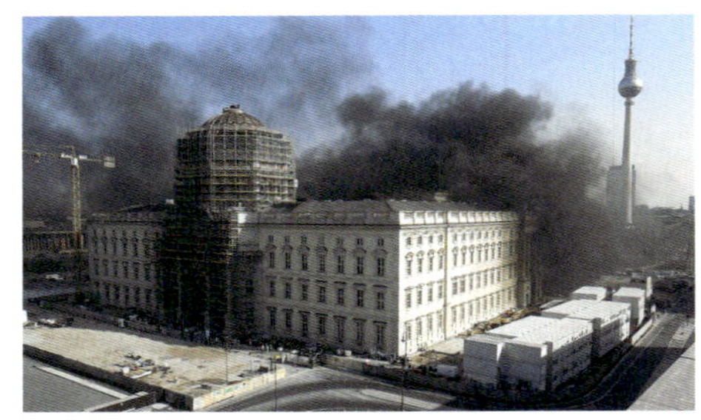

Progress at the construction site experienced so many delays due to capacity problems of the firms involved, but also arising from deficiencies in the planning and execution above all of the house technology that in June of 2019 the Foundation board together with the president of the Federal Office for Building and Regional Planning and the responsible secretary of state from the Federal Ministry of the Interior, Building and Community, declared that they would advise the Foundation board to delay the phased opening of the Humboldt Forum by an entire year to September of 2020. In contrast to the bad tidings from other major construction projects in the region of the German capital, this news was received by the media with calm and understanding.

On 14 (and 15) September 2019, the Humboldt Forum Foundation gave one final blast of the trumpets prior to the planned opening in 2020, namely the festivities surrounding the 250th birthday of Alexander von Humboldt. About 7000 people participated in the birthday party, which included exhibitions, concerts, performances, podium discussions, hackathons and much more. The various appearances, live acts and installations took place in the now completed Grand Foyer, in Hall 1 located on the corner facing the Lustgarten, in the staircase hall and in the special exhibitions area, and provided some sense of the future potential of these spaces. The event was a successful overture and provided multifaceted insights into the upcoming programme and profile of the Humboldt Forum.

On a Wednesday morning in spring of 2020, the world seemed to stand still – at least for those observing the building site of the reconstructed Berlin Palace via WebCam. Around 9:45 AM on 8 April, when a gigantic cloud of black smoke poured from Portal 1 on the south side of the building, the Internet page crashed, overloaded by hundreds of thousands of users. Just a half hour later, the nightmare was over, the fire extinguished. Was it a blessing in disguise that the fire had broken out on the exterior, at the passageway of the Portal, during work with hot tar? In any event, there was damage 'only' to exterior areas, as well as to plasterwork in the passageway. No one was injured. Without delay, mockers quipped that the sandstone had now acquired a lovely patina …

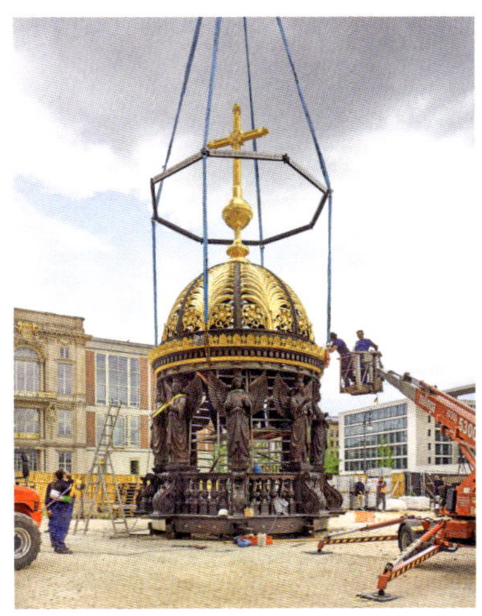 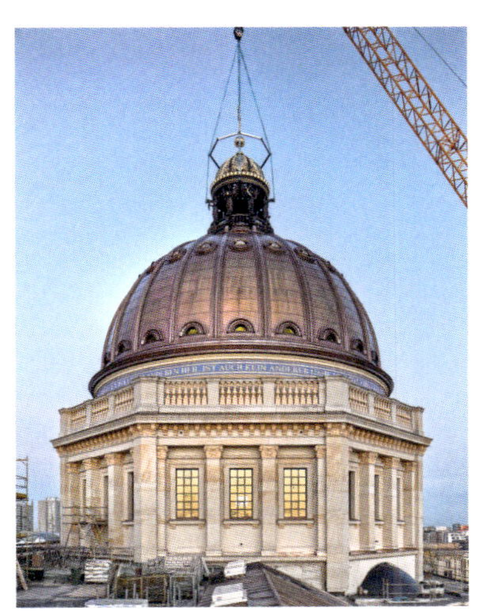 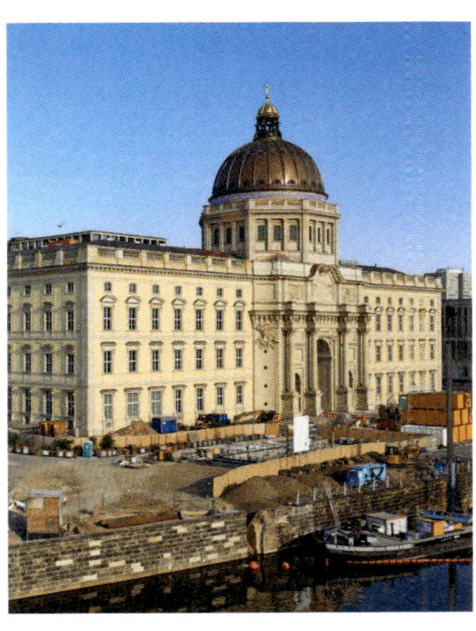

Finally, after protracted back-and-forth, 29 May was the day for action: an oversized mobile crane lifted the intricate lantern with its golden cross onto the cupola. All day long, hundreds of people had waited for this moment on Schinkelplatz and in front of the European School of Management and Technology in the former Staatsratsgebäude (the former East German State Council Building). At around 9 PM, once the steel and bronze structure had been assembled on the ground, the crane hoisted the finished cupola lantern – consisting of a rounded balustrade, cherubim, their wings forming a circle, and finally a baldachin formed of gilded vegetal forms, topped by an imperial orb-globe with its cross – upward into the reddened evening sky.

Beginning on 9 September, enthusiastic onlookers have been able to appreciate the fully finished west portal with its cupola, which again displays its old splendor in a new form. Missing now is only the armorial cartouche above the central portal, the sandstone figures on the columns, and those on the rotunda of the cupola – and its green copper patina. That, however, will take a while – thirty years, according to experts. When it appears, it will be seen by a new generation.

The Floor Plans of the Building

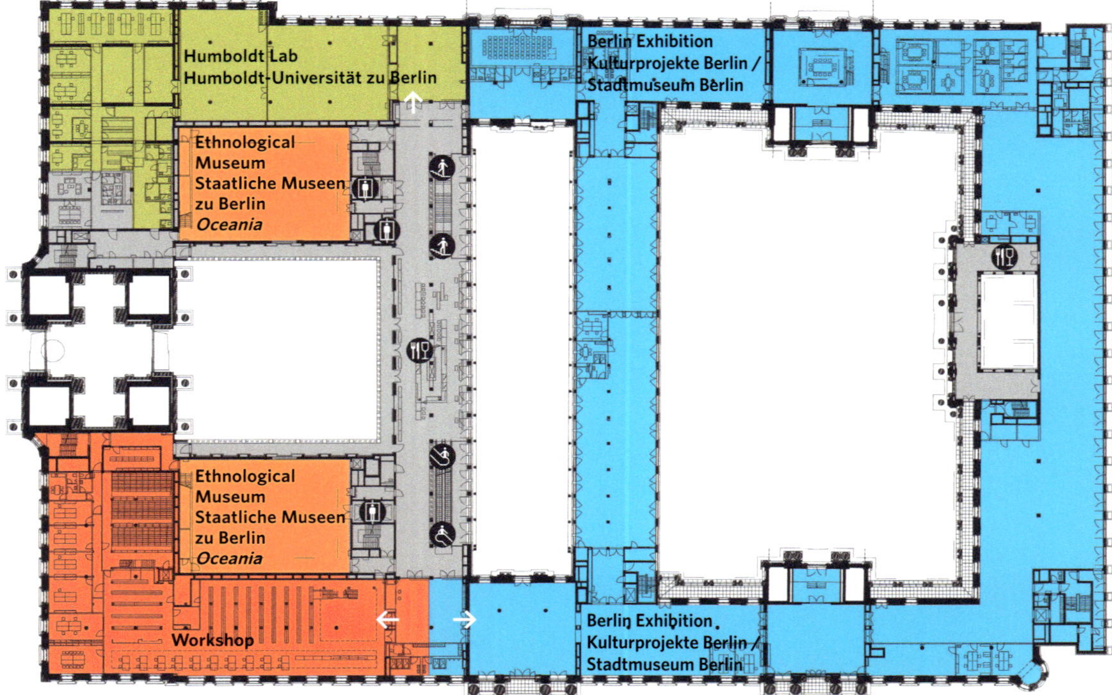

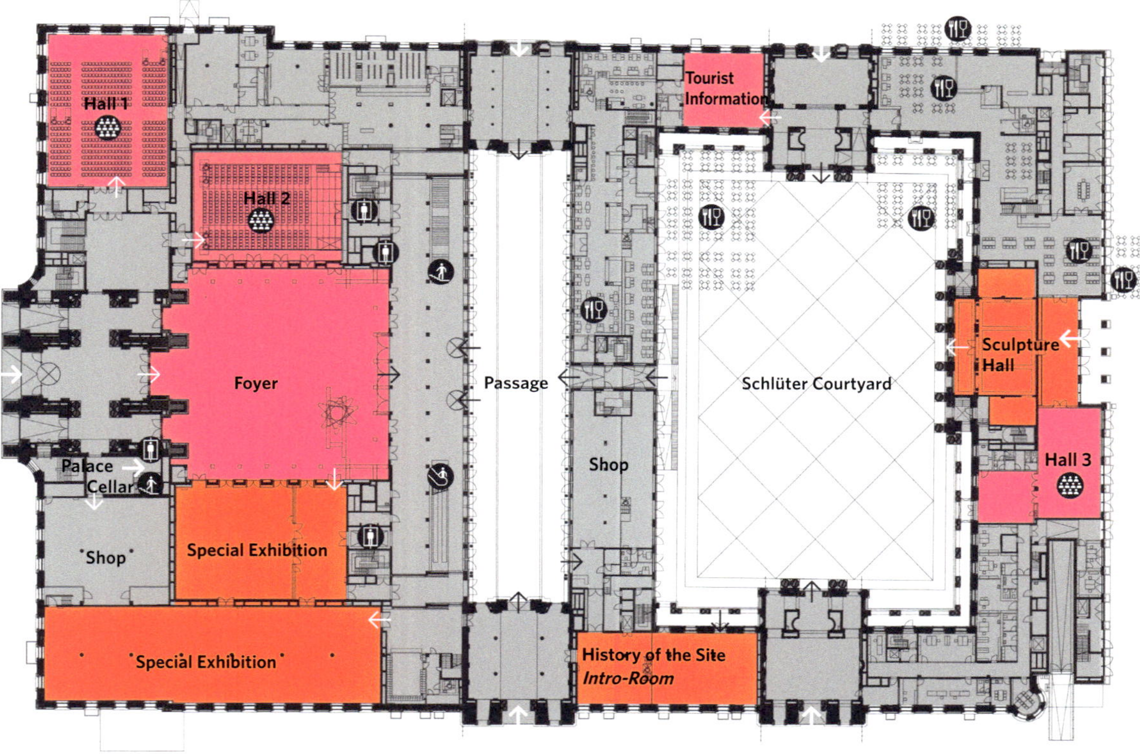

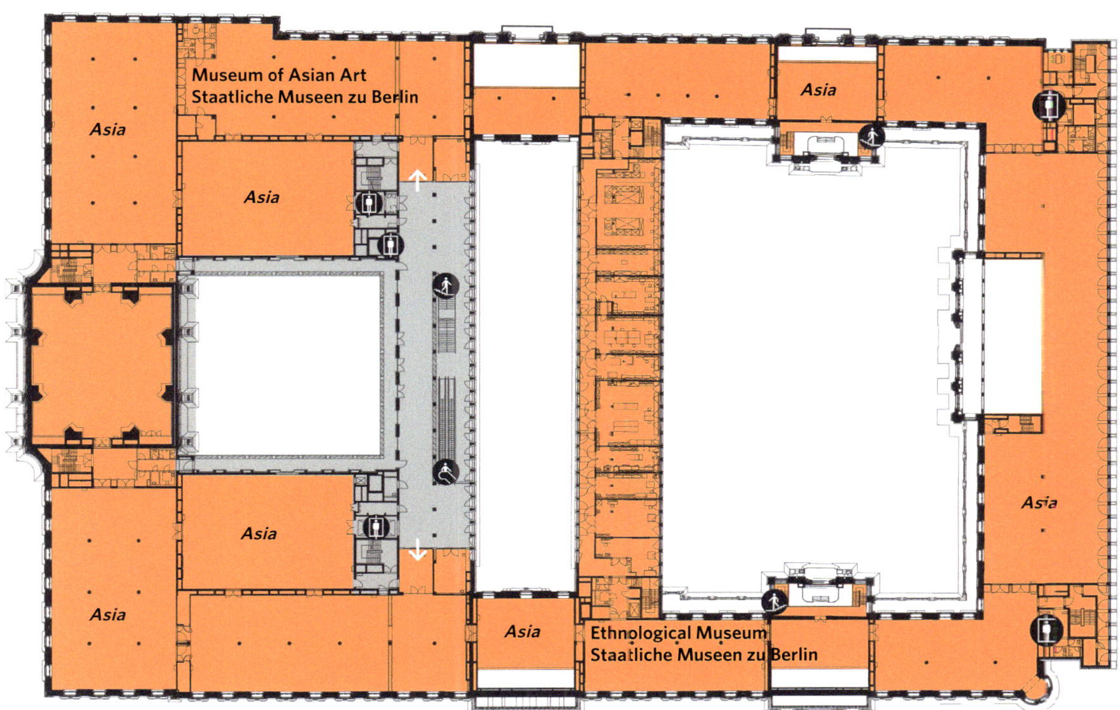

Third Upper Floor
Museum of Asian Art
Staatliche Museen zu Berlin
Asia
Asia
Asia
Asia
Asia
Asia
Asia
Asia
Ethnological Museum
Staatliche Museen zu Berlin

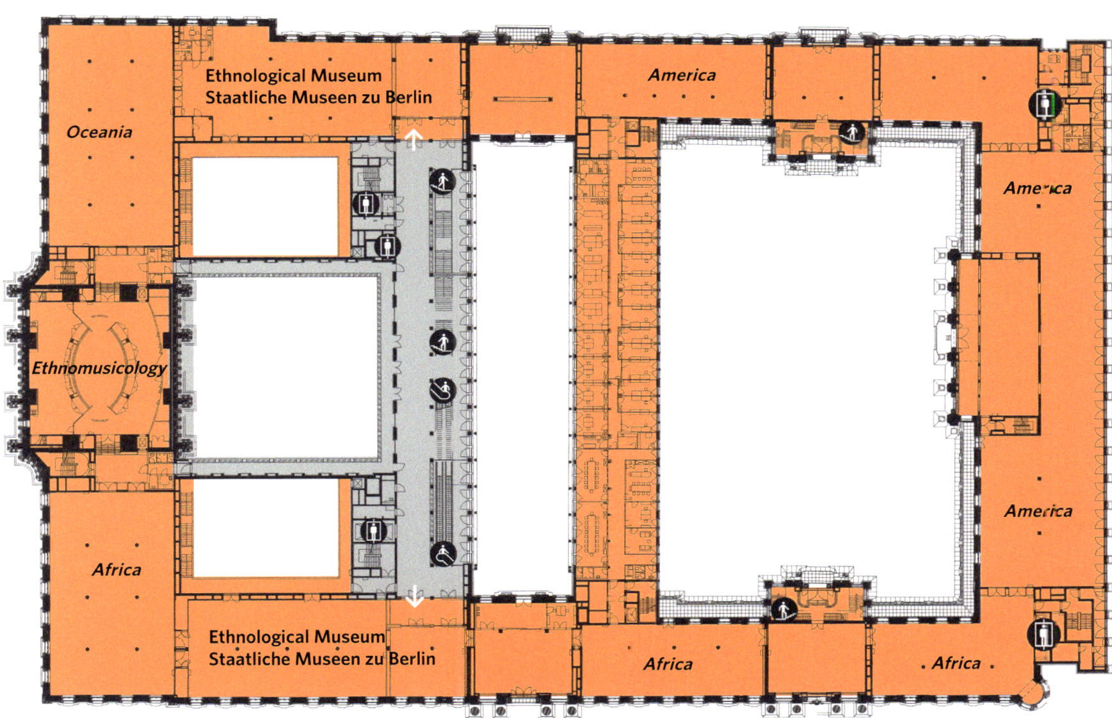

Second Upper Floor
Ethnological Museum
Staatliche Museen zu Berlin
Oceania
America
America
Ethnomusicology
America
Africa
Ethnological Museum
Staatliche Museen zu Berlin
Africa
Africa

The Authors

Wilhelm von Boddien initiated the reconstruction of the Berlin Palace. In 1992, he founded the association of friends Förderverein Berliner Schloss e.V. (Association Berliner Schloss e.V.), and serves as its executive director. Since 2004, the Förderverein has successfully worked to raise funds from all over Germany.

Professor Dr. Horst Bredekamp is a professor of art and visual history at the Humboldt-Universität zu Berlin. Together with Neil MacGregor and Hermann Parzinger, he served as a founding director of the Humboldt Forum in the Berlin Palace from 2015 until 2018.

Professor Dr. Hartmut Dorgerloh has been the general director and chairman of the board of the Stiftung Humboldt Forum im Berliner Schloss (Humboldt Forum Foundation in the Berlin Palace) since 2018. From 2002 until 2018 he was general director of the Stiftung Preussische Schlösser und Gärten Berlin-Brandenburg (Prussian Palaces and Gardens Foundation). An art historian and cultural manager, he has also taught at the Humboldt-Universität zu Berlin as an honorary professor since 2004.

Lavinia Frey is the managing director of programme and projects of the Stiftung Humboldt Forum im Berliner Schloss (Humboldt Forum Foundation in the Berlin Palace). A cultural manager and former theatre director, she was the chief culture officer of Humboldt Forum Kultur GmbH from 2016 until 2018, and managing director from 2016 until 2019.

Hans-Dieter Hegner has been chief technology officer at the Stiftung Humboldt Forum im Berliner Schloss (Humboldt Forum Foundation in the Berlin Palace) since 2016. A construction engineer, he was formerly responsible for construction engineering, sustainable building, building research and questions related to building culture as the head of a division for the German Federal Ministry of Transport, Building and Urban Affairs.

Professor Dr. Lars-Christian Koch is director of the collections of the Staatliche Museen zu Berlin im Humboldt Forum (Berlin

State Museums in the Humboldt Forum). An ethnomusicologist and ethnologist, he teaches ethnomusicology at the University of Cologne as an extraordinary professor, and as an honorary professor at the Berlin University of the Arts.

Neil MacGregor was director of the British Museum in London from 2002 until 2015. From 2015 until 2018, he served as a founding director of the Humboldt Forum Foundation in the Berlin Palace together with Horst Bredekamp and Hermann Parzinger.

Professor Dr. Hermann Parzinger is a prehistorian, and has been president of the Stiftung Preussischer Kulturbesitz (Prussian Cultural Heritage Foundation) since 2008. Alongside Horst Bredekamp and Neil MacGregor, he was a member of the founding directorate of the Humboldt Forum Foundation in the Berlin Palace from 2015 until 2018.

Dr. Gorch Pieken is research director at the Centre for Military History and Social Sciences of the Bundeswehr (German Armed Forces) in Potsdam. From May 2018 until December 2020, he was delegated as senior curator of the inaugural exhibition of the Humboldt Lab in Humboldt Forum at Humboldt-Universität zu Berlin.

Dr. Judith Prokasky has worked for the Stiftung Humboldt Forum im Berliner Schloss (Humboldt Forum Foundation in the Berlin Palace) since 2014 as a curator in the area of the history of the site. An art historian, she was active earlier as a researcher and curator for various museums and cultural and educational institutions.

Manfred Rettig was the founding chair and CEO of the Stiftung Berliner Schloss – Humboldt Forum (Berlin Palace Foundation – Humboldt Forum) from 2009 to 2016. As head of the relocation staff of the Federal Construction Ministry, the architect and city planner coordinated federal construction measures in Berlin, and headed the Bundesbaugesellschaft Berlin mbH (Federal Construction Corporation) as technical manager from 2001 until 2008.

Paul Spies has been director of the Stadtmuseum Berlin (City Museum of Berlin) and chief curator for the Federal State of Berlin at the Humboldt Forum since February 2016. Born in Amsterdam, he co-founded the art history firm D'Arts after graduating from university in art history, and remained there for 21 years. He was director of the Amsterdam Museum from 2009 until 2015.

Franco Stella is the architect of the reconstruction of the Berlin Palace as the Humboldt Forum. He is professor of architectural and urban design: he has taught in Venice (IUAV) and Genoa. Since 1975 he has directed his own studio in Vicenza and since 2009 also in Berlin. In the 1990s he was a member of the jury of the competitions 'Spreebogen' and 'Spreeinsel' for the restoration of Berlin's function as the capital of Germany.

York Stuhlemmer, an architect with a degree in engineering, heads his own architectural practice. Prior to that, he worked in the office of his father Rupert Stuhlemmer (who died in 2018), which performed essential preliminary work on the planning of the historic facade on commission from the association of friends Förderverein Berliner Schloss e.V.

Johannes Wien is chief of finances and of the fundraising office of the Stiftung Humboldt Forum im Berliner Schloss (Humboldt Forum Foundation in the Berlin Palace), and was CEO from 2016 until 2018. Earlier, the prehistorian headed the division and the ministerial office of the Federal Ministry of Transport, Building and Urban Affairs, where he was a division head with the Ministry sustainability officer.

Bernhard Wolter is head of the press and public relations office of the Stiftung Humboldt Forum im Berliner Schloss (Humboldt Forum Foundation in the Berlin Palace). Prior to that, he managed the supervisory board of the Bundesbaugesellschaft Berlin mbH (Federal Construction Corporation), was a division head with the Federal Office for Building and Regional Planning (BBR), and contributed to the establishment of the Stiftung Humboldt Forum beginning in 2009.

Image Credits

pp. 7, 79, 87, 167, 215, 230 above and middle: SHF/Marco Urban; pp. 8–9, 10–11, 16–17, 22–23, 37, 56–57, 60, 64, 66–67, 86, 236 below middle, 241 right: SHF/GIULIANI I VON GIESE; pp. 12–13, 15, 18, 20–21, 24–25, 27, 63, 88–89, 104, 106–107, 154, 156, 157, 241 left, middle: © Stefan Müller, Berlin; pp. 19, 54–55, 58–59, 75, 78, 90, 91, 96, 131–133, 134 below, 135 middle, 136–149, 153, 155, 159–165, 225, 226, 227 above, 230 left, 234 right, 235 right, 237 right: SHF/Stephan Falk; pp. 28–29, 30–31, 32–33, 35, 36, 38, 39, 68–69, 70–71, 101, 176–177, 178–179, 209–213, 230 middle right, 230 below left and below right, 235 left, 236 above and below right, 237 left, 240 above and below left: SHF/David von Becker; pp. 43–50, 233 left: © Franco Stella Architetto; pp. 51, 92–93, 103, 238 right: SHF/Rolf Schulten; pp. 52–53, 85: © Wilhelm von Boddien; pp. 73 above, 74, 76–77: SHF/architect: Franco Stella with FS HUF PG; p. 73 below: BBR, Wettbewerb HUF, Architekturmodell, Franco Stella, 2008, photographer: Torsten Seidel; p. 81: bpk/Luftbild Berlin GmbH; p. 82 above left: bpk/Carl Weinrother; p. 82 above right and middle, 111 above and middle, p. 223 left: akg-images; p. 82 below: Brandenburgisches Landesamt für Denkmalpflege und Archäologisches Landesmuseum, Bildarchiv, 126/220 A 02; p. 83 above: Landesarchiv Berlin, F Rep. 290 (01) Nr. 0071420/ photograph: unknown; p. 83 middle: bpk/Herbert Fiebig; p. 83 below: Photonet.de/Lehnartz; p. 84: haddenhorstfotografie. de; pp. 94–95, 97, 228, 229 right, 232: SHF; p. 98: Benjamin Zibner; p. 99: SHF/Benjamin Zibner; pp. 109 above, 121 below: © Stiftung Stadtmuseum Berlin; p. 109 below: © Stiftung Stadtmuseum Berlin, reproduction: Oliver Ziebe, Berlin; p. 110: © Stiftung Stadtmuseum Berlin, reproduction: Michael Setzpfandt, Berlin; p. 111 below: © Stiftung Preußische Schlösser und Gärten Berlin-Brandenburg/Oberhofmarschallamt/ Verwaltung der Staatlichen Schlösser und Gärten (1927–1945); p. 112 below: Bundesarchiv, Bild 183-J31381/photographer: unknown; p. 112 below: bpk; p. 113 above: Bundesarchiv, Bild 183-R0519-191/photographer: Klaus Franke; p. 113 below: picture alliance/dpa-Zentralbild/Paul Glaser; p. 115 above: bpk/Interflug-Luftbildarchiv; p. 115 below: © bpk/Gerhard Kiesling/Hans Vent, Menschen am Strand, 1975 and Lothar Zitzmann, Weltjugendlied, 1975: VG Bild-Kunst, Bonn 2020; pp. 117, 119, 120, 121 above: © Stiftung Preußische Schlösser und Gärten Berlin-Brandenburg; p. 118: Bezirksamt Mitte von Berlin, Stadtentwicklungsamt, Fachbereich Kataster und Vermessung, Stückvermessungshandriss, Abteilung II, Block 12, Blatt 11 (1879); p. 122 above left: Brandenburgisches Landesamt für Denkmalpflege und Archäologisches Landesmuseum, Bildarchiv, Neg.-Nr.: 60 d 37/1476.015; p. 122 above right: Bundesarchiv, Bild 183-08243-0007/photographer: Igel; Eva Kemlein; p. 122 middle: Brandenburgisches Landesamt für Denkmalpflege und Archäologisches Landesmuseum, Bildarchiv, Neg.-Nr.: 126/193 A 08; p. 122 below: Montage Büro Stuhlemmer Architekten; p. 123 above: TrigonArt BauerPraus GbR; p. 123 below: York Stuhlemmer; pp. 124, 125: Zeichnung Büro Stuhlemmer Architekten; pp. 126–127, 128 above, 129: Büro Stuhlemmer Architekten; p. 128 left below left: reproduced from: Goerd Peschken: *Das königliche Schloß zu Berlin*, Vol. I, Munich 1992, p. 297; p. 128 below right: reproduced from: Goerd Peschken: *Das königliche Schloß zu Berlin*, Vol. I, Munich 1992, p. 304; pp. 134 below, 204–205: SHF/Alexander Hartmann; p. 135 below: Benjamin Zibner; pp. 150–151, 240 right: SHF/Hi.Res.Cam; p. 169: Holger Talinski/laif; pp. 170, 187: © Staatliche Museen zu Berlin, Ethnologisches Museum/SHF, digital reproduction: Jester Blank GbR; p. 173: © Kulturprojekte Berlin und Stiftung Stadtmuseum Berlin, photograph: Alexander Schippel; p. 174: photograph: Mathias Heyde, HU Berlin, Zoologische Lehrsammlung; pp. 180–181: Stiftung Preußischer Kulturbesitz/Stefan Müchler; p. 182: © Staatliche Museen zu Berlin, Museum für Asiatische Kunst/bpk/Jürgen Liepe; pp. 184, 186: © Staatliche Museen zu Berlin, Ethnologisches Museum, bpk/Fotograf: Dietrich Graf; pp. 185, 234 left: © Staatliche Museen zu Berlin, Ethnologisches Museum/ bpk/Martin Franken; pp. 188–189, 238 middle: © Staatliche Museen zu Berlin, Museum für Asiatische Kunst/SHF, digital reproduction: Jester Blank GbR; pp. 190–191: © Staatliche Museen zu Berlin, Ethnologisches Museum/David von Becker; pp. 192–193: © How & Nosm/Kulturprojekte Berlin und Stiftung Stadtmuseum Berlin, photograph: Alexander Schippel; pp. 194–195: © Privatbesitz Dimitri Hegemann/Kulturprojekte Berlin und Stiftung Stadtmuseum Berlin, photograph: Alexander Schippel; pp. 196–197: © Kulturprojekte Berlin und Stiftung Stadtmuseum Berlin, design: krafthaus Das Atelier von facts and fiction/Lothar Zitzmann, Weltjugendlied, 1975: VG Bild-Kunst, Bonn 2020; pp. 198–199, 200–201: © Studio für Animation und Interaktion schnellebuntebilder; pp. 202–203: © Universitätsbibliothek der Humboldt-Universität zu Berlin, Historische Sammlungen – Signatur: Hdschr. Koll. 290/SHF, digital reproduction: Jester Blank GbR; pp. 206–207: Catherine Feff/SHF/Alexander Hartmann; p. 217: bpk/Christine Kösser; p. 218: Stiftung Preußischer Kulturbesitz, Ralph Appelbaum Associates/malsyteufel; p. 219: SHF, Stiftung Preußischer Kulturbesitz, exhibition design: Ralph Appelbaum Associates/ malsyteufel, architect: Franco Stella with FS HUF PG; p. 223 middle: Bundesarchiv, Bild 183-12003-05/photographer: Martin Schmidt; p. 223 above right: akg-images/Reimer Wulf; p. 223 below right: ullstein bild – Peter Meißner; p. 224 left: Lars Ø. Ramberg; p. 227 below: SHF/Bildschön; p. 229 left: Stiftung Preußischer Kulturbesitz, photograph: Sebastian Bolesch; p. 231 left: Inspirationsraum Audio Lounge, Vorstudie WELT DER SPRACHEN im Humboldt-Forum, Zentral- und Landesbibliothek Berlin/TRIAD 2013; p. 231 right: Inspirationsraum Sprachlabor, Vorstudie WELT DER SPRACHEN im Humboldt-Forum, Zentral- und Landesbibliothek/TRIAD 2013; p. 233 above and below right: Juri Reetz/Förderverein Berliner Schloss e.V.; p. 234 middle: Gritt Ockert/Förderverein Berliner Schloss e.V.; p. 236 left: © Tim Trantenroth, Entwurf Nr. 1389 (untitled)/SHF; p. 236 middle above: © An Seebach/ Christiane Stegat, GLOBAL BAROCC – CCORAB LABOLG/SHF; p. 236 below middle: © Stefan Sous, ZEITMASCHINE, SHF/ GIULIANI | VON GIESE; p. 236 above right: © Kang Sunkoo, Statue of Limitations, SHF/David von Becker; p. 236 below right: © Christiane Dellbrügge/Ralf de Moll, Die Architekten, SHF/David von Becker; p. 238 left: © Stiftung Preußische Schlösser und Gärten Berlin-Brandenburg/Roland Handrick; p. 239: Ludwig Zepner, Peter Strang, Rudi Stolle, Heinz Werner/ Staatliche Porzellan-Manufaktur Meissen/Klaus Tänzer; pp. 242–243: SHF/böing gestaltung, Berlin; frontispiece: photographer: Christina Kleßmann

Colophon

Edited by Stiftung Humboldt Forum im Berliner Schloss

Concept and project management
Bernhard Wolter

Text editing
Bernhard Wolter, Susanne Müller-Wolff

Picture editing
Oksana Grewul, Susanne Müller-Wolff

Captions
Bernhard Wolter

Floor plans
FSPG Franco Stella Projektgesellschaft

1st edition

www.humboldtforum.org

© Stiftung Humboldt Forum im Berliner Schloss, Unter den Linden 3, 10117 Berlin, and Prestel Verlag, Munich · London · New York, 2020, A member of Penguin Random House Verlagsgruppe GmbH Neumarkter Strasse 28 · 81673 Munich

In respect to links in the book, Penguin Random House Verlagsgruppe/the Publisher expressly notes that no illegal content was discernible on the linked sites at the time the links were created. The Publisher has no influence at all on the current and future design, content or authorship of the linked sites. For this reason Penguin Random House Verlagsgruppe/ the Publisher expressly disassociates itself from all content on linked sites that has been altered since the link was created and assumes no liability for such content.

A CIP catalogue record for this book is available from the British Library.

www.prestel.de

Editorial direction Prestel
Markus Eisen

Copyediting
Donald Goodwin

Translation
Ian Pepper

Design and layout
Thomas Manss

Typesetting
Kösel Media GmbH, Krugzell

Production management
Cilly Klotz

Cover photo
Stiftung Humboldt Forum im Berliner Schloss

Separations
Ludwig : media gmbh, Zell am See

Printing and binding
Kösel GmbH & Co. KG, Krugzell

Typeface
Mercury, Whitney

Paper
170 g/qm Garda Matt Ultra

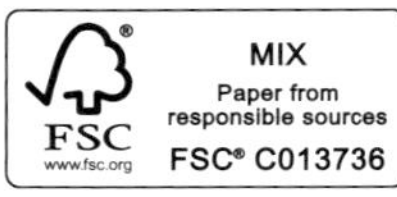

Penguin Random House Verlagsgruppe
FSC® N001967

ISBN 978-3-7913-5836-9
(German edition)
ISBN 978-3-7913-5837-6
(English edition)
Printed in Germany